Millwork
Handbook

Millwork Handbook

John E. Hiro

 Sterling Publishing Co., Inc. New York

DEDICATION

This book is dedicated to Suzanne, Kathleen, Mary, and Christine.

Library of Congress Cataloging-in-Publication Data

Hiro, John E.
    Millwork handbook / by John E. Hiro.
       p.   cm.
    Includes index.
    ISBN 0-8069-8698-0
    1. Windows—Amateurs' manuals. 2. Doors—Amateurs' manuals.
    3. Moldings—Amateurs' manuals. I. Title.
    TH2270.H65   1993
    694'.6—dc20   92-45042
                                                CIP

10 9 8 7 6 5 4 3 2 1

Published by Sterling Publishing Company, Inc.
387 Park Avenue South, New York, N.Y. 10016
© 1993 by John E. Hiro
Distributed in Canada by Sterling Publishing
% Canadian Manda Group, P.O. Box 920, Station U
Toronto, Ontario, Canada M8Z 5P9
Distributed in Great Britain and Europe by Cassell PLC
Villiers House, 41/47 Strand, London WC2N 5JE, England
Distributed in Australia by Capricorn Link Ltd
P.O. Box 665, Lane Cove, NSW 2066
Manufactured in the United States of America
All rights reserved

Sterling ISBN 0-8069-8698-0

Contents

Window Units   11

Acknowledgments

Special thanks to Mary Margaret Hiro for her assistance in the creation of the graphics and to Rosemary Hiro for her editorial expertise. The following individuals all contributed to making this book a reality:

Bill and Betty Welch	Welch Design	
Kurt Hersher		Stelco Ind.
Paul Devan		Stelco Ind.
Bob Monk		B.W.I.
Barry Mirsky		Thermo-Vu
Bob Spindler		Cardinal IG
Jeff Lowinski		AAMA

Introduction

Millwork is considered to be any product that has been machined at a mill. A review of the construction budget for any structure will reveal the importance of millwork in today's marketplace. Expenditures for millwork are significant, whether they be for a new home or a remodelling job in the basement. Most of the cost is associated with windows, doors, and mouldings.

It has always amazed me that we spend so little time planning our millwork purchases. We often rely on a home-center clerk or the neighborhood carpenter to tell us which product to use and how much to pay. We don't install those windows or doors ourselves because we feel we do not have the technical expertise. Because we rely on others and have very little knowledge of what is involved, the wrong product may be selected or the installation may not be complete.

This book describes and illustrates the fundamentals of sound millwork planning: how to select the right product, ensure that it is installed correctly, and perform small repair jobs on it. It examines the different types of door and window available and shows you how to select the one best suited for the particular situation. It also includes a section on mouldings that will show you how to accentuate your door or window or, for that matter, any room in your home. This information will help you reap the greatest possible dividends from the time and money spent—something that is essential in today's economic climate.

John Hiro

Safety Guidelines

Do not attempt any of the work outlined in this book without a thorough knowledge of and a strict adherence to safety measures. This includes the following:

1. Always wear safety glasses or goggles when woodworking. When using loud power equipment, wear hearing protectors. Wear a dust mask when sanding or doing other operations that produce a lot of dust.
2. Read the instructions that come with all tools and follow the manufacturer's safety and operating information.
3. Use the safety equipment on all power tools, such as guards and hold-downs.
4. Do not wear loose clothing or jewelry when working with power tools. They can get caught in the moving parts of the power equipment and cause injury.
5. Never work with power tools when you are under the influence of drugs or alcohol. Always pay attention to the job at hand.

WINDOW UNITS

1
Basic Information

One of the keys to selecting the proper window unit is understanding the components of the unit (Illus. 1-1). A window unit is a combination of several parts: the frame, one or more sash, the hardware, the glazing material, and the weather stripping. It's important to look at a window's parts separately because each component plays a specific part in a successful installation.

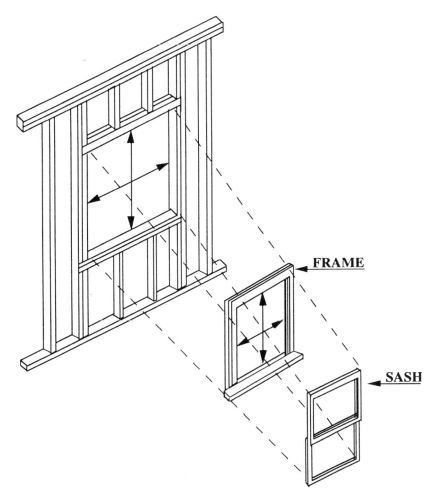

Illus. 1-1. Double-hung window unit.

FRAME

SASH

FRAME

The frame contains all the other components and is the part of the window unit that is fastened to the wall (Illus. 1-2). Frame parts are described according to the area of the window unit they are located in. The "head" section is made up of all the horizontal components at the top. The "side" sections (usually a left and right side as viewed from the outside) consist of all the vertical components. The "sill" section is made up of all the horizontal components at the bottom.

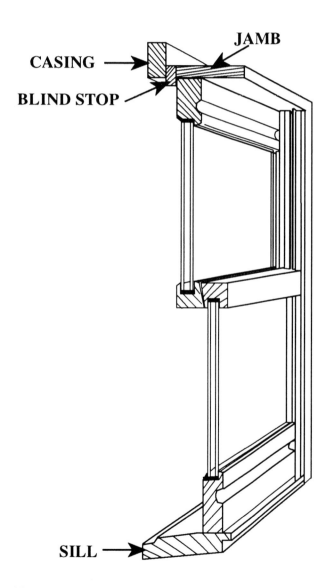

CASING

JAMB

BLIND STOP

SILL

Illus. 1-2. Wood, double-hung window unit.

The wood double-hung window frame shown in Illus. 1-2 includes blind stops. There are three pieces in a single frame; one piece is a "head" blind stop and two pieces are "side" blind stops. Manufacturers may have different names for these add-on frame parts, but they are usually described satisfactorily with the terms *head*, *sill*, and *sides*, along with a brief description.

The main components that make up a window frame are the *jamb*, *stop*, *casing*, and *sill*. The jamb is the main member forming the frame. The outer surface of the jamb meets the wall framing. A window frame usually consists of one head jamb and two side jambs.

The function of the stop varies according to how the window is operated. Its normal function is to stop the sash from falling in or out of the unit and to provide a surface on which to install weather stripping. The window frame stop should not be confused with the interior trim stop, which may be added after the window is installed.

The casing is the outermost component of a window frame. Its main function is to provide a method for attaching the frame to the structure, as well as providing the area against which the siding butts and onto which a combination storm window unit is installed. The window frame casing should not be confused with the interior trim casing, which is added after the window is installed. Only wooden window frames are manufactured with casing. Aluminum, vinyl, and clad-wood window units use a "fin" method of installation (Illus. 1-3).

The sill is the main structural member of a frame at the bottom. It is normally the most heavily constructed portion of the frame because it supports the weight of the window unit over its width. The sill is pitched towards the exterior to allow for water drainage. The sill is usually just long enough to fit under the side jambs and, in wooden windows, the side casing. At times, it is necessary to extend the sill past its normal limits to facilitate joining one window to another. These sill extensions are called *long horns*.

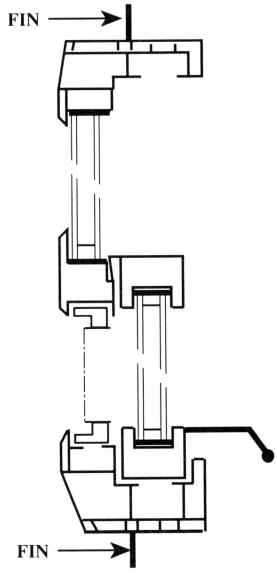

FIN ➔

FIN ➔

Illus. 1-3. A section view of a vinyl single-hung window unit.

The frame of a window unit has many functions. It provides a square environment for the sash and weather stripping to operate in. It also offers protection from the elements around its entire perimeter. It provides the means of attaching the window unit to the building, and it forms the surface against which the exterior siding rests.

The frame of a window will operate independently of all other parts. You can leave a frame attached to a structure while replacing all the other parts of the unit and end up with a brand-new window unit.

It's very important to keep your window frames in good shape. Wood sills may allow water to accumulate and eventually rot. Aluminum frames may start to pit because of the environment. Be aware of the condition of your window unit frames. They are the most difficult of all to replace.

SASH

The sash contains the glass or other glazing material. It may open to allow ventilation. All window units except directly set windows include one or more sash, depending on how the window operates.(The term "window" is sometimes used interchangeably with the term "sash." For clarity, refer to the window and sash as a window unit.)

The sash often provides a surface for attaching operating hardware and weather stripping. Sash may be made of aluminum, vinyl, wood, or clad wood.

Sash that open are called "venting" or "operating." Sash that do not open are referred to as "fixed," "stationary," or "non-venting."

Double-hung and sliding window units include at least two (one pair) sash: a top and bottom or a left and right. Casement, awning, and other projecting window units contain at least one sash.

The horizontal members that make up a sash are called the rails. The vertical members are referred to as the stiles (Illus. 1-4).

The glazing material (normally glass) is installed in the sash in various ways. Originally, glass was installed from the outside. A bead of bedding compound was placed around the perimeter of the opening, followed by the glass. Glazier's points were driven into the sash against the glass and putty was applied around the perimeter. With the introduction of insulating glass, many new glazing techniques evolved. Most include the use of a glazing bead to take the place of putty. Some make use of a vinyl gasket which totally surrounds the glass. Some sash are reglazeable and some are not.

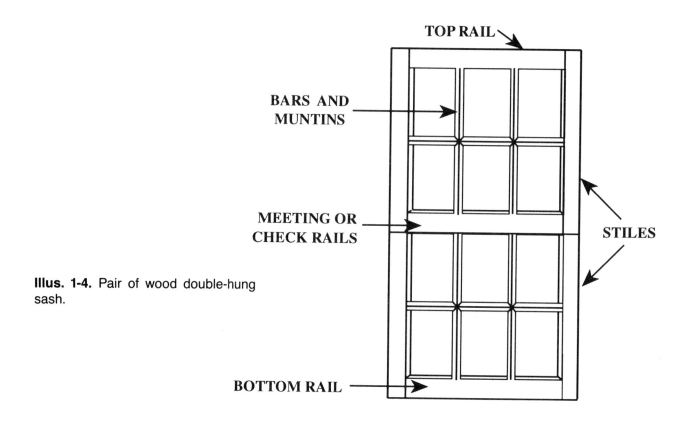

TOP RAIL

BARS AND MUNTINS

MEETING OR CHECK RAILS

STILES

Illus. 1-4. Pair of wood double-hung sash.

BOTTOM RAIL

Illus. 1-5. Window grille.

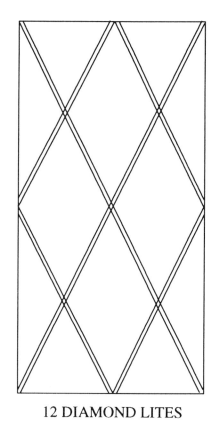

8 DIVIDED LITES

12 DIAMOND LITES

You should know exactly how your windows are glazed. If you break a piece of glass, you may have to purchase and refinish an entirely new sash or you may be able to reglaze it yourself. These are important considerations in your window selection.

A sash may contain a single piece of glass (called a one-light sash) or it may contain multiple lights. The parts of a sash that create the multiple-light appearance are called bars and muntins. A one-light sash can also be converted into a multiple-light sash through the use of grilles.

If a window has a pair of double-hung sash, it is classified according to the number of lights in the sash. Illus. 1-6 shows a pair of double-hung sash that would be specified as six lights over one light or 6/1. Some common light configurations for double-hung units are 1/1, 2/2, 4/4, 6/1, 6/6, and 8/8.

Cottage-style, double-hung sash are relatively common in Colonial homes. They differ from normal double-hung sash in that the top sash is smaller than the bottom sash, and the divided light pattern varies accordingly. Light configurations of 6/9 and 8/12 are common.

THE HARDWARE

The hardware allows the sash to operate (open and close). Illus. 1 shows a double-hung window unit with hardware consisting of channels mounted to the side of the frame, allowing the sash to go up and down. It also includes a counterbalance system made up of weights and cords. Different types of window have different hardware; this is described in Chapter 3.

GLAZING MATERIAL

The glazing material or glass is the largest area

Illus. 1-6 (above left). A pair of wood double-hung sash with a light configuration of 6/1. **Illus. 1-7 (above right).** Cottage double-hung window unit with a sash ratio of 6:9.

of any window unit. It has been improved greatly over the last 20 years. Chapter 4 contains a thorough description of glazing material available today.

WEATHER STRIPPING

The weather stripping is what keeps the energy usage and cold drafts to a minimum. It may be attached to both the frame and the sash. Some types of window unit are much more energy-efficient because they allow for a greater use of weather stripping.

CONFIGURATION

A window unit may be constructed of a single frame or multiple frames joined together horizontally or vertically. When two side jambs are joined together to create a multiple-frame opening, this section is called a "mullion" (Illus. 1-8).

Window units with mullions can be classified as "mullion," "twin, or two wide," "triple, or three wide," "quad, or four wide," or "quint, or five wide" (Illus. 1-9). Additional single units can be added to make "six wides" or "seven wides," etc.

A "picture window" unit is a triple window unit with a fixed central section surrounded by operating window units. The central section is usually wider than the flanking sections.

Window units may also be joined at the head and sill areas. This is called "stacking" and may be used to create a "window wall" effect.

By combining various individual sizes of window unit, almost any overall size is possible. Because there are so many possibilities, the manufacturers are not able to list them all. If you have a specific requirement, look the specifications over and come up with a combination of single frames that will meet the requirement.

Bows and Bays

Who hasn't been impressed with the grandeur of a large bow or bay window unit overlooking a magnificent view? These window types create exciting architectural expressions from both the interior and exterior of a home (Illus. 1-10 and 1-11).

Bow and bay window units are made up of individual frames with angled mullion sections (Illus. 1-12). The same single units that make up mullions and triples, etc., are joined to create the semicircle or angle of the window. The head and sill sections are held together with "head and seat boards." These plywood members add rigidity and keep the weather outside. Head and seat boards should be well insulated on the exterior during installation. It is common to add a

Illus. 1-8. A mullion section on a wood double-hung window.

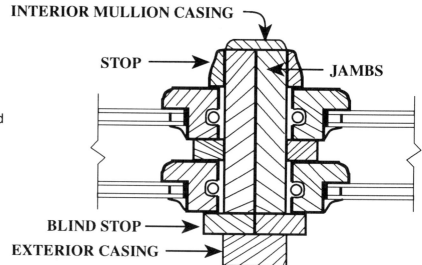

INTERIOR MULLION CASING

STOP

JAMBS

BLIND STOP

EXTERIOR CASING

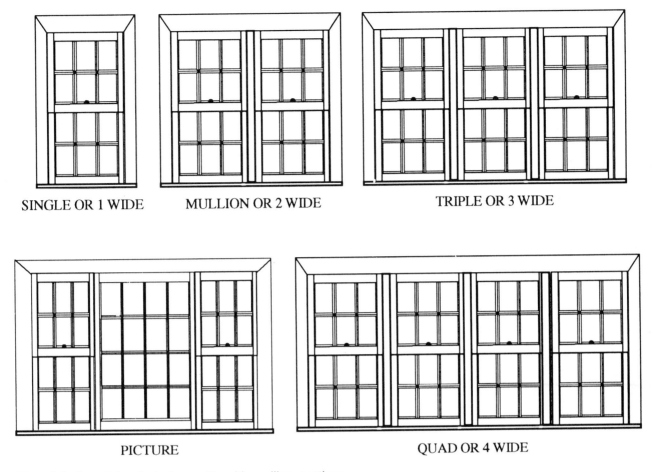

SINGLE OR 1 WIDE MULLION OR 2 WIDE TRIPLE OR 3 WIDE

PICTURE QUAD OR 4 WIDE

Illus. 1-9. A variety of window units with mullion sections.

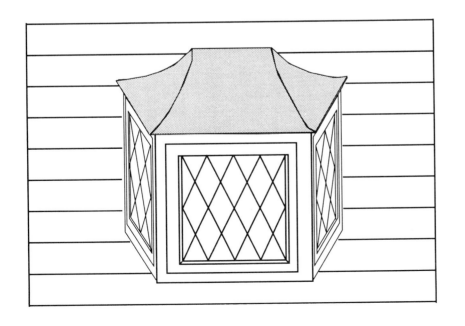

Illus. 1-10. Bay window unit.

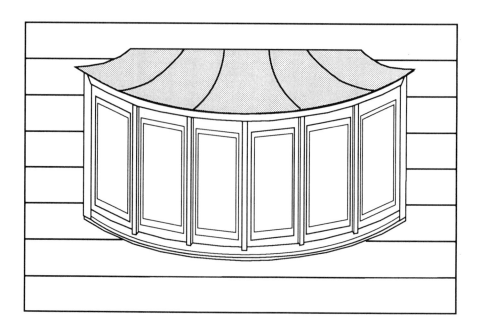

Illus. 1-11. Bow window unit.

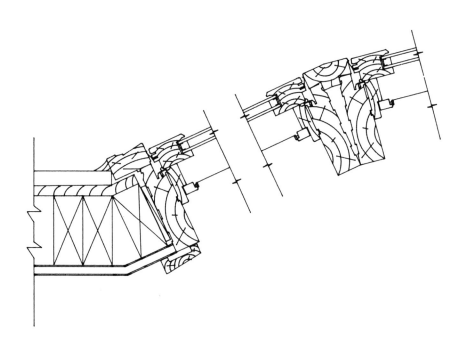

Illus. 1-12. An angled mullion section on a bow window unit. (*Courtesy of BiltBest Windows*)

roof over the head board and to provide some kind of framing to accept insulation under the seat.

Bow and bay units are usually casement or double-hung units. They are available in aluminum, vinyl, wood, and clad wood.

These are true projecting window units; that is, they project out, away from the exterior wall. These projections vary, based on the num-

ber of frames in a bow unit or the angle of projection in a bay unit (normally 30, 45, 60, or 90 degrees). When planning for the use of these units, be sure you have the space needed to accommodate the projection. Also, if you choose a casement window unit, the sash will project even farther out from the foundation and may create a hazard to pedestrian traffic.

Bow and bay window units are normally installed so that the seat board is approximately two to three feet above the floor. This creates a window seat effect. Another method is to align the bottom of the window with the floor of the house, creating a "walk in" or "walk out" effect. This requires special framing under the window unit and is used to create an expansive feeling within a room (Illus. 1-13).

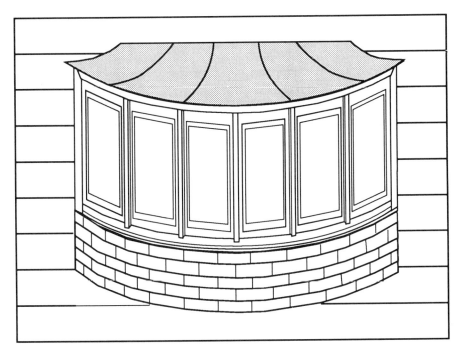

Illus. 1-13. Walkout bow window unit.

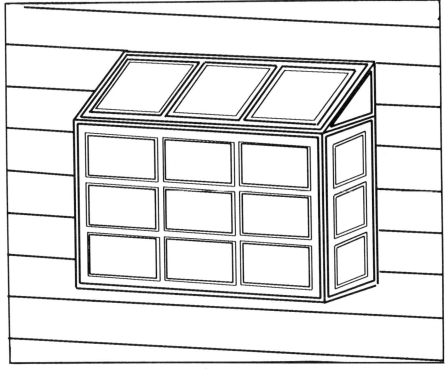

Illus. 1-14. Greenhouse window unit.

Another type of bay window unit is the *greenhouse*, *box bay*, or *garden window unit* (Illus. 1-14). It is made up of a middle section joined at 90 degrees to a left and right flanking section. Different manufacturers incorporate special features such as a glass roof or special shelves to accommodate the growing of plants. This type of window unit is an attractive addition to any window plan.

Since a bow or bay window unit projects out from a wall, most of its weight is hanging out in space. Special steps must be taken during installation to support this weight and prevent gravity from ultimately pulling the unit away from the house. Follow the manufacturer's installation instructions carefully. Some manufacturers provide an internal cable support system; others depend on external "knee brackets."

MEASUREMENTS OF IMPORTANCE

In the United States, feet and inch dimensions are used to measure window units. Twelve inches equal one foot. The foot sign is ′, and the inch sign is ″. The common tape measure (use a good one) breaks down inches into 32nds, 16ths, 8ths, quarters, and halves. Become familiar with reading a ruler. Window units are manufactured to tolerances of $1/32″$ or closer.

Measurements of millwork should always be stated in the same way, that is, the width or horizontal size followed by the height or vertical size. A window unit with a sash 24″ wide by 38″ tall would be listed as 2/0 × 3/2 or 2′0″ × 3′2″ or 24″ × 38″ or 2438, always with the horizontal measurement first.

The "callout" size of a window unit is the size shown in a catalogue and the size used for ordering. The callout size of a mullion (two wide) or triple (three wide) window unit would be given as follows: the designation as a mullion or triple followed by the single unit size, or the single unit size followed by a "2 wide" or "3 wide." If two single units 2/0 × 3/2 were joined together

to make a mullion, this unit might be called a mullion, 2/0 × 3/2. Each manufacturer has his own method of listing multiple units. Just remember that the size shown refers to the sash-opening size of a single unit.

Accurate measurements are essential to ensure a satisfactory installation. Window manufacturers supply many different dimensions to aid in planning, and once these dimensions are understood, window units can be installed with confidence.

In order to fully understand the measurement system used by window manufacturers, we must be cognizant of a major difference between wood windows and aluminum, vinyl, or clad-wood windows. (The frame of a wooden window is made of wood. The frame of an aluminum window is made of aluminum. Clad-wood windows have aluminum or vinyl as exterior material.) Illus. 1-15 shows a vinyl window with a fin frame and a wood window with exterior casing or brick mould. The overall measurement of the fin frame *excludes* the fin, while the overall measurement of the wood frame *includes* the casing or brick mould.

Overall Size

The overall size (or "unit size" or "unit dimension") is the overall width × the overall height of the entire window unit *excluding* any fins but including any exterior casing (Illus. 1-16 and 1-17). This measurement indicates the exact dimension of the unit as viewed from the exterior. This is also the measurement of that part of the window unit that fits within the exterior siding, and, therefore, becomes critical in replacement applications.

Frame Size

The frame size is a measurement of the overall width × the overall height *excluding fins* on aluminum, vinyl, or clad-wood windows, and *excluding casing* on wood windows.

Sash-Opening Size and Sash Size

The "sash-opening size" is the measurement of the area within a frame that accepts the sash. The width is measured between the interior

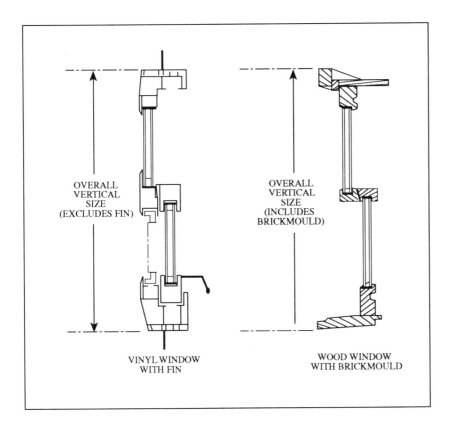

OVERALL
VERTICAL
SIZE
(EXCLUDES FIN)

OVERALL
VERTICAL
SIZE
(INCLUDES
BRICKMOULD)

VINYL WINDOW
WITH FIN

WOOD WINDOW
WITH BRICKMOULD

Illus. 1-15. Vinyl window unit with fin, and wood window unit with brick mould.

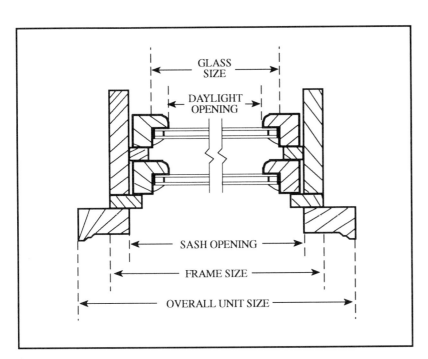

GLASS
SIZE

DAYLIGHT
OPENING

SASH OPENING

FRAME SIZE

OVERALL UNIT SIZE

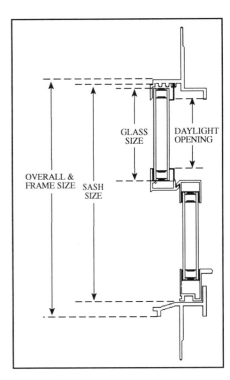

GLASS
SIZE

DAYLIGHT
OPENING

OVERALL &
FRAME SIZE

SASH
SIZE

Illus. 1-16 (above left). A section view of a wood double-hung, horizontal window unit. **Illus. 1-17 (above right).** A section view of an aluminum single-hung, vertical window unit.

faces of the side jambs. The height is measured between the interior face of the head jamb and the interior face of the sill where it comes in contact with the outermost surface of the sash bottom rail. The sash size is the measurement of the sash. The sash-opening size is usually the size that is listed by the manufacturer in his product-description code.

Since double-hung window units are made up of two sash, care must be taken in determining the sash-opening size when you only have the sash to work with. The top and bottom sash overlap at the center, and this causes the bottom sash to be vertically larger by two inches. It is best to work with the top and bottom sash together.

Local building codes may mandate minimum ventilation requirements or you may want to know these figures for planning purposes. You can approximate these measurements by using the sash size of venting sash. Some manufacturers will also provide this information.

Glass Size

The "glass size" is the actual size of the piece of glass within a single sash from stile to stile horizontally and rail to rail vertically. Even though a sash may contain divided lights, the glass size is stated as if there were only one light of glass. The glass size is stated in inches, width × height. The size of a piece of glass is usually larger than the visible glass area because there is a recess in the stiles and rails to accept the glass.

The glass size is often used as a reference to determine window unit size. If you are replacing a sash or window unit, the glass size of the existing unit is one of the measurements you should take to your supplier.

Local building codes may mandate minimum natural lighting areas or you may want to know these areas for planning purposes. The glass size dimension will provide this information.

Daylight-Opening Size

The "daylight-opening size" is the actual visible

area of the piece of glass within a single sash from stile to stile horizontally and rail to rail vertically. Even though a sash may contain divided lights, the daylight-opening size is stated as if there were only one light of glass. The daylight opening size is stated in inches, width × height.

The daylight-opening size is important for the specification of grilles because they will fit exactly within the daylight opening. This measurement is also used by some manufacturers in place of the glass size.

Clear or Egress Opening

The "clear" or "egress" opening is the measurement of the amount of space available within a fully open window unit to provide an unobstructed exit to the outside. The size is stated two ways: width × height or square footage. This measurement is important for the planning stage of your window installation because many local building codes require minimum egress sizes, especially in sleeping areas.

Rough Opening

The "rough opening" (Illus. 1-18) is the most widely used measurement of all. It reflects the manufacturer's recommendation of the size of the hole in a framed wall necessary to accept the window unit. Generally, the rough opening is ½"

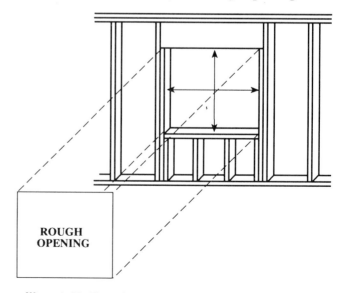

Illus. 1-18. Rough opening.

to 1″ wider and higher than the frame size. The rough opening is the measurement you need when framing a wall to accept a window unit.

If you want to replace a unit and need to determine the rough opening of the window unit which is already installed, you must remove the interior trim and expose the wall framing. You can then measure the existing rough opening. It is possible to estimate the rough-opening size of an existing window, but this is best left to professionals.

Manufacturers usually provide the rough-opening size needed to accommodate a single window unit. Openings for mullion and wider units, however, must be computed in accordance with the formula provided by the manufacturer (Illus. 1-19).

Masonry Opening

The "masonry opening" is the manufacturer's recommendation of hole size necessary to accept a window unit placed in a block, brick, stone or poured concrete wall. It is usually approximately ½ to 1″ larger than the overall size of the unit. It should be noted that there is a difference between masonry walls and masonry *veneered* walls. It is common today to install a brick wall as a veneer over a wood-frame wall. In this type of construction, rough-opening dimensions rather than masonry-opening dimensions are used because the window unit will be installed into a wooden wall.

Wall Thickness or Wall Construction

Window units have a third dimension (in addition to width and height) which is crucial to a successful installation: the depth of the frame (Illus. 1-20). This measurement is the wall thickness or wall construction, and must be provided by you when the window units are ordered.

The easiest way to determine the wall construction is to look upon the wall as a "sandwich," the center of which is the framing lumber. Work out from the center towards the interior and exterior and add all the parts that create this sandwich. Working towards the interior, add the dimensions of all the parts until you get to the interior face of the wall. Working towards the exterior, add the dimensions of all the parts until you get to the siding. Do not include the siding itself in the wall-construction formula.

As an example, let's consider a wall made of

Multiple Units

Double and triple units—All single units shown above are also available in 2 and 3-wide units. Determine rough and masonry openings as indicated below.

TWO WIDE

Rough Opening		Masonry Opening	
Width	Height	Width	Height
Add all Rough Opening Widths and Subtract 1″	Same as single unit	Add all Rough Opening Widths and Subtract 1½″	Same as single unit

THREE WIDE

Rough Opening		Masonry Opening	
Width	Height	Width	Height
Add all Rough Opening Widths and Subtract 2″	Same as single unit	Add all Rough Opening Widths and Subtract 2½″	Same as single unit

THREE WIDE UNITS

Rough Opening		Masonry Opening	
Width	Height	Width	Height
Add all Rough Opening Widths and Subtract 2″	Same as single unit	Add all Rough Opening Widths and Subtract 2½″	Same as single unit

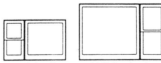

TWO WIDE UNITS

Left hand unit   Right hand unit
(As viewed from the outside.)

Rough Opening		Masonry Opening	
Width	Height	Width	Height
Add all Rough Opening Widths and Subtract 1″	Same as single unit	Add all Rough Opening Widths and Subtract 1½″	Same as single unit

Illus. 1-19. Typical instructions for determining the rough opening of multiple window units. (*Courtesy of Marvin Windows*)

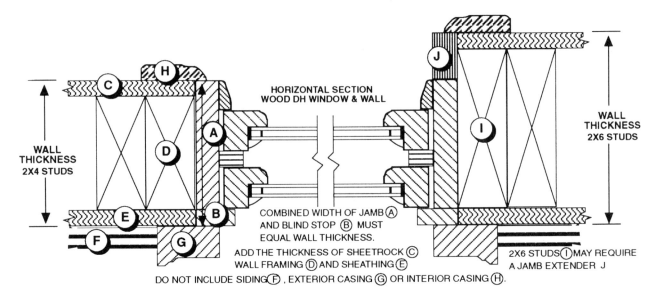

HORIZONTAL SECTION WOOD DH WINDOW & WALL

WALL THICKNESS 2X4 STUDS

WALL THICKNESS 2X6 STUDS

COMBINED WIDTH OF JAMB Ⓐ
AND BLIND STOP Ⓑ MUST
EQUAL WALL THICKNESS.
ADD THE THICKNESS OF SHEETROCK Ⓒ
WALL FRAMING Ⓓ AND SHEATHING Ⓔ
DO NOT INCLUDE SIDING Ⓕ , EXTERIOR CASING Ⓖ OR INTERIOR CASING Ⓗ.

2X6 STUDS Ⓘ MAY REQUIRE
A JAMB EXTENDER J

Illus. 1-20. Wall thickness of a window unit.

2×4s with ½″ thick Sheetrock® mounted to the inside and ½″ thick sheathing (plywood) mounted to the outside. The sandwich will consist of the width measurement of the 2×4 (3½″) plus the thickness of the Sheetrock (½″) plus the thickness of the sheathing (½″), for a total of 4½″. Add ¹⁄₁₆″ for building paper, etc., and the specified wall construction or wall thickness becomes 4⁹⁄₁₆″. This is the most common wall-construction size in use today. If 2×6s were used instead of 2×4s in the example, the middle of the sandwich would be 5½″ instead of 3½″. This would change the overall wall thickness to 6⁹⁄₁₆″. If ¼″ thick panelling were used over the Sheetrock on the interior, ¼″ would have to be added to the wall thickness.

If you plan to replace a window unit and need to determine the existing wall thickness, measure from the inside edge of the siding to the face of the interior wall. Be cautious, because frame thicknesses have changed considerably in the last 50 years.

Window units are generally manufactured to accommodate a basic wall thickness of 4⁹⁄₁₆″. Wider walls are accommodated with an accessory called a *jamb extender*. These extenders can be ordered along with the window unit or fabricated on the job.

2
Selection Factors

The factory-assembled window unit is a relatively new product. Until the 1930s most windows were shipped knocked down from the lumberyard and assembled on the job by carpenters. They were limited in design and size, and were not energy-efficient. They were made of wood or steel.

Today's window unit is much more functional and efficient. It may be made of wood, metal, or plastic, and prices vary dramatically. The only way you can select the proper window to fit your needs and budget is to understand all the variables before you reach a decision.

A window unit should be graded on the following: its ability to provide light, ventilation, a view and security; its architectural appearance; its energy efficiency and how easily it can be maintained. These factors are discussed below.

LIGHT

The main reason for installing window units is to provide light. Artificial light just can't match that wonderfully airy feeling given off by a naturally illuminated room. Take advantage of modern materials and always consider how to get the most effective use of light when planning for your window use. The ideal objective is to create uniform daylight across an entire room.

Maximizing Light

Follow these guidelines to maximize light:

1. Pay attention to the east-west orientation of your window openings relative to the rising and setting sun. During the summer in the Northern Hemisphere, the sun rises in the northeast and sets in the northwest; in the winter, it rises in the southeast and sets in the southwest. Remember also that the height of the sun changes with the seasons. The sun is higher in the summer. A little planning will allow you to make the best use of the light available (Illus. 2-1).
2. A south-facing window unit admits the most light (in the Northern Hemisphere). However, it also admits the most heat. Both these factors must be carefully weighed.
3. One large opening is preferable to several small openings. This is the best way to avoid contrasting areas of high brightness and semi-dark areas (Illus. 2-2).
4. Windows in more than one wall within a room provide a more effective and even light source (Illus. 2-3).
5. For planning purposes, assume that sunlight will penetrate a room approximately twice the vertical measurement of the window unit. Therefore, a 4′ tall window will admit sunlight approximately 8′ into the room.

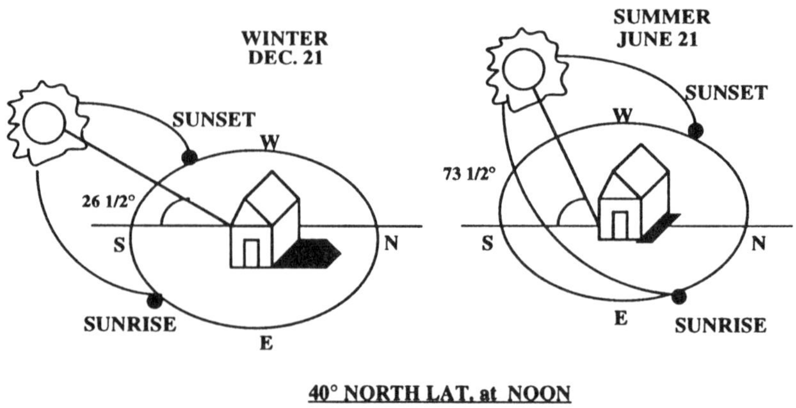

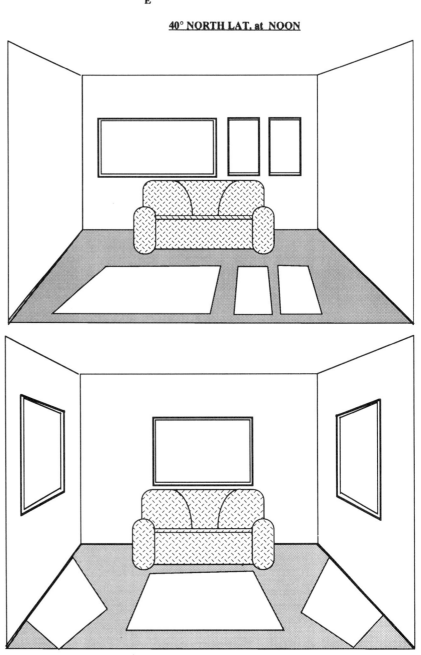

WINTER DEC. 21

SUNSET

W

26 1/2°

S   N

SUNRISE

E

SUMMER JUNE 21

SUNSET

W

73 1/2°

S   N

E   SUNRISE

40° NORTH LAT. at NOON

Illus. 2-1. The height of the sun changes with the seasons.

Illus. 2-2. One large opening is preferable to several small openings.

Illus. 2-3. Window units in more than one wall within a room provide a more effective and even light source.

28

6. Horizontally oriented windows (wider than tall) provide a broader distribution of light. Vertically oriented windows (taller than wide) provide narrow but deep penetration (Illus. 2-4).

7. The higher you place any window on a wall, the deeper the light will penetrate into the room (Illus. 2-5).

8. Locate draperies so that they do not block any light when they are opened.

9. Lightly colored wall and floor treatments will distribute light more evenly throughout a room. This reflected light is an important consideration in evening out your room lighting. Flat paint finishes will dissipate glare.

10. Plan to light a specific work area from either the right or left. Lighting from behind creates shadows, and from the front causes glare and eye strain (Illus. 2-6).

11. Very bright, *uneven* light creates glare. Uneven light will create a dramatic effect within a room, but it may be difficult to live with.

12. Consider roof window units in planning for a natural light source (Illus. 2-7).

13. Screens are necessary for ventilation, but greatly inhibit light. Use half-screens if

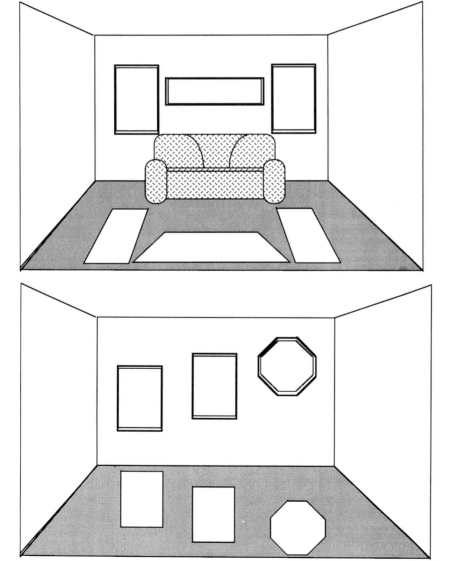

Illus. 2-4. Vertically oriented window units provide narrow but deep penetration.

Illus. 2-5. The higher you place the window on a wall, the deeper the light will penetrate into the room.

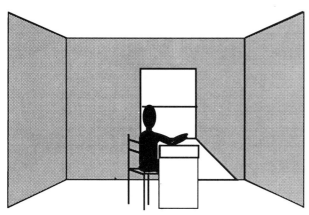

Illus. 2-6. Lighting from behind creates shadows, and from the front causes glare and eye strain.

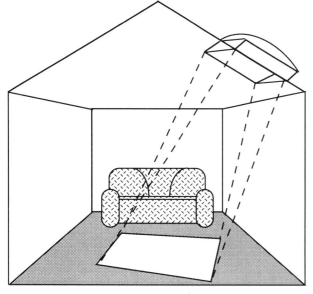

Illus. 2-7. Roof window units make a good source of natural light.

possible or eliminate screens altogether if you don't plan to open that window.

VENTILATION

Natural ventilation is a major consideration in ensuring our comfort in the summer months. The number, size, and placement of window units are key elements in a ventilation plan and must be coordinated with landscaping (the placement of plants and trees so as to encourage or prevent the flow of air), north-south orientation, and building shape. In most locations, the prevailing summer breeze comes from a different direction than the winter wind. You can design the landscaping and window location to block undesirable winter winds while taking advantage of cooling summer breezes.

Pressure or temperature differences cause air to move. The windward side (the side or direction from which the wind is blowing) of your home has higher air pressure than the leeward side (the side opposite the windward side). Air flows naturally from high- to low-pressure areas. You can take advantage of this air movement by locating window units on opposite exterior walls. To speed the movement of air, the openings through which the air leaves should be larger than those through which it enters (Illus. 2-8).

Obstacles in the path of moving air cause it to change direction and slow down. These obstructions include trees, shrubbery, fences, screens, walls, and furniture. Since the cooling effect of air depends on its speed, obstructions to the prevailing summer breeze should be minimized (Illus. 2-9).

Ventilation in a structure may be natural or mechanically induced, or often both. Warm air tends to rise, and this characteristic can be used to aid air movement. Air entering through the first-floor windows can be directed up to higher levels, creating a pleasant breeze as it travels. This effect is also possible with the use of a whole-house exhaust fan (Illus. 2-10).

The angle at which the air enters and leaves the room is a controlling influence on the pattern of air movement within the room, and this angle

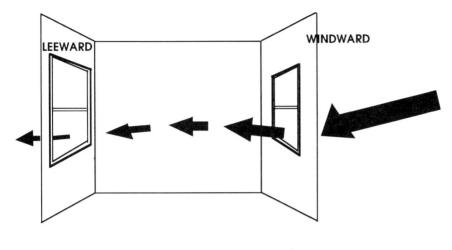

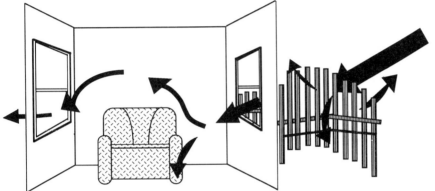

LEEWARD

WINDWARD

Illus. 2-8. To speed the movement of air, the openings through which the air leaves should be larger than those through which it enters.

Illus. 2-9. Try to minimize obstructions to the prevailing summer breeze.

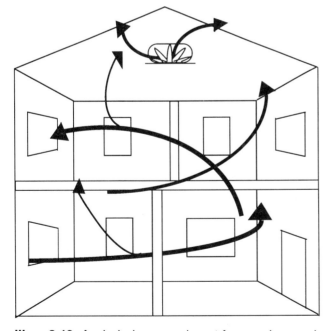

Illus. 2-10. A whole-house exhaust fan can be used to direct air entering through first-floor windows up to higher levels.

depends on the location and type of windows. If the windward window is located close to the floor and the leeward window is high on the opposite wall, air will follow that pattern. Local building codes may mandate a minimum amount of ventilation depending on which room the window unit is located in.

Maximizing Ventilation

Follow these guidelines to maximize ventilation:

1. Locate the house and ventilation openings to take full advantage of prevailing summer breezes. Determine the high- and low-pressure areas as defined by the shape of the house and its orientation to the prevailing wind.

2. Plan landscaping, interior partitions, and furniture locations so that they do not interfere with air movement. If possible, locate

the home so that existing hills and buildings divert only the prevailing *winter* wind.

3. Create a clear vertical path for air movement from the first floor to the highest point in the house. Consider whole-house fans or skylights for this purpose.

4. Use windows to direct the flow of air across a room at the level of occupancy. Directly opposite the occupant is best. Next best is in adjacent walls as far as possible away from corners (Illus. 2-11).

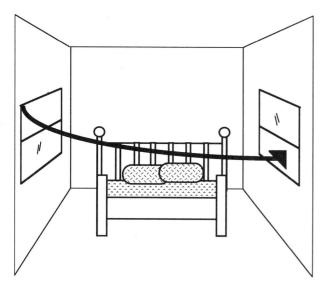

Illus. 2-11. The best way to direct the flow of air across a room at the level of occupancy is to place the window directly opposite the occupant.

VIEW

One of the major considerations in selecting and placing your window is the pleasure you will derive from the view it affords. Whether you are standing at the kitchen sink or sitting in your favorite chair in the family room, you should take advantage of the most beautiful scenery available. Conversely, the view from outside into the house must be considered when planning, for privacy.

Properly designed and placed windows allow the outside to become part of the decor. However, you don't want to be tilting your head or shielding your eyes in order to see what's on the other side of the glass. Careful planning is

called for when considering how best to take advantage of the view.

Maximizing the View

Follow these guidelines to maximize the view:

1. Use windows with vertical rather than horizontal lines. Horizontal lines, as found in double-hung and awning windows, obstruct the view more severely than the vertical lines found in casement and sliding window units. Other considerations may mandate windows with horizontal lines, but if view is your major concern, use window units with vertical lines.

2. Use nonventing units whenever ventilation is not needed. You can often use larger-sized fixed windows and you will not need a screen. Screens obstruct views. Consider whether you will be looking through a window from a seated position or while standing. Your height of eye can vary by approximately two feet, depending on your position (Illus. 2-12).

3. If the window location is already set and you are not satisfied with the view, consider changing the landscaping to create a pleasant environment.

4. While sunsets and sunrises are very beautiful, they are also hard on the eyes. Anticipate the inconvenience and plan accordingly.

5. Colonial lights (grilles) are attractive architectural features, but may have an adverse effect on the view. Consider using them only in windows that can be seen from the street.

6. Use a glass door in place of a window. Glass doors contain more glass area and are therefore the ultimate means of expanding apparent room size; also they allow unobstructed views from almost any position.

7. Consider the placement of windows in relation to exterior doors to allow for observing unwanted visitors.

SECURITY AND SAFETY

Window units are the least secure area of the exterior wall. If someone wishes to gain access

The vertical lines of casement windows are typical of a contemporary architectural style.

Plenty of glass and light colors create a bright, airy environment. (Photo courtesy of Velux-America, Inc.)

A

Energy-efficient glazing plays an important role in millwork planning. (Photo courtesy of Velux-America, Inc.)

Natural lighting creates the perfect environment in this modern kitchen. (Photo courtesy of Johnson Pocket Door Hardware.)

B

Note how the circle heads add just the right decorative touch to these casement windows. (Photo courtesy of Weather Shield MFG, Inc.)

Patio doors, transoms, and skylights, blended into an elegant porch setting. (Photo courtesy of Velux-America, Inc.)

Fenestration is the arrangement of windows and doors in a building. As shown in this example, fenestration can create a strikingly beautiful environment.

Millwork should be decorative as well as functional. (Photo courtesy of Weather Shield MFG, Inc.)

D

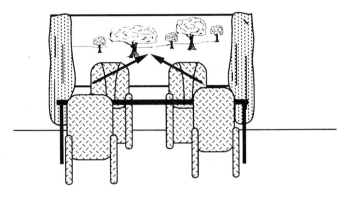

Height of eye seated in dining room
3' - 8" to 4' - 2"

Illus. 2-12. Your height of eye varies by approximately two feet, depending on your position.

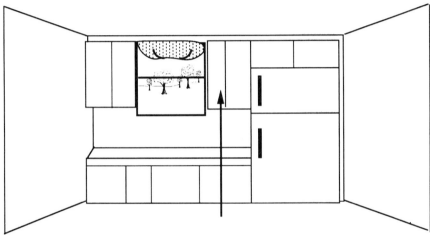

Height of eye standing
4' - 8" to 5' - 6"

by breaking a window, he will. Aside from using metal grates or an alarm system, all that can be done is to be sure to have sash locks and use them.

The glass used in window units can be dangerous. Recently, many building codes have adopted the use of "tempered" glass in any window unit that comes within 18″ of the floor. Tempered glass is more resistant to breakage than regular glass and crumbles when it breaks. Broken pieces of tempered glass have smooth rather than sharp edges. Be sure to check with your local building department before replacing or installing any window unit in close proximity

(24″) to the floor. Many window manufacturers offer safety glazing as a special order option.

Windows may, in the case of fire, become an important emergency exit. Most building codes now mandate the minimum number and size of windows and their location above the floor in any room used for sleeping. This makes a great deal of sense, and has probably saved many lives. The sizes of these windows are referred to as "egress" or "clear opening," and are usually quoted in the manufacturer's specifications. Check with your local building-code official. To provide additional safety, put a sturdy piece of furniture below an emergency window exit so that children can easily reach the sill (Illus. 2-13).

Another safety concern is a window unit that projects outward or inward from the exterior wall. These are generally casement, awning or hopper window units, and they constitute a potential hazard if they project into an area of pedestrian traffic. If you anticipate traffic, place projecting windows high enough off the ground to prevent an accident.

Privacy may be very important, depending on the room involved. Plan to use obscure glass or some type of shading device in that case.

Maximizing Security and Safety

Follow these guidelines to maximize security and safety:

1. Make sure that your window units have sash locks, and get in the habit of locking a window each time you close it.
2. Consider that your window units may have to be used as emergency exits. They should be sized accordingly, and the sill should be located close enough to the floor to allow access.
3. Use tempered safety glass in any window unit located within 18 to 24″ of the floor.
4. Be careful not to locate projecting windows in the way of pedestrian traffic.
5. Consult your local building code official to

ensure that your window unit installation meets legal requirements.

ARCHITECTURAL APPEARANCE

Today's window units can make an important architectural statement. The shape, size, and placement of the window units all play a role in how your home appears. The arrangement of window units in a building is known as the fenestration, and should be carefully planned (Illus. 2-14). As a general rule, vertical window lines such as those achieved with casement or sliding window units are considered to be contemporary (Illus. 2-15), while horizontal lines achieved with double-hung or awning window units are considered traditional or Colonial (Illus. 2-16).

Window units may create a relatively weak area in the framework of a building. Structural considerations such as framing dimensions are best addressed by a qualified contractor, engineer, or architect. You can also obtain pertinent information from your local building inspector (Illus. 2-17).

Another item to be addressed in the fenestration-planning stage is the use of windows to realize a passive solar gain (to take advantage of the sun's energy in order to effect a net gain in the home's heating system). If this is your main goal, southern orientation may sup-

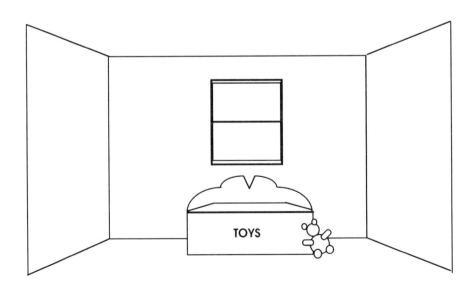

Illus. 2-13. Provide a secure piece of furniture below an emergency exit so children can easily reach the sill.

Illus. 2-14. Carefully plan the arrangement of window units in your building.

Illus. 2-15. Window units with vertical lines are generally considered to be contemporary.

Illus. 2-16. Window units with horizontal lines are considered traditional.

Illus. 2-17. Structural considerations may be necessary for unique window shapes and sizes.

plant architectural appearance as your major consideration. It is possible to obtain additional warmth by using windows to collect the sun's energy and the interior structure to store and distribute that energy throughout the house. This system becomes an integral part of your home and should be engineered by a competent professional (Illus. 2-18).

Achieving the Best Architectural Appearance

Follow these guidelines to achieve the best architectural appearance for your home:

1. Take the time to sketch elevations of your home, whether for new construction or re-

Illus. 2-18. A system can be devised that will use the window units to collect the sun's energy and the interior structure of the house to store and distribute the energy throughout the house. (*Courtesy of Velux-America, Inc.*)

modelling. See how different combinations of windows will appear from the exterior.

2. Research product availability through your local supplier. Many manufacturers provide descriptive literature to aid you in your search.

3. Be sure to consult a professional if structural or solar considerations are involved.

ENERGY EFFICIENCY

Historically, the least energy-efficient parts of our homes have been the doorways and window units. Window units and doorways are, however, becoming more energy-efficient, due to upgraded glazing materials and weather stripping.

Certain types of operating window unit are inherently more energy-efficient than others. For example, tilting, double-hung window units are usually less efficient than casement units. This is because the hardware and sash on the double-hung window must provide a slight space to allow the sash to tilt inward, while the casement window closes tightly against the entire frame perimeter. The casement window, however, provides a significantly different architectural expression and is considerably more expensive than the double-hung window.

Energy efficiency varies not only according

to how the window unit is operated, but also from manufacturer to manufacturer. Some window makers have large research and development departments to keep them on the cutting edge of new technology. You may pay a little more for their product now, but you will be eventually compensated by the savings in energy.

Window and glass manufacturers have made enormous advances over the past 20 years. The insulating glass now available—including the glass with special coatings—has more than doubled the energy efficiency of glazing surfaces. Also, there is now a method of comparing glazing surfaces that relies on "U," "R," and "air infiltration" values to help gauge the effectiveness of energy-saving construction. (See Chapter 4.)

The location and sizing of window units relative to the sun's path and the prevailing wind may have a lot to do with energy efficiency. Plan carefully. Several years ago I purchased a 40-year-old home with many large window units. The second story of this house contained all the bedrooms, which were uncomfortably cold during our first winter. The following spring I purchased and installed a supplemental heating system for the bedrooms. I also upgraded all the windows on the northwest (prevailing winter wind) side of the second story by installing insulated, glazed, fully weather-stripped casement units. Since the windows had been changed, the supplemental heating system, which was on a thermostat, never went on. I could have saved all the money I spent for the heating system if I had only trusted the ability of my window units to keep out the elements.

Maximizing Energy Efficiency

Follow these guidelines to maximize the energy efficiency of your window unit:

1. Compare the energy efficiency of the window unit from one manufacturer to another and from one type of unit to another.
2. Use fixed (nonventing) units whenever ventilation is not important.
3. Use the window unit of the smallest practical size.
4. Carefully check glazing options.
5. Install storm panels on older window units.

EASE OF MAINTENANCE

Manufacturers have invented many labor-saving features for window units. Two aspects of maintenance—cleaning the glass and painting—are described below.

Glass Cleaning

The ability to wash both sides of a piece of glass from inside the house is one of the most important considerations today. Manufacturers now offer this feature for many operating types. It will cost more on some models, but the window washer in your family will definitely think it's worthwhile, especially on second floor units. If your window is double- or single-hung, you will also sacrifice some energy efficiency in order to have the sash tilt inward for washing.

Paint-Free Exteriors

Probably next on the list of maintenance savers is a prepainted metal, vinyl, or wood exterior. To explore this option we'll divide window units into five categories: 1, aluminum; 2, vinyl; 3, wood with the exterior surface of the frame and sash "clad" with vinyl or aluminum; 4, wood with the exterior *frame* surface "clad" and the exterior *sash* surface coated with a special, long-lasting paint; and 5, wood with the exterior surfaces prime-coated or not painted at all.

Types 1, 2, and 3 will require the least amount of attention over the years. Type 4 will provide at least 10 years of maintenance-free use. Type 5 will need to be painted along with the rest of your home's exterior.

Window Grilles

Another maintenance time-saver in wide use

today is the window grille. By simply installing a grille, you can convert a one-light sash into a multilight sash. Grilles may be made of wood, aluminum, or vinyl, and fit either on the glass or in between two lights of insulating glass. They allow for easy washing and painting and are usually less expensive than multiple lights that are individually glazed. Grilles are available in divided and diamond patterns, and also come in custom styles. Grille profiles change from manufacturer to manufacturer. (See Illus. 1-5 on page 16.)

Minimizing Maintenance

Follow these guidelines to minimize window-unit maintenance:

1. Become familiar with manufacturer's list of options and take advantage of those that will prove useful.
2. When considering paint-free exterior treatments, make sure that you are satisfied with the color of the window unit you select. These window units cannot be easily repainted.

3
Types of Window Unit

Windows can be categorized according to the type of material their frames are made of and how they are operated. Both are described below.

MATERIAL CONSTRUCTION

Window units are usually made of several materials, but each unit is put into a specific category according to the type of frame it has. A window unit will be classified as aluminum, vinyl, wood, or clad wood. Steel window units are still being produced, primarily for the fire-resistant market, but are not considered in this section.

Aluminum Window Units

The largest portion of all the window units being manufactured in the United States today, commercial and residential as well as storm products, is aluminum window units. The Second World War created an enormous demand for and supply of aluminum and, when the war ended, products such as aluminum window units evolved. Aluminum provided all the strength and design flexibility of wood and steel, but had less bulk and weight. The construction boom which followed in the 1950s solidified aluminum's position as a major material in the industry. Aluminum combination (triple-track) storm window units were very popular then, as they are today. Primary (prime) window units, such as the single-hung, awning and slider-window units, soon became prevalent over a wide section of the country, and today almost every conceivable operating window unit is made of aluminum.

Aluminum creates an energy challenge in some climates because it is a highly thermally-conductive material—that is, if it's cold outside, the window frame will allow the cold to travel through the aluminum to the inside. When this cold gets inside, condensation has a good chance of developing and heat is wasted. To deal with this problem, aluminum window manufacturers have created a *thermal break* within the frame and possibly also the sash. Thermal breaks are constructed of a nonconductive material such as plastic, and the resulting frame is then made up of an outer and inner frame with the break in the middle. Another method of "thermalizing" an aluminum window unit is to cover its surface in vinyl, thus limiting the aluminum's contact with the air. Illus. 3-1 shows five methods of creating thermal breaks.

The emergence of aluminum window units

There are several ways of making Thermalized windows, depending upon how the thermal break is constructed. The cross-sections below show five types of thermal break construction:

Type 1 is a "unitized" prime and storm Thermalized combination window, consisting of a single-glazed or double-glazed prime window with insulating glass, and a storm window, supplied as one unit. The frame has a built-in thermal break and the air space between the prime window and the storm window provides insulation in the usual manner provided by double-glazing.

Type 2 is a Thermalized prime window with insulating glass and a plastic thermal break in both the frame and sash.

Type 3 also uses insulating glass. It has a thermal break in the frame and uses vinyl cladding as the thermal break for the sash members.

Type 4 uses insulating glass and provides a thermal break by having vinyl cladding on both the frame and the sash members.

Type 5 uses insulating glass and a thermal break in the frame which serves a dual purpose by extending out and covering the sash members, giving them insulation at the same time.

Illus. 3-1. Five methods of creating thermal breaks. (*Courtesy of American Architectural Manufacturers Association*)

TYPES OF THERMAL-BREAK ALUMINUM WINDOWS

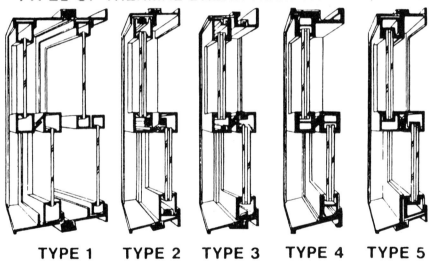

TYPE 1   TYPE 2   TYPE 3   TYPE 4   TYPE 5

has meant less work for the American home-owner. First, the combination storm-and-screen window unit eliminated the task of changing wood screens and storm windows every spring and fall. Then, prime aluminum window units introduced maintenance-free exterior and interior surfaces, reducing dramatically painting time.

When selecting an aluminum window unit, pay attention to its color. Manufacturers do not advise repainting aluminum window units, so the color you choose cannot be changed. Standard colors are white, beige and brown, but many other colors are available on special order.

Aluminum window units normally use a nailing fin or flange system for installation. They present a rather narrow-frame profile from the exterior.

Vinyl Window Units

These strong, lightweight, and durable window units have been improved considerably since they were first manufactured in the 1970s and are popular in the residential—and especially the replacement window market. Vinyl window units are now available in almost every operating type. Limit your vinyl window acquisitions to products that have "welded" corners, which means that the horizontal and vertical frame members have been welded together to create strength and weather resistance. This represents a vast improvement over the old method of only screwing the joint together.

Because it is lightweight and relatively inexpensive, vinyl has become the leading material in the replacement-window-unit market. There are many manufacturers who specialize in this aspect of the industry and gear their production to custom requirements. Very often, these manufacturers will sell directly to the homeowner, and substantial savings can be realized.

Vinyl, which is much less thermally conductive than aluminum, is actually an efficient insulator. The frames and sash on vinyl window units do not require thermal breaks. Maintenance is limited to washing. Painting is not required and also not suggested by the manufacturers. Standard colors for vinyl window units are white, beige and brown. Vinyl window units normally use a nailing fin or flange system for installation. They present a rather narrow-frame profile from the exterior.

Several wood-window manufacturers are now introducing vinyl window units into their product line. This indicates that this relatively new product has a bright future.

One drawback to the vinyl window unit is its inability to accept a natural stain finish on the interior. Several manufacturers have compensated for this by adhering wooden members to the frame and sash on the interior of the unit. Stain can then be applied and a true wood appearance realized.

Wood Window Units

Wood (usually pine) has always been a preferred material for the manufacture of window units because of its availability, strength, workability and insulating characteristics. Wood window units are used primarily in residential and lightly commercial districts. They are available in every operating type.

Wood is much less thermally conductive than aluminum and about on a par with vinyl. The frames and sash of wood window units do not require thermal breaks. Maintenance includes painting, which, depending on your outlook, may become the deciding factor in your window acquisition. If you want to be able to change your interior or exterior color, select a wood window unit. If, however, you do not like painting, you will be better served by a vinyl, aluminum, or clad product.

Wood window units are normally installed by nailing through the exterior casing. They present a relatively wide-frame profile from the exterior. Consider this factor when planning your fenestration. It is normally not advisable to mix wood window units with other types in the same elevation because their frame profiles will not match.

Clad Wood Window Units

Clad-wood window units represent the latest innovation within the wood-window industry. Cladding came about as a response to the maintenance-free aluminum and vinyl window units. Wood-window-unit manufacturers now use aluminum and vinyl as exterior cladding materials to eliminate the necessity of painting. There is not much difference between vinyl and aluminum cladding. Base your decision on factors other than the cladding material.

Illus. 3-2 shows two casement frames, one wood and one clad with aluminum. Note that the cladding is placed on top of the wood frame and

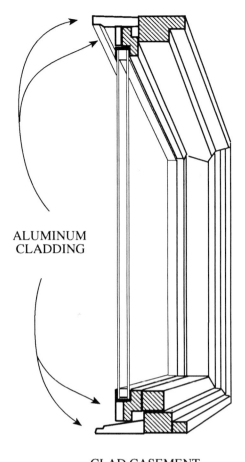

ALUMINUM
CLADDING

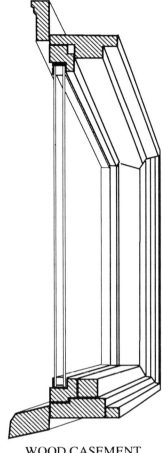

Illus. 3-2. Casement window unit frames.

CLAD CASEMENT   WOOD CASEMENT

located only on the exterior of the frame and sash. This is because of thermal conductivity. The objective is to keep the cold outside and use the natural insulating tendencies of wood to ensure energy efficiency. Also note that the profile of the clad window unit, as viewed from the outside, is narrower than the profile of the wood unit.

Exterior maintenance of clad window units is limited to washing only. The interior has to be painted or stained. A clad window unit comes in standard colors of white, beige and brown, but many other colors are available on special order.

It should be noted that aluminum and vinyl window unit manufacturers are now offering an interior clad product; that is, they are taking an aluminum or vinyl unit and applying wood to the inside. Theoretically, the same result is achieved with this reverse application.

Clad-wood window units normally use a nailing fin or flange system for installation.

Approximately 50 percent of the primary window units sold in the United States during 1990 were wood or clad wood, 33 percent were aluminum, and 17 percent were vinyl or other materials.

OPERATING CHARACTERISTICS

Windows open from the top, side, bottom, or not at all. Each operating type has advantages and limitations, not to mention cost variations. Take advantage of your supplier's displays to find each of the windows featured below.

Double-Hung Window Unit
Construction
The double-hung window unit consists of a sin-

gle frame in which two sash (a top and bottom) slide vertically past each other (Illus. 3-3). The two sash meet in the vertical center of the window when closed unless they are "cottage-style." The frames can be joined together (side by side) to create multiple openings. Double-hung window units are readily available in wood, clad wood, vinyl and aluminum (Illus. 3-4).

"Cottage-style" double-hung window units differ from the standard unit in that the top and bottom sash are of unequal size. Usually, the top sash is smaller than the bottom sash. This style is found most frequently in Colonial architecture (Illus. 3-5).

Use

Double-hung windows are primarily found in the residential and light commercial market, usually in traditional or Colonial designs. (The "residential" market refers to single-family homes, while the "light commercial" market refers to multifamily low-rise construction, as well as offices and retail stores.)

Sizes

The double-hung window unit is the most popu-

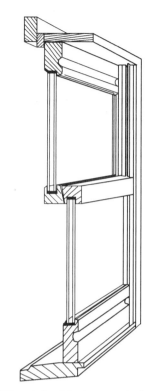

Illus. 3-4. Wood double-hung window unit.

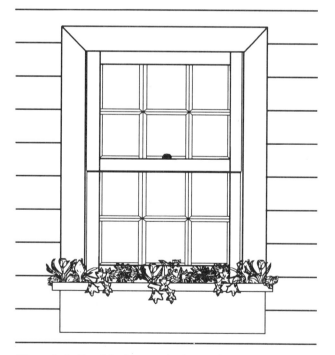

Illus. 3-3. Double-hung window unit.

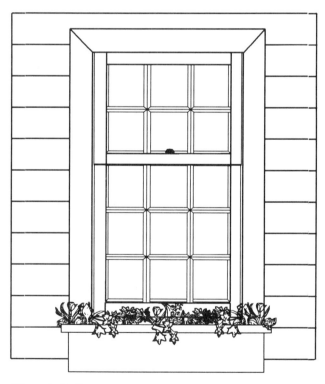

Illus. 3-5. Cottage double-hung window unit with a sash ratio of 6:9.

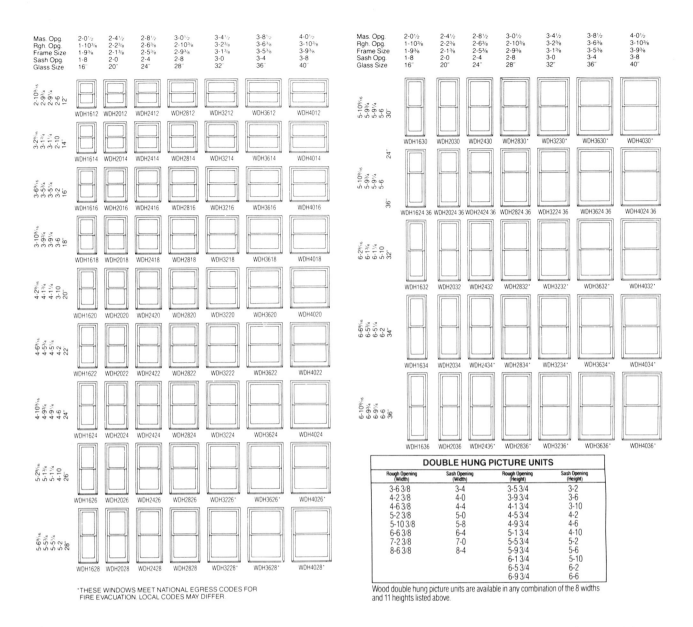

Illus. 3-6. The size listing for wood double-hung window units. (*Courtesy of Marvin Windows*)

lar of all window units in use today, and there are a large number of standard sizes which should meet all requirements. Illus. 3-6 shows the standard sizes of wooden double-hung windows offered by one manufacturer. These single-window units can be joined together to create wider units, or special sizes can be ordered.

It's interesting to note that triple-hung window units are also available but are not widely used. They are very similar to double-hung window units except that three sash operate. They are most often used in very tall openings.

Hardware
Hardware is generally located within or on the sides of the frame, and consists of channels in which the sash slide and a counterbalancing mechanism to aid in raising and lowering the sash and keeping them open in any desired position. Since the 1940s, this system has evolved from weights and cord to one of several balance

45

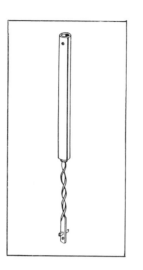
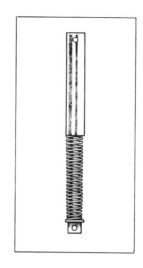
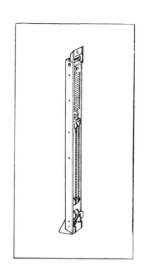

Illus. 3-7. Spiral, spring, and block-and-tackle balance mechanisms. (*Courtesy of American Architectural Manufacturers Association*)

mechanisms: "spiral," "spring," and "block and tackle" (Illus. 3-7). Some windows do not have this counterbalance and use friction within the channels to obtain similar results.

Much of the double-hung hardware of today allows for the tilting in of the sash to facilitate cleaning and painting. Sash locks, mounted on the check rail, and sash lifts, mounted on or in the top and bottom rails, are often (but not always) provided by the manufacturer.

Weather Stripping
The weather stripping may be located on the frame or sash but is most commonly found on both. A double-hung window unit is a difficult window to weather-strip because space must be provided for the sash to slide and tilt. The sash come together at only one location—the "check" or "meeting" rail—and this area should surely be weather-stripped. Also, the top of the top sash and the bottom of the bottom sash should be covered. Vertical weather stripping is normally provided by the channels.

Ventilation
Ventilation is available through only 50 percent of the sash opening, although this may be through the top, bottom, or both. This ventilation system can be used to direct incoming air and avoid drafts.

View and Light
Double-hung window units do not allow as much view and light as more vertically oriented win-

dow units. The area where the sash meet may obstruct any view.

Maintenance
Double-hung window units must be washed from the outside, unless the hardware allows the sash to be tilted in. This option, called "tilt in" or "tilt and take out" (Illus. 3-8) is worth considering. A window with a tilt-in sash is slightly less energy-efficient, but is much more convenient. If you decide on the tilt option, be sure you are familiar with the operation of this feature. Many problems can result from incorrect engagement of the sash within the channels. Even if the hardware allows for removal of the sash, use only the tilt option and leave the sash in the frame whenever possible. This may require that you bring a chair along with you to support one sash while you are cleaning the other, but it will prevent a "sprung" balance that is not easy to repair. When a "sprung" balance occurs, the spring mechanism becomes detached from its track and snaps upwards, where it hangs limply. Ask your sales representative to demonstrate this tilting feature completely.

Keep paint away from the channels and weather stripping. Lubricate channels with a silicone product if necessary.

Operation Technique
If a double-hung window unit is directly accessible, it is normally quite easy to operate. How-

Illus. 3-8. Double-hung tilting window unit.

ever, if furniture or a countertop is in the way, as when the unit is over a sink, operation may become difficult. Try the window unit before you buy it. A switch to a casement or awning window unit for an awkward location may be warranted.

Storm Window Units and Screens
Storm window units and screens are installed on the exterior of the frame. They are available from either the window unit manufacturer or many third-party vendors.

Energy Efficiency
Double-hung window units are generally less energy-efficient than casement and awning window units. Their energy-efficiency ratings may vary dramatically among different manufacturers.

Cost
Double-hung window units cost less than other types of window per square foot of window opening. This is because of less sophisticated hardware.

Advantages of Double-Hung Window Units

1. They are less expensive.
2. They are simple to operate and maintain.
3. They can provide indirect ventilation if used in conjunction with a combination storm-and-screen window unit or a shade.
4. The sash do not project from the frame, causing a hindrance to pedestrians or furniture.

Disadvantages of Double-Hung Units
1. Only 50 percent of the sash on double-hung window units allows for ventilation.
2. The horizontal lines at meeting rails may obscure the view.
3. Double-hung window units cannot be cleaned from inside the house unless tilting hardware is used.
4. An open window unit will not prevent rain from entering.
5. A double-hung window unit is hard to open if access to the window is limited.
6. Egress from a double-hung window unit is limited to only half the frame area unless the sash are removed.
7. Open sash do not catch the available wind.

Single-Hung Window Unit
A single-hung window unit is very similar to a double-hung window unit except that only one sash (the bottom sash) is now operating (Illus. 3-9). The logic is that since only 50 percent of the sash in a double-hung window unit can be open at any one time, why waste money on two operating sash? It is also claimed that one operating sash makes for a more energy-efficient window unit. These windows are generally available in aluminum or vinyl and are only rarely seen in wood. They are less expensive than double-hung window units and are commonly used in the southern United States in residential construction.

Horizontal-Sliding Window Unit
Construction
This type of window unit is also called a "glider," "slider" or "slide-by." In this type of window unit, two or more sash (usually two) slide horizontally past each other (Illus. 3-10). In some types, one of the sash may be fixed

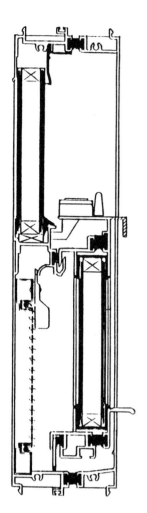

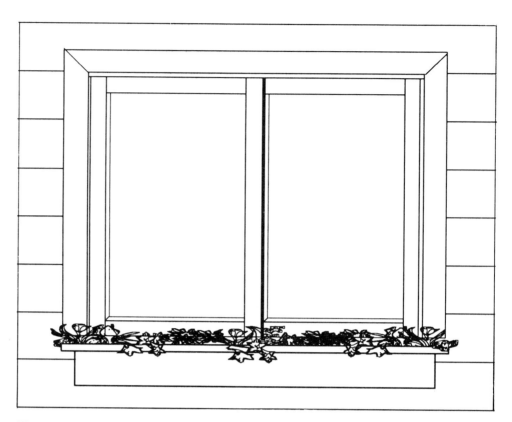

Illus. 3-9 (above left). Section view of aluminum single-hung window unit. (*Courtesy of Acorn Building Components*) **Illus. 3-10 (above right).** Horizontal-sliding window unit.

(nonmovable). When both sash operate, they can be removed for cleaning, which may be an important factor, especially on upper floors. Be sure to inquire whether one or both sash operate, because different manufacturers offer one or the other. The two sash meet in the horizontal center of the window unit when closed. The frames can be joined together (side by side) to create multiple openings. Horizontal-sliding window units are readily available in wood, clad wood, vinyl, and aluminum (Illus. 3-11).

Use
Horizontal-sliding window units are very popular in multifamily residential construction. They are also commonly found on porches and breezeways of single-family homes. Their vertical lines create a more contemporary than traditional fenestration.

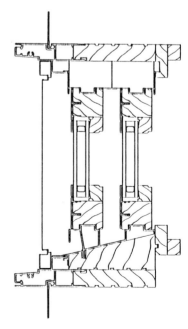

Illus. 3-11. Aluminum-clad horizontal-sliding window. (*Courtesy of Semling-Menke Co.*)

48

Sizes

Horizontal-sliding window units come in fewer standard sizes than double-hung window units. Check the available sizes before creating construction plans. Wide sizes are readily available (Illus. 3-12).

Hardware

No balancing device is necessary because gravity keeps the sash in the track. The sash ride horizontally in a top and bottom track. At least one sash is removable by pushing it up and swinging it in. Sash locks mounted on the meeting stiles and sash pulls mounted on or in the left- and right-side stiles are often (but not always) provided by the manufacturer.

Weather Stripping

Weather stripping may be located on the sash, frame, or both, as well as on the track. A horizontal-sliding window unit is difficult to weather-strip because space must be provided for the sash to slide and tilt. The sash come together at only one location—the "check" or "meeting" rail—and this area should surely be weather-stripped.

Ventilation

Ventilation is available through only 50 percent of the sash opening. The ventilation system on a horizontally sliding window unit is not as effective as that on other types of window unit.

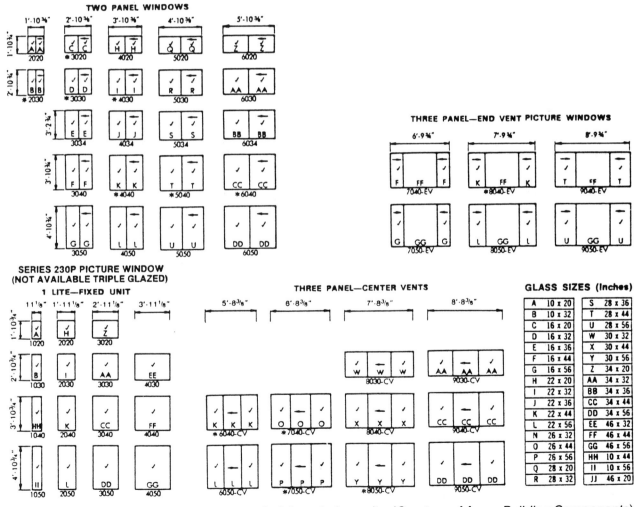

Illus. 3-12. Size listing for aluminum horizontal-sliding window units. (*Courtesy of Acorn Building Components*)

View and Light

These window units allow for more view and light than horizontally oriented windows. Vertical obstructions are less disruptive to viewing.

Maintenance

These window units can only be washed from the exterior unless the hardware allows for removing the sash. A window unit with removable sash is worth considering. You normally sacrifice energy efficiency when both sash are removable, but these types of window unit can be washed much more easily. Keep paint away from the channels and weather stripping. Lubricate channels with a silicone product on a regular basis because friction is the major force working against easy operation. Vacuum and clean the bottom channel frequently.

Operation Technique

If a horizontal-sliding window unit is directly accessible, it is normally quite easy to operate. However, if furniture or a countertop is in the way, the window unit may become difficult to operate. Try it before you buy it. It may be more convenient to use a casement or awning window unit for that location.

Storm-Window Units and Screens

Storm windows and screens for horizontal-sliding window units vary widely, depending on the manufacturer. They may be installed on the frame or sash, on the interior or exterior. They are normally available only from the manufacturer and should be purchased along with your window units.

Energy Efficiency

Horizontal-sliding window units are usually less energy-efficient than casement and awning units, but are more energy-efficient than a double-hung unit. Ratings may vary dramatically among different manufacturers.

Cost

Horizontal-sliding window units cost less per square foot of window opening than any other type of window unit. This is because the hardware for these windows is less expensive than the hardware for other types of window unit.

Advantages of Horizontal-Sliding Window Units

1. They are less expensive than other window units.
2. They are simple to operate and maintain.
3. The sash do not project from the frame, causing a hindrance to pedestrians or furniture.
4. Wide horizontal sizes are easily accommodated within single windows.
5. Large units, with both sash removed, allow the window to be used for access of furniture or supplies into the building. They are very convenient for upper stories.
6. Horizontal-sliding window units afford a better view than a double-hung window unit.

Disadvantages of Horizontal-Sliding Window Units

1. Only 50 percent of the window unit allows for ventilation.
2. They cannot be cleaned from the inside unless the sash are removable.
3. An open window unit will not prevent rain from entering.
4. They are hard to open if access to the window unit is obstructed by furniture.
5. Egress is limited to only half the frame unless both sash are removed.
6. The open sash do not catch the available wind.
7. They are susceptible to water infiltration at the bottom track.

Casement Window Unit

Construction

A casement window unit projects outward (Illus. 3-13). It usually has one sash (some manufacturers put in more than one sash) per frame, with frames joined together to create multiple openings. The sash open out like a door. Casement window units are readily available in wood, clad wood, vinyl and aluminum (Illus. 3-14).

Use

These window units are sold primarily to the residential and light commercial market. Their

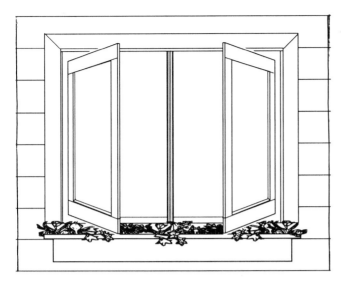

Illus. 3-13. Casement window unit.

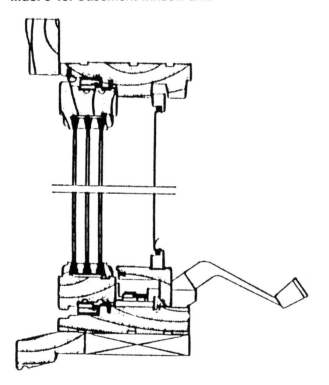

Illus. 3-14. Section view of a triple-glazed wood casement window unit. (*Courtesy of WeatherShield Manufacturing*)

vertical lines create a more contemporary than traditional fenestration.

Sizes

Casement window units are sold in an enormous number of standard sizes that should cover all requirements. Any single-casement window unit can be joined to any other single-casement unit to accommodate special size requirements. This is possible even though the manufacturer does not show that combination in his specifications. Sash widths are somewhat limited due to weight restrictions of the hardware. Join several single-window units to create wide widths.

Since casement sash may be hinged to either side jamb, you can specify whether you want the sash to open to the left or right (as viewed from outside). Manufacturers indicate this hinging by using a triangle. The symbol ▶ indicates that the sash is hinged on the right; ◀ indicates hinging on the left. If no triangle is shown, the manufacturer is stating that the sash will be shipped nonventing unless you specify otherwise. Usually you can change the standard hinging patterns by simply making the request. If you change a nonventing sash to a venting sash, you will be charged extra; the converse is also true. You should be able to change a left hinge to a right hinge for no extra charge (Illus. 3-15).

Hardware

The hardware for casement window units has changed dramatically over the years. It has evolved from sash which were manually swung open to push-bar assemblies to the present-day roto-gear operators. Sash are attached to frames at the top and bottom with a slide mechanism that is actuated by a roto-handle.

Sash locks are located on the projecting sash stile. As the vertical height of the window unit increases, more than one sash lock will be provided to ensure a tight, uniform fit when the sash are closed and locked.

The hardware should allow for sash to be rigidly held open at any position. All parts should be rust-resistant. Modern hardware should allow for the sash to be opened a full 90 degrees and far enough from the side jamb to allow your arm to reach out and clean the glass from the inside. Check that your new window units have this feature.

PERMA-SHIELD®CASEMENT WINDOW BASIC UNIT SIZES

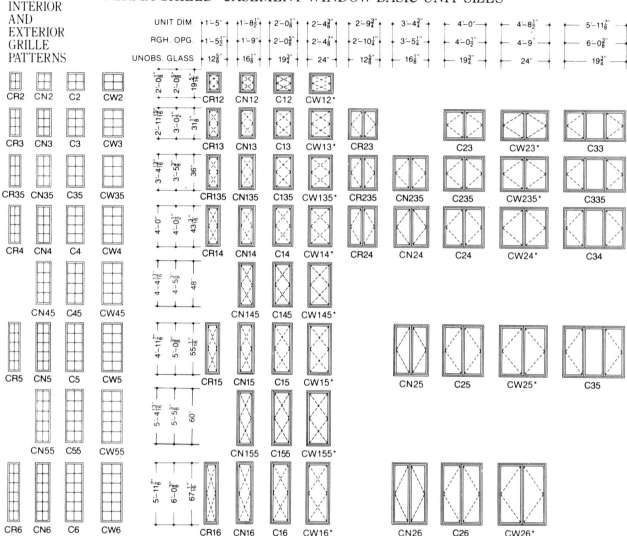

Illus. 3-15. Size listing for vinyl-clad casement window units. (*Courtesy of Anderson Windows, Inc.*)

Problems can result if sash locks are not disengaged before the sash are opened. Stripped gears are a common consequence, and you should order extra hardware if you are buying a house full of casement window units.

Many manufacturers now provide numerous hardware color options. Solid brass, dark and light bronze, and other colors are commonplace. Check with your supplier.

Weather Stripping
The weather stripping is located on the frame and sash. Casement window units are generally more energy-efficient because their design allows for full-perimeter weather stripping combined with the sealing effect of the latching device. This type of window unit differs from double-hung and slider window units in that it does not slide and its fit can be much tighter.

Ventilation
Ventilation is possible through almost 100 percent of the sash opening. Also, the projecting sash allows the collecting and directing of air moving parallel to the exterior wall. This

method of ventilation is superior to that for double-hung window units.

View and Light
Casement window units allow a better view and light than more horizontally oriented units. Vertical obstructions are less disruptive to the view. However, screens on casement window units are always full-height and can affect both the view and light. Plan to remove them when insects are not a factor.

Maintenance
These window units can be washed from the inside if the hardware allows for enough space on the hinge side of the sash. Be sure to check specifications before you buy the window unit. Keep paint away from the hardware and weather stripping. Lubricate the hardware with a product specified by the manufacturer.

Operating Technique
These window units are the easiest of all to operate. As long as you can reach the handle, you can open the sash.

Storm Window Units and Screens
The screens are installed on the inside and can be easily removed. The storm panels ride piggy-back on the exterior of the sash or are mounted in the same location as the screens. Both are normally available only from the manufacturer and should be purchased along with the window units.

Energy Efficiency
Casement window units are generally the most energy-efficient of all operating types. However, ratings may vary dramatically among different manufacturers.

Cost
These window units cost relatively more per square foot of window opening than other types of window unit. This is because of more sophisticated hardware and construction.

Advantages of Casement Window Units

1. They are very easy to operate.
2. They provide greater and more efficient ventilation.

3. They provide a better view than double-hung window units.

Disadvantages of Casement Window Units

1. Their sash width is somewhat limited due to the weight restrictions of hardware. This may affect egress.
2. An open window unit can allow rain to enter.
3. These projecting window units can create a dangerous obstacle to pedestrian traffic.
4. Their open sash are subject to damage in high winds.

Awning Window Units

Construction
An awning window unit projects outward (Illus. 3-16). It generally has one sash (some manufacturers put in more than one sash) per frame with the frames joined together (both horizontally and vertically) to create multiple openings. The sash are hinged to the frame so that

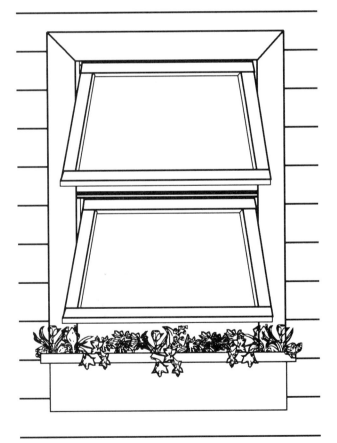

Illus. 3-16. Awning window unit.

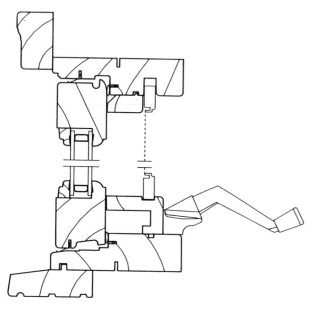

Illus. 3-17. Section view of wood awning window unit. (*Courtesy of Marvin Windows*)

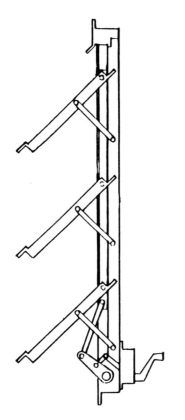

Illus. 3-18. Hardware for multi-sash aluminum awning window unit. (*Courtesy of American Architectural Manufacturers Association*)

the bottom of the sash swings outward like an awning. Awning window units are readily available in wood, clad wood, vinyl and aluminum. Wood units usually contain one sash per frame (Illus. 3-17), while aluminum window units contain multiple sash (Illus. 3-18).

Use

Awning window units are sold primarily to the residential and light-commercial markets and are used equally in contemporary and traditional fenestration. They are very commonly used on porches and breezeways. Awning window units can be mounted high off the floor as in a bathroom and still be easily opened.

Sizes

Awning window units are sold in a fair number of standard sizes which, when joined to other awning window units either vertically or horizontally, should cover all requirements. For special needs, check the manufacturer's specification sheet. Sash heights are somewhat limited due to weight restrictions of hardware. Join several window units to create greater height (Illus. 3-19).

Since awning sash may be venting or nonventing, manufacturers indicate this hinging by using a triangle: ▲ indicates an awning sash which is hinged at the top. If no triangle is shown, the manufacturer is stating that the sash will be shipped nonventing unless you specify otherwise. If you change a nonventing sash to a venting sash, you will be charged extra; the converse is also true.

Hardware

The hardware for awning window units has changed dramatically over the years. It has evolved from sash that were manually swung open to push-bar assemblies to the present-day roto-gear operators. During the 1950s, 60s and 70s, it was common to have multiple sash controlled by a single operator. Today, it is just as common to control each sash with a separate operator, and hardware is of a stronger, more durable design. Sash are attached to frames at the sides with a slide mechanism that is actuated by a roto-handle or a push rod. Sash locks

VENT AND FIXED SIZES

ROUGH OPENING(mm)		902	1 054	1 207	1 359
	FRAME(mm)	889	1 041	1 194	1 346
	ROUGH OPENING	2'11-1/2"	3'5-1/2"	3'11-1/2"	4'5-1/2"
	FRAME	2'11"	3'5"	3'11"	4'5"
	GLASS	30"	36"	42"	48"
451 / 432 15-3/4" 15" 12"		3012CA	3612CA	4212CA	4812CA
552 / 533 19-3/4" 19" 16"		3016CA	3616CA	4216CA	4816CA
603 / 584 1'11-3/4" 1'11" 18"		3018CA	3618CA	4218CA	4816CA
654 / 635 21-3/4" 21" 20"		3020CA	3620CA	4220CA	4820CA
756 / 737 25-3/4" 25" 24"		3024CA	3624CA	4224CA	4824CA

ADDITIONAL FIXED SIZES

ROUGH OPENING(mm)		902	1 054	1 207	1 359
	FRAME(mm)	889	1 041	1 194	1 346
	ROUGH OPENING	2'11-1/2"	3'5-1/2"	3'11-1/2"	4'5-1/2"
	FRAME	2'11"	3'5"	3'11"	4'5"
	GLASS	30"	36"	42"	48"
1 060 / 1 041 3'5-3/4" 3'5" 36"		3036CA	3636CA	4236CA	4836CA
1 213 / 1 194 3'11-3/4" 3'11" 42"		3042CA	3642CA	4242CA	4842CA
1 365 / 1 346 4'5-3/4" 4'5" 48"		3048CA	3648CA	4248CA	4848CA
1 518 / 1 499 4'11-3/4" 4'11" 54"		3054CA	3654CA	4254CA	4854CA
1 670 / 1 651 5'5-3/4" 5'5" 60"		3060CA	3660CA	4260CA	4860CA
1 873 / 1 854 6'1-3/4" 6'1" 68"		3068CA	3668CA	4268CA	4868CA (5/8 IG)

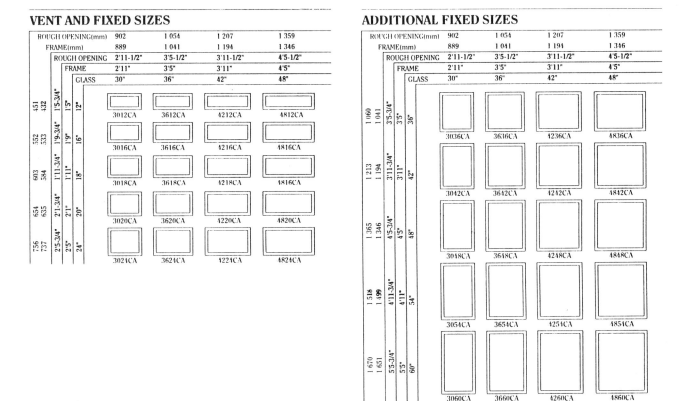

Illus. 3-19. Size listing for aluminum-clad awning window units. (*Courtesy of Pella Windows and Doors*)

are located on the projecting sash rail. As the width of the window unit increases, more than one sash lock is provided to ensure a tight, uniform fit when the sash is closed and locked.

The hardware should allow for sash to be rigidly held open at any position. All parts should be rust-resistant. Modern hardware should allow the sash to be opened a full 90 degrees and far enough from the head jamb to allow your arm to reach out and clean the glass from the inside.

Problems can result if the sash locks are not disengaged before you open the sash. Stripped gears are a common consequence, and you should order extra hardware if you are buying a house full of awning window units.

Many manufacturers now provide numerous hardware color options. Solid brass, dark and light bronze, and other colors are commonplace. Check with your supplier.

Weather Stripping
The weather stripping will be located on the frame and sash. Awning window units are generally more energy-efficient because their design allows for full-perimeter weather stripping combined with the sealing effect of the latching device. This type of window unit differs from double-hung and slider window units in that it does not slide, so the fit can be much tighter.

Ventilation
Ventilation is possible through almost 100 per-

cent of the sash opening. Also, the projecting sash allows it to be open in inclement weather without admitting the elements. This is the best window unit for use in the rain.

View and Light
It allows less expansive views and light than more vertically oriented units because horizontal obstructions are more disruptive to the view. Screens are always full-height and can affect both view and light. Plan to remove them when insects are not a factor.

Maintenance
Awning window units can be washed from the inside as long as the hardware allows. Be sure to check its specifications before you buy the window unit. Keep paint away from the hardware and weather stripping. Lubricate the hardware with a product specified by the manufacturer.

Operating Technique
These window units are very easy to operate. As long as you can reach the handle, you can open the sash.

Storm Window Units and Screens
The screens are installed on the inside and can be easily removed. The storm panels ride piggyback on the exterior of the sash or are mounted in the same location as the screens. Both are normally available only from the manufacturer and should be purchased along with the window units.

Energy Efficiency
Awning window units are generally among the most energy-efficient of all. However, ratings may vary dramatically among different manufacturers.

Cost
Awning window units cost more than most of the other types of windows. This is because of their more sophisticated hardware and construction.

Advantages of Awning Window Units
1. They are very easy to operate.
2. They can be opened for ventilation in the rain.
3. They can be located very high off the floor to accommodate obstructions but still be easily operated.
4. They can be joined horizontally or vertically to other windows.

Disadvantages of Awning Window Units
1. Their sash height is somewhat limited due to weight restrictions of hardware. This may affect egress.
2. These projecting window units can create a dangerous obstacle to pedestrian traffic.
3. The open sash are subject to damage in high winds.
4. The open sash collect dirt and debris.

Hopper Window Units
Hopper window units are similar to the awning window units described above, except that the sash are hinged, so that the top of the sash swings inward (Illus. 3-20). They have limited use because the inwardly open position interferes with furniture placement and pedestrian

Illus. 3-20. Fixed and hopper window unit.

traffic. The unit's one useful feature is to provide a means to direct incoming air upwards, thus preventing drafts across a room.

Hopper window units are common in schools, offices, and institutions and are generally constructed of wood, aluminum, or steel. Their hardware is not sophisticated, consisting of a hinge and latch assembly.

Since hopper sash may be venting or nonventing, manufacturers indicate this hinging by using a triangle: ▼ indicates a hopper sash which is hinged at the bottom. If no triangle is shown, the manufacturer is stating that the sash will be shipped nonventing unless you specify otherwise. If you change a nonventing sash to a venting sash, you will be charged extra; the converse is also true.

Jalousie

The jalousie window unit is also similar to the awning window unit (Illus. 3-21). However, instead of one operating sash, jalousie windows have a number of horizontal glass slats, all of which are operated simultaneously by a crank assembly. The slats open out in the same fashion as an awning. These window units can be opened for ventilation in the rain.

Weather-stripping problems have precluded the use of the jalousie window unit in regions with harsh winter climates. They are normally found on porches and breezeways and are generally constructed of aluminum.

Basement Window Unit

The basement window unit is also similar to the awning window unit (Illus. 3-22). It consists of a frame containing a single sash, which opens inward. Generally, the sash is reversible, in that it can be hinged at the top (like an awning, directing the air downwards) or at the bottom (like a hopper, directing the air upwards), depending on the user's preference. Basement window units come in a limited number of sizes and usually accommodate 16″ long concrete-block construction. They may be made of wood, aluminum, or steel. Screens and storm panels are available.

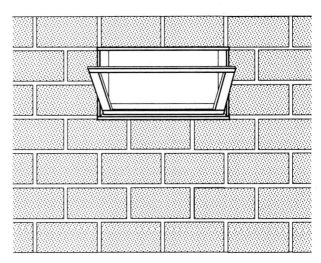

Illus. 3-22. Basement window unit.

These are very functional but unsophisticated window units that are relatively inexpensive. In addition to their use as basement windows, they are commonly found in garages, cabins, and utility buildings.

Special frames may be available from the

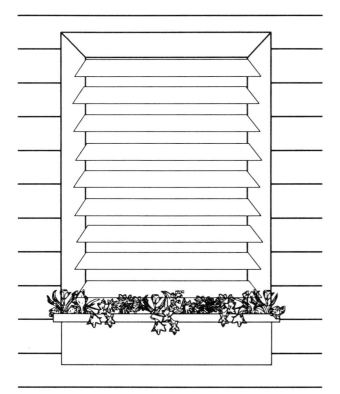

Illus. 3-21. Jalousie window unit.

manufacturer to be installed within the form work prior to pouring the concrete walls of the basement. This system ensures an accurate fit into the masonry wall.

Barn-Sash and Slip-Head Window Units

These are the most economical of all wood window units. A barn-sash window unit is really created on the job site. The window frame may be part of the building framing or added on by the installer. Only the sash is purchased and then joined to the frame with hinges or stops.

The slip-head window unit (Illus. 3-23) consists of a frame with a slot in the top and a single sash that opens by being pushed up through the head of the frame and into the pocket between the wall framing, which is hidden. Both the barn-sash and slip-head units are used when low price is the main concern, as in barns and cabins. They are not widely available.

Illus. 3-23. Slip-head window unit.

Tilt-Turn Window Units
Construction
This type of window unit has been used for years in Europe, but is a fairly new product in the United States. A tilt-turn window has one sash per frame; the frames are joined together (both horizontally and vertically) to create multiple openings (Illus. 3-24). The sash open in two different ways: at the top like a hopper unit and at the side like an inward-swinging casement unit. This is a heavy-duty product constructed of substantially thicker stock. Tilt-turn window units are readily available in wood and aluminum (Illus. 3-25).

Use
Tilt-turn window units are sold to the residential and commercial market. Their heavy-duty construction and dual venting function allow for widespread use.

Sizes
Tilt-turn window units come in a limited selection of sizes. Consider joining frames to create the size you need.

Hardware
Tilt-turn window units have very sophisticated

Illus. 3-24. Tilt-turn, dual-action window unit.

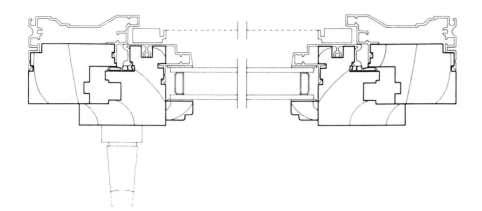

Illus. 3-25. Section view of an aluminum-clad tilt-turn window unit. (*Courtesy of Marvin Windows*)

hardware. Turn the handle one way, and the sash tilts slightly in at the top, allowing secure ventilation. Turn the handle a little more, and the sash opens inward like a door, allowing full ventilation, easy cleaning, and a possible emergency exit. Tilt-turn window units are also available for institutional use with hardware that can be locked with a key.

Weather Stripping
The weather stripping may be located on either the frame or the sash but is most commonly found on both. Tilt-turn window units are heavily weather-stripped to prepare them for their proposed use.

Ventilation
There is ventilation through almost 100 percent of the sash opening, or through only the top if tilted in.

View and Light
These window units allow a great deal of view and light, just slightly less than a casement window unit.

Maintenance
These window units can be easily washed from the inside. Keep paint away from the hardware and weather stripping. Lubricate hardware in accordance with manufacturer's specifications.

Operating Technique
If the window unit is directly accessible, it is normally quite easy to operate, although it may be too sophisticated for small children. The sash

opens inward and may interfere with furniture and draperies.

Storm Window Units and Screens
The screens are installed on the exterior of the frame, and storm panels are mounted on the exterior of the sash. Both are normally available only from the manufacturer and should be purchased at the same time as the window units.

Energy Efficiency
Tilt-turn window units are generally among the most energy-efficient window units. The sash is held tightly closed along its entire perimeter by the hardware. Ratings may vary dramatically among different manufacturers.

Cost
Tilt-turn window units cost more per square foot of window opening than other types of window. This is because their hardware is sophisticated and they are constructed for heavy duty.

Advantages of Tilt-Turn Window Units

1. They have several options for ventilation.
2. They are easy to clean from the inside.
3. They allow an expansive view and light.
4. They perform well in wind and temperature extremes.

Disadvantages of Tilt-Turn Units

1. The inward-opening sash may adversely affect furniture placement.
2. They are expensive.
3. They come in a limited selection of sizes.

Fixed Window Units

Construction

Fixed window units are also referred to as "non-venting units," "picture units," "direct sets," "flexiframes," and "spandrels," as well as several other names, by different manufacturers. There are two basic types of fixed window unit: "stationary frame and sash" and "direct set" windows (Illus. 3-26).

A "stationary frame and sash" unit consists of a frame containing a sash which does not open. This type of window is usually joined (either horizontally or vertically) to operating window units to create a large opening. Common configurations include placing the fixed unit between two operating units of any type to create a picture-window unit (Illus. 3-27) or placing the fixed unit above an awning or hopper to create a "window wall" effect (Illus. 3-28). Its use is limited only by your imagination.

A "direct set" unit consists of a frame and no sash. The glass is set directly into the frame and does not open. This type of unit is often used independently of other windows and allows for a great variety of shapes and sizes (Illus. 3-29).

Both types of window unit are readily avail-

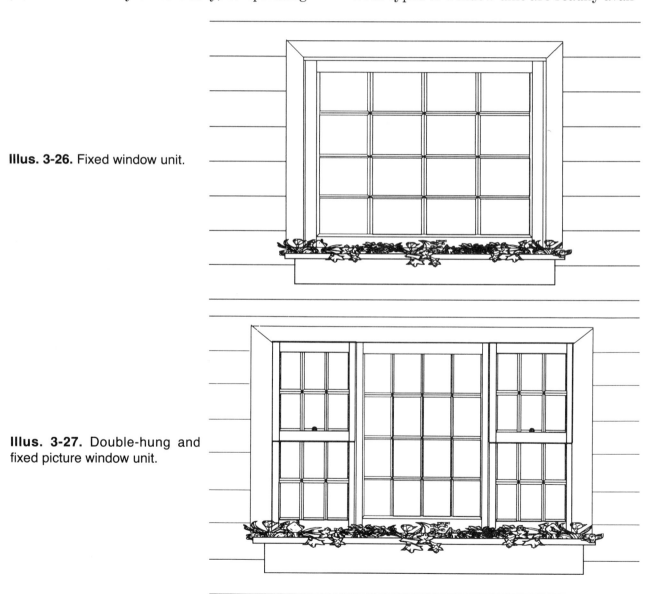

Illus. 3-26. Fixed window unit.

Illus. 3-27. Double-hung and fixed picture window unit.

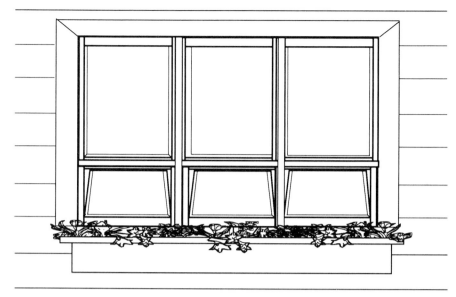

Illus. 3-28. Hopper and fixed window wall unit.

able in wood, clad wood, vinyl and aluminum.

Use
Fixed window units are sold primarily to the residential and light-commercial market.

Sizes
Fixed window units are available in an enormous number of standard sizes that should cover all requirements. Any fixed frame and sash unit can usually be ordered joined to any other single operating unit to accommodate special size requirements. This is possible even when the manufacturer does not show that combination in its specifications. Unique sizes and shapes of direct set units are available as a special order.

Hardware and Weather Stripping
Fixed window units don't have hardware, because the sash do not operate. Weather stripping is provided around the total perimeter and should be more efficient because the sash don't vent.

Ventilation
Ventilation is not provided by these units.

View and Light
Depending on their location, these units allow a more expansive view and light than operating windows.

Maintenance
These window units can only be washed from the outside.

Storm Window Units
Storm window units can be installed on the outside or inside. They are normally available only from the manufacturer and should be purchased along with the window units.

Energy Efficiency
Fixed window units are generally the most energy-efficient of all types. However, ratings may vary dramatically among different manufacturers.

Cost
Fixed window units range drastically in cost per square foot. A basic rectangular shape is relatively inexpensive, while a fancy circle or oval can be very costly. It definitely pays to look at all the options and manufacturers when choosing a unique design.

Advantages of Fixed Window Units

1. They allow a more expansive view and more light.

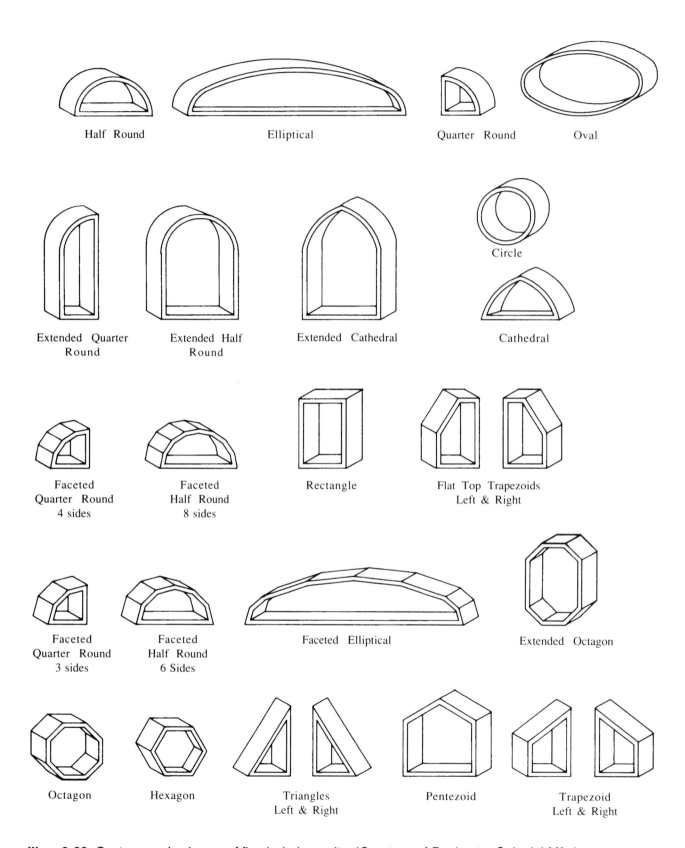

Half Round

Elliptical

Quarter Round

Oval

Extended Quarter Round

Extended Half Round

Extended Cathedral

Circle

Cathedral

Faceted Quarter Round 4 sides

Faceted Half Round 8 sides

Rectangle

Flat Top Trapezoids Left & Right

Faceted Quarter Round 3 sides

Faceted Half Round 6 Sides

Faceted Elliptical

Extended Octagon

Octagon

Hexagon

Triangles Left & Right

Pentezoid

Trapezoid Left & Right

Illus. 3-29. Custom-made shapes of fixed window units. (*Courtesy of Rochester Colonial Mfg.*)

2. They enhance the architectural appearance of the house.

Disadvantages of Fixed Units

1. They give no ventilation or egress.
2. They must be cleaned from the outside.

Circle-Head or Round-Top Window Units

Construction

A circle-head or round-top window is also referred to as an "eyebrow window" or other names created by manufacturers. There are two basic types of circle-head window unit: true circle-heads and created circle-heads. A true circle-head consists of a single frame with a semicircular head jamb and a sash with a semi-circular top (Illus. 3-30). It may be a casement, double-hung, or other kind of window. A created circle-head is an operating unit (or units) that is vertically joined to a single fixed unit with a semicircular head (Illus. 3-31). This method of creating a round-top window allows for a great number of size variations and provides a single circle top over multiple operating units. However, the horizontal lines created by joining the two frames may impede the view and affect the architectural appearance of the unit. Both true and created circle-head window units are readily available in wood, clad wood, vinyl and aluminum.

Use

Circle-head window units are used primarily by

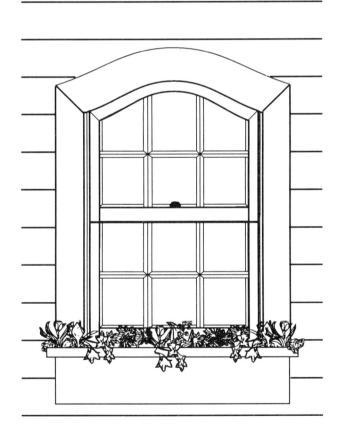

Illus. 3-30. True circle-head double-hung window unit.

Illus. 3-31. Created circle-head double-hung window unit.

the residential and light commercial market. The addition of a circle top greatly enhances fenestration.

Sizes
True circle-heads are available in a limited number of sizes, but fixed circle-head units are available in a large number of standard sizes which should cover all requirements.

View and Light
The true circle-head is better for the view because it does not contain the horizontal interruption necessary in the created circle-head.

Cost
Circle-head windows are relatively expensive, with the true circle-head being the most costly.

Skylights and Roof Window Units

Terminology
Before skylights and roof window units can be described, the following terminology must be understood.

The *roof slope* (also called pitch) is the number of inches a roof drops in one foot of run. Use a level and rule to determine the pitch in the area where you want to mount the skylight. Hold the level horizontally, perpendicular to the peak with one end touching the roof. Measure 12″ along the level out from the roof and then measure down from this point back to the roof, creating a right triangle with the roof line as the hypotenuse. The last measurement, from the level down to the roof, will be the slope (Illus. 3-33). If your last measurement is 4″, the slope is described as 4″ in 12″, 4:12, 4/12, or 33.3 degrees. Most skylight and roof window units have minimum slope requirements of 3/12 or 4/12.

Flashing is metal, plastic, or rubberized asphalt stripping which is designed to interact with the skylight and the roof surface to provide a weathertight seal. It may or may not provide a means for attaching the skylight to the roof. It may be an integral part of the skylight (self-flashing) or a part to be added on later (step flashing, to name just one type) (Illus. 3-34 and 3-35).

Metal flashing may be manufactured of aluminum, copper, or lead. Different types of roofing material and extreme roof pitches require different types of flashing. When skylight or roof window units are located within close proximity to one another (6 to 8″) special flashing systems are used.

A *curb*, as it relates to skylight and roof window units, is a frame positioned on top of the roof around the perimeter of the hole (Illus. 3-36). It may be made of wood, vinyl, or aluminum. It raises the glazed surface above the most serious ice, snow, and flowing rain conditions,

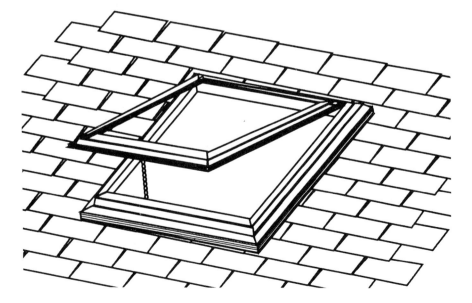

Illus. 3-32. Ventilating skylight.

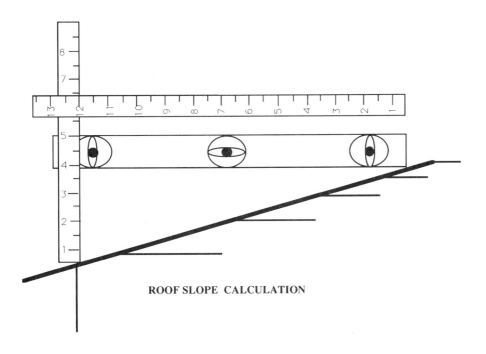

ROOF SLOPE CALCULATION

Illus. 3-33. Calculating roof slope.

Illus. 3-34. Metal self flashing. (*Courtesy of Thermo-Vu Skylights*)

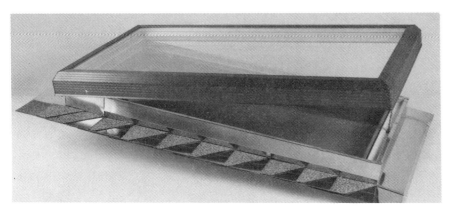

Illus. 3-35. Metal step flashing. (*Courtesy of Thermo-Vu Skylights*)

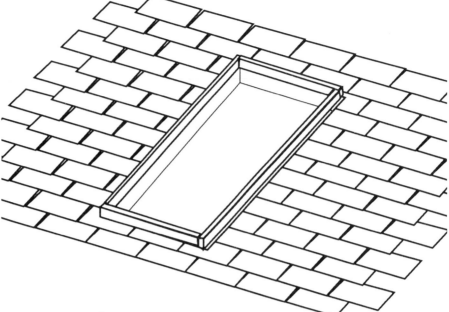

Illus. 3-36. Skylight curb.

and provides a rigid surface to support the skylight.

Some curbs are provided by the installer and are usually made up of 2 × 4s on edge. However, more often than not, curbs are provided by the manufacturer and are an integral part of the skylight. Roof pitches below 3/12 or in excess of 6/12 usually require special curbing and flashing.

Construction

Skylight and roof window units are manufactured in many different styles and materials. For the sake of clarity, here they are divided into two categories: Unframed and Framed.

Unframed units are less expensive and encompass a large portion of those in use today.

Illus. 3-37. A self-flashing, unframed, nonventing skylight. (*Courtesy of APC Corp.*)

They are made *totally* of plastic and consist of a thermally formed dome of one, two, or more sheets of plastic with an insulating air space between each layer. Unframed skylights are usually nonventing. They may or may not require a curb, but if a curb is required, it is usually provided by the installer. The least expensive models have no curb, sit directly on the roof, and are self-flashing (Illus. 3-37). The plastics used are either polycarbonates such as Lexan or acrylics such as Lucite™ or Plexiglas™. Plastic skylights are lightweight and easy to handle. They are usually easy to install.

Framed skylights and roof window units differ from unframed models in that they have a frame (usually metal or vinyl) which contains the glazing surface. Glazing may be dome-shaped plastic (Illus. 3-38) or flat glass (Illus. 3-39). Framed skylights and roof window units may be fixed or operating.

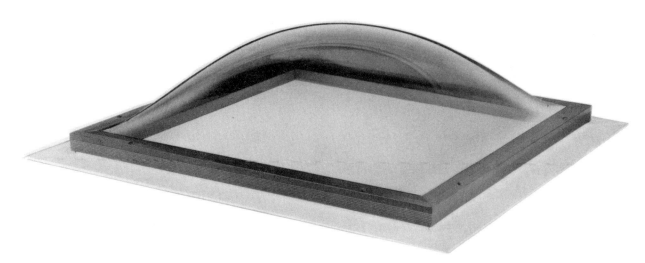

Illus. 3-38. A self-flashing, framed, domed skylight. (*Courtesy of Wasco Products*)

Illus. 3-39. A self-flashing, framed, glass skylight. (*Courtesy of Wasco Products*)

An important consideration in choosing your glazing material is strength. Tempered glass is stronger than regular glass, and some plastic glazing materials are stronger still. Laminated glass is also available. Be sure to check with your local building inspector to ensure you are meeting all the requirements of the code. There are many different stock shapes available, from squares and rectangles to circles, triangles, hexagons, octagons, and trapezoids. Some manufacturers also offer custom shapes and sizes.

Installation

Installation is the critical component in creating a successful skylight or roof window unit. Many of the problems associated with skylight and roof window units are a direct result of faulty installation. If you plan to open your roof, be sure you understand every aspect of the installation beforehand. Check the manufacturer's instructions carefully. They should be clear and precise.

Use

Skylights and roof window units have become very popular in the last 20 years, spreading from the commercial into the residential market. From sunrooms and greenhouses to privacy lighting for the bathroom and bedroom, skylight and roof window units make up one of the most rapidly growing segments of the market. Closets and hallways can now be naturally illuminated. If your home is located close to other homes, you can now add a window unit without sacrificing privacy. All you need is access to your roof, attic, or pitched sidewall.

Sizes

Skylights and roof window units are generally available in widths from 2 to 4′ and heights from 2 to 5′, with other sizes possible as special orders. The most important consideration in sizing a skylight is the spacing of your roof rafters or trusses. Make sure you know this measurement. Modification of the roof framing to accommodate the window unit requires knowledge and skill. Plan carefully and pay close attention to the manufacturer's instructions.

Hardware

There are many different types of hardware option, depending on the manufacturer. Venting units fall in two separate categories: "simple venting" and "pivot venting" units (Illus. 3-40

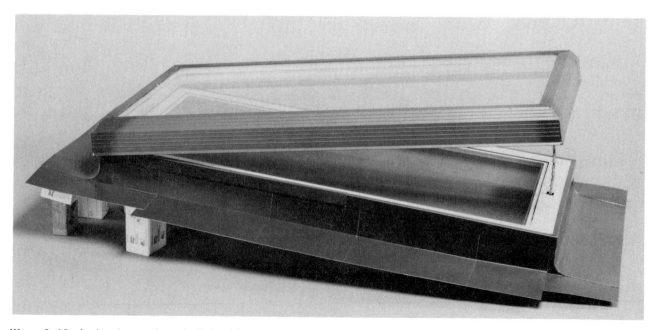

Illus. 3-40. A simple venting skylight. (*Courtesy of Thermo-Vu Skylights*)

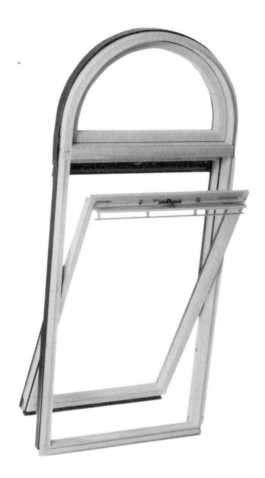

Illus. 3-41. Pivoting, venting roof window. (*Courtesy of Velux-America, Inc.*)

and 3-41). Simple venting units allow the bottom of the sash to open approximately 10″. Pivot units allow the same function with the additional option of pivoting the window totally open on its horizontal axis so that the bottom of the sash moves out and the top of the sash moves in. This allows for inside cleaning if the unit is accessible, as well as greater ventilation. Other hardware options include extension poles (Illus. 3-42) for reaching operators high in a ceiling or, if you want the ultimate, electric operators with sensors that detect rain and automatically close your skylight and roof window units.

Weather Stripping

The weather stripping is critical if you are to have a successful installation. You are putting a window unit in direct contact with ice, snow,

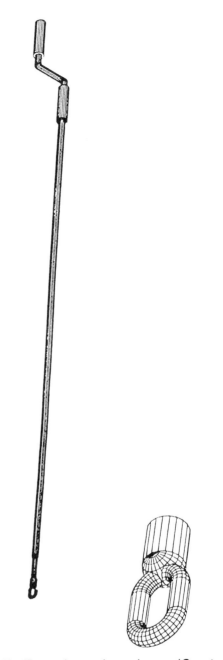

Illus. 3-42. Extension pole and eye. (*Courtesy of Wasco Products*)

and running water. As you consider different manufacturers, pay close attention to the weather stripping.

Ventilation

Ventilation is another important consideration in skylight and roof window unit selection.

69

While the vent option is an added expense, it may make the most sense in the long run. Skylights and roof window units are located in the place in the house that best takes advantage of the natural flow created when air heats up and rises (Illus. 3-43). By allowing that heated air to exit the house at the ceiling, you will create a very comfortable breeze in the summer months.

Another consideration is the prevention of condensation. When outside temperatures fall, the skylight's glazing surface will become colder than the interior room air which comes in contact with it. If that interior air contains substantial humidity, water will condense on the colder glazing surface. There are two methods for eliminating this condensation: either drying or venting the interior air. Venting the interior air is not possible with nonventing units. Some units have an integral condensation gutter which collects and stores water until it evaporates (Illus. 3-44). Condensation should be an important consideration in your planning, because skylights and roof window units are very susceptible to it.

Illus. 3-43. Ventilating skylights encourage air flow.

Illus. 3-44. A sectional view of a skylight. (*Courtesy of APC Corp.*)

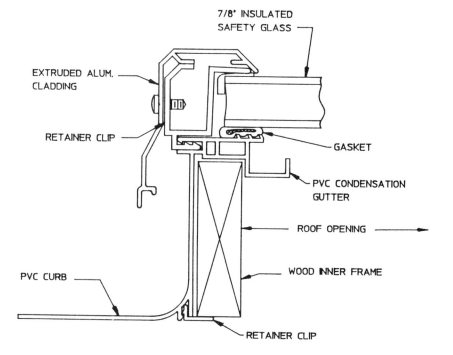

7/8" INSULATED SAFETY GLASS

EXTRUDED ALUM. CLADDING

RETAINER CLIP

GASKET

PVC CONDENSATION GUTTER

ROOF OPENING

WOOD INNER FRAME

PVC CURB

RETAINER CLIP

70

View and Light

The view is totally dependent upon the placement of the window relative to the living space. View potential is not normally a major concern unless the roof is also the sidewall of the living space.

These window units were invented to allow access to more light throughout the solar season than other window units in the house. They allow up to six times more than units in a vertical sidewall. Their potential to provide natural and dramatic lighting accents is almost unlimited.

Plan to provide a roof opening or openings equal to approximately 10 percent of the room's square footage (width × length). Frequently, light shafts will have to be created to channel light through the roof and attic into the living space. The walls of these shafts can be angled to create broad or narrow areas of illumination.

Be aware of the effects of the sun at different times of the year. Manufacturers offer many different types of glazing material to allow you to take direct advantage of, diffuse, or reflect the sun's illumination.

Maintenance

If the unit is not a pivot unit, it must be washed from the outside. However, if the window unit provides only light and no view, a washing once or twice a year may be sufficient.

Keep paint away from the hardware and weather strip. Lubricate the hardware with a product specified by the manufacturer.

Operating Techniques

How easily venting window units can be operated is determined by where they are located. Manufacturers have devised several methods of operating venting units. Study the options. You may have to decide between the use of a 12′ extension pole in a cathedral ceiling or an electronic device that automatically opens your window unit when the temperature reaches a preset limit.

Storm Window Units, Screens, and Shades

Screens are installed on the inside of venting units. Some are framed and must be removed so that the glass can be washed. Some screens roll up like a shade and are much more convenient. Storm panels are generally available, and since insulating glass is common, these storm panels provide for triple glazing.

Shades are an important consideration. They provide both privacy and protection from direct summer sunlight. They may be a fabric or a venetian-blind type, and may be located on the sash or between the lights of glass. Outside awnings are also available. All options are normally available only from the manufacturer and should be purchased along with the window units.

Energy Efficiency

The energy efficiency of skylight and roof window units is dependent on glazing material, solar orientation, local climate, and optional accessories. These window units generally make very effective solar collectors. Their weather stripping is normally very tight due to the precarious location of the unit. Ratings may vary dramatically among different manufacturers.

Cost

Skylight and roof window units range in cost per square foot from very inexpensive to expensive, depending on the materials used and options selected.

Advantages of Unframed Skylights and Roof Window Units

1. They are less expensive than framed skylights and roof window units.
2. They are relatively easy to install.
3. Their lighter weight allows for easy handling.

Disadvantages of Unframed Skylights and Roof Window Units

1. Venting unframed skylights and roof window units are not readily available.
2. Their dome-shaped glazing surface may not complement the architectural appearance of the house.

3. The view through plastic glazing material is less clear than through glass.
4. Domed glazing may allow condensation to form between layers of plastic.

Advantages of Framed Skylights and Roof Window Units

1. They are available in many glazing options, both glass and plastic.
2. They are available in several venting options.
3. Flat glazing surfaces are available. These surfaces may have less negative impact on architectural appearance and offer more optical clarity.
4. They can be installed in extreme roof slopes with special curbs and flashing.

Disadvantages of Framed Skylights and Roof Window Units

1. They are more expensive than unframed skylights and roof window units.
2. They are heavier than unframed skylights and roof window units.

3. They are more complicated to install than unframed skylights and roof window units.

Gable Louvres and Window Units

Attic space requires ventilation which is commonly provided by the gable louvre. This is not really a window unit, but it is typically ordered at the same time and deserves to be included.

Construction

Gable louvres (Illus. 3-45) consist of a frame with slats installed, creating a louvred effect. Screening is installed directly on the interior of the frame. Louvred units are available in wood or aluminum and in many shapes, including rectangles, triangles, circles, and more decorative designs.

Gable window units (Illus. 3-46) (often called octagon window units) are either fixed or venting. Fixed gable window units consist of a frame with glass installed directly within. The venting unit consists of a frame and sash which open in the same fashion as an awning window unit. Gable window units are available in wood, clad

Illus. 3-45. Gable louvre.

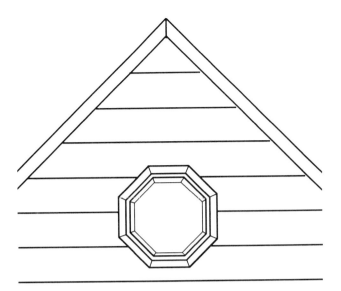

Illus. 3-46. Gable or octagon window unit.

wood, vinyl, and aluminum, and are usually circular or octagonal.

Use
Gable louvres and window units are sold primarily to the residential and light commercial market. Louvres are normally located in the very top of each gable end, although special venting chores in other sections of the house can be handled with this product. The window units are now used more for their aesthetic value. They may be located to specifically light a small interior space such as a stairway landing or foyer. They are often glazed with colored or leaded glass to create a unique architectural impression.

Sizes
Gable louvre units are available in a wide variety of sizes and shapes. Gable window units are quite limited in size. The nonventing window unit is really the same as the direct-set type, and is available in specialized sizes or shapes.

The sizing of louvred units requires some planning. The commonly used formula for determining the amount of "free air" ventilation in a gable-style roof attic is to divide the total square footage of all the ceilings in the house by 300. For example, if all your ceiling space equals 1,200 square feet, you would need 1,200 ÷ 300, or 4 square feet of free air. This formula refers to free, unobstructed air. Since louvres and screens effectively block some of the free air, you must multiply the result by 2.25 to determine the amount of louvred space necessary. In this example, 4 square feet × 2.25 equals 9 square feet.

Now, divide this answer by the total number of louvred units, normally two. Therefore, in this example 9 square feet divided by 2 equals 4.5 square feet per louvre. This formula assumes no other attic ventilation. If ridge or soffit vents are used, new calculations are required.

Hardware
The hardware for the venting window unit is usually a simple push bar awning assembly.

Weather Stripping
The weather stripping is installed on the venting window unit only.

Ventilation
Ventilation is the only thing a gable louvre unit provides. Don't block the attic space in the winter months, because a properly vented space will impede the formation of roof ice both inside and out.

View and Light
Gable window units are relatively poor providers of views or light.

Maintenance
Lubricate the hardware for the operating window unit with a product specified by the manufacturer. Keep the screens over the louvre clean, to allow maximum air flow.

Storm Window Units and Screens
Screens are installed on the inside of the operating window and the louvre. Storm window units are not generally available.

Energy Efficiency
Operating gable window units are about as energy-efficient as awning units. However, ratings may vary dramatically among different manufacturers.

Cost

The louvred units have a relatively low cost per square foot. The gable window units range in cost, depending on the type of glazing used and whether they are venting or fixed.

Storm Window Units

Not too long ago a storm window was the only way to increase a window unit's energy efficiency. Today, weather stripping and glazing materials have been improved enough to substitute for a storm window. However, there are still many benefits to be derived from these windows.

Storm windows can be divided into two categories: panels and combination units. Storm panels consist of a single piece of glass or plastic glazing material surrounded by an aluminum, wood, or vinyl frame. The framing material provides rigidity and an area that may be weather-stripped to provide a tight seal with the sash. Storm panels are also referred to as RDG (Removable Double Glazing) and Piggyback. They are usually found on projecting window units but are available for any type of window unit.

Today's storm panels are designed to be mounted directly on a sash and ride piggyback with the sash as it opens. This installation creates a dead air space between the sash and storm panel which adds greatly to the insulating value of the glass area. You may be able to retrofit existing window units with storm panels.

Some manufacturers use storm panels to create a triple glazing effect—that is, the storm panel is put over a sash glazed with insulating glass. The third layer of glass, however, offers only marginal improvement over two layers.

One benefit of storm panels is that they allow for the use of authentic divided lights within a sash without the need for expensive individual lights of insulating glass. Another potential benefit is the cost of replacing a storm panel versus the cost of replacing a light of insulating glass. If the window is located near the basketball court or baseball field, a storm window may make more sense.

There are three disadvantages of using storm panels in place of insulating glass. First, you must wash four rather than two glazing surfaces. Second, there is the possibility that condensation may form on the interior of the storm panel. Third, a storm panel does not provide the same insulating value as insulating glass.

Combination units (Illus. 3-47), also called "triple track" units, consist of a frame containing one or more sash along with a half screen. The sash slide in a track and are held open by mechanical means. The storm unit frame is mounted on the exterior of the window unit frame. These units are usually found on double-hung and sliding window units. Their design allows for ventilation and insulation by simply sliding the sash or screen into operating position. They are usually made of aluminum, although combinations of aluminum and wood or vinyl are available.

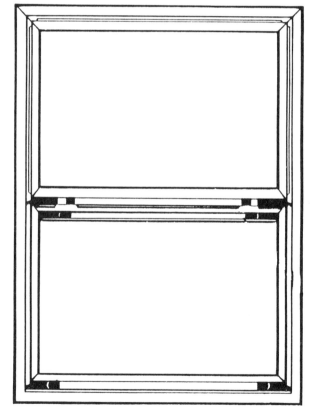

Illus. 3-47. Combination storm-and-screen window unit.

One advantage of using a combination unit is that it is not necessary to remove storm panels and install screens in the summer. Simply slide one of the storm panels out of the way and slide the screen into position, and you're all set for another six months.

Another benefit is the chance to use a half rather than a full screen. Screens obstruct views, and a half screen provides screening only where it is absolutely needed.

While half screens are better for views, they do not allow the user to take full advantage of the ventilating effect of a double-hung unit. When the bottom and top sash are each partially open, a ventilating flow of air may be created, with cool air entering through the bottom and warm air exiting through the top.

The major reason for using a combination storm unit is its ability to provide additional insulation around the entire sash opening. Storm panels provide insulation only to the glass area, while combination units, because they are mounted on the frame, cover not only the glass but also the openings all around the sash. This aids greatly in providing a much more weathertight installation. You should consider the use of combination storm and screen units on all double-hung and sliding window units even if insulating glass is used. The benefits derived from the built-in screen and full-frame weatherproofing are, in my estimation, definitely worth the added expense.

Screens

Screens are usually sold in conjunction with window units. They are generally framed in aluminum, but may also be framed in vinyl or wood. Screening material is either metallic or fibreglass, and is available in several colors.

Since a proper fit is essential, you should order screens at the same time window units are being ordered. If you are purchasing six or more window units with the same size screen, consider buying an extra screen to put in storage as insurance against a later problem.

If you have a broken screen, first try to replace just the screening material while saving the frame. If you need a complete replacement, visit your retailer with the name of the window manufacturer, the window operating type, the sash opening size, and the glass size. Hopefully, the screens will still be available from the manufacturer. If that approach fails, try a local hardware store, where a new screen may be made.

Warning: Screens are intended to exclude insects. They are not designed to restrain children or pets. Serious injuries can result if a screen gives way while being leaned against.

Dual Window Units

A dual window unit is a "prime" window unit and a storm unit that are incorporated into the same frame. (A prime window unit is the primary window within an opening; a storm window unit is a secondary window.) This is more energy-efficient than a prime window unit used by itself.

Replacement Window Units

The term "replacement window" sounds somewhat specialized, but in actuality any new window unit can become a replacement unit if it takes the place of an existing unit. Replacing a complete window requires working from the exterior of the home (often on a ladder) and dealing with units that may not be exactly the same size as the original unit.

"True" replacement window units operate the same as other units described in this section with one important difference: The frame of the replacement unit is designed to fit *within* an existing window frame. Their use is feasible only if the frame of the original window is sound. Almost any size can be manufactured to meet requirements, and installation is accomplished from the interior of the home. "True" replacement window units offer enormous labor-saving potential (Illus. 3-48).

These replacement units are available in aluminum, vinyl, wood, and clad wood. Prefinished exterior colors include bronze, white, and almond, as well as custom colors. The interior of the units is available in the same colors, as well as natural wood.

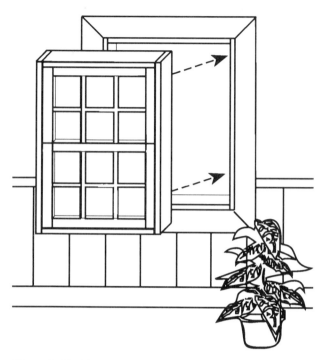

Illus. 3-48. Replacement double-hung window unit.

Most "true" replacement windows are designed to fit within old double-hung window unit frames, because double-hung window units have been the most commonly used in the past. Also, double-hung frames are easily adapted to the installation of a new unit.

As we have seen, a window unit is made up of several parts. Often only one or two parts of a unit are replaced, and immediate benefits are realized. For example, old sash and hardware in a double-hung unit can easily be replaced with new, insulating glazed sash and side channel hardware to create a more efficient and convenient window unit at a relatively moderate price.

Specialty Window Units

Modern technology in the manufacture of insulating glass and innovative thinking on the part of manufacturers have resulted in several specialty products which should be noted here. While these products don't fit every design or budget, they can make an impressive architectural expression.

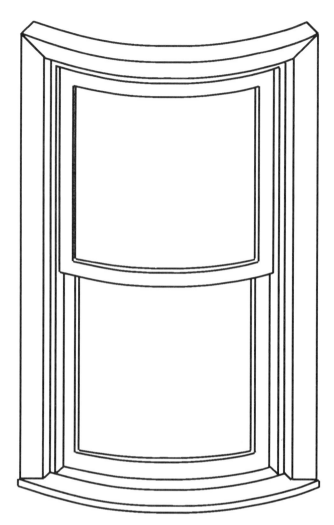

Illus. 3-49. Curved-glass, single-hung window unit.

Curved glass window units provide a true radius frame, sash, and glass area (Illus. 3-49). They are available as single-hung or fixed units, and in a limited number of sizes. They allow for a true semicircular appearance and can follow the curve of a circular wall.

Corner window units have glass which is actually formed into a 90-degree angle, thus allowing the window unit to cover the corner of a room (Illus. 3-50). They are available as fixed units only, and in a limited number of sizes. They allow for a "glass" corner rather than the typically framed corner, and are useful in special bay window unit applications.

Illus. 3-50. Fixed, corner window unit.

4
Glazing

The largest area of any window unit is the glass or glazing surface. The quality of this glazing material plays a critical role in your view potential and personal comfort and should be carefully considered in the planning stage of your window purchase. In the past, there were very few choices to make when it came to a glazing system. Now, however, due to recent technological advances, there are many options to choose from.

The best glazing products for window units will provide the greatest clarity along with the most cost-effective energy efficiency. Desirable performance characteristics of glass depend on the type and location of your home. In a northern climate, the objective is to save on heating costs by lessening heat loss through the glass during the winter months at night. In the south, the objective is to save on air conditioning costs by lessening solar gain during the day. In order to explore specific options, you need to become familiar with the following terminology.

SINGLE PANE

The term "single pane" (or "single glazing" or "monolithic glass products") is one of many designations that may be given to regular glass.

Such glass has a thickness of usually $\frac{3}{32}$ or $\frac{1}{8}''$. This was the standard glazing material for many years, and is still prevalent today. Since glass is a relatively poor insulator, it is usually necessary to use storm windows in conjunction with this glazing in order to create a comfortable installation.

To compensate for wind load resistance, the larger the light of glass, the thicker the glass must be. A picture window unit with operating flankers would have $\frac{3}{32}''$ glass in the flank sash and $\frac{3}{16}$ or $\frac{1}{4}''$ glass in the one-light central section.

INSULATING GLASS

Without a doubt, the major factor in making glazing surfaces more energy-efficient is the use of insulating glass (Illus. 4-1). Two or more pieces of glass are joined together around an inorganic spacer, and the whole light is coated around its perimeter with sealants that hold the two pieces of glass together and provide a barrier to minimize moisture-vapor transmission into the airspace cavity. This hermetically sealed airspace between the pieces of glass provides enormous insulating value. Heat loss

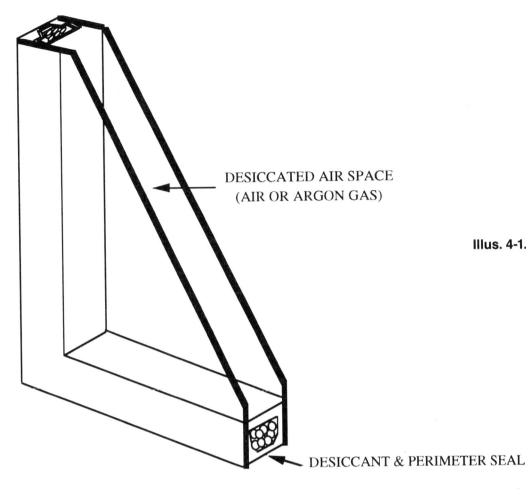

DESICCATED AIR SPACE
(AIR OR ARGON GAS)

Illus. 4-1. Insulating glass.

DESICCANT & PERIMETER SEAL

through the glass area is reduced by over 50 percent compared to a single pane.

Much has been written about the importance of having a very wide airspace. The truth is that an airspace of approximately ½ to ⅝″ provides optimum insulation. Combine this airspace with two pieces of ⅛″ thick glass and the result is an ideal overall thickness of ¾ to ⅞″. This airspace is sealed and will not readily admit water vapor. A desiccant (chemical drying agent) is included in the spacer to keep the air dry.

The thermal efficiency of insulating glass can be enhanced by infusing argon gas into the space between the lights. Quantifying the increased insulating value requires product-by-product comparison, but in general efficiency can be increased by 5 to 47 percent. Check the manufacturer's test data. Considerable experimentation is now being done with krypton gas as an even greater insulator than argon.

When air is replaced as the insulator between the two lights of glass, the thickness of the space may also change. Krypton gas, for example, seems to reach optimum insulating value with a space of only ¼″, thereby creating an overall insulating light thickness of ½″.

Another method of increasing efficiency is the use of a nonmetallic spacer between the lights of glass. The metal edge acts as a channel through which outside cold is transmitted to the inside edges of the glass. By eliminating or insulating this metal edge, energy can be saved. This phenomenon is referred to as "edge conductance."

One major benefit of insulating glass is a higher indoor glass-surface temperature during the winter, resulting in greater comfort and less condensation potential on the indoor glass surfaces.

LOW-EMISSIVITY OR HIGH-PERFORMANCE GLASS

Within the last 10 years, the efficiency of insulating glass has been increased by the inclusion of a transparent, microscopically thin, metallic coating applied to the inner surface of one of the pieces of glass in the insulating glass unit. In layman's terms, glass with this metallic coating has the ability to reflect heat back towards its source. If the heat source is your heating system on a cold winter night, much of the heat energy that would ordinarily be transferred out through the glass is now reflected back, thus saving energy. If, on the other hand, the source of heat is the sun on a hot summer afternoon, that heat energy will be absorbed by the coating and reflected back outdoors, resulting in savings on your air conditioning bills. Some manufacturers call this type of glass "low E" (low-emissivity) glass, and others refer to it as "HP" (high-performance) glass.

These coatings also have the ability to lessen ultraviolet light to varying degrees. There are different types of low-E glass coating, depending on the primary need: winter heating or summer cooling. All low-E glass coatings are invisible from inside the home, but some may create a bluish grey outdoor reflected color. Here, again, window manufacturers will use different names to describe their glazing system. Some common names are "Sun Glass," "Northern," or "Southern." If you are in doubt, compare the technical data on winter and summer U values, along with the optical characteristics of the glass as published by the window or glass manufacturer.

HEAT MIRROR GLASS

Here is another of the new technologies of insulating glass. Instead of applying a coating to the inner surface of one of the lights of glass in the insulating unit, this system actually suspends a piece of clear film midway between the two lights of glass in the airspace. This film has all the energy-reflective qualities of the coating on low-E glass, and it creates two airspaces rather than one.

Products are now being developed which combine low-E and heat mirror technology to create even greater efficiency.

WINTER NIGHTTIME HEAT LOSS: U AND R VALUES

To quantify the relative insulating values of different glazing combinations in a cold, winter, nighttime period, we measure the *amount of heat transfer* through the glass from inside to outside. This is the *U value*. This measurement is taken at the center of the glass and is expressed numerically. The lower the U value, the better the insulating capability.

A reciprocal value is a number so related to another that when they are multiplied together, the answer is 1. The reciprocal of the U value is the *R value*. It is a measurement of the glazing material's *resistance to heat transfer* through the center of the glass. The higher the R value, the better the insulating capability. U and R insulating values are used in the classification of other building products as well as glass products.

SUMMER DAYTIME SOLAR HEAT GAIN: SHADING COEFFICIENT AND RELATIVE HEAT GAIN

These specifications are important to those who want to save on air conditioning by increasing the efficiency of their glazing material in reducing the effect of the sun. The "relative heat gain" is a mathematical formula used by glass and window manufacturers to indicate the amount of heat gain through a window unit's glazing system from outside to inside. The lower the number, the better the unit is for reducing heat gain. The "shading coefficient" states the relative difference between the solar heat gain through the window unit being tested and a single light of clear, ⅛" glass. The lower the number, the better the window unit is preventing the entry of solar heat.

VISIBLE LIGHT TRANSMISSION AND REFLECTANCE

These measurements help us to quantify how

the view is affected when coatings are applied to glass. "Visible light transmission" is expressed as a percentage of visible light through the subject glass surface versus a clear, unglazed opening. The lower the number, the more interference with view. As an example, a single piece of ⅛″ thick, clear glass allows 90 percent of the visible light transmission of an unglazed opening.

"Visible light reflectance" measures the amount of visible light that is reflected by the glazing surface. It is stated in two ways: as a percentage of visible light reflected back outdoors, or reflected back indoors.

ULTRAVIOLET TRANSMISSION

Ultraviolet light represents only 3 percent of the energy in sunlight, but it can contribute to the weathering and fading of materials like fabric. Some glass products have the ability to reduce UV light transmission to varying degrees. The measurement of this ability is referred to as "ultraviolet transmission." It may be stated as the percentage of the amount allowed through, or the amount blocked by, the glass.

MISCELLANEOUS GLAZING SYSTEMS

Many window manufacturers offer more than one glazing product to accommodate specific requirements. There are bronze- or grey-tinted glasses which may be used alone or in conjunction with low-E glass in exceptionally warm, sunny climates. This combination results in a lower shading coefficient, relative heat gain, and UV transmission, but allows less visible light transmission and may create a slightly tinted appearance when viewed from the outside. Naturally, there are tradeoffs in any glazing system.

High-tech glazing systems can be very expensive. Whether or not you should spend the money depends on your climate and energy costs. You should use at least insulating glass in any area which is heated or air-conditioned. If considering a more advanced glazing system, weigh its cost against the potential savings and act accordingly. Many window manufacturers have made low-E, argon-filled, insulating glass their standard product because the amount of money that will ultimately be saved outweighs the initial expense.

The glass is only one of several factors that play a part in determining the energy efficiency of a window unit. Overall energy efficiency depends as much on the sash, frame, and installation as it does on the glass.

Tables 4-1 and 4-2 describe different glazing combinations. These are general figures and do not indicate every type of glass available from every manufacturer. Use these charts to determine the relationships between certain products and their insulating and view properties.

WINTER "U" VALUE COMPARISONS

GLASS TYPE	WINTER "U" VALUE*
SINGLE PANE	1.11
CLEAR IG; 2 PANE; AIR FILL	0.49
CLEAR IG; 3 PANE; AIR FILL	0.32
LOW E IG; 2 PANE; AIR FILL	0.31
LOW E IG; 2 PANE; ARGON FILL	0.25
LOW E IG; 3 PANE; AIR FILL	0.23
LOW E IG; 3 PANE; ARGON FILL	0.19

NOTE: All glass 1/8" thick. IG air space 1/2"

* "U" Value expressed in BTU / hr / ft² / °F

Table 4-1. Winter "U"-value comparisons of different glazing combinations. (*Courtesy of Cardinal IG*)

Insulating Glass Type	% Visible Transmittance	Visible Reflectance %		Solar Energy %		* Summer "U" Value	Shading Coefficient	** Relative Heat Gain
		Out	In	Transmission	Reflected Out			
Clear	81	15	15	71	13	0.55	0.89	185
Low E	78	11	12	57	20	0.25	0.73	150
Low E Sun	44	14	14	30	25	0.27	0.41	86
Bronze Glass	62	10	13	54	9	0.56	0.72	152
Bronze & Low E	59	9	10	44	15	0.26	0.60	124

Note: All glass 1/8" thick. Low E products are Argon filled.

* "U" Value expressed in BTU / hr / ft² / °F

** Relative Heat Gain expressed in BTU / hr / ft²

Table 4-2. Comparing the optical properties and summertime performance of different glazing systems. (*Courtesy of Cardinal IG*)

DIVIDED LIGHTS

Many fenestration applications call for the use of divided lights within a sash. There are several ways to create these divided lights, whether it be using individual lights of glass or a grille system. Illus. 4-2 shows the type of divided lights one manufacturer offers, and your research will uncover other methods. The most important considerations in choosing between real lights and grilles are the architectural appearance and the ease of washing. You usually sacrifice one while attaining the other.

MAINTENANCE AND WARRANTIES

The only maintenance involved for insulating glass is keeping it clean. Even though there are four glass surfaces, you only have to wash two because the interior space is sealed. A failure in a light of insulating glass usually starts to show itself gradually as a foggy area which you cannot clean. This indicates that the seal around the two pieces of glass has failed and water vapor is entering the space and condensing on the interior glass surface. There is no sure repair for this condition, and the entire light of insulating glass must be replaced.

Many glass and window manufacturers issue warranties covering the integrity of their insulating glass for a period of years (ten years is common). If you purchase windows with insulating glass, become familiar with this warranty. Be sure to save both the receipt of purchase showing the type of glazing and a copy of the warranty.

Insulating glass failures are not uncommon. At the time of purchase you should know how the glazing is to be replaced. Some sash are reglazeable, while others are designed to be discarded and replaced. These facts are not usually contained in the advertising literature, and you should ask for a demonstration at the time of purchase. If your new window purchase includes at least six sash of the same size, consider buying an extra light of insulating glass or an extra sash and storing it (along with an extra screen and an extra set of operating hardware) as insurance against future problems.

If you are buying a new home, ask about the window units. What company manufactured them? Where were they bought? What type of glazing do they contain? What type of warranty do they have? These facts may seem unimportant at the time of purchase, but they will become very important if you have an insulating glass failure.

If you don't know what kind of glazing you presently have, inspect the glass. Look at the perimeter of a light of glass. Do you see a metallic spacer? If so, you have insulating glass. Since some insulating glass does not contain this metallic spacer, place a finger from one hand on the outside edge of the glass and a finger from the

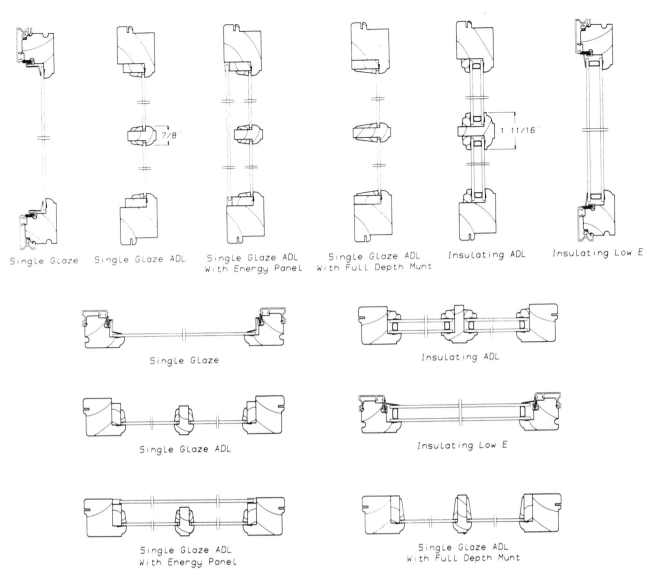

Illus. 4-2. Section view of glazing options for wood-clad casement window unit. (*Courtesy of Marvin Windows*)

other on the inside edge. If you feel a thickness of ½″ or more, you have insulating glass.

Information about the insulating glass is sometimes inscribed on the metal spacer. Careful examination may identify the glass or window manufacturer and the date of manufacture. Another area to check is the corner of the glazing surface. Information is sometimes etched on the glass.

CONDENSATION

One of the most annoying problems that occurs with window units is condensation on the glass. As regards glazing, the higher the indoor glass temperature, the less likelihood of condensation. Insulating glass or at least a storm window unit can help to eliminate this problem. Low-E coatings and argon gas are even more successful.

5

Measuring Energy Efficiency

The international oil crisis of the 1970s has had far-reaching effects on the window-manufacturing industry in the United States. Just as with automobiles, energy efficiency has become a major consideration in the selection of window units. Only you can make the final determination of the correct product for your environment at a price you can afford. By comparing data from different manufacturers, you should be able to predict which type of window unit will be more economical.

Glazing options and storm window units were described in their appropriate sections. Consider these products carefully, because they can make an energy-efficient product more energy-efficient. This section presents an overview of the efficiency of various types of window unit and the methods of determining that efficiency.

U AND R, AND AIR INFILTRATION VALUES

The amount of heat transfer through the window unit is the "U" value. The lower the U value, the better the insulating capability.

A reciprocal value is a number so related to another that when they are multiplied together, the answer is 1. The reciprocal of the U value is the "R" value. It is a measurement of the window's resistance to heat transfer. The higher the R value, the better the insulating capability. Just as with glazing materials, U and R measurements are used to help describe the energy efficiency of the *entire* window unit.

When comparing data from manufacturers, make sure that all are reporting on a consistent basis. Their energy statistics should list the type of testing, the test lab used, and the portion of the window unit where measurements were taken. The U and R values for entire window units will usually be different than those for glazing materials only because they include the sash and frame as well as the space around the sash. These measurements present the most meaningful indicator of a window unit's energy efficiency.

One of the factors affecting the unit's overall efficiency is how tightly the sash, frame, and weather stripping fit together while still providing ease of operation. Higher-quality construction usually reflects a tighter fit. Tests are conducted with pressure applied to the exterior of the unit; the resulting numerical score is called the "air infiltration" value. The lower the number, the more efficient the unit.

ENERGY EFFICIENCY OF OPERATING WINDOW UNITS

Certain operating types of window unit are inherently more energy-efficient simply because of their design. Casement units can be locked and sealed tightly by full-perimeter weather stripping. Double-hung units must always allow space to slide up and down and are usually not as weathertight as casement units. Following are operating window units listed from most to least efficient as they relate to air infiltration: fixed, roof, casement, awning, slider, single-hung, and double-hung.

This is a generic list. In order to be certain of your installation, you must compare product to product and manufacturer to manufacturer. There are significant differences.

ENERGY EFFICIENCY AND MATERIAL TYPE

Window units are usually made of several materials, but each unit falls into a specific category depending on the type of frame. It will either be aluminum, vinyl, wood, or clad wood. Steel window units are still being produced, primarily for the fire-resistant market, but are not considered here.

Table 5-1 compares the energy efficiency of aluminum, thermalized aluminum, wood, and vinyl units. Note that the thermal break is the crucial link to energy efficiency in cold climates. Table 5-2 indicates the heating and cooling costs for two typical communities in the United States with different window types. These charts indicate how important your material selection can be. They offer only general figures, however. Compare the specific figures supplied by the manufacturers you are researching.

California is the only state in the United States with an energy efficiency labelling system similar to that found on major appliances.

OVERALL WINDOW UNIT WINTER "U" VALUES

Glass Type	Glass "U" Value	"U" VALUE FOR ENTIRE WINDOW UNIT			
		Aluminum Frame No Thermal Break	Aluminum Frame With Thermal Break	Wood Frame	Vinyl Frame
Single Pane	1.11	1.31	1.09	0.90	0.87
Regular IG (2 pane)	0.49	0.87	0.64	0.49	0.46
Low E IG (2 pane)	0.25	0.71	0.49	0.34	0.31
Low E IG (3 pane)	0.13	0.64	0.42	0.28	0.25

ASSUMPTIONS:

1. All glass is 1/8" thick. IG air space is 1/2". Low E is Argon filled.
2. Window size is 36" X 48".
3. Heat loss based on 50% from glass, 25% from frame conductance and 25% from edge conductance.
4. Calculations based on LBL window 3.1 computer program.

Table 5-1. A comparison of the energy efficiency of aluminum, thermalized aluminum, wood, and vinyl window units. (*Courtesy of Cardinal IG*)

Typical Energy Savings, single glazed aluminum unit vs. various types of glass in a wood unit for two different sections of the country.

Glass Type	"U" Value Glass	"U" Value Unit	Madison, Wisconsin		
			Heating Cost $	Cooling Cost $	% Saving
Single pane (Aluminum)	1.11	1.30	$213	$84	-
Single pane (Wood)	1.11	0.90	$126	$87	29%
Clear IG (Wood)	0.49	0.49	$35	$82	61%
Low E IG (Wood)	0.25	0.34	$5	$74	73%

Glass Type	"U" Value Glass	"U" Value Unit	Lake Charles, Louisiana		
			Heating Cost $	Cooling Cost $	% Saving
Single pane (Aluminum)	1.11	1.30	$42	$205	-
Single pane (Wood)	1.11	0.90	$22	$212	5%
Clear IG (Wood)	0.49	0.49	$2	$205	16%
Low E IG (Wood)	0.25	0.34	($5)	$186	27%

NOTES: 1. Analysis based on LBL "RESFEN" program, beta version.
2. 60 ft^2 window on each elevation.
3. Overall window performance calculated using LBL Window 3.1 with residential size wood frame window, aluminum spacer, 1/8" glass, 1/2" air space. All Low E type units Argon filled.
4. Natural Gas Heat @ 0.50 $/therm.
5. Electric Cost @ 0.09 $/kwh.
6. All glazing data based on wood frame window.
7. Analysis based on indoor baseline temperature conditions: winter 70°F, summer 78°F.

Table 5-2. A comparison of the heating and cooling costs for two typical communities in the United States with different types of window units.

All windows and exterior doors sold in California will soon be labelled. This practice should be used throughout the country. It would certainly help clarify what has been a most confusing part of the industry.

6

Buying Window Units

Window units are expensive. A new home or large remodelling job can result in substantial expenditures for windows. Investigation can pay great dividends. The following story will prove this point. I was called in to advise on the procurement of 36 window units to be used as replacements on two large porches of a home. The homeowner knew nothing about window units except that the contractor told her to purchase a specific type and that she was quoted a price of $12,500 by the retailer. She had no idea whether this was high, low, or just right.

We first discussed the material to be used. The homeowner decided on wood window units because they were already installed in the remainder of the home. Next, we determined which type of operating unit to use. She chose three types: awning, casement, and fixed, depending on their location. Based on those selections, we worked with the contractor to develop a list of rough opening sizes.

We researched several manufacturers and came up with prices of approximately $8,000 for clad and $6,800 for nonclad window units. Since the exterior trim of the home was a bright yellow color, it was decided that clad windows were

not necessary because the trim would have to be painted on a regular basis anyway and the windows could be incorporated into that task. The $6,800 for the nonclad window units was considerably less than the $12,500 cited by the retailer.

Now that we were sure of the material and operating type, we did a little more research on size. Many of the awning window unit rough openings were approximately 5′ tall, and the only way to fill up this space was to stack three awning units vertically (one on top of the other). Finally, we found one manufacturer who made a size that was large enough to allow us to use only two high awning units. This saved considerably more money and brought the cost down to $4,800.00.

The windows were installed. The entire cost, *including labor*, did not reach the $12,500 originally quoted for material only.

Every installation project does not offer this opportunity for savings, but the only way to approach an acquisition is with as much information as possible. Your knowledge can make a substantial difference.

There is no general formula that shows you how to save money. Compare products based on all the factors discussed in this book and choose the best unit for your specific circumstances at the price you can afford.

Window units may be purchased from several sources: manufacturers, distributors, lumberyards, and home centers. Don't assume that you automatically get the cheapest price from a manufacturer or distributor. Compare all sources. Often, the best source for your window unit purchase is the company that provides the most service. Displays, sales assistance, delivery, and warranty service are important factors to consider.

WINDOW SELECTION

ROUGH OPENING

Width_____   Height_____

WALL THICKNESS

Framing_____ Sheathing_____ Sheetrock_____ Other_____ Total_____

MATERIAL

Aluminum   Vinyl   Wood   Clad Wood

COLOR
EXTERIOR   White   Bronze   Almond   Natural   Other_____
INTERIOR   White   Bronze   Almond   Natural   Other_____

OPERATING TYPE

Double Hung Casement   Awning   Slider   Other_____

GLAZING TYPE

Single Pane Clear IG   Winter LowE Summer LowE Other_____

DIVIDED LIGHTS

None   Authentic   Grilles   # of lights_____ Other_____

EXTRAS

Screen   Storms   Shades   _____ _____

MANUFACTURER

Window ID#_____ Price $_____   Delivery_____

Warranty   Installation Instructions   Sales Clerk_____

Table 6-1. Window unit selection checklist.

REPLACEMENT WINDOW SELECTION

EXISTING WINDOW DATA

Material_____ Operating Type_____

Sash Size_____ Glass Size_____

Overall Size (Exterior Measurement) Width_____ Height_____

Sketch of existing window unit:

NEW WINDOW DATA

MATERIAL	Aluminum	Vinyl	Wood	Clad Wood
COLOR				
EXTERIOR	White	Bronze	Almond	Natural	Other_____
INTERIOR	White	Bronze	Almond	Natural	Other_____
OPERATING TYPE	Double Hung	Casement	Awning	Slider	Other_____
GLAZING TYPE	Single Pane	Clear IG	Winter LowE	Summer LowE	Other_____
DIVIDED LIGHTS	None	Authentic	Grilles	# of lights____	Other_____
EXTRAS	Screen	Storms	Shades	_____ _____

Window ID#_____ Price $_____ Delivery_____

MANUFACTURER

Warranty   Installation Instructions   Sales Clerk_____

Table 6-2. Replacement window unit checklist.

BUYING GUIDELINES

Let's imagine that you're adding a new family room to your home. You plan to install an entertainment center along one entire wall. You enlist the services of a general contractor, who then hires subcontractors to handle special jobs such as the electricity and flooring. You would never ask the flooring contractor to pick out an appropriate carpet for the floor, or the electrical contractor to pick out an appropriate TV and stereo system. Why, then, when the window units are equally as expensive and important to your comfort, would you let the contractor determine which type to install? This is a decision you should make yourself.

You should bring along certain information when shopping for window units. Tables 6-1 and 6-2 will help you to provide the details a supplier will need to give you a price or place an order.

Table 6-1 provides a checklist of items that are pertinent to buying new window installations. Know the rough opening and wall thickness of the window unit. The remaining factors can be decided at the supplier's. The window unit identification number at the bottom of the form provides a space for the manufacturer's identifying code for the product being quoted. Make sure that this is accurately indicated. Very often, there are only subtle differences between a 2- and 3-wide unit or between a bronze and white unit. Since these windows will probably have to be specially ordered and manufactured, the orders cannot be changed or cancelled. You will probably have to leave a deposit, so double-check all the specifications and maintain a written record of the transaction.

Table 6-2 provides a similar format for replacement windows. Here you need to provide information about the existing unit so that an accurate replacement can be found. When shopping for replacement windows, take along a photo or sketch of the old unit. This can be a big help to the salesperson.

7

Installation Guidelines

The best installation instructions are created by the manufacturer and are supplied with the product to be installed. Table 7-1 contains an excellent set of installation instructions supplied by Marvin Windows, Warroad, Minnesota. The manufacturer's warranty is also included. Don't use these instructions for any product other than the double-hung window unit described. They merely illustrate how thorough these instructions can be. You will find that other manufacturers do an equally fine job of providing a full set of directions.

These instructions contain the following information:

1. The window unit is warranted for one year from the date of purchase. Make sure you save your receipt.
2. The consumer has the responsibility to inspect the product for defects when it arrives and to protect the product from moisture or excessive dryness. The consumer must also seal all wood surfaces with paint or varnish. If he or she doesn't carry out these responsibilities, the warranty may not apply.
3. The company will replace any defective item, including hardware, within one year of purchase, "in the white," or unfinished.
4. There is a size limitation. If you ordered a custom size greater than the largest size shown in the manufacturer's price catalogue, no warranty applies.
5. Insulating glass has a much longer warranty period of 10 years. The consumer is responsible for reglazing labor.
6. How to receive warranty service from the manufacturer.
7. If the window unit is not installed in accordance with the manufacturer's instructions, the warranty is voided.
8. A list of the tools required.
9. The consumer should leave the shipping straps attached while installing the unit.
10. The rough opening size.
11. The step-by-step installation procedures for different types of window. Note that "fin" installation of a clad unit (which would be the same as for an aluminum or vinyl window unit) is different than that for a wood window unit.
12. Installation technique in a masonry wall.
13. How to remove sash.
14. Painting and staining guidelines.

Ask to see a set of installation instructions and a warranty from each window manufacturer you are considering. The effort they put into these directions provides an insight into their commitment to the consumer. Even if you are not going to install the windows yourself, you should be able to monitor the performance

LIMITED WARRANTY

MILLWORK (WOOD PARTS)

Marvin millwork is warranted for one year after sale to be of high-quality workmanship and materials, and to be free from defects which might render it unserviceable. Of course, natural variations in color or texture of woods are not defects. We suggest that all millwork be inspected upon arrival and before installation and finishing.

So that you will be fully protected by our Limited Warranty, it is the homeowner's responsibility to properly care for and protect new woodwork against moisture or excessive dryness, and to see that top and bottom edges and all surfaces of doors and windows are thoroughly painted or varnished. THIS LIMITED WARRANTY SHALL NOT APPLY IF (1) THE NEW WOOD-WORK IS NOT SO PROTECTED FROM MOISTURE OR EX-CESSIVE DRYNESS; OR (2) THE CONSUMER FAILS TO SEE THAT THE TOP AND BOTTOM EDGES AND ALL SUR-FACES OF DOORS AND WINDOWS ARE THOROUGHLY PAINTED OR VARNISHED.

Some stains are not compatible with the Marvin "prime coat" and, therefore, if doors and windows are to be stained, DO NOT apply stain on top of Marvin's "factory prime." Instead, order your windows and doors "not primed" and apply stain only if the windows are unprimed. THIS LIMITED WARRANTY SHALL NOT APPLY IF STAIN IS APPLIED ON TOP OF MARVIN'S FACTORY PRIME.

If your windows and doors are ordered with Marvin "factory prime," a GOOD-QUALITY top coat must be applied as soon as possible after installation. The top coat of QUALITY PAINT should be applied as recommended by the paint manufacturer. THIS LIMITED WARRANTY SHALL NOT APPLY IF A GOOD QUALITY TOP COAT IS NOT APPLIED AS SOON AS POSSI-BLE AFTER INSTALLATION.

For one year, we agree to repair or replace, in the white (unfin-ished), without charge, any items which may be defective. The company, however, cannot, under any conditions, be responsi-ble for repainting, refinishing, or other similar activities neces-sary to complete the replacement. Please notify us at once if we have made an error or if any millwork proves to be unsatisfactory.

HARDWARE (METAL, NYLON AND VINYL PARTS)

While all window and door hardware is manufactured by others, it is the company policy to provide a warranty against defect or error in workmanship for one year after sale. Replace-ment for defective hardware will be supplied free of charge for one year after sale. The company, however, will not, under any conditions, be responsible for installation, repainting, refinish-ing, or other similar activities necessary to complete the re-placement. It will be the homeowner's responsibility to com-plete the replacement.

DEALER'S NOTE: In all cases, the replacement hardware will be invoiced at the regular price and full credit will be issued when the defective hardware has been returned.

SIZE LIMITATION

THIS LIMITED WARRANTY DOES NOT APPLY WHEN WE ARE FURNISHING WINDOW UNITS OR A COMPONENT THEREOF IN A SIZE WHICH IS GREATER IN WIDTH OR GREATER IN HEIGHT THAN THE LARGEST SIZE SHOWN FOR THAT WINDOW SPECIES IN OUR PRINTED PRICE CATALOG. IN THE CASE OF SUCH GREATER SIZE, THERE SHALL BE NO WARRANTY OF ANY KIND, WHETHER IM-PLIED OR OTHERWISE, WITH RESPECT TO A WINDOW AND ANY COMPONENT THEREOF.

INSULATING GLASS

All insulating glass is warranted against failure of the air seal for a period of ten years from date of manufacture. Should there be a failure of the air seal within the warranty period, the company shall supply either the insulating glass only or the glass in sash at the company's option. The company will not, under any circumstances, be responsible for installation, repainting, re-finishing, or other similar activities necessary to complete the replacement. It will be the homeowner's responsibility to com-plete the replacement.

The company will furnish either the insulating glass only or the insulating glass in sash only, as the case may be, free of charge, F.O.B. the original point of delivery.

Table 7-1 (here and pages 93–98). Instructions for installing a double-hung window unit. (*Courtesy of Marvin Windows*)

Cracked or broken glass is not covered by the warranty.

GENERAL PROVISIONS

THE EXPRESS WARRANTIES SET FORTH HEREIN ARE IN LIEU OF ALL OTHER WARRANTIES, EXPRESS OR IMPLIED, INCLUDING, WITHOUT LIMITATION, ANY WARRANTIES OF MERCHANTABILITY OF FITNESS FOR A PARTICULAR PURPOSE. ALL SUCH OTHER WARRANTIES, TO THE EXTENT PERMITTED BY LAW, ARE HEREBY DISCLAIMED AND EXCLUDED BY MARVIN WINDOWS. ANY IMPLIED WARRANTIES WHICH ARE NOT EXCLUDED HEREBY, DUE TO OPERATION OF LAW, ARE LIMITED IN DURATION TO THE DURATION OF THE EXPRESS WARRANTY PROVIDED HEREIN FOR THE PRODUCT WARRANTED.

THE REMEDIES SET FORTH ABOVE ARE THE SOLE AND EXCLUSIVE REMEDIES PROVIDED HEREUNDER, AND MARVIN WINDOWS SHALL NOT BE LIABLE FOR ANY FURTHER LOSS, DAMAGES OR EXPENSES, INCLUDING INCIDENTAL OR CONSEQUENTIAL DAMAGES, DIRECTLY OR INDIRECTLY, ARISING FROM THE USE OF ITS PRODUCTS.

Some states do not allow limitations on how long an implied warranty lasts, so the above limitation on the duration of any implied warranties not excluded hereby, due to operation of law, may not apply to you. Some states do not allow the exclusion or limitation of incidental and consequential damages, so the above exclusion of incidental and consequential damages may not apply to you. This warranty gives you specific legal rights, and you may also have other rights, which vary from state to state.

To make a claim under this Limited Warranty, you must contact the contractor who installed the product or the Marvin Window distributor or dealer from whom the product was purchased, or, if these persons are not known, contact:

> Customer Service Manager
> Marvin Windows
> Warroad, Minnesota 56763

Provide the following information to the person contacted:
  (a) Your name, address, and telephone number;
  (b) Description of product for which claim made;
  (c) Date of purchase of product (approximate if exact date not known);
  (d) Name of Marvin Window dealer or distributor from whom purchased (if known);
  (e) Nature of product failure; and
  (f) In the case of "insulating glass," provide the date of manufacture as stamped on the metal spacer between the panes of glass.

Table 7-1 continued.

INSTALLATION INSTRUCTIONS

IMPORTANT! Read these instructions thoroughly before beginning to install a double-hung unit. Failure to install as recommended will void any warranty, written or implied. Refer to the Marvin Window Limited Warranty Policy for Warranty information.

CHOOSE THE METHOD OF INSTALLATION YOU DESIRE:

YOU WILL NEED TO SUPPLY:

Level
Hammer
Tape measure
Flat screwdriver
A good-quality silicone caulk and a gun
Nails 8d common or 10d common (20)
Screws—No. 7 × ¾" (20)
Wood shims
Safety glasses
2" Roofing nails (clad units)
Drip cap
Masonry clip

NOTE: Leave any strapping bands on a double-hung unit until it is positioned in the rough opening. This will help keep the side jambs in position.

PREPARE ROUGH OPENING

1. The width of the rough opening should be 1″ wider than the outside measurement of the frame. The height of the rough opening should be ½″ higher than the outside measurement of the frame. If needed, block the rough opening on both the sides and bottom to fit the frame.

INSTALLING THE UNIT

2. WOOD DOUBLE HUNG—Place the unit into the rough opening. The exterior edge of the jamb should be flush with edge of the opening. The brick mould casing should rest snugly against the sheathing. Clip strapping bands and remove.

   CLAD DOUBLE HUNG—Install a nailing fin on the head jamb, jamb, and sill in the groove provided on the clad frame. The lip of the nailing fin should be towards the inside of the window. Tap it into place using a wood block and hammer. See illustration 1.

   Position the metal secure corners on the back side of the nailing fin. Fold over the tabs to secure the corners. See illustration 2.

   Place the unit into the rough opening. The nailing fin should lay flat against the sheathing.

3. WOOD DOUBLE HUNG—Secure the lower corner of the frame through the exterior casing with one #10 galvanized nail. See illustration 3. Do not drive the nail all the way in. Place a level on the sill and level it by shimming under the sill beneath the jambs. Plumb the unit by placing the level vertically against the frame. Shim the window at side jambs and at the check rail. Shims should not bow the window frame. Recheck the window for level and plumb. See illustration 4.

   CLAD DOUBLE HUNG—Nail through the holes provided on the nailing fin, with 2″ roofing nails. Do not drive the nails all the way in. Level and shim as above.

4. On multiple window units it is extremely important to shim under all mull posts.

5. Measure the window diagonally from corner to corner. The measurement should be the same in both directions. The window frame should be installed without twisting to ensure proper operation. See illustration 5.

6. Finish nailing the window into the opening through

Table 7-1 continued.

94

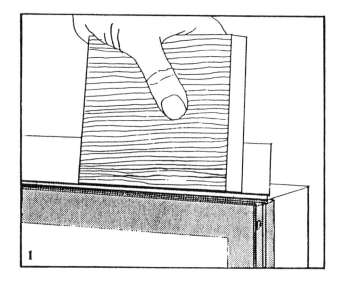

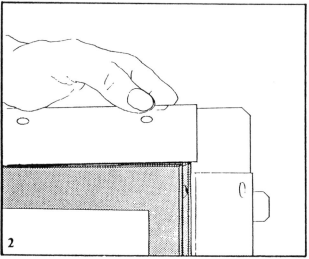

the exterior casing, when installing wood double hungs; or through the nailing fin, when installing clad double hungs.

7. Insulate loosely around the unit on the interior side. Insulation should not exert pressure on the jambs. Marvin Windows does not recommend the use of expandable foam insulators. Apply interior trim (not included).

8. Install a drip cap above the head jamb with roofing nails.

9. A good quality caulk should be applied around exterior casing to seal the unit against the wall.

10. Remove sash and finish as soon as possible after installation.

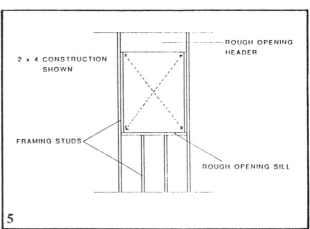

INSTRUCTIONS FOR INSTALLING WOOD OR CLAD DOUBLE HUNG WITH MASONRY CLIPS INTO A MASONRY OPENING

PREPARE OPENING

11. WOOD DOUBLE HUNG—The width of the masonry opening should be 3⅛″ wider than the outside measurement of the frame and 1⁵⁄₁₆″ higher than the frame height.

CLAD DOUBLE HUNG—The masonry opening should be ½″ wider than the outside measurement of the frame and ¼″ higher than the frame height.

12. WOOD DOUBLE HUNG—Attach masonry clips to the frame, lip side up, about 4″ from the end of the jamb using No. 7 × ¾″ screws. On frames with a standard 4⁹⁄₁₆″ jamb, clips should be flush against the brick mould casing. On frames with wider than 4⁹⁄₁₆″ jambs, clips should be placed to extend 1¼″ beyond the jamb. Follow the same procedure at the opposite end of the jamb. Secure the remainder of

Table 7-1 continued.

the masonry clips about 15″ apart for operating units and 24″ apart for picture units. Install the remaining clips on the head jamb.

CLAD DOUBLE HUNG—Place masonry clips in the groove on the aluminum part of the jamb. Tap into place with a hammer until secure. See illustration 6. Fasten into place with No. 7 × ¾″ screws. The first clip should be placed 4″ from the end of the jamb, the remainder of the clips should be spaced about 15″ apart for operating units and 24″ apart for picture units. Frames with a 6⁹⁄₁₆″ jamb width should be installed with 10″ masonry clips.

13. Square the unit before it is fastened permanently in the opening. Level the sill and plumb the jambs. See illustration 7. Bend the masonry clips around the studs with your hand or a hammer. Nail the masonry clip in the lower corner of the frame into the stud. Do not drive the nail all the way in. See illustration 8.

14. Recheck for level and nail the masonry clip into the stud on the opposite bottom corner of the unit.

15. Measure the window diagonally from corner to corner. The measurements should be the same in both directions. See illustration 5. The window frame should be installed without twisting to ensure proper operation.

16. Complete nailing the masonry clips in place.

SHIM THE UNIT

17. When the unit is secure in the opening it will be necessary to shim the unit from the interior. Shims should be placed on both sides of the jambs, at the check rail, and between the frame and rough opening.

On multiple window units it is extremely important to shim under mull posts.

Be careful not to cause the jambs or header to bow in or out. Bowed jambs will result in improper sash operation.

INSULATE THE UNIT

18. Insulate loosely around the unit on the interior side. Insulation should not exert pressure on the jambs. Marvin Windows does not recommend the use of expandable foam insulation.

Install a drip cap above the head jamb with roofing nails.

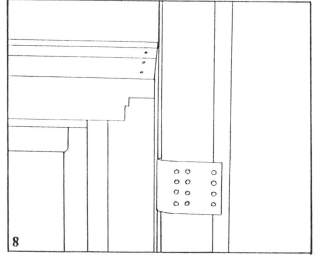

Table 7-1 continued.

19. A good quality caulk should be applied around exterior casing to seal the unit against the siding.

20. Remove sash and finish as soon as possible after installation.

WOOD DOUBLE HUNG WITH POLYCRON EXTERIOR FINISH

21. You may follow instructions for installing a double hung into a masonry opening using masonry clips to avoid damage to the Polycron finish. If nails are driven through the Polycron finish they should be countersunk and resealed.

DOUBLE-HUNG SASH REMOVAL AND SASH REPLACEMENT

REMOVING BOTTOM SASH

1. To remove sash raise the bottom sash about 3″. Depress the vinyl jamb liner with your hands and gently pull the top of the sash towards you to a horizontal position.

2. Lift one side of the sash and remove the sash from the jamb liner.

REMOVING TOP SASH

3. Lower top sash about halfway down the frame. Depress the jamb liner at the top of the sash. Pull the sash gently, but firmly, towards you to a horizontal position. Lift one side and remove. See illustration 9.

4. SASH REPLACEMENT—NOTE: WHEN REPLACING SASH, BOTH SASH PINS MUST BE POSITIONED ABOVE THE LOCKING TERMINAL ASSEMBLY LOCATED IN JAMB HARDWARE. Replace top sash first in track closest to the exterior of the building.

   A. Hold sash in horizontal position.
   B. Place one sash pin above locking terminal assembly.
   C. Raise opposite side of the sash and place the sash pin above locking terminal assembly on that side.
   D. Tilt sash up and depress vinyl jamb liner. Push sash gently into place.
   E. Pull sash down slightly to engage hardware.
   F. Repeat above procedure for bottom sash.

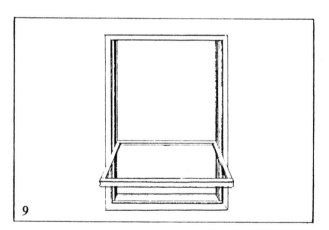

9

Table 7-1 continued.

GENERAL PAINTING & STAINING INSTRUCTIONS

Finish paint on primed or bare wood windows and doors must be applied immediately following installation to avoid damage to the wood parts. Lap the finish coat ¹⁄₁₆″ onto the glass for a proper moisture seal. Marvin factory-applied primer is designed to provide a good base for field-applied paints. Lacquer and varnishes should not be used over primed parts.

IT IS EXTREMELY IMPORTANT THAT YOU DO NOT paint locks, weather stripping, jamb liners, Patio or Terrace door screen channels and sills or any surface which has an abrasive or sliding contact with another surface. Paints, stains, and varnishes contain solvents which cause plastics or vinyls to lose their flexible qualities, making them brittle. Even momentary contact between the finish and the plastic will cause this to occur.

Abrasive cleaners or solutions containing solvents should not be used on Marvin products.

The exterior surfaces of Marvin clad and Marvin Polycron finished wood windows and doors come to you with a virtually maintenance-free exterior finish. However, the interior must be painted or stained and varnished by carefully following these instructions.

Before finishing, bare wood window and door surfaces must be clean and dry. Remove handling marks, debris, or effects of exposure to moisture by sanding lightly with 3/0 or 5/0 sandpaper and clean before applying your choice of finish.

EXTERIOR

PAINTING: Use only a high-quality oil base or latex paint. To provide good adhesion of paint, a prime coat should be applied. Paint with sash open (or removed) and do not close until thoroughly dry. Apply one coat of primer (if not factory primed) and two coats of top-quality paint according to the paint manufacturer's instructions. NOTE: Do not paint over top of Marvin clad or Marvin Polycron finishes. If you must, contact Marvin Windows for proper instructions.

STAINING: We do not recommend the use of stain on exterior surfaces.

INTERIOR

PAINTING: Use only a high-quality oil base or latex paint. To provide good adhesion of paint, a prime coat should be applied. Paint with sash open (or removed) and do not close until thoroughly dry. Apply one coat of primer and two coats of top-quality paint according to the paint manufacturer's instructions.

STAINING: Apply stain according to the paint manufacturer's instructions. Apply as many coats of stain as necessary to achieve the desired color. After the stain is thoroughly dry, apply at least two coats of varnish.

Table 7-1 continued.

of your contractor by being familiar with the installation procedures. Remember, an improper installation voids a warranty, regardless of who completed the procedure.

Whether or not you should install a window unit yourself is a question only you can answer. A review of the installation instructions will help you make up your mind. If you decide to enlist the services of a contractor, you should still buy the windows yourself. Most of the time, the contractor is happy to have you make the purchase, and you can now oversee the selection and warranty process. Discuss this with your contractor first so that you are in full agreement.

If you are installing a new window unit, consult your local building inspector to find out if you need a permit. If you do need a permit, you will probably have to submit information on the window units. If you are replacing an existing window, you probably will not need a permit, but it never hurts to check.

8
Certification Agencies

There are two additional considerations when buying window units. First, are you purchasing a product that was designed to be used in your environment? Second, how can you grade the overall quality of the unit?

Manufacturers provide answers to these questions by testing their window units and publishing the results. In order to ensure that these test results are meaningful, the manufacturers have created minimum standards against which the window is judged. These minimum standards change, depending on the proposed use of the product. If, for example, you are buying a window unit to be located on the 30th floor of a high-rise office building with its extremely high wind loads, you need a much stronger product than you would for a bedroom window on the second floor of your home.

There are two major product certification agencies within the window industry. Both have been around for over 50 years and play a vital role in quality assurance. The first is the National Wood Window and Door Association (NWWDA), 1400 East Touhy Avenue, Des Plaines, Illinois 60018. NWWDA is made up of manufacturers of wood and clad wood window units (as well as doors). The second is American Architectural Manufacturers Association (AAMA), 1540 Dundee Road, Palatine, Illinois 60067. AAMA is made up of manufacturers of aluminum and vinyl window units (as well as other products).

Each of these groups provides similar services to its membership and the consumer. Here's how AAMA describes itself:

The American Architectural Manufacturers Association (AAMA) is a trade association dedicated to serving the interests of the building envelope market. Its membership consists of manufacturers of residential, commercial, industrial and monumental products, organized into five divisions: Architectural Window, Curtain Wall and Store Front; Residential/Commercial Window and Door; Skylight and Space Enclosure; Mobile/Manufactured Housing Components; and Residential Siding Products.

In serving both the new construction and remodelling markets AAMA:

1. *develops voluntary guide specifications, product performance standards, and application and maintenance references.*
2. *sponsors a Certification Program to ensure product quality and customer acceptance.*
3. *promotes energy conservation aspects of building envelope products.*
4. *keeps the building community, code groups and regulatory bodies, and the public informed about the merits and proper application of fenestration products and about AAMA's industry standards and guide specifications.*
5. *publishes over 50 voluntary standards, guidelines, etc.*

Table 8-1 outlines the performance requirements and testing procedures as well as the classification and designations of various types of aluminum and vinyl window certified by AAMA. This is more information than you may actually need, but it is presented here for anyone who wants a complete look at all the steps a manufacturer takes to assure the customer of a quality product.

NWWDA provides similar services for the

PERFORMANCE REQUIREMENTS AND TESTING

AAMA Voluntary Specifications

AAMA pioneered in the development of voluntary standards for the establishment of performance requirements for aluminum windows. In recent years the scope of AAMA's standards has been expanded to include performance requirements for vinyl as well as aluminum windows. These requirements are detailed in ANSI/AAMA 1002.10–83, *Voluntary Specifications for Aluminum Insulating Storm Products for Windows and Sliding Glass Doors,* ANSI/AAMA 101–88, *Voluntary Specifications for Aluminum Prime Windows and Sliding Glass Doors,* AAMA 101V–86, *Voluntary Specifications for Polyvinyl Chloride (PVC) Prime Windows and Sliding Glass Doors,* and AAMA GS–001, *Voluntary Guide Specifications for Aluminum Architectural Windows.* The ANSI/AAMA voluntary specifications are submitted for a national consensus review and are approved by the American National Standards Institute. They form the basis for the AAMA window certification programs.

Performance Testing

All AAMA-designated window types must meet performance requirements for air leakage, water penetration and uniform structural loading. Architectural windows specified in AAMA GS-001 must also meet performance requirements for deflection under uniform loading. The ability of windows to meet these primary performance requirements is determined by tests described briefly in the following paragraphs.

The tests for air leakage, water penetration, and uniform loading are all conducted in the same type of test chamber. The test chamber essentially is a well-sealed box with one open side in which, or against which, the test window is installed and sealed. The box is equipped with a controllable blower, which may be reversible and which is designed to provide the specified test air-pressure difference across the test window. The chamber is equipped with a device for measuring the test pressure and a device for measuring air flow. The system is designed to provide constant air flow at a fixed pressure for the period required to obtain readings of air flow and pressure difference. A general arrangement of the test chamber is shown in Figure 72.

Air Leakage Tests

Air leakage tests are conducted in accordance with ASTM E 283, *Standard Test Method for Rate of Air*

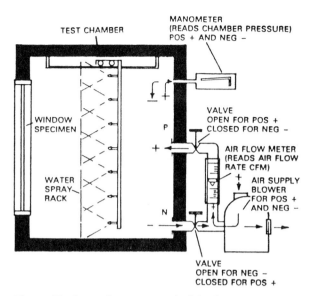

Figure 72. General arrangement of testing apparatus.

Leakage Through Exterior Windows, Curtain Walls, and Doors. This standard calls for air leakage to be measured with a pressure difference of 1.57 psf across the test window, unless otherwise specified. AAMA adheres to the 1.57 psf requirement for all residential and commercial windows, and for all storm windows above performance class 10. For performance class 10 storm windows the test is conducted at a pressure difference of 0.57 psf. 1.57 psf is also used for testing heavy commercial double-hung and horizontal-sliding windows. All other heavy commercial windows and all architectural windows are tested with a pressure difference of 6.24 psf, which is the pressure equivalent of approximately a 50 mph wind. Leakage per foot of crack length is determined. These wind velocities are much higher than those which normally occur, which means that windows in actual use will give excellent resistance to air leakage under average weather conditions.

Water Drainage Tests

Tests to measure the water drainage of externally applied storm windows are conducted in accordance with ASTM E 331, *Test Method for Water Penetration of Exterior Windows, Curtain Walls, and Doors by Uniform Static Air Pressure Difference.* Water is sprayed uniformly against the exterior surface of the window while the specified air pressure is applied across the window. The water is sprayed for a period of three minutes.

Table 8-1 (here and pages 102 and 103). Performance requirements, testing procedures, and classification of aluminum and vinyl window units. (*Courtesy of AAMA*)

Satisfactory performance means that no water over-flows the interior edge of the test-buck sill during the test. For class 10 and 15 external units the test pressure is zero. For class 20 and above the test pressure is 10% of the design pressure. The water drainage test is not applicable to internally applied storm windows, or residential, commercial, heavy commercial or architectural windows.

Water Resistance Tests

Tests to measure the resistance to water penetration of residential and commercial windows are conducted in accordance with ASTM E 547, *Test Method for Water Penetration of Exterior Windows, Curtain Walls, and Doors by Cyclic Static Air Pressure Differential.* Four test cycles are used, each cycle consisting of five minutes with the specified pressure applied and one minute with the pressure released, during which the water spray is continuously applied. Water is sprayed uniformly against the exterior surface of the window at a minimum rate of five gallons per hour per square foot of window area.

Tests to measure the resistance to water penetration of heavy commercial and architectural windows are conducted in accordance with ASTM E 331. In these tests, water is sprayed uniformly against the exterior surface of the window at a minimum rate of five gallons per hour per square foot of window area at the specified air pressure difference for a period of 15 minutes.

Satisfactory performance in all cases means that there shall be no penetration of water into the plane of the innermost face of the test window or through the window frame during the specified test period.

Uniform Load Deflection Tests

Uniform load deflection tests are conducted in accordance with ASTM E 330, *Test Method for Structural Performance of Exterior Windows, Curtain Walls, and Doors by Uniform Static Air Pressure Difference.*

This test is applied only to the architectural-grade windows described in AAMA GS-001. An air pressure equal to the design pressure is applied to the exterior side of the window for a period of 10 seconds. Under this condition no framing member of the window shall deflect more than 1/175 of its span.

AAMA requires a minimum air pressure of 30 psf for this test. This represents the velocity pressure of a 108 mph wind.

Uniform Load Structural Tests

Uniform load structural tests are also conducted in accordance with ASTM E 330. In this test method, an air pressure equal to 1.5 times the design pressure is used in order to provide an essential safety factor in the window design. The window is tested with the load applied first to the exterior side and then to the interior side, or vice versa. The minimum duration of load application required by AAMA is 10 seconds.

As its name implies, the purpose of this test is to determine the structural adequacy of the window. A window will have satisfactorily passed the test if upon completion there is no glass breakage; permanent damage to fasteners, hardware parts, support arms or actuating mechanisms; there is no other damage which would cause the window to be inoperable; there is no permanent deformation of any main frame, sash or ventilator member in excess of 0.4% of its span for windows conforming to ANSI/AAMA 101-88 and 0.2% of its span for windows conforming to AAMA GS-001.

Structural tests are required on all grades of windows.

Test Sample Sizes

The AAMA voluntary specifications establish minimum test sizes at which the various performance requirements of all windows are to be measured. The test sizes assure a desired level of quality for windows and provide a uniform basis for product comparisons. The minimum test sizes are listed along with the primary performance requirements. In the window certification programs sponsored by AAMA the minimum test sizes required by the specifications, or the manufacturer's largest production size, whichever is larger, must be used for qualifying tests.

Forced Entry Resistance

Forced entry resistance features are mandatory in some parts of the country and are desired in many other parts of the country where security is a problem. Where these features are needed, AAMA 1302.5, *Voluntary Specifications for Forced-Entry Resistant Aluminum Prime Windows* or ASTM F 588-85 (Performance Level 10) should be specified. These specifications are applicable to both aluminum and vinyl windows. If governing code requirements conflict with the AAMA specifications the code will obviously govern.

Safety Drop Test

(For vertically operating secondary window sash in dual

Table 8-1 continued.

windows only.) When the glazed sash is allowed to "free fall" the maximum distance provided by latch positions, it shall automatically stop in the next-lower latch position on the first attempt and the glass shall be unbroken or, if broken, all pieces retained in the insert.

Thermal Performance Tests

Thermal performance tests are optional. However, the use of thermally improved windows continues to grow throughout the country in all types of buildings and consequently the need for testing is growing in a like manner. AAMA thermal performance testing covers the measurement of condensation resistance and thermal transmittance. The standard test for condensation resistance is AAMA 1502.7, "Voluntary Test Method for Condensation Resistance of Windows, Doors and Glazed Wall Sections," and for thermal transmittance is AAMA 1503.1, "Voluntary Test Method for Thermal Transmittance of Windows, Doors and Glazed Wall Sections."

Specific Window Requirements

In addition to primary and high-performance requirements there are a number of other requirements which relate to specific windows. These are requirements which concern the structural capabilities of windows and their hardware to perform their operations satisfactorily under the conditions to which they will be subjected. These requirements and the methods of test used to check them are not included in the selection guide but can be found in the specifications for specific windows.

Performance Requirements for Prime Windows

Primary performance requirements and optional performance requirements for prime windows are given on the pages which follow. These requirements are identical for aluminum windows as specified in ANSI/AAMA 101-88 and vinyl windows as specified in AAMA 101V-86.

Primary performance requirements are covered in Section 2.1 of the AAMA voluntary specifications. In this section the minimum requirements for structural adequacy, water penetration resistance and air infiltration resistance are specified for the various window types and performance classes.

Optional performance requirements are covered in Section 3. This section prescribes the water resistance and uniform structural load test requirements necessary to obtain performance class designations higher than the minimum prescribed in Section 2.1.

Both Sections 2.1 and 3, and the minimum test size requirements for all windows, are reproduced in their entirety in this selection guide since they provide the essential data needed by the architect in selecting and specifying windows.

Not reproduced in this guide are Section 1, Section 2.2 and the Appendix of the AAMA voluntary specifications.

ANSI/AAMA 101-88 and AAMA 101V-86 Aluminum and Vinyl Prime Windows

Classifications and Designations

PRODUCT SYMBOL SYSTEM							
Product Type		**Grade**		**Performance Class**			
Product Code	Product	Designation	Description	Class (Design Pressure)	R	C	HC
A	Awning	R	Residential	15	•		
C	Casement	C	Commercial	20	•	•	
DH	Double (Single) Hung	HC	Heavy Commercial	25	•	•	
VS	Vertical Slide			30	•	•	
F	Fixed			35	•	•	
HS	Horizontal Sliding			40	•	•	•
P	Projected			45	•	•	•
TH	Top Hinged			50	•	•	•
VP	Vertical Pivoted						
GH	Greenhouse						
JA	JAL-Awning						
J	Jalousie						
DA	Dual Action						

Table 8-1 continued.

PRIMARY PERFORMANCE REQUIREMENTS

Window/Door Designation (1)	Design Pressure lbf/ft²(Pa)	Structural Test (4) Pressure lbf/ft²(Pa)	Water Resistance Test Pressure lbf/ft²(Pa)(5)	Air Infiltration Test Pressure lbf/ft²(Pa)	Maximum Rate (2)
AWNING					
A-R15	15 (718)	22.5 (1077)	2.86 (137)	1.57 (75)	0.37
A-C20	20 (958)	30 (1437)	3.00 (143.6)	1.57 (75)	0.37
CASEMENT					
C-R15	15 (718)	22.5 (1077)	2.86 (137)	1.57 (75)	0.37
C-C20	20 (958)	30 (1437)	3.00 (143.6)	1.57 (75)	0.37
C-HC40	40 (1915)	60 (2873)	6.00 (287.3)	6.24 (299)	0.37
DOUBLE-HUNG					
DH-R15	15 (718)	22.5 (1077)	2.86 (137)	1.57 (75)	0.37
DH-DW-R15	15 (718)	22.5 (1077)	2.86 (137)	1.57 (75)	0.37
DH-C20	20 (958)	30 (1437)	3.00 (143.6)	1.57 (75)	0.37
DH-DW-C20	20 (958)	30 (1437)	3.00 (143.6)	1.47 (75)	0.37
DH-HC40	40 (1915)	60 (2873)	6.00 (287.3)	1.57 (75)	0.37
SLIDERS					
HS-R15	15 (718)	22.5 (1077)	2.86 (137)	1.57 (75)	0.37
HS-DW-R15	15 (718)	22.5 (1077)	2.86 (137)	1.57 (75)	0.37
HS-C20	20 (958)	30 (1437)	3.00 (143.6)	1.57 (75)	0.37
HS-DW-C20	20 (958)	30 (1437)	3.00 (143.6)	1.57 (75)	0.37
HS-HC40	40 (1915)	60 (2873)	6.00 (287.3)	1.57 (75)	0.37
PROJECTED					
P-R15	15 (718)	22.5 (1077)	2.86 (137)	1.57 (75)	0.37
P-C20	20 (958)	30 (1437)	3.00 (143.6)	1.57 (75)	0.37
P-HC40	40 (1915)	60 (2873)	6.00 (287.3)	6.24 (299)	0.37
TOP-HINGED					
TH-C20	20 (958)	30 (1437)	3.00 (143.6)	1.57 (75)	0.37
TH-HC40	40 (1915)	60 (2873)	6.00 (287.3)	6.24 (299)	0.37
VERTICALLY PIVOTED					
VP-C20	20 (958)	30 (1437)	3.00 (143.6)	1.57 (75)	0.37
VP-HC40	40 (1915)	60 (2873)	6.00 (287.3)	6.24 (299)	0.37
VERTICAL-SLIDE					
VS-R15	15 (718)	22.5 (1077)	2.86 (137)	1.57 (75)	0.37
VS-DW-R15	15 (718)	22.5 (1077)	2.86 (137)	1.57 (75)	0.37
GREENHOUSE WINDOW					
GH-R15	15 (718)	22.5 (1077)	2.86 (137)	1.57 (75)	0.37
JAL-AWNING WINDOW					
JA-R15	15 (718)	22.5 (1077)	2.86 (137)	1.57 (75)	0.37
JALOUSIE WINDOW					
J-R15	15 (718)	22.5 (1077)	2.86 (137)	1.57 (75)	0.37
FIXED WINDOWS					
F-R15	15 (718)	22.5 (1077)	2.86 (137)	1.57 (75)	0.15
F-DW-R15	15 (718)	22.5 (1077)	2.86 (137)	1.57 (75)	0.15
F-C20	20 (958)	30 (1437)	3.00 (143.6)	1.57 (75)	0.15
F-DW-C20	20 (958)	30 (1437)	3.00 (143.6)	1.57 (75)	0.15
F-HC40	40 (1915)	60 (2873)	6.00 (287.3)	6.24 (299)	0.15
DUAL-ACTION					
DA-R15	15 (718)	22.5 (1077)	2.86 (137)	1.57 (75)	0.37
DA-C20	20 (958)	30 (1437)	3.00 (143.6)	1.57 (75)	0.37
DA-HC40	40 (1915)	60 (2873)	6.00 (287.3)	6.24 (299)	0.37

1. "DW," where used, indicates dual window.

2. Air infiltration rate is cfm per foot of operating ventilator or sash crack length except for fixed windows, jalousie windows, and sliding-glass doors, which shall be cfm per square foot of area. In dual windows, only the operating sash of the designated primary window or the area of the designated fixed primary window is to be used in determining the sash crack or square footage.

3. Air infiltration rate is cfm per square foot of finished window opening in plane of the wall.

4. Structural Test Pressure shown are for both positive and negative loads. After each specified loading, there shall be no glass breakage, permanent damage to fasteners, hardware parts, support arms or actuating mechanisms or any other damage which could cause the window to be inoperable. There shall be no permanent deformation of any main frame, sash or ventilator member in excess of 0.4% permanent deformation requirement, which applies to the primary window members only.

5. Where the manufacturer offers or specifies an insect screen, the water resistance test is to be performed both with and without the insect screen in place. In dual windows, where an exterior insect screen is offered by the manufacturer, the dual window unit must be tested with the screen in both the summer and winter modes.

Table 8-1 continued.

wood window and door industries. The actual certification programs are also similar. Table 8-2 provides the certification data for wood and clad wood window units as set forth by NW-WDA. Once again, this may be more information than you actually need, but it does give you a complete look at all the steps a manufacturer takes to assure the consumer of a quality product.

NWWDA Industry Standard for Wood Window Units I.S. 2-87
NATIONAL WOOD WINDOW & DOOR ASSOCIATION

1. Purpose

1.1 The purpose of this standard is to establish nationally recognized standard performance requirements for materials, construction, and assembly of wood window units for the guidance of producers, distributors, architects, builders, and the public; to avoid delays and misunderstandings; and to effect economies from the producers to the ultimate users through a wider utilization of these standard requirements.

2. Scope and Classification

2.1 Scope. This standard provides minimum performance requirements for wood window units. It includes all types and classes of window units. Provisions are included in the Appendix for labelling or otherwise identifying each window unit which fully complies with this standard.

2.2 Classification. The types of wood window units covered by this standard are listed below and are described in Section 6.

Awning Window Units	Horizontal-Sliding Window Units
Casement Window Units	Non-Operative Window Units
Decorative Window Units	Pivot Window Units
Double-Hung Window Units	Single-Hung Window Units
Hopper Window Units	Turn-tilt Window Units

2.2.1 Designs, Layouts, and Sizes. Window units are designed and produced by individual manufacturers and fabricators and vary widely in designs, layouts, sizes, and methods of manufacture and do not lend themselves to rigid standardization. Individual manufacturers' literature should be consulted for this information.

2.2.2 Classes. In addition to the types of window units listed in paragraph 2.2, window units are also classified based on different levels of performance (see Sections 4.3 and 4.4).

3. General Requirements

3.1 All wood windows which are certified, or otherwise indicated or represented as conforming to this standard, shall meet or exceed all the applicable requirements of this standard.

3.2 Wood. The wood parts of the window units shall be manufactured from Ponderosa Pine or other suitable lumber which has been kiln-dried to a moisture content of between 6% and 12% at time of machining.

3.2.1 Grading.

3.2.1.1 Sash and Frame Parts. All exposed sash and frame parts, unless a factory opaque finish is applied, shall be free from blue stain, knots, or surface checks larger than 1/8 inch deep by 2 inches in length (3 mm × 50 mm). Structurally sound defects are permitted. Fingerjoints are permitted in both sash and frame parts.

3.2.2 Tolerances. A tolerance of plus or minus 1/32 inch (± 0.8 mm) from the specifications of the windows tested will be permitted for all window unit parts.

3.2.3 Adhesives. The adhesives used in the manufacture of finger-jointed and/or edge-bonded parts shall meet or exceed the wet use adhesive requirements as defined in the latest revision of ASTM D-3110, "Adhesives Used in Non-Structural Glued Lumber Products."

3.2.4 Preservative Treatment. All wood parts of window units, except inside stops and inside trim, shall be water-repellent-preservative treated, after machining, in accordance with the latest revision of NWWDA Industry Standard I.S.4, "Water Repellent Preservative Treatment for Millwork."

3.3 Weather strip. All operative window units shall be weather-stripped. Weather stripping shall be made, at the option of the manufacturer, with any suitable mate-

---

Both English and Metric (SI) units are listed in this Standard. Where confusion or conflict occur, English units are to be taken as the standard. Metric conversions are approximate equivalents.
A list of the names and addresses of the sponsors of standards referenced in this publication appears in the appendix of this Standard. Copies of referenced standards may be obtained by writing to the appropriate sponsor.

Table 8-2 (here and pages 106 and 107). Certification data for wood and wood-clad window units. (*Courtesy of NWWDA*)

rial that has the performance qualities and durability reasonably adequate for normal and continuous operation. The weather strip shall be installed in the window frame, or window sash, or both, and shall effectively enable the unit to meet the air and water infiltration requirements for the performance level specified.

3.4 Hardware. The requirements for hardware shall be as specified in the requirements for each type of window unit. Latching devices which are the same or are equal to those which allowed the unit to pass the performance test specified in Section 4 shall be furnished by the manufacturer of the unit. All hinges, latches, and operating devices, including screws, shall be made of non-rusting material or steel protected by a rust-resistant finish.

3.5 Glazing Material.

3.5.1 Unless otherwise specified, glass shall conform to the requirements of ASTM C 1036-85 and shall be of appropriate thickness as recommended by the glazing material supplier for the size of the window.

3.5.2 Insulating Glass. Sealed insulating glass shall meet or exceed the requirements of the latest revision of ASTM E-774, "Specifications for Sealed Insulating Glass Units." Each insulating glass unit shall be permanently labelled with a name or code identifying the insulating glass manufacturer.

3.6 Screen Panels. Insect screen panels shall be provided when specified or in accordance with each manufacturer's usual practice. When aluminum-framed insect screens are specified, they shall meet or exceed the requirements of the latest revision of ANSI A201.1, "Specifications for Aluminum Tubular Frame Screens for Windows" (SMR 1004), sponsored by the Screen Manufacturers Association.

3.7 Double-Glazing Panels (Storm Panels). Double-glazing panels shall be provided when specified or in accordance with each manufacturer's usual practice. Glass shall meet or exceed the requirements of Section 3.5.1.

3.8 Glazing Materials and Procedures. Glazing materials (i.e., bedding, putty, etc.) and procedures shall be in accordance with each manufacturer's usual practice and specification.

4. Performance Requirements, Test Methods and Classes

4.1 Window Unit Test Sample. Window units tested for compliance with this standard shall be stock units produced by the manufacturer or fabricator. The test window may be caulked, primed, and/or painted prior to testing. When actual production units are not prepared in the same manner as the sample tested, adequate instructions must be provided to subsequent assemblers, installers, finishers, etc., to provide the same performance factors as the sample test, i.e., caulking, painting, priming, etc.

4.1.1 Window Test Size. A casement, awning, hopper, tilt-turn, decorative, pivot, or non-operative window sample submitted for testing shall be of the largest unit frame area for which conformance is desired. A double-hung or single-hung window sample submitted for testing shall be of the greatest width and of the largest unit frame area, in that width, for which conformance is desired. A horizontal-sliding window sample submitted for testing shall be of the greatest height and of the largest unit frame area, in that height, for which conformance is desired. Unit frame area is defined as the overall area (width times height) of the unit, excluding interior and exterior trim.

4.1.2 Additional glazed sash must be submitted with the window unit for testing if single lite sash are submitted in the window unit and conformance is desired for divided lite sash or vice versa or if conformance is desired for glazing systems which differ from those submitted in the window test unit.

4.2 Performance Test Methods—General.[1]

4.2.1 Mounting Procedures. The unit is to be mounted for testing in a manner simulating the field installation of the unit. The unit shall be installed in a wood buck-surround simulating the rough window opening or may be installed directly into the test chamber wall. The unit shall be installed plumb, square and level, in strict accordance with the manufacturer's installation instructions. Interior trim and other interior wall finishings shall not be used, to permit visual inspection of the wall side of the unit during testing. All joints between the test unit and the wood buck or test chamber shall be thoroughly sealed to prevent extraneous air or water leakage.

4.2.2 Order of Testing. The following order of testing must be followed. (The unit must be thoroughly dried prior to air infiltration and water-penetration tests.)

1. Preliminary Loading.
2. Air Infiltration.
3. Water Penetration.
4. Physical Load Testing.
5. Qualification testing for sash systems[2] not submitted in the test unit.
   a. Conversion from single to divided lite sash or vice versa—repeat test 4 above[3].
   b. Conversion to different glazing system—repeat tests 3 and 5 above[2].

Table 8-2 continued.

Note 1: The ASTM tests referenced herein are laboratory tests under defined conditions. The results of these tests may or may not be duplicated in the field depending upon environmental conditions and proper installation and handling of the window unit.

Note 2: Sash system means the stiles and rails are identical to those in the unit tested and the only variables are glazing methods and bar arrangements.

Note 3: Glazed sash may be tested in the unit or by mounting them separately to the test chamber.

4.3 Performance Test Criteria.

4.3.1 Preliminary Loading. After installation is complete, the window shall be checked to ensure that it is in operating condition by unlocking, opening, closing, and locking each operating sash five (5) times. For single-hung, double-hung, and horizontal-sliding windows, the operating force required to move each sash shall not exceed that amount specified for the selected grade level found in Table 1. The window exterior shall be subjected to five (5) loading cycles in accordance with the procedures established in ASTM E-330, under the uniform static air-pressure difference specified for the selected grade level found in Table 1. Prior to continuing the test sequence, the unit shall again be checked for proper operation in accordance with the paragraph above.

4.3.2 Air Infiltration. The unit shall be in a closed and locked position during the test. The unit shall be tested in accordance with the latest revision of ASTM E-283 (Standard Test Method for Rate of Air Leakage Through Exterior Windows, Curtain Walls, and Doors). Air leakage shall not exceed that shown in Table 1 for the grade level selected when tested under a uniform static air-pressure difference of 1.57 pounds per square foot (75 PA).

4.3.2.1 The leakage for window units with an operating sash(es) shall be measured per linear foot of sash crack.

TABLE 1
GRADES OF PERFORMANCE*

	Grade 20[1]	Grade 40[2]	Grade 60[3]
Preliminary (Design) Load: (Minimum test pressure sustained without damage, psf)	13.3	26.6	40
Operating Force (Pounds of force)	25	30	35
Air Infiltration: (Maximum infiltration at test pressure)	0.34	0.25	0.10
Water Penetration: (Minimum test pressure sustained without leakage, psf)	2.86	4.43	6.24
Structural Performance: (Minimum pressure sustained without damage, psf)	20	40	60

GRADES OF PERFORMANCE*
(Metric Units)

	Grade 20[1]	Grade 40[2]	Grade 60[3]
Preliminary Load: (Minimum test pressure sustained without damage, Pa)	638	1277	1920
Operating Force (Newtons)	111	133	156
Air Infiltration (Maximum infiltration at test pressure)	5.26×10^{-4}	3.81×10^{-4}	1.55×10^{-4}
Water Penetration: (Minimum test pressure sustained without leakage, Pa)	137	215	300
Structural Performance: (Minimum test pressure sustained without damage, Pa)	960	1920	2880

*The loads and levels prescribed in this table are actual quantities to be applied or measured during testing and do not include consideration of safety factors.

1. Suitable for residential construction.
2. Suitable for light commercial construction.
3. Suitable for heavy commercial construction.

Table 8-2 continued.

What does all this technical data mean to the consumer? It means that a "certified" window unit offers the best assurance possible that you'll be getting a serviceable product that has been tested to meet minimum standards and will provide years of satisfactory use if installed in the proper environment. Certification is not a guarantee or warranty, but it does provide that extra information needed to select a window maker.

Some manufacturers are too small to afford the certification process. Does this mean that their product is defective? Not necessarily, but someone who is new to window buying should probably concentrate on certified products.

You can tell whether or not a window unit is certified by the certification stamp. Illus. 8-1 shows the AAMA stamp. Illus. 8-2 shows the NWWDA stamp. Look for them in advertising and on the product itself.

There are other certification programs within the window industry, but none is as widespread as the two described. Feel free to write to either of the above associations to request literature.

Illus. 8-1 (above left). AAMA certification stamp. (*Courtesy of American Architectural Manufacturers Association*) **Illus. 8-2 (above right).** NWWDA certification stamp. (*Courtesy of National Wood Window and Door Association*)

9
Post-Installation Maintenance

Once a window unit is installed, it does not usually require very much maintenance. Keep it clean, painted, and lubricated in accordance with the manufacturer's recommendations and it will serve you well for many years. There are only a few problems that may arise.

REPLACEMENT PARTS

Hopefully, you will never have to replace any part of your window unit, but if you do, it will be necessary to provide certain information to your supplier. The best source of this information is your original sales invoice, so it is important that you save this document. But if you don't have it, try to supply the following information:

1. *The window manufacturer.* Look over the entire window unit carefully to find the manufacturer's name. If there is insulating glass, look between the two lights of glass on the exposed metal edge and in all the corners. It is not uncommon to find no manufacturer's name, but this presents a real challenge if you are looking for an authentic replacement part. Question your neighbors. If you live in a subdivision of homes built by the same contractor, your neighbor probably has the same window units and may have this information.

2. *The date of manufacture.* Once again, you may find pertinent information between the two lights of insulating glass. Other than that, the year your home was built will be the key. If your window unit is more than 25 years old, the chances of finding authentic replacement parts are remote but still worth a try.

3. *The material type.* Inform your supplier as to whether the window unit is aluminum, vinyl, wood, wood clad with aluminum, or wood clad with vinyl.

4. *The operating type.* Inform your supplier as to whether the window unit is casement, awning, double-hung, slider, etc.

5. *The sash opening size (width × height).* Measure the space occupied by the sash from side jamb to side jamb and head jamb to sill.
6. *The glass size (width × height).* Measure the size of the piece of glass within a sash, exclusive of bars and muntins.
7. *The glass type.* Inform your supplier as to whether the glass is insulating or single-pane.
8. *A sketch or photo of the window unit.*

Armed with this information, do one of two things: Either write to the manufacturer describing your problem and requesting a solution, or visit the local retail supplier who was most likely to have sold your window unit in the first place. Only deal with someone who has a thorough understanding of what you are looking for. If, as is often the case, you are unable to purchase an authentic replacement part, there are many generic parts available which still may do the job.

MAINTENANCE PROBLEMS

Following are some common maintenance problems and their solutions:

1. *Broken screen.* Screening material and the hardware needed to install it are readily available. Pay special attention to the color of your old screening and try to match it as closely as possible. If the frame of the screen is broken, first try to have it repaired. If this fails, visit your local hardware store, where a new, similar design can probably be made. Bring very accurate measurements.
2. *Broken glass.* If you are able to determine how the sash is to be reglazed, you can buy a new piece of glass precut to the correct size or a new piece of insulating glass from your hardware store or glass company and install it yourself. Otherwise, call in a professional glazier. Remember, some sash are not reglazeable and must be replaced. This can present a real problem if you are unable to determine the manufacturer.
3. *Bad insulating glass seal.* This manifests itself as dirty spots between the lights of glass that cannot be cleaned. The glass must be replaced. Proceed as with broken glass above. Remember, however, that most manufacturers warrant against this problem for approximately 10 years. It may be worthwhile to try and ascertain the manufacturer's name and proceed with the warranty process.
4. *Malfunctioning hardware.* This is probably the most frustrating of all maintenance problems and the most difficult to solve. There are so many parts to a window unit that it's extremely difficult to have generic replacement parts for all of them. You should disassemble your hardware and take it to two or three full-service hardware stores or lumberyards in your area. They may have encountered this problem before and found a solution. Two other sources for replacement window and door hardware are: Blaine Window Hardware, 1919 Blaine Drive, Hagerstown, Maryland 21740, and Stry-Buc Industries, 550 Church Lane, Yeadon, Pennsylvania 19050. Both companies specialize in current and obsolete hardware.

If all your attempts at procuring replacement hardware end in failure, you still have three options. If you cannot replace the hardware, replace the entire window, or remove the hardware from another window unit in the house that is not as critical.

You should consider purchasing an extra set of hardware any time you order a large quantity of window units. Wheels such as those found in sliding units and gear assemblies in awning and casement window units are especially prone to problems.
5. *Rotting frames.* If wood window unit frames are not protected from the elements, they may begin to decompose. They should be carefully inspected on an annual basis for any problems. Look at the exterior of the frame following a rainstorm to ensure that water is not collecting there. Any rotted parts should be replaced.

CONDENSATION

In order for you to fully understand condensation's relationship to window units, the technical terms used should be clarified. *Condensation* is the fog that may appear on the glass of windows. Aside from blocking your view, it can drip onto furniture or the floor, and even freeze. Condensation occurs when moist air touches a surface that is colder than the dew point of the air. If the surface temperature of the glass is below freezing, the condensation will appear as frost.

Humidity is water vapor mixed with air. Warm air can hold more water vapor than cold air. *Relative humidity* is a term that indicates the amount of water vapor in the air compared to the amount required for full saturation. For example, 50 percent relative humidity means that the air is holding half the amount of water vapor it could hold. *The dew point* is the temperature at which the water vapor in the air begins to condense. For our purposes here, the critical measurement of the dew point temperature is taken at the frame or glass of the window unit.

Window units are the first place in a home on which condensation appears. The opportunities for condensation to appear on window units can be lessened in two ways: either by lowering the relative humidity of the air within the building or raising the temperature of the interior glass surface above the dew point.

Relative humidity can be lowered by making a concerted effort to limit the release of moisture into the interior air. Some specific suggestions are:

1. Use a kitchen fan while cooking and a bathroom fan while bathing. Make sure both are vented to the outside.
2. Vent the clothes dryer to the outside.
3. Limit the use of humidifiers and vaporizers.
4. Allow air to circulate. Don't cover heat registers. Leave drapes open.
5. Make sure the attic is adequately vented.
6. Even though it's not energy-efficient, allow the colder (and dryer) outside air to enter the home.

The best way to raise the temperature of the interior glass surface is to upgrade to double- or triple-pane glazing. Storm window units used in conjunction with single-pane or insulating glass can pay great dividends.

There are many charts published by the window manufacturers showing the likelihood of condensation under different climatic conditions and with different glazing combinations. These are helpful except that they all depend on a measurement of the relative humidity within the structure. This reading is not easily accomplished by the layperson, so you should take a trial-and-error approach to solving the problem. The following anecdote will show what I mean. I was called in to investigate a condensation complaint in a relatively new home with clad wood window units and insulating glass. The homeowner had not experienced any difficulty through the first part of the winter, but had recently noticed large amounts of condensation on two windows during the night. I asked if there were any unusual sources of water and when he said there were not, we inspected the house. The basement was dry and the attic space seemed well vented. A trip through the bedrooms revealed a youngster in bed with the flu. Right next to the bed was a vaporizer that had recently been purchased to ease the child's congestion. I explained that this appeared to be the problem and suggested we see what happened when they finally put the vaporizer away.

A telephone call a week later confirmed our hunch. Since the vaporizer had been turned off, no condensation had formed. It appears that the vaporizer added just enough extra water vapor to cause condensation to form during the night when the temperature of the glass fell.

If you are faced with a condensation problem, investigate. Look for water vapor sources that can be eliminated. The condensation problem in the story just related was easily corrected. Unfortunately, some condensation difficulties are not so easily treated. Newer houses are more susceptible to condensation because they are more tightly constructed. They allow less of the colder (and dryer) outside air in and trap more of the warmer (and wetter) inside air. If you are experiencing constant condensation on your window units, this condition is probably more severe than what you are seeing. Condensation can and does occur in other areas of the home, but those spots are often hidden from view. If the problem persists, don't treat it lightly. You must do everything possible to lower the relative humidity of the air within the building.

DOORWAYS

10
Basic Information

A doorway is the only millwork item that is absolutely mandatory for every structure used for habitation (Illus. 10-1). Our prehistoric ancestors realized that the entrance to their cave was a crucial element to comfortable and efficient housing. Too large an opening would admit too much cold air and be less secure in an attack, while too small an opening would make entry difficult when carrying heavy loads of food or firewood. A southern orientation for a doorway was by far the most desirable in colder climates.

Our comfort requirements haven't changed in the ensuing years, but our approach to doorway selection has certainly become more sophisticated. Now, it seems that aesthetic rather than utilitarian requirements mandate our preference. Various doorway options are presented in this section to help you make the correct choice.

FUNCTION OF DOORWAYS

The primary, utilitarian function of a doorway is to provide an entrance and exit through and separation between two environments. This separation is desirable for several reasons: 1, protection from cold, heat, sound and insects; 2, privacy; 3, security; 4, safety; and 5, aesthetics.

In addition to these primary functions, new demands have been placed upon some of our doorways. Many are now used to supply *light*, *ventilation*, and *view*.

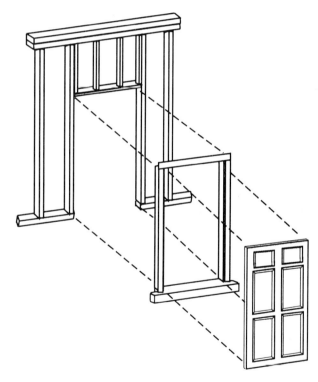

Illus. 10-1. A doorway.

You must carefully consider the functions of each doorway when planning your purchase because all doors are not suited to serve all functions. For example, while a louvre door is a beautiful and efficient closet door, allowing air to circulate freely within the enclosed space, it

115

is not an acceptable bathroom door because it affords very little privacy.

Aesthetics

For many centuries, the aesthetic value of doorways has been as important as the functional value (Illus. 10-2). A recent trip to the castles of Ireland made me extremely aware of the value ancient craftsmen placed on functional aesthetics. Beautiful portals are common adornments to these majestic structures.

In the period following the Second World War in the United States, great emphasis was placed on plain-looking doorways. Now, door treatments appear to be evolving towards the more ornate, both inside and outside the home. Manufacturers have been quick to notice this change and are creating high-tech products to meet these more flamboyant tastes. Another part of the doorway that has undergone substantial change in recent years is the glazing system. Authentic leaded glass, even in insulating lights, is now common in many patterns.

It is impossible to cover all the new, ornate doorway designs in this book. Check with your local building-material suppliers. They can provide samples or photos of the very latest designs. Your choice today is much greater than it was only 15 years ago.

Illus. 10-2. This doorway is functional and aesthetically pleasing. (*Courtesy of Morgan Products*)

11
Types of Door Construction

CONSTRUCTION CLASSIFICATION

There are three basic types of door construction: core, stile and rail, and glass. Each type of door construction is commonly found in both interior and exterior doorways, and is described below.

Core Construction

Core construction is the most widely used. It consists of three components:

1. An internal frame (usually wood or steel) made up of two or more horizontal members called rails and two or more vertical members called stiles. This frame is visible only at the outer edge of the door.
2. A core filled with various materials. This core may be hollow, solid, or insulating, depending on the materials used.
3. Two faces, called skins or veneers, which make up the decorative surface of the doorway. These veneers may be wood, aluminum, vinyl, steel or fibreglass.

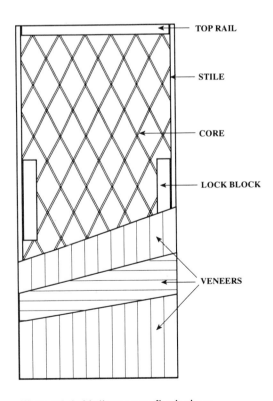

TOP RAIL

STILE

CORE

LOCK BLOCK

VENEERS

Illus. 11-1. Hollow-core flush door.

117

Illus. 11-1 shows one type of core-constructed door called a "hollow-core flush door." This door is a wood frame within which a honeycomb material is placed and onto which a wood veneer is adhered. Two wooden lock blocks have been added next to the stiles in order to provide a solid surface through which to drill the lock hole. Also, the veneer is made up of three very thin layers with the grains running perpendicular to each other. The combination of the core with three layers on each side makes this a seven-ply construction. Other combinations such as three- and five-ply are also common.

The term "flush door" indicates that both faces of the door are smooth, or flush. It is common to use other faces in conjunction with hollow cores. Moulded designs, with panels actually formed in the skin, are produced out of hardboard and adhered to a frame to create an entirely different appearance (Illus. 11-2).

The term "hollow core" is used because the core is not solid, only a cardboard, honeycomb material, or blocking which supports the veneer. Other core types of doorway serve different functions, such as temperature and sound insulation, and may be made of wood, particleboard, insulating foam, or a specialty product to provide protection from fire, X rays, etc. Illus. 11-3 shows a solid, particleboard core door with five-ply construction.

In order to install glass into core-constructed doors, a hole is cut through the veneers and core and a glazed light is installed. Panels may also be created in this fashion. There are hundreds of combinations available, including some very fancy designs using leaded insulating glass and panels that appear to be hand-carved. They can be incorporated into a new door or added to an

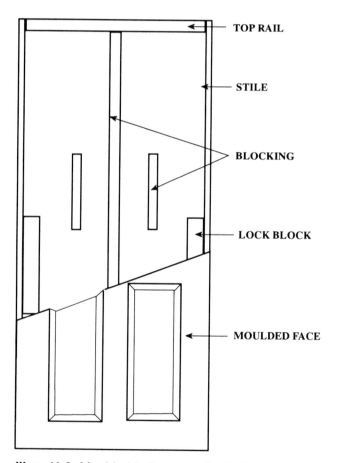

Illus. 11-2. Moulded hollow-core flush door.

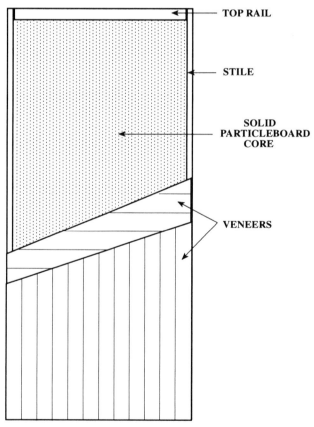

Illus. 11-3. Solid-core flush door with five-ply construction.

existing door. There are manufacturers who specialize in creating these lights and panels even though they don't make the doors. Be sure to ask your retailer for all the brochures so that you have an understanding of the current options.

Another method of creating simulated panels is to mount mouldings to the surface of the door face in the shape of the desired panel. From a distance, it appears that there is actually a raised panel in the door. These simulated panels are called "plants" and were quite common prior to 1980, especially on steel-veneered, insulated core doors (Illus. 11-4).

zontal members (rails) and vertical members (stiles), along with one or more panels or glazing surfaces. The stiles and rails are joined together with dowel (Illus. 11-5) or mortise-and-tenon (Illus. 11-6) joints. Dowelling is by far the most widely used technique. The stiles and rails are grooved to accept the panels.

True stile-and-rail doors are made almost exclusively of wood. The individual stiles and rails are either a solid one-piece construction (Illus. 11-7) or veneered construction (Illus. 11-8). Solid stiles and rails are more liable to warp

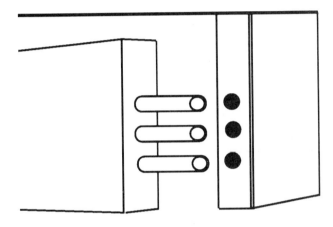

Illus. 11-5. Dowel joint.

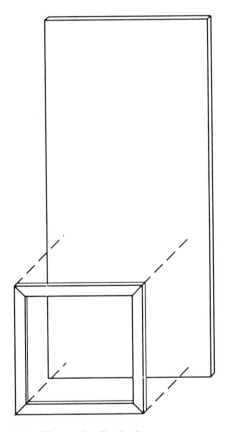

Illus. 11-4. Plants for flush doors.

Stile-and-Rail Construction

Stile-and-rail construction has been around much longer than core construction and is usually a more expensive manufacturing technique. This construction design consists of hori-

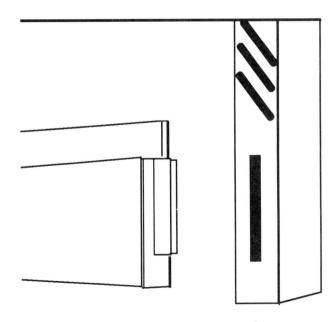

Illus. 11-6. Mortise-and-tenon joint.

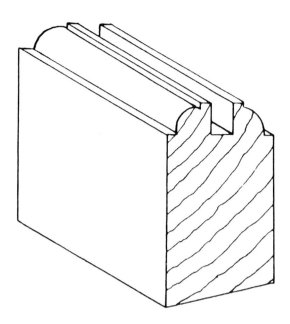

Illus. 11-7. A one-piece stile or rail. (*Courtesy of National Sash and Door Jobbers Association*)

than veneered stiles, and the veneering technique allows for the use of aesthetically blemished wood under the skins. Veneered stiles were very uncommon 20 years ago, but today, with supplies of clear lumber shrinking and manufacturing technology advancing, they are becoming the norm.

Panels, especially on exterior stile-and-rail doors, have also undergone some high-tech modification in recent years. Lamination prevents cracks and splits in the panel from extending completely to the other side.

Panels may be raised or flat, and must not be firmly attached to the stiles or rails. They float within the grooves to allow for the natural expansion and contraction of the wood. This may make a mess of the finish of a new door because the panels can shrink substantially during the heating season. You may apply a coat of paint or stain in the summer and then find a rectangle of raw, unfinished wood appearing around the perimeter of the panel once the heat is put on in the winter. A simple touchup is called for.

Glass Construction

Glass construction is the system commonly found on patio and storefront doors, usually those made of aluminum. This type of construction differs from the other two in that the frame of the door fully encompasses the main feature, which is the glass. Horizontal members are still called rails and vertical members stiles, but all they really do is provide stiffness and a channel to accept the glass.

Illus. 11-9 shows the sill section of a sliding glass doorway. Note the U-shaped channels holding the glazing gasket and the insulating glass. In order to reglaze this type of construction, you must fully disassemble the stiles and rails (usually by unscrewing the joints) to get at the glass. There are some wood and vinyl manufacturers who also use glass construction.

Illus. 11-8. Veneered stile and rail around a laminated panel. (*Courtesy of National Sash and Door Jobbers Association*)

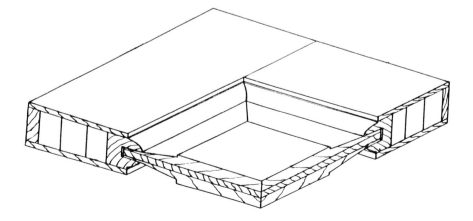

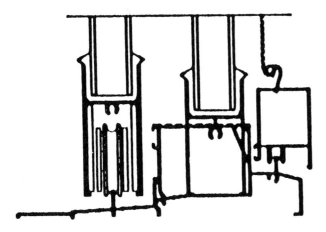

Illus. 11-9. Section view of a glass patio doorway. (*Courtesy of American Architectural Manufacturers Association*)

MATERIAL CLASSIFICATION

Doorways are similar to window units in that they are constructed of aluminum, vinyl, wood, and clad wood. In addition, there are two new types of material to consider: "insulating steel" and "insulating fibreglass." *Insulating steel doors* have revolutionized the exterior-door market in the last 25 years. Illus. 11-10 shows how the manufacturer incorporates the core construction technique by combining a steel skin over a foamed-in-place, insulated core located within a wood frame. The energy efficiency of this door has surpassed any other type of door.

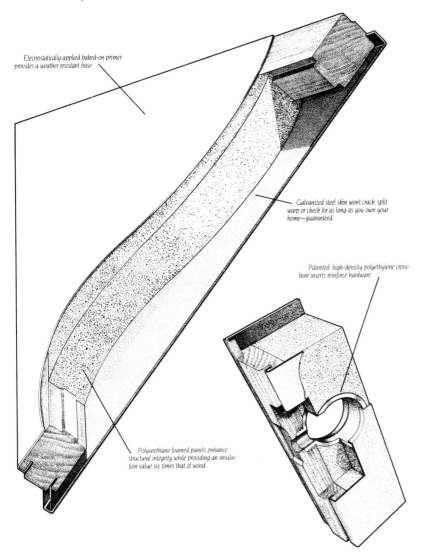

Electrostatically applied baked-on primer provides a weather resistant base.

Galvanized steel skin won't crack, split, warp or check for as long as you own your home—guaranteed.

Patented, high-density polyethylene cross-bore inserts reinforce hardware.

Polyurethane foamed panels enhance structural integrity while providing an insulation value six times that of wood.

Illus. 11-10. Insulated steel door. (*Courtesy of Peachtree Doors and Windows*)

The major drawback to a steel door is the impossibility of applying a natural-looking, stain finish to it. This problem has now been overcome with the *insulating fibreglass door* (Illus. 11-11). Insulating fibreglass doors feature construction and energy efficiency similar to insulating steel doors, with the added feature of an exterior surface that looks grained and will accept a coat of stain.

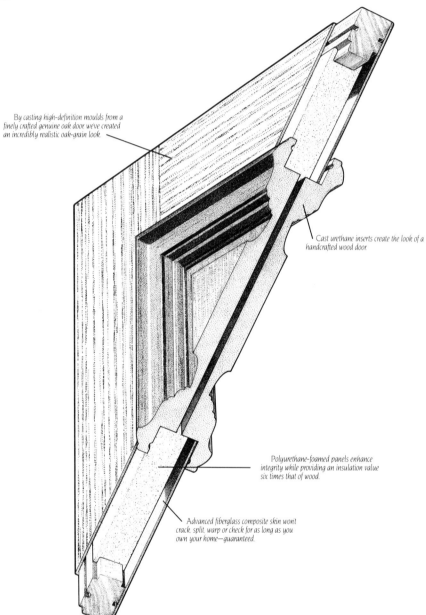

By casting high-definition moulds from a finely crafted genuine oak door we've created an incredibly realistic oak-grain look.

Cast urethane inserts create the look of a handcrafted wood door.

Polyurethane-foamed panels enhance integrity while providing an insulation value six times that of wood.

Advanced fiberglass composite skin won't crack, split, warp or check for as long as you own your home—guaranteed.

Illus. 11-11. Insulated fibreglass door. (*Courtesy of Peachtree Doors and Windows*)

12
General
Classifications

For purposes of this text, doorways are divided into four types: patio doorways, architectural doorways, exterior doorways, and interior doorways.

The doorways that will be covered are all "production doorways"; that is, they are not custom-built and are widely available from large manufacturers. Each is described below.

PATIO DOORWAYS

A relatively recent addition to the doorway market is the patio doorway. Also referred to as "glass doors," these units are available in sliding and swinging designs. They have become very common over the past 40 years.

Patio doorways could just as well have been covered in the window section of this book. Their primary purpose is to supply light, ventilation, and view rather than a major means of access or egress. Patio doorways are most commonly found opening onto a deck, patio, or porch. Like all doorway products in recent years, they have evolved into a large variety of types. Below are descriptions of sliding and swinging patio doorways.

Sliding Patio Doorways
Construction
Sliding patio doorways consist of a frame (often called a buck) and two, three, or four glass door panels (Illus. 12-1). The panels are either stationary (signified by the letter O) or operating (signified by the letter X) as viewed from the outside. These door panels slide open horizontally, so only 50% of the opening can emit fresh air or allow access at any one time. Some manufacturers make the opening panels reversible (slide to the left or the right). This practice serves two functions: It aids in inventory control and, more important to the consumer, it allows for the operating door to be changed from one side to the other in years to come.

Sliding patio doorways are generally available in aluminum, vinyl, wood and clad wood. Screens are commonly supplied along with the unit.

Use
They are very common in areas where large expanses of light and ventilation are desired, and are found mostly in residential and light commercial structures. They can be used as large windows on porches and breezeways.

Illus. 12-1. Sliding patio doorway.

Sizes

The panels of sliding patio doorways are limited in width to three sizes: 2′6″; 3′0″, and 4′0″. By combining panels, many overall sizes can be created (Illus. 12-2).

Manufacturers offer different size options. Some make the 12′0″ wide unit with four 3′0″ panels rather than three 4′0″ panels. This makes a considerable difference in the amount of ventilation you will derive (50 percent versus 33⅓ percent), so be sure you know which configuration you are receiving. Single, fixed panels are available from some manufacturers. They may be installed next to a sliding door unit and are used to continue the glass effect even when there is not enough space to fit another complete patio unit.

Sliding glass doors vary in height from 6′0″ to 8′0″, depending on the desired effect and the traditional size used in that part of the country. The most popular size is 6′8″ (80″).

Many manufacturers now offer a replacement-size patio unit to fit within old rough openings.

Hardware

The hardware for sliding patio doorways consists of a device to hold the stationary panels in place and wheels to allow the sliding panel to operate smoothly. The track is usually preattached to or formed in place with the frame head and sill. A handle and locking device for the operating door is normally included, as is the screen hardware.

A word of caution about replacing hardware: The wheels take a considerable beating and are subject to failure. Jot down the name of the manufacturer and keep any pertinent literature so you will be able to order authentic replacement parts should the need arise. Optional hardware for sliding glass doorways includes key locks and other security devices.

You should know whether your operating panel is reversible. By simply changing the wheels to the other end of the operating panel and flipping it upside down, you may be able to change the side of the unit that opens. This may become important in the future to facilitate new pedestrian patterns or furniture changes. Of course, the stationary panel and screen must also be reversed.

Weather Stripping

Weather stripping plays an important role in the success of these doorways. Because this unit contains a large operating panel which must slide, significant space is left open to air infiltration around its perimeter. Manufacturers approach this problem in various ways, but effi-

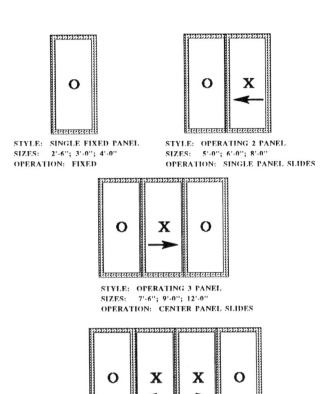

STYLE: SINGLE FIXED PANEL
SIZES: 2'-6"; 3'-0"; 4'-0"
OPERATION: FIXED

STYLE: OPERATING 2 PANEL
SIZES: 5'-0"; 6'-0"; 8'-0"
OPERATION: SINGLE PANEL SLIDES

STYLE: OPERATING 3 PANEL
SIZES: 7'-6"; 9'-0"; 12'-0"
OPERATION: CENTER PANEL SLIDES

STYLE: OPERATING 4 PANEL
SIZES: 10'-0"; 12'-0"; 16'-0"
OPERATION: BOTH CENTER PANELS SLIDE

Illus. 12-2. By combining the panels of sliding patio doorways, many overall sizes can be created.

cient weather stripping is essential to your comfort. Check it carefully.

Another area of concern is the perimeter of the screen. There must be a complete seal or insects will crawl between the screen and the panel or the frame.

Ventilation, View, and Light

Ventilation, view and light are the main reasons for buying these doorways. Even with only 50 percent of the opening providing ventilation, a significant volume of fresh air is accessed.

Maintenance

The exterior of the glass must be washed from the outside. Keep paint far away from the weather stripping and tracks. The bottom track should be kept clean and well lubricated with a silicone or Teflon product in accordance with manufacturer's recommendations. This is especially important, because excessive wear of the rollers causes severe operating problems.

Storm Panels and Screens

Storm panels are available and come in two types. The first type is the individual panel that mounts directly on the X or O panel. The second type is a full storm unit, which is like another patio door unit mounted to the exterior of the primary unit. Neither is very common nowadays because insulating glass makes patio units more energy-efficient.

Screens are generally supplied along with the door by the manufacturer. Generic replacement screens are available, but they will never fit as well as a specific product.

Energy Efficiency

The energy efficiency of sliding patio doorways is dependent on many variables. Since so much of this product is glass, the glazing type plays a large role in its efficiency. Consider low-E insulating glass in all climates. The insulating value in both summer and winter conditions along with the added protection against the damaging effects of ultraviolet light make low-E insulating glass the right choice.

Also of critical importance is the weather stripping system. Study the manufacturer's air infiltration data carefully in order to find the most efficient system. If you are considering an aluminum-framed unit, use a thermalized product.

Cost

Sliding patio doorways usually cost less per square foot of wall opening than swinging patio door units, but can vary greatly depending on material and glazing type.

Swinging Patio Doorways

Construction

Swinging patio doorways consist of a frame and one, two, or three glass door panels (Illus. 12-3). The panels are either stationary (signified by the letter O) or operating (signified by the letter X) as viewed from the outside. The operating door panel swings (usually towards the inside). Regardless of the number of panels, only one actually swings.

This system, with two or three total panels, allows for a screen to be located on the outside of

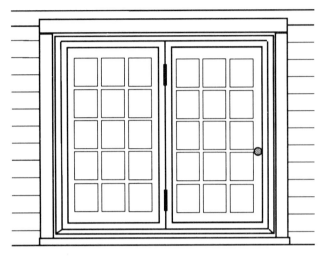

Illus. 12-3. A swinging patio doorway which opens out.

the unit. This screen is the same size as the operating door and can be rolled out of the way to allow for easy entrance and exit, or it can be pushed in front of the operating door opening to allow for insect-free ventilation.

Another type of swinging patio doorway is the "French-style" doorway (Illus. 12-4). This design allows two adjoining doors to swing open

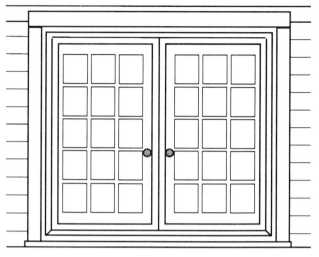

Illus. 12-4. French swinging patio doorway.

simultaneously. Since there is no frame member where the two doors come together, a piece of T astragal (Illus. 12-5) is attached to one of the doors to provide weatherproofing. This T astragal also contains hardware that allows the door to which it is attached to be rigidly locked in place. With one door locked in place, you still have the other door for entering and exiting. If you want to open both doors for ventilation or to move large objects, simply disengage the locks at the T astragal and swing both open.

Applying screens to a French-style exterior doorway is not as easy as with other sliding or swinging patio doorways. Since both doors can be opened, there is no area into which to slide a screen when the doorways are in use, so you must order a set of swinging screen doors which

Illus. 12-5. T astragal. (*Courtesy of Marvin Windows*)

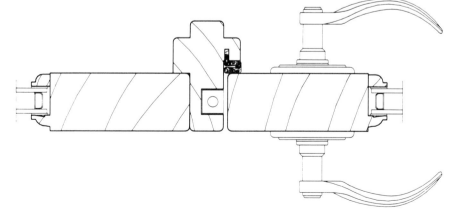

are manufactured with their own frame and T astragal. These screens are available from only a few of the patio-door manufacturers, but can be ordered from storm and screen door makers. Be sure to compare this added cost when comparing products.

Swinging patio doors are generally available in insulated steel, insulated vinyl, wood, and clad wood.

Sidelights and Transoms

Manufacturers also offer sidelights to match both types of swinging patio unit. A sidelight is the same as a fixed frame and sash except that it aligns perfectly with the doorway height. The purpose of sidelights is to provide a wider door without enlarging the operating door.

Transoms, which are like sidelights but are placed over the head jamb of the unit, are also available. These provide additional light and different architectural expression.

Use

Swinging patio doorways are common where large expanses of light and ventilation are desired, and are used mostly in residential and light commercial structures. They can also be used as large windows on porches and breezeways. French-style doors are commonly used as interior doorways between a heated room and an enclosed porch.

Sizes

The panels for swinging patio doorways are usually available in three widths: 2′0″, 2′6″, and 3′0″. By combining panels, many overall sizes can be created (Illus. 12-6 and 12-7). Swinging glass doorways vary in height from 6′0″ to 8′0″, depending on the desired effect and the traditional size used in that part of the country. The most popular size by far is 6′8″ (80″), and this vertical measurement is common throughout the entire door industry.

Hardware

The hardware for swinging patio doorways con-

sists of hinges and a locking device. Optional security devices are available. Since these units are always shipped preassembled, only the lock and screen need to be mounted on the site.

If the door swings out, make sure the hinges are weather-resistant and that the hinge pin is nonremovable, for security.

Weather Stripping

Manufacturers have different methods of weather stripping. Compare the systems carefully. Efficient weather stripping is essential to your comfort.

Swinging patio doors are generally more efficient than sliding units because the operating panel can be securely fastened against the weather stripping. French-type swinging units, because they depend on a T astragal for insulation between the doors, are more difficult to weather-strip.

Ventilation, View, and Light

Ventilation, view and light are the main reasons for buying these doorways.

Maintenance

The exterior of the glass is washed from the outside. Keep paint far away from the weather stripping and tracks.

Storm Panels and Screens

Storm panels are available in two types. The first type is the individual panel that mounts directly on the X or O panel. The second type is a full storm unit, which is like another patio door unit mounted to the exterior of the primary unit. Neither is very common nowadays, because insulating glass makes patio units more energy-efficient.

Screens are generally supplied along with the door by the manufacturer. Generic replacement screens are available, but they will never fit as well as a specific replacement product.

French-type doorways require special screening and only a few doorway manufacturers provide that along with the doorway. You may have to purchase these screens from a man-

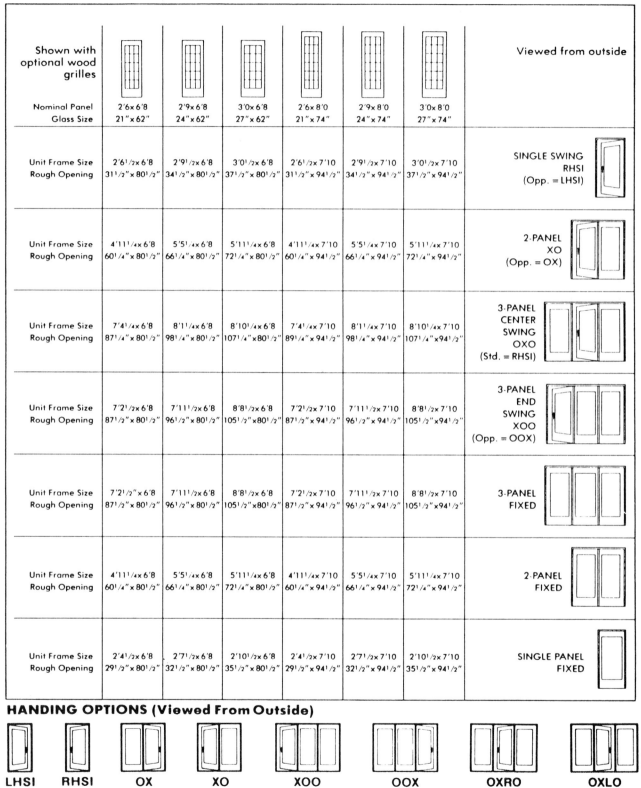

Shown with optional wood grilles Nominal Panel Glass Size	2'6 x 6'8 21" x 62"	2'9 x 6'8 24" x 62"	3'0 x 6'8 27" x 62"	2'6 x 8'0 21" x 74"	2'9 x 8'0 24" x 74"	3'0 x 8'0 27" x 74"	Viewed from outside
Unit Frame Size Rough Opening	2'6¹/₂ x 6'8 31¹/₂" x 80¹/₂"	2'9¹/₂ x 6'8 34¹/₂" x 80¹/₂"	3'0¹/₂ x 6'8 37¹/₂" x 80¹/₂"	2'6¹/₂ x 7'10 31¹/₂" x 94¹/₂"	2'9¹/₂ x 7'10 34¹/₂" x 94¹/₂"	3'0¹/₂ x 7'10 37¹/₂" x 94¹/₂"	SINGLE SWING RHSI (Opp. = LHSI)
Unit Frame Size Rough Opening	4'11¹/₄ x 6'8 60¹/₄" x 80¹/₂"	5'5¹/₄ x 6'8 66¹/₄" x 80¹/₂"	5'11¹/₄ x 6'8 72¹/₄" x 80¹/₂"	4'11¹/₄ x 7'10 60¹/₄" x 94¹/₂"	5'5¹/₄ x 7'10 66¹/₄" x 94¹/₂"	5'11¹/₄ x 7'10 72¹/₄" x 94¹/₂"	2-PANEL XO (Opp. = OX)
Unit Frame Size Rough Opening	7'4¹/₄ x 6'8 87¹/₄" x 80¹/₂"	8'1¹/₄ x 6'8 98¹/₄" x 80¹/₂"	8'10¹/₄ x 6'8 107¹/₄" x 80¹/₂"	7'4¹/₄ x 7'10 89¹/₄" x 94¹/₂"	8'1¹/₄ x 7'10 98¹/₄" x 94¹/₂"	8'10¹/₄ x 7'10 107¹/₄" x 94¹/₂"	3-PANEL CENTER SWING OXO (Std. = RHSI)
Unit Frame Size Rough Opening	7'2¹/₂ x 6'8 87¹/₂" x 80¹/₂"	7'11¹/₂ x 6'8 96¹/₂" x 80¹/₂"	8'8¹/₂ x 6'8 105¹/₂" x 80¹/₂"	7'2¹/₂ x 7'10 87¹/₂" x 94¹/₂"	7'11¹/₂ x 7'10 96¹/₂" x 94¹/₂"	8'8¹/₂ x 7'10 105¹/₂" x 94¹/₂"	3-PANEL END SWING XOO (Opp. = OOX)
Unit Frame Size Rough Opening	7'2¹/₂ x 6'8 87¹/₂" x 80¹/₂"	7'11¹/₂ x 6'8 96¹/₂" x 80¹/₂"	8'8¹/₂ x 6'8 105¹/₂" x 80¹/₂"	7'2¹/₂ x 7'10 87¹/₂" x 94¹/₂"	7'11¹/₂ x 7'10 96¹/₂" x 94¹/₂"	8'8¹/₂ x 7'10 105¹/₂" x 94¹/₂"	3-PANEL FIXED
Unit Frame Size Rough Opening	4'11¹/₄ x 6'8 60¹/₄" x 80¹/₂"	5'5¹/₄ x 6'8 66¹/₄" x 80¹/₂"	5'11¹/₄ x 6'8 72¹/₄" x 80¹/₂"	4'11¹/₄ x 7'10 60¹/₄" x 94¹/₂"	5'5¹/₄ x 7'10 66¹/₄" x 94¹/₂"	5'11¹/₄ x 7'10 72¹/₄" x 94¹/₂"	2-PANEL FIXED
Unit Frame Size Rough Opening	2'4¹/₂ x 6'8 29¹/₂" x 80¹/₂"	2'7¹/₂ x 6'8 32¹/₂" x 80¹/₂"	2'10¹/₂ x 6'8 35¹/₂" x 80¹/₂"	2'4¹/₂ x 7'10 29¹/₂" x 94¹/₂"	2'7¹/₂ x 7'10 32¹/₂" x 94¹/₂"	2'10¹/₂ x 7'10 35¹/₂" x 94¹/₂"	SINGLE PANEL FIXED

HANDING OPTIONS (Viewed From Outside)

LHSI RHSI OX XO XOO OOX OXRO OXLO

Illus. 12-6 and 12-7 (opposite page). By combining panels, many overall sizes can be created. (*Courtesy of Peachtree Doors and Windows*)

128

AUTHENTIC FRENCH DOOR SYSTEM

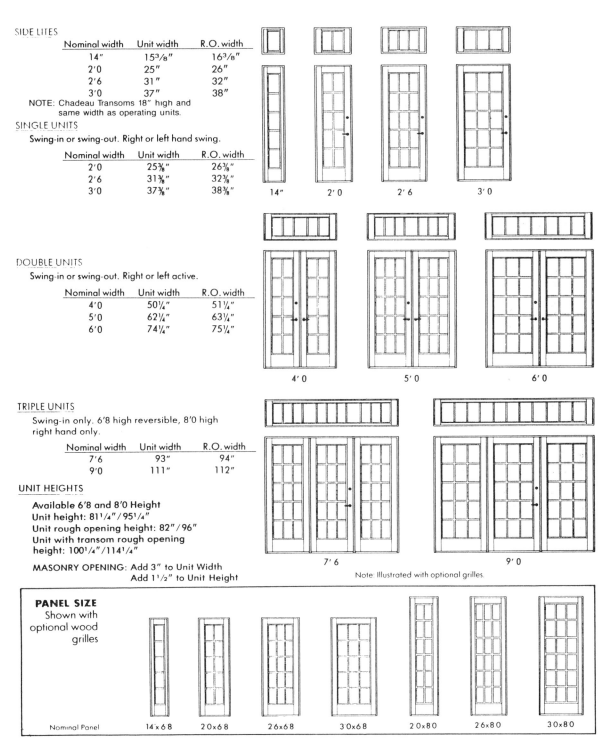

SIDE LITES

Nominal width	Unit width	R.O. width
14″	15³⁄₈″	16³⁄₈″
2′0	25″	26″
2′6	31″	32″
3′0	37″	38″

NOTE: Chadeau Transoms 18″ high and same width as operating units.

SINGLE UNITS

Swing-in or swing-out. Right or left hand swing.

Nominal width	Unit width	R.O. width
2′0	25³⁄₈″	26³⁄₈″
2′6	31³⁄₈″	32³⁄₈″
3′0	37³⁄₈″	38³⁄₈″

14″   2′0   2′6   3′0

DOUBLE UNITS

Swing-in or swing-out. Right or left active.

Nominal width	Unit width	R.O. width
4′0	50¼″	51¼″
5′0	62¼″	63¼″
6′0	74¼″	75¼″

4′0   5′0   6′0

TRIPLE UNITS

Swing-in only. 6′8 high reversible, 8′0 high right hand only.

Nominal width	Unit width	R.O. width
7′6	93″	94″
9′0	111″	112″

UNIT HEIGHTS

Available 6′8 and 8′0 Height
Unit height: 81¼″ / 95¼″
Unit rough opening height: 82″ / 96″
Unit with transom rough opening
height: 100¼″ / 114¼″

MASONRY OPENING: Add 3″ to Unit Width
Add 1½″ to Unit Height

7′6   9′0

Note: Illustrated with optional grilles.

PANEL SIZE
Shown with optional wood grilles

Nominal Panel	14x68	20x68	26x68	30x68	20x80	26x80	30x80

Illus. 12-7.

ufacturer other than the one who made the primary unit.

Energy Efficiency

The energy efficiency of swinging patio doors is dependent on many variables. Since so much of this product is glass, the type of glass used plays a large role in its efficiency. Strongly consider using low-E insulating glass in all climates. The insulating value in both summer and winter conditions, along with the added protection against the damaging effects of ultraviolet light, make low-E glass the ideal choice.

Also of critical importance is the weather stripping system. Study the manufacturer's air infiltration data carefully in order to find the most efficient system. If you are considering an aluminum-framed unit, use a thermalized product.

Cost

Swinging patio doorways usually cost more per square foot of wall opening than sliding patio doorways but can vary greatly, depending on material and glazing type.

Advantages of Sliding Patio Doorways

1. They allow for the greatest amount of light and view.
2. They allow for good secondary access and exit, especially for large items.
3. They generally cost less per square foot of wall space than windows.

Disadvantages of Sliding Patio Doorways

1. They are less energy-efficient than some types of window.
2. They take away wall space from furniture.
3. They require more expensive shades.
4. Only 50 percent or less of a sliding patio doorway is available for ventilation.
5. An open door will allow rain to enter.
6. Sliding patio doors provide less security than other types.

Disadvantages of Swinging Patio Doorways

Swinging patio doorways have all the disadvan-

tages cited above for sliding patio doorways, plus two additional disadvantages:

1. Their swing radius lessens space available for furniture.
2. French-style doorways require a sophisticated screening technique.

Optional Items for Patio Doorways

Security against unwanted visitors is a common concern of patio doorway owners, and manufacturers have come up with many options to take the place of a broom handle. Glazing options are the same as with window units. Remember that a great portion of a patio doorway is made of glass, and if temperature extremes exist in your climate, use the type of glass that will best save energy.

Tempered glass in patio doorways is mandated by law and not optional. This type of glass is much tougher than regular glass and, if it is broken, crumbles into pieces that are not nearly as sharp as regular glass shards would be.

Divided lights are commonly used in patio doorways and may be authentic or created with grilles. Both are readily available. Some manufacturers offer custom-divided light designs.

Sidelights of various sizes are generally available, offering almost unlimited overall size potential when used in conjunction with patio units. Rectangular and circle-head transoms as well as true circle-head doors are available and provide fenestration opportunities.

Warning: *Large expanses of glass are potentially dangerous to humans and their pets. Certain light conditions may cause the glass to become invisible, and serious injuries can result from collisions. Take special steps to identify the glass surface to pedestrians.*

ARCHITECTURAL DOORWAYS

The term "architectural doorway" is often given to doors used in commercial or institutional buildings. Hospitals, hotels, schools, and fancy office buildings are a few of the places that use architectural doorways. An architectural doorway is generally a beefed-up version of a residential doorway. They have to withstand rougher-than-normal treatment in their commercial surroundings, and special steps are usually taken in construction to ensure dependability. Architectural doorways come in exterior and interior designs.

Construction

Architectural doors most frequently have a core construction. They may have a hollow or solid core. Glass construction is also used, mainly in entrances.

The internal frames of core doors are made of either wood or steel. The stiles and rails are often wider than those found in residential versions.

Hollow-core doors have a honeycomb core material which is much more substantial than that found in residential doors. The only function the core serves is to support the veneer and keep it from collapsing (Illus. 12-8). Hollow cores create the lightest door possible, which is easier to hang and designed to provide aesthetic separation between rooms. More specialized functions are provided by solid cores.

Solid cores in wood-veneered architectural doors can be made of wood-composite materials such as particleboard, or wood blocks, or noncombustible mineral material for fire-proofing, or lead for X-ray proofing, or insulation for deadening sound. Steel-veneered architectural doors offer similar core options as well as an insulating foam core.

Solid cores provide more support for the door, resulting in a tougher product which is also much heavier than a hollow-core door. Hinges and doorway frames must be strengthened to support these doors. They all provide significantly improved sound- and thermal-insulating qualities, as well as more resistance to warping (Illus. 12-9).

Fire-retardant cores are a common specialty of many residential as well as architectural doorways. Sound-dampening cores are used when there is a need for extreme sound separation from the surroundings. A normal solid core

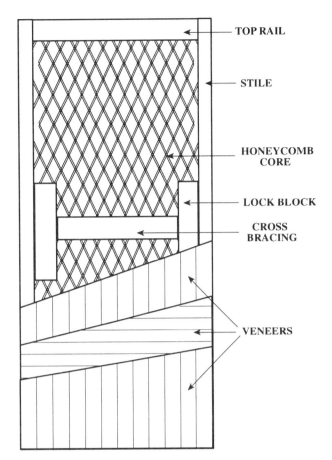

Illus. 12-8. Architectural, hollow-core flush door.

will provide considerable protection, but not enough for the sound recording studio or the president's private conference room. A sound-dampening core has an audio insulator at its center.

Lead cores are specific to X-ray protection in the hospital or physician's office. The office walls contain lead insulation and the lead-core door continues the protection throughout the perimeter of the room.

There is a new door on the market which simulates stile-and-rail construction but is in reality built around a laminated core which can be engineered to be sound- and fire-retardant. This door provides a rather unusual architectural appearance (Illus. 12-10).

Veneers

The veneers for architectural doorways are

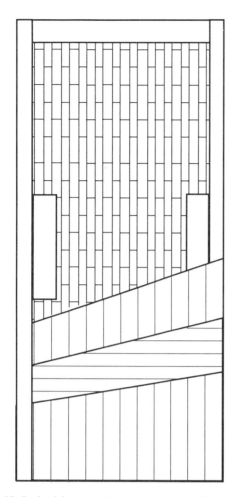

Illus. 12-9. Architectural, wood-stave solid-core flush door.

Illus. 12-10. Architectural doorway with stile-and-rail look. (*Courtesy of Jessup Door Company*)

Illus. 12-11. Rotary-cut veneers. (*Courtesy of National Sash and Door Jobbers Association*)

usually made of wood, steel, or plastic laminate. Wood veneers may be created from various species of tree. Mahogany, birch, cherry, oak and walnut are common, but almost any wood is available at a price. Color and grain characteristics are prime considerations since the ultimate effect is purely aesthetic.

The manufacture of wood veneers is an industry unto itself. Several methods are used, each of which creates a different grain configuration. Rotary cutting is a method in which the log is turned on a lathe-like device while a very sharp, fine blade peels layer after layer away from the core. Rotary cutting usually results in a wild grain pattern, depending on the type of wood used (Illus. 12-11).

Slicing is an entirely different method of obtaining veneers, in which the log is straight-cut along its length into thin pieces. The slicing technique results in a face with relatively straight grain at the edges and broad circular lines in the middle (Illus. 12-12).

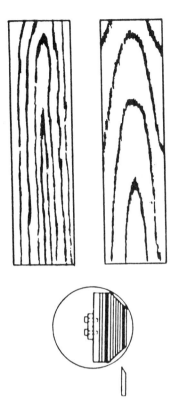

Illus. 12-12. Plain-sliced veneers. (*Courtesy of National Sash and Door Jobbers Association*)

Other cutting styles may be used to create veneers, but they are really variations of rotary cutting and slicing.

It should be noted that a wood door skin is usually made up of more than one piece of veneer. As pieces come off the cutting machines, they are grouped in the same order as they were cut from the log and then joined together along their vertical edge to create the final product, which becomes the door skin. If you look carefully at the face of a door, you may be able to see where the pieces are joined. It's not uncommon to see four or six pieces making up the face of a 3′0″ wide door. By keeping the pieces of veneer in sequential order, it is possible to minimize the visual transition and even to enhance the overall appearance.

Types of Veneer
Plastic veneers are manufactured of a laminated mica product similar to that used on kitchen countertops. They are used when a very durable, chemical-resistant surface is desired. Many colors and patterns are available.

Steel veneers are commonly used in commercial installations, especially where a painted, rather than a wood-grained, stain finish is called for. Veneers generally range in thickness from 16 to 20 gauge. Today, raised panels are being formed into steel skins, and this new design can add a distinctive flair to a commercial application.

Sizes of Architectural Doors
Since architectural doors are often custom-manufactured for a specific job, they are not limited in size to any standards. In a practical sense, however, there are "normal," or more frequently used, sizes.

Hollow-core doors are usually 1⅜″ or 1¾″ thick. Normal widths run from 1′0″ to 3′0″ in 2″ increments, and heights from 6′0″ to 8′0″ with 6′8″ as a good average. Normal maximum size is 4′ wide × 8′ tall.

Solid-core doors are usually 1¾″ thick. They normally run in widths from 2′0″ to 3′0″ in 2″ increments, and in height from 6′0″ to 8′0″ with 6′8″ as an average. Solid-core doors normally have a maximum width of 4′0″ and a height of 10′0″.

Doorway Frames
The doorway frames for architectural doors may be somewhat specialized, depending on the function the door serves. They may be wood or aluminum, but are often manufactured of steel, even if a wood doorway is used.

Hardware
The hardware for architectural doors is usually not provided by the door manufacturer. Hinges, knob sets, locks, automatic closers, viewers, kick plates and push plates are just a few of the hardware items that need to be considered along with the door. This is a specialty unto itself, since building codes often mandate minimum hardware requirements for commercial installations. The hardware for architectural doors is normally specified by the architect along with the door list.

Weather Stripping

The weather stripping for architectural doors is normally contained on the doorway frame rather than the door. It is important that both exterior and interior doors have weather stripping, not only for thermal insulation but also for soundproofing. When you put an automatic closer on a solid-core doorway, you must cushion the area against which the door closes or the impact will create unwanted sound and vibration. Sound-dampening cores work well, but the area around the doorway must also be protected from sound transmission.

Ventilation, View, and Light

Ventilation, view and light are not prime considerations in the specification of architectural doors, but there are occasions when each must be considered. Ventilation is provided by a framed louvre assembly which is inserted into the door. There are different styles of louvre assembly, depending on need. View and light are provided in a similar fashion. Holes are cut through the door and vision panels inserted (Illus. 12-13).

Maintenance

The maintenance of architectural doors is dependent upon the material used. Each door should be sealed on all six sides (top, bottom, two edges, and two faces), and that seal should be maintained with touch-ups as needed throughout the life of the door. This practice will inhibit the flow of moisture into and out of the frame and core and is the critical step in preventing warpage.

Keep paint away from the hardware and weather strip. Lubricate hinges and locks as recommended by the manufacturer.

Cost

Architectural doors cost substantially more than similar residential doors. This is because of the heavy-duty construction involved in commercial installations.

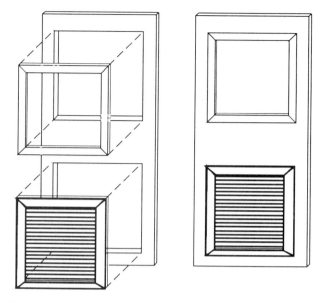

Illus. 12-13. Installing a light and louvre in a flush door.

EXTERIOR DOORWAYS

Every structure has at least one exterior doorway. These units play an important role in our personal comfort because they are really a continuation of the exterior wall of the home and are the only thing standing between us and the elements. The positioning of exterior doorways in the center of a structure makes them the focal point of the fenestration of the home. Therefore, aesthetics may play an important role in selection. Exterior doorways are manufactured in all construction and material types. For purposes of this text, they are divided into three categories: core, stile-and-rail, and storm, screen, and garage doorways. Each type is described below.

Core Residential Exterior Doorways

Core construction for exterior doorways consists of three components:

1. An internal frame (usually wood or steel) made up of two or more horizontal members called rails and two or more vertical members called stiles.
2. A core filled with various materials. This core may be hollow, solid, or insulating, depending on the materials used.

3. Two faces, called skins or veneers, which make up the decorative surface of the door. These veneers may be wood, aluminum, vinyl, steel or fibreglass. Aluminum- and vinyl-faced doors are covered in the Storm and Screen Doorway section.

Insulated-Core, Steel-Veneered Doorways

Steel-veneered doorways (commonly referred to as "steel entry doorways") are available in several core types. Practically speaking, however, only the type with an insulated core is used for exterior installation in residential and light commercial construction. Introduced in the late 1960s, these doorways have become the most popular type in use today for new residential construction. They were originally available only with flush skins, but are now offered with a wide variety of formed panels and fancy light inserts.

Construction

These doors have a very innovative construction technique. First, an internal frame (usually wood) is assembled. It includes blocks to support the future installation of the locks. This frame is then covered by two steel skins, one on each side. The skins may be flush, or panels may have been formed into them under extreme pressure within a large press. These two skins must not touch each other, in order to protect against the thermal conductivity of steel. If you look carefully at an insulated-core steel door, you will see this skin separation at the edges.

At this stage of construction, the core is hollow. If there is to be a light in the door, the skins are cut and the light frame is installed.

Now comes the innovative part of the construction. A nozzle is inserted through a hole in the bottom rail and a precise amount of liquid foam is injected into the hollow core. As this liquid dries, it expands to fill every hollow inside the door and provide an excellent insulating material, which is also quite dense. The foam serves to bond the stiles, rails, and faces together into a rigid panel. The completed door includes bottom weather stripping and cutouts for the lock and hinges.

Illus. 12-14 shows the vertical and horizontal cross-sections of an insulated-core steel door and frame. Note how the light is installed and the raised panel is embossed into the steel face. There are other types of light which may be installed after the door is manufactured. These lights usually have a raised moulding surrounding the glass.

Veneers

The veneers for insulated-core, steel residential doorways are usually 22- or 24-gauge steel. As these doors become more popular, manufacturers are expanding the styles of stamped panels. At least one manufacturer offers a steel door with an oak hardwood veneer overlaid on top of the steel face. This model takes advantage of the insulated construction while still providing a natural wood surface.

Sizes

Insulated-core, steel residential doors are generally limited to only three sizes: 2'6" × 6'8", 2'8" × 6'8", and 3'0" × 6'8". Some manufacturers offer 3'6" or 3'8" widths and 7'0" heights, but only in limited veneer designs. There is such a small selection of this type of door primarily because these sizes make up over 95 percent of the entry doors in the United States and the cost of creating a die to manufacture another size in the press is exorbitant. Other size options are available through the use of sidelights and transoms.

All these doors are 1¾" thick, which is standard for entry units.

Sidelights and Transoms

Sidelights and transoms may be used to enhance the amount of light admitted by entrance doorways as well as to create an unusual architectural appearance. These items are constructed in the same fashion as the doors and provided as a package by the manufacturer. Each sidelight or transom comes in its own frame. Some manufacturers offer ventilating sidelights, which open out in the same fashion as a casement window.

Illus. 12-15 gives an indication of the side-

Illus. 12-14. Section view of a steel entry door. (*Courtesy of Peachtree Doors and Windows*)

Head

Sill

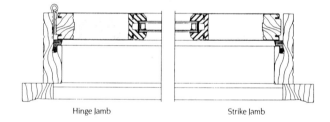

Hinge Jamb   Strike Jamb

lights and transoms available from one manufacturer. Note that various configurations result in many size options.

Doorway Frames

The doorway frames for insulated-core, steel residential door are important considerations when choosing a unit. By their very nature, steel-faced doorways are not "field trimmable." This means that they are not meant to be cut down to fit within your existing frame. Manufacturers always supply a weather-stripped frame to accompany the door. Since this frame will play an important role in the overall performance of the doorway, you should compare its features carefully to other models.

Hardware

The hardware for insulated-core, steel residential doorways is partially provided by the door manufacturer. Since the frame is included, the door is prehung and hinges are installed. Accessories such as knob sets, locks, automatic closers, viewers, kick plates, and push plates must be ordered separately.

Care should be taken that items such as door knockers are bolted through the door because the core of these doors is not meant to hold a wood screw.

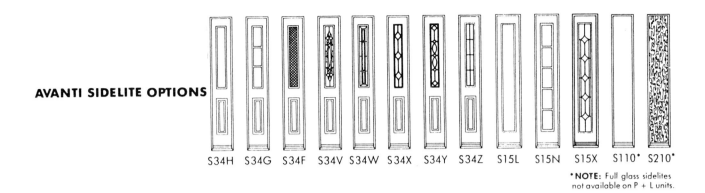

AVANTI SIDELITE OPTIONS

S34H S34G S34F S34V S34W S34X S34Y S34Z S15L S15N S15X S110* S210*

*NOTE: Full glass sidelites not available on P + L units.

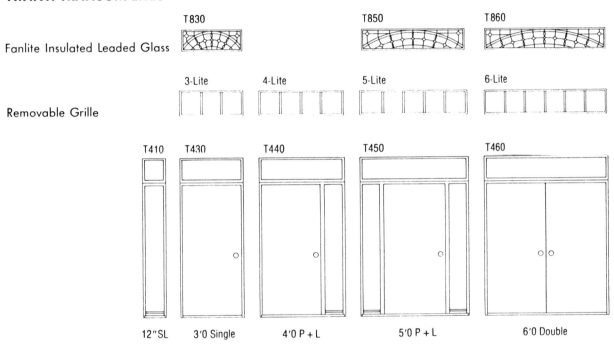

AVANTI TRANSOM LITES

Fanlite Insulated Leaded Glass

T830   T850   T860

Removable Grille

3-Lite   4-Lite   5-Lite   6-Lite

T410 T430   T440   T450   T460

12"SL   3'0 Single   4'0 P + L   5'0 P + L   6'0 Double

Illus. 12-15. Sidelight and transom options. (*Courtesy of Peachtree Doors and Windows*)

Weather Stripping

The weather stripping for insulated-core, steel residential doorways is always provided by the manufacturer. The doorway has a sweep or bulb-like insulator at the bottom edge which attaches to the top of the sill to form a tight bond (Illus. 12-16). Some sills may even be adjustable up or down to ensure that the insulator and top of the sill form a tight bond even though there may be some settlement in the structure. The head and side jambs are weather-stripped to create a seal around the door when it is closed.

There are two types of weather stripping commonly used: "magnetic" and "compression." In the first system, the magnetic property of the steel face is used to form a bond between the weather stripping and the door. Compression weather stripping is made of a bulky, pliant material that compresses and spreads out when the door is closed. Either system is successful in providing a draft-free environment.

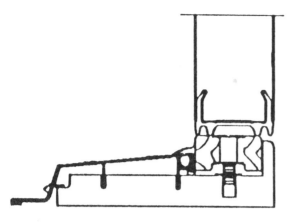

Illus. 12-16. Steel door weather stripping at sill.

Ventilation, View, and Light

Ventilation, view and light are usually not prime considerations in the specification of these doorways, but there are occasions when each must be considered. Ventilation is provided by opening the door, which means a screen door must be used. Light is limited only by the amount of glass in the door. Sidelights and transoms can add an enormous amount of light.

Maintenance

The maintenance of insulated-core, steel residential doorways is limited to painting and lubricating as needed. These doors come with a factory-applied prime coat and must be given their final coat of paint after installation. The manufacturer usually affixes a label to the door advising of the recommended type of paint. Don't take chances with the paint; use what the manufacturer recommends.

The steel skins of these doorways are similar to automobile fenders. If you hit them hard enough, they will dent. These blemishes can be repaired with the same material you would use to fill the fender. Ask your local auto supply dealer for suggestions.

Keep paint away from the hardware and weather stripping. Lubricate hinges and locks as recommended by the manufacturer.

Early designs of these doorways came with a flush steel skin and depended on plants (plastic mouldings) to create the effect of a panel. If a storm door is installed over the steel door and the sun shines directly on the door, enough heat may be generated to melt or disfigure the plants. Be on the lookout for excessive heat buildup in the cavity created by these two doors. Provide ventilation if needed.

Security

An exterior doorway is a prime target for thieves. Be sure that your lock is effective; add a dead bolt if necessary. The lock blocks within these doors usually allow for the location of a dead bolt above the regular lock, but be sure to test them first. If in doubt, ask your supplier.

If you do use a dead bolt and you have a large light of glass in your door, consider a keyway on both the interior and exterior. With this system, a thief cannot break the glass and disengage the dead bolt. The disadvantage of the two keyway system is the extra time it takes to unlock the door from the inside.

If you are particularly concerned with security, consider having no glass in your door, but add a viewer or sidelights to allow you to see who is outside. The sidelights would also provide some light.

Energy Efficiency

Insulated-core, steel residential doorways are the industry leader in energy efficiency. While comparisons are difficult due to nonstandardized testing techniques, it is certain that the foam core material is a more efficient thermal insulator than wood or any other core material to date. The energy efficiency of any particular type of insulated-core, steel residential door does depend on the amount of glass, the doorway frame, and the weather stripping.

Steel-door manufacturers, unlike window manufacturers, do not publish energy efficiency data based on standard criteria, so you must rely a great deal on your own ability to spot a well-constructed and weather-stripped doorway. The energy efficiency lost through poor construction will not be compensated for by an insulating core.

One advantage of these doors is that they come prehung in their own frame. Theoretically, they should fit well and provide sufficient weather stripping.

Cost

Insulated-core, steel residential doorways range in cost from low to high, depending largely on panel design and light inserts. There are leaded glass inserts that might add $1,000 to the cost of the unit. Compare different doors and you'll end up with the right product at a fair price.

If you want to replace an exterior door within your home, it's important to remember that you must also buy the frame with these steel doors. That's an added expense both in material and labor, but you are receiving a complete package that will probably be more energy-efficient. If the existing frame is fine and you want to save it, you'll have to use another type of door.

Warranty

Manufacturer warranties for insulated-core, steel residential doors are quite good, ranging from five years to a lifetime. Remember that they are limited and cover certain doors under certain circumstances. Be sure to ask your supplier about the warranty for the door you are considering. Also, be sure to get a copy of the warranty and file it away with your copy of the sales invoice.

Insulated-Core, Fibreglass-Veneered Door

Insulated-core, fibreglass-veneered doors (commonly referred to as "fibreglass entry doors") have evolved in the last 10 years as an additional product within the steel door industry. One of the drawbacks of steel doors is that they can take only a limited number of paint finishes. It is quite difficult to obtain the appearance of natural wood as you would with a stain finish. Fibreglass skins were created to help solve this problem. They have wood-grain lines moulded into their face and readily accept certain types of stain finish to give a wood-like appearance.

Construction

These doors are constructed very similarly to the steel doors outlined above. This is the same core construction. The only difference is that these doors have veneers made of fibreglass rather than steel. The completed door still includes bottom weather stripping and cutouts for the lock and hinges.

Illus. 12-17 shows vertical and horizontal cross-sections of an insulated-core fibreglass door and frame. Note how the light is installed and the raised panel is embossed into the fibreglass face.

Illus. 12-18 shows the same door with a different panel and light treatment. These inserts have a raised moulding surrounding each of them, which creates a distinct appearance.

Veneers

The veneers for insulated-core, fibreglass residential doors, as described by their manufacturers, are made up of "fibreglass-reinforced composite materials, compression-moulded under high pressure." They actually have wood graining etched into their faces as well as lines in the corners to make it appear that they are wood stile-and-rail doors. If they are stained and finished properly, they look authentic.

Sizes

Insulated-core, fibreglass residential doors are generally limited to only three sizes: 2′6″ × 6′8″, 2′8″ × 6′8″, and 3′0″ × 6′8″. Some manufacturers may offer more in the future but for now these will have to do. Other size options are available through the use of sidelights and transoms.

All these doors are 1¾″ thick, which is standard for entry units.

Sidelights and Transoms

Sidelights and transoms may be used to enhance the amount of light admitted by entrance doorways as well as to create an exceptional architectural appearance. Fibreglass sidelights and transoms are still being introduced by the manufacturers, so check with your retail supplier for an up-to-date design sheet.

Doorway Frames

The doorway frames for insulated-core, fibreglass residential doorways are important considerations when choosing a unit. At this time, only one manufacturer offers a fiberglass

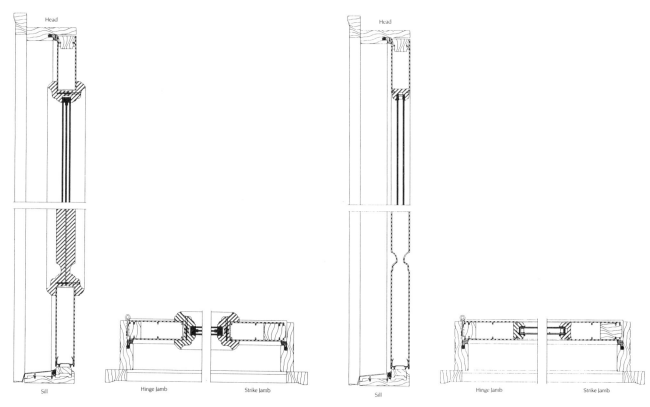

Illus. 12-17 (above left). Section view of a fibreglass entry door. (*Courtesy of Peachtree Doors and Windows*)
Illus. 12-18 (above right). Insulated fibreglass entry door with raised moulding inserts. (*Courtesy of Peachtree Doors and Windows*)

door which is "field trimmable." This means that if buying a door from all other manufacturers, you must buy a frame along with the door. Since this frame will play an important role in the overall performance of the doorway, compare its features carefully to other models.

Hardware
The hardware for insulated-core, fibreglass residential doors is partially provided by the door manufacturer. If the frame is included, the door is prehung and hinges are installed. Items such as knob sets, locks, automatic closers, viewers, kick plates and push plates must be ordered separately. Care must be taken that items such as door knockers are bolted through the door because the core of these doors is not meant to hold a wood screw.

Weather Stripping
The weather stripping for insulated-core, fibreglass residential doorways is provided by the manufacturer if a frame is purchased along with the door. Unlike steel doorways, magnetic weather stripping is never used on fibreglass doorways. Different types of compression weather stripping are the standard for fibreglass doorways.

Ventilation, View, and Light
Ventilation, view and light are usually not prime considerations in the specification of these doorways, but there are occasions when each must be considered. Ventilation is provided by opening the door, which then necessitates a screen door. Light is limited only by the amount of glass in the door. Sidelights and transoms can add an enormous amount of light.

Maintenance

The maintenance of insulated-core, fibreglass residential doors is limited to painting and lubricating, as needed. These doors come with a label advising the suggested finishing technique. Some manufacturers even offer a finishing kit. Don't take chances with the stain or paint. Use only what the manufacturer recommends.

Keep paint away from the hardware and weather stripping. Lubricate hinges and locks as recommended by the manufacturer.

Security

An exterior doorway is a prime target for thieves. Be sure that your lock is effective. Add a dead bolt if necessary. The lock blocks within these doors usually allow for the location of a dead bolt above the regular lock, but be sure to measure the space first. If in doubt, ask your supplier.

Energy Efficiency

The energy efficiency of insulated-core, fibreglass residential doors is equal to that of steel-skin doors.

Cost

Insulated-core, fibreglass residential doorways cost more than steel doorways. If you want to replace an exterior door and save the existing frame, investigate these fibreglass models. Already, one manufacturer's product allows for field trimming of up to ½″ in width and even more in height. This may permit you to use this new design without having to replace the existing frame.

Warranty

Manufacturer warranties for insulated-core, fibreglass residential doorways are quite good, ranging from five years to a lifetime. Remember that they are limited and cover certain products under certain circumstances. Be sure to ask your supplier about the warranty for the products you are considering. Also, be sure to get a copy of the warranty and file it away with your copy of the sales invoice.

Core, Wood-Veneered Exterior Doors

Core, wood-veneered exterior doors have been the doors of choice for the price-conscious consumer for many years. Their function has always been more utilitarian than decorative, but recent upgrades in light and panel inserts allow for a more aesthetic product at the lower end of the pricing spectrum. Since they can be field-trimmed to almost any size, this type of door is well suited to nonstandard size applications as well as for replacements. The use of solid-core, wood-veneered doors in exterior construction has diminished significantly in recent years due to the introduction of insulated-core, steel and fibreglass-veneered doors with their higher insulating values.

Construction

Core, wood-veneered doors are constructed just like the two exterior doors described above. Internal frames of wood, a core, and veneers are joined together to create the door. Overall they may be three, five, or seven-ply. It should be noted that all adhesives used in exterior construction must be water-resistant, exterior adhesives.

Lights and panels are installed by cutting holes into the door and inserting framed modules.

Veneers

The veneers for core, wood-veneered doors are made either of wood or wood-composite materials such as hardboard. Common woods for veneers are lauan, birch and oak.

Cores

The cores of core, wood-veneered doors are either hollow or solid, but hollow-core doors are very seldom used on the outside because they lack sufficient structural and insulating value. Solid cores may be made up of wood blocks or a wood-composite material such as particleboard.

Sizes

Core, wood-veneered doors are available in a nearly unlimited variety of sizes. The manufacturers are quite flexible and can supply anything up to 4′0″ × 8′0″. Exterior doors usually come in three widths—2'6", 2'8", or 3'0"—and any height between 6'0" and 8'0", with 6'8" being the most popular. Almost all exterior doors are 1¾" thick, but are also available in thicknesses from 1⅜" to 2¼".

These doors are easily field-trimmed and are, therefore, well suited as replacement doors, especially when price is an important consideration. Be careful when cutting down these core doors. The stiles and rails of the internal frames are joined with metal fasteners that may come in contact with your saw blade. Also, the stiles and rails are normally only about 1" wide, so if more than ½" is cut off any edge, the stile or rail must be replaced.

Sidelights and Transoms
Sidelights and transoms are uncommon in this type of doorway. They are possible, however, through the use of light inserts.

Doorway Frames
The doorway frames for core, wood-veneered doorways are made of steel or, more commonly, wood. They may be included with the door (as in a prehung unit) or purchased separately. If you are purchasing a new frame, make sure it is well weather-stripped. If you are keeping the old frame, now is the time to install a modern weather-stripping system. Check with your local supplier. There are many new weatherproofing products on the market specifically designed for retrofitting.

Hardware
The hardware for core, wood-veneered doors is similar to that on other exterior units. Hinges will be provided on prehung units, but all else must be purchased separately. Solid-core wood doors will hold a wood screw, so additions such as door numbers can be directly attached without through-bolting.

Weather Stripping
The weather stripping for core, wood-veneered doors is normally not supplied with the door unless it is prehung.

Ventilation, View, and Light
Ventilation, view, and light are usually not prime considerations in the specification of these doorways, but there are occasions when each must be considered. Ventilation is provided by opening the door, which means a screen door must be used. Light is limited only by the amount of glass in the door. Sidelights and transoms can add an enormous amount of light.

Maintenance
The maintenance of core, wood-veneered doors is limited to staining or painting and lubricating as needed. Each door should be sealed on all six sides (top, bottom, two edges and two faces), and that seal should be maintained with touch-ups as needed throughout the life of the door. This practice will inhibit the flow of moisture into and out of the frame and core and is the critical step in preventing warpage.

Keep paint away from the hardware and weather stripping. Lubricate hinges and locks as recommended by the manufacturer.

Table 12-1 shows maintenance instructions for wood doorways as published by The National Wood Window and Door Association.

Security
Core, wood-veneered doors provide the same type of security as steel and fibreglass-veneered doors. Make sure your lock is effective and provide yourself with a means of identifying callers before the door is fully opened.

Energy Efficiency
Solid-wood core doors are generally less energy-efficient than insulated core steel or fibreglass models. Comparisons are difficult due to non-standardized testing techniques and the effects of glazing materials. You must rely a great deal on your own ability to spot a well-constructed and weather-stripped product. The energy efficiency lost through poor construction will not be compensated for by an insulating core.

Cost
Core, wood-veneered doors are generally the least expensive doors on the market, depending on the veneer used (hardboard-composite material and lauan are the least expensive). The

How to
Store, Handle, Finish, Install and Maintain Wood Doors

STORAGE AND HANDLING

1. Doors shall always be stored flat and in clean, dry surroundings. Protect from dirt, water, and abuse. If stored for long periods, doors must be sealed with a non-water based sealer or primer.

2. Doors shall not be exposed to excessive moisture, heat, dryness, or direct sunlight.

3. Doors shall always be handled with clean hands or while wearing clean gloves.

4. Doors shall be lifted and carried, not dragged across one another.

FIELD FINISHING

1. Prior to finishing, insure that the building atmosphere is dried to a normal, interior relative humidity. Insure that the doors have been allowed to equalize to a stable moisture content.

2. Prior to finishing, remove all handling marks, raised grain and other undesirable blemishes by completely block sanding all surfaces with a 100 to 150 fine grit abrasive.

3. Certain species of wood, particularly oak, contain chemicals which react unfavorably with certain finishes causing dark stain spots. Where possible, the species/finish combination should be tested prior to finishing the doors. Notify your finish supplier or door supplier immediately if any undesirable reaction is noticed. Do not continue with the finishing until the problem is resolved.

4. In order not to induce warpage, avoid dark stains or dark colored paints on door surface exposed directly to sunlight.

5. In order to prevent blemish magnification, avoid extremely dark stains in light colored wood species.

6. Water based sealer or prime coats should not be used. Water based top coats should only be used over surfaces that have been completely sealed with a non-water based sealer or primer.

7. A first coat of a thinned clear sanding sealer, followed by light block sanding, will minimize subsequent handling marks and promote the uniformity of subsequent stain coats.

8. All exposed wood surfaces must be sealed, including top and bottom rails.

9. To achieve the desired results of color uniformity, finish build, gloss and reduce the frequency of refinishing, obtain and follow finish manufacturer's recommendations.

10. Be sure the door surface being finished is satisfactory in both smoothness and color after each coat before applying the next coat.

11. Certain wood fire doors have edges, and possibly crossbands under the face veneer, which contain fire retardant salts. These salts are usually hygroscopic and will take on excess moisture in a damp atmosphere. The salts will concentrate at the surface and form whitish crystals that can interfere with the finish. Before finishing, remove the salt crystals with a damp cloth, followed by drying and light sanding.

INSTALLATION

1. The utility or structural strength of the doors must not be impaired in fitting to the opening, in applying hardware, in preparing for lights, louvers, or plant-ons or other detailing.

2. Use a minimum of one hinge for each 30 inches of door height on all exterior doors and all solid core doors. When using three or more hinges, they are to be equally spaced. Interior hollow core doors weighing less than fifty pounds and not over 7'6" in height may be hung on two hinges.

3. Clearances between door edges and door frame shall be a minimum of 1/16 inch on the hinge edge, 1/8 inch on the latch edge and top rail.

4. All hardware locations, preparations for hardware, and methods of hardware attachment must be appropriate for the specific door construction. Templates for specific hardware preparation are available from hardware manufacturers, NWMA, or DHI.

5. Apply the sealer, primer, or first coats of the required finish, on exterior doors, immediately after fitting, cutting for hardware, weatherstripping, etc., and before the installation of any hardware.

6. When light or louver cutouts are made for exterior doors, they must be protected in order to prevent water from entering the door core. Metal flashing at the bottom of the cutout is one satisfactory method.

MAINTENANCE

1. Most finishes on exterior doors deteriorate relatively quickly. In order for exterior doors to continue receiving the protection required, inspect the condition of exterior finishes at least once a year and refinish as often as needed to maintain the protective integrity of the finish.

2. Insure that doors continue to swing freely, do not bind in the frame and that all hardware remains functional.

Table 12-1. (*Courtesy of National Wood Window and Door Association*)

Illus. 12-19. Modern stile-and-rail doors. (*Courtesy of Morgan Products*)

price may be substantially increased by adding light and panel inserts.

Warranty

Manufacturer warranties for core, wood-veneered doors generally run for one year from the date of purchase. Remember that they are limited and only cover certain defects under certain circumstances. Be sure to ask your supplier about the warranty for the doors you are looking at. Also, be sure to get a copy of the warranty and file it away with your copy of the sales invoice.

Stile-and-Rail Exterior Doors

This type of door has been around for centuries. The joinery technique has evolved to the present-day dowel construction, but the designs have remained the same since the castles of Europe. These were the most popular outer doors in the United States prior to the introduction of insulated-core, steel and fibreglass units. In recent years, manufacturers have greatly expanded the available designs of stile-and-rail doors.

Illus. 12-19 shows some of the newer models. Notice the extensive use of leaded and etched glass. These new glazing systems may also be found in other types of outer door. They consist of a triple-glazing system featuring a piece of tempered glass on each side of a piece of leaded glass. This provides a good degree of insulation as well as protection for the leaded light (Illus.

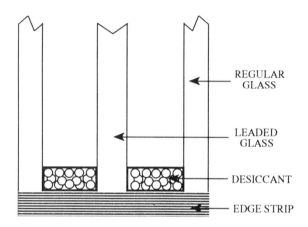

Illus. 12-20. Triple-glazed leaded glass.

12-20). Be sure to ask your supplier to show you the entire range of stile-and-rail doors. There are many quality manufacturers of exterior stile-and-rail doors with a wide range of products. Stile-and-rail doors are also referred to as "panel doors" if they do not contain any glass, and as "sash doors" if they do.

Construction

Exterior stile-and-rail doors consist of horizontal members (rails) and vertical members (stiles), along with one or more panels or glazing surfaces. The stiles and rails are joined together with dowel or mortise-and-tenon joints. Dowelling is by far the most widely used technique. The stiles and rails are grooved to fit the panels and glazing.

True stile-and-rail doors are made almost exclusively of wood. Illus. 12-21 shows the names

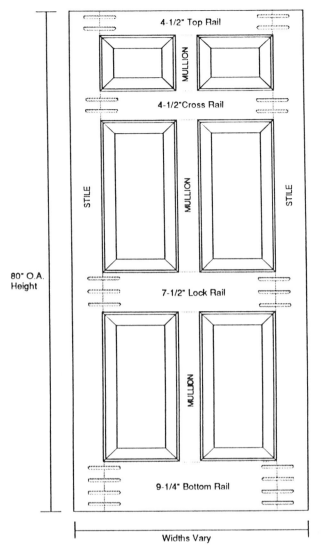

Illus. 12-21. Typical construction of a fir six-panel doorway. (*Courtesy of Morgan Products*)

of the parts of a typical six-panel stile-and-rail doorway, along with the location of the dowels.

Exterior stile-and-rail doors are commonly available in oak, mahogany, fir, hemlock and pine, although all designs are not available in all species. Some doors, depending on the wood species, are treated with a water-repellent and wood-preservative solution.

Panels

The panels may be flat, or, more commonly, raised. Illus. 12-22 shows a laminated raised panel frequently used in outer doors. Notice that it is made of two half-panels joined to resist checking and cracking. The overall thickness of this panel is 1¼", which provides more insulation as well as a more aesthetically pleasing design.

Another type of laminated panel is shown in Illus. 12-22. Laminated panels are a relatively recent addition to stile-and-rail door construction, and single-thickness panels with raises run on each side are still widely available.

Panels are described by their orientation within the door: horizontal or vertical. The X-shaped panel arrangement commonly found in the bottom of sash doors is called a crossbuck. Carved raised panels containing intricate designs are now becoming popular (Illus. 12-23).

Stiles and Rails

Illus. 12-24 shows the stiles and rails commonly found on exterior stile-and-rail doors. These are finger-jointed, edge-glued stiles and rails. Finger jointing is a method of utilizing short pieces of lumber by cutting joints in each end and then gluing those joints together to form longer, more usable lengths. A properly formed finger joint is at least as strong as the wood it is made of and is resistant to warpage.

Edge gluing is a method of creating a wide board out of several narrow ones. Once again, glue is used to produce a tight bond that is strong and resistant to warpage.

The stiles and rails are completed by installing edge strips made from the same species of

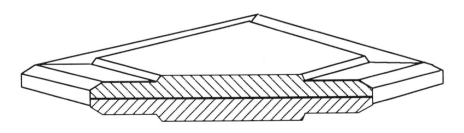

Illus. 12-22. Laminated raised panel.

145

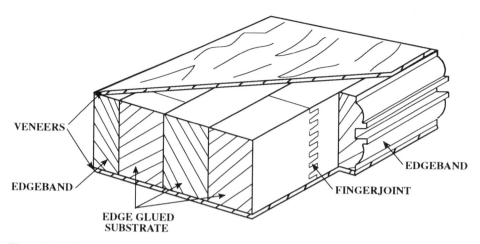

Illus. 12-23 (left). Carved panels on a fir door. **Illus. 12-24 (above).** Veneered stile and rail.

wood as the veneer on both the outer and inner edges. The interior edge strip with the moulded design is referred to as the "sticking."

Although this method is widely used, some manufacturers still use one-piece stiles and rails in their doors, which allow for greater trimmability later. You can usually tell which method was used, by looking at the top or bottom edge of the door.

Sizes

Exterior stile-and-rail doors are available in a nearly unlimited variety of sizes. The manufacturers can usually supply anything up to 4'0″ × 10'0″, although it is much more cost-efficient to work within standard-size guidelines. Exterior doors usually come in three widths—2'6″, 2'8″, or 3'0″—and any height between 6'6″ and 8'0″, with 6'8″ being the most popular. Almost all exterior doors are 1¾″ thick, but thicknesses from 1⅜ to 2¼″ are possible. The vast majority of front doors are 3'0″ × 6'8″, and back or service doors are 2'8″ × 6'8″. These doors are easily trimmed on the spot and are, therefore, well-suited to be replacements.

Sidelights and Transoms

Sidelights and transoms are common accompaniments in doorways. Many entranceways use an all-panel door with sidelights at each side to provide security, light, and view all together.

Frames

The frames for exterior stile-and-rail doorways are usually made of wood. They may be included with the door as a prehung unit or purchased separately. If you are buying a new frame, make sure it is well weather-stripped. Doorway frames are often enhanced with decorative trim.

Dutch Doors

Dutch doors are made from stile-and-rail doors. They consist of a top and bottom section, each opening independently of the other (Illus. 12-25). These doors originated in Europe and probably opened onto the family barnyard. The top section could be opened to allow light and ventilation, while the bottom section remained closed to the animals. Today, their function is primarily decorative.

Dutch doors require additional hardware to join the two sections together so they can be opened as if they were a single unit. You should take special precautions in finishing these doors to prevent warpage, which may make them inoperable.

Illus. 12-25. Dutch doorway.

Hardware

The hardware for outer stile-and-rail doorways is similar to that used for other exterior units. Hinges will be provided on prehung doors, but hinges for all other units must be purchased separately. Stiles and rails will hold a wood screw, so accessories such as door numbers can be directly attached without through-bolting.

Energy Efficiency

Exterior stile-and-rail doorways are generally less energy-efficient than insulated core, steel, or fibreglass models, but how the door fits into the door frame and which type of weather stripping it has are the most important factors in creating an efficient doorway.

Cost

Outer stile-and-rail doorways range in cost from low to high, depending on the species of wood and the glazing system. The least expensive type is a fir or hemlock, all-panel, unglazed door.

Warranty

Manufacturer warranties for exterior stile-and-rail doors generally range from one to five years from the date of purchase. Doors with new, laminated parts sometimes have extended warranties. Know what the warranty says before you buy the door, and save any documentation you may need to exercise your rights in the future.

Maintenance

Tables 12-2–12-12 offer an excellent compilation of finishing, maintenance, and repair information by Morgan Products.

Exterior oak doors require greater care in finishing and maintenance because of the nature of red oak. The exterior finish should be inspected every six months; if the surface feels rough or has become dull or if any evidence of wood surface checking occurs, it is time to apply another coat of finish. The door surface should be completely, but lightly, sanded and wiped free of dust before additional coats of finish are applied. Don't neglect the edges of the door; they are just as important as the face.

Storm-and-Screen Doors

It's amazing how much money is spent on homes to keep out insects. Part of this expenditure is spent on screen doors. Steps are also taken to improve a home's environment by eliminating drafts through the use of storm doors. The combination storm-and-screen door was devised to incorporate both functions into the same unit. Individual screen or storm doors are still manufactured, but the combination unit is by far the most widely sold. Illus. 12-26 shows two common designs of wood models, but there are dozens of other patterns available.

Construction

Construction of storm-and-screen doors may be of core, stile-and-rail, or glass. They can be made of wood, vinyl, or aluminum, but in many cases are a combination of two or three materials. They range from expensive, very rigid, highly energy-efficient doors to low-priced, hollow-core models. Only you can decide which type will best serve your climate and your bud-

continued on page 165

Glazing Instructions

Reglazing Broken Door Lites

Replacing a broken pane of window glass is a relatively simple task. To make the job as easy as possible it's advisable to remove the door from the frame and repair it on a workbench. Lay the door on the bench with the interior of the door facing up.

It is important to replace broken glass with tempered glass or plexiglass. A glass kit is available with replacement sticking if requested. You can custom order pre-cut glass from most lumber yards carrying our products or from a local glass shop.

1. While wearing heavy-duty leather work gloves and safety goggles, pull free any loose glass from the shattered door pane.

Next, remove the nailed wood bead from around the glass. To remove the nailed in bead, pry it off with an old chisel or rigid-blade putty knife. (See Fig. #1.)

Figure #1

2. After removing the wood bead, pull free all of the remaining glass from the broken pane. Now scrape down the sash and muntin rabbets to the bare wood using a chisel held perpendicular to the surface. Try to avoid digging into and gouging the wood. (See Fig. #2.)

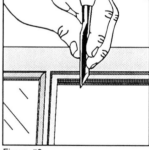
Figure #2

3. Next, using a flexible blade putty knife, apply a 1/8" thick bead of glazing compound (not putty) in the rabbets around the opening. Compound is preferred over putty since it doesn't dry brittle and it resists cracking and shrinking. (See Fig. #3.)

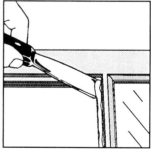
Figure #3

Tables 12-2–12-12 (here and pages 149–164). Finishing, maintenance, and repair information for stile-and-rail doorways. (*Courtesy of Morgan Products*)

Reglazing Broken Door Lites

4. While wearing gloves, position the glass pane in the opening. For a good seal, press down gently to eliminate any air pockets that may appear in the compound. (See Fig. #4.)

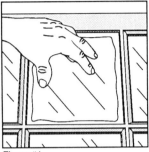

Figure #4

5. Using a wood block and hammer tap the short pieces of wood bead into the top and bottom of the opening. Then, bow the longer pieces to insert the ends into the corners of the opening. Snap in place and fasten with 3/4" to 1" finishing nails, one every 4" on center. (See Fig. #5.)
Note: It may be necessary to pre-drill nail holes in bead to help prevent splitting of wood when installing.

Figure #5

6. Nails should be driven into wood at approximately a 45° angle using caution not to hit edge of glass or surrounding area. (See Fig. #6.)

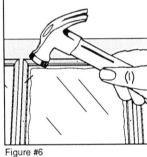

Figure #6

7. Clean off the excess compound which may have squeezed onto the glass or wood. Allow the compound to dry, then apply the paint so that it extends about 1/16" onto the glass to form a moisture seal. This will help protect the compound and seal the glass from excessive moisture. (See Fig. #7.)

Figure #7

Table 12-2 continued.

Door Repair

Repairing Surface Marks or Checks

Most surface marks from handling are easily removed:

●————— Material Needed

1. Knife
2. Wood Shims or slivers
3. Exterior Glue
4. Plastic wood or stainable wood filler. (See your local paint or finish store.)
5. Household type electric iron used for ironing clothes
6. 120 to 150 grit sandpaper

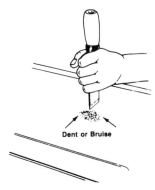

Figure #1

●————— Procedure

1. If deep bruise or mark, use knife point and perforate in and around mark. (See Fig. #1.)
2. Moisten with water and carefully apply hot iron to raise grain. Set iron around medium temperature. Be careful not to scorch door.
3. Repeat step two several times until mark is shallow enough to fill.
4. Fill with plastic wood or stainable wood filler.
5. Sand with grain.
6. If open check or similar mark - open surface with knife and insert glue, wood shim, fill and sand with grain. (See Fig. # 2 and #3.)

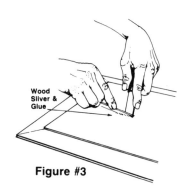

Figure #2

●————— Quality Repair

1. Slivers selected should be color matched and grain matched so that stain take on sliver will be uniform with door.
2. Sand only with the grain.
3. Repairs should be blended into the door.
4. No more than (2) slivers should be placed in any one opening.
5. Glue is applied to both sides of sliver before inserting into opening.
6. All excess glue should be REMOVED immediately, to avoid sealing the wood which prevents the take of stain.

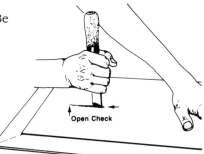

Figure #3

Table 12-3.

Door Repair

Repair of Snipes or Checks on Raised Panels

Testing for Defective Glue Line

To test for defective glue line on separated panel, insert shim knife or other sharp bladed implement in separation. Tap end of knife with hammer. If glue line splits open - replace panel. Follow steps below. (See Fig. #4.)

Repairing Panel Snipe or Check

Required Materials

1. Knife
2. Wood shims or slivers
3. Exterior type glue
4. Plastic wood or a stainable wood filler
5. 120 to 150 grit sand paper

Procedure

1. Open surface of snipe or checks with sharp bladed instrument.
2. Insert glued shim edge and trim to face of panel.
3. Fill with plastic wood.
4. Sand with grain.

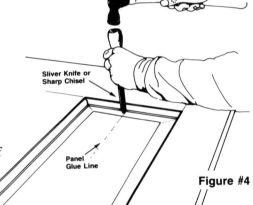

Sliver Knife or Sharp Chisel

Panel Glue Line

Figure #4

Note: Most surface openings that develop need only be filled with plastic wood or wood filler that is stainable and matches wood color.

Table 12-4.

Repairing Loose Panels

Wood panels are designed to float. In the rare instance where a panel becomes too loose it can be tightened up. (See Fig. #5.)

● ——————— Material Needed

1. 1/2" to 3/4" finish brads
2. Punch (nail set)
3. Hammer
4. Plastic wood or stainable wood filler
5. 120 grit sand paper

● ——————— Procedure

1. Properly align the loose panel.
2. Drive brad into sticking at a point just under the panel edge.
    Note: It may be necessary to pre drill especially for oak.
3. A single brad at center top and bottom of the panel will be sufficient.
4. Counter sink brad into sticking.
5. Fill with plastic wood and sand it. (See Fig. #5.)

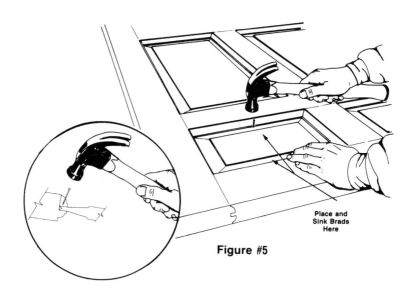

Place and
Sink Brads
Here

Figure #5

Table 12-5.

Door Repair

Repairing Out of Line
Bars, Panels and Mullions

Remember that the interior components of stile and rail doors are designed to "float" so that during climactic changes the wood components can move without stressing. Therefore, occasionally during handling, these components can shift out of line. Generally, adjustments are simply made. (See Fig. #6.)

● ——— Material Needed

1. Panel block or block of wood with leather or non-marking rubber on one end.
2. Hammer
3. Straight edge 3' and longer (to help align panels and mullions).

● ——— Procedure

1. Place panel block or leather covered wood block against component ridge and tap into position. (See Fig. #7.)
   Note: Be careful not to destroy or mark component.

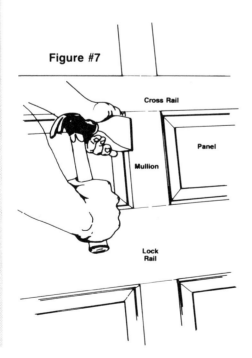

Figure #7

Cross Rail

Panel

Mullion

Lock Rail

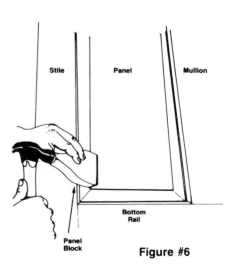

Stile   Panel   Mullion

Bottom Rail

Panel Block

Figure #6

Table 12-6.

Repairing End Checks
Splits and Cracks

Suggested repairs for out of warranty doors.

Most splits, checks and cracks, if not clear through, will not alter the structural value of the door. These problems can be solved simply by wood shimming; using a good exterior glue, or filling with plastic wood or stainable wood filler.

Examples of repairable openings:

Stile Cross Check. This is not a defect as long as it does not continue the entire width of piece. Simply fill with plastic wood or stainable wood filler and the problem should not worsen. (See Fig. #16.)

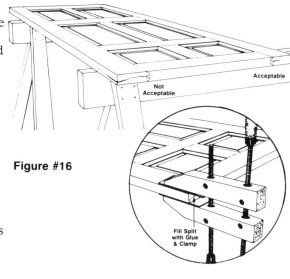

Figure #16

Buried Pitch Pocket is only a defect when it extends over three-fourths of the width of the piece. Simply plug with wood shim using a good exterior glue and plastic wood filler. (See Fig. #17.)

Figure #17

Table 12-7.

Door Repair

Repairing End Checks Splits and Cracks (cont).

Glue Line Snipe is a remote possibility, but when evident is usually at the end of a stile or rail. To test for complete line failure insert a knife into split and tap. If failure present, entire piece will separate. If glue line is within 2-1/2" of the inside edge of the stile it is normally secure because it is held by the dowel. The same holds true for rail splits. (See Fig. #18 and Fig. #19.)

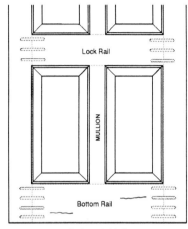

Easily repairable if a short surface check.

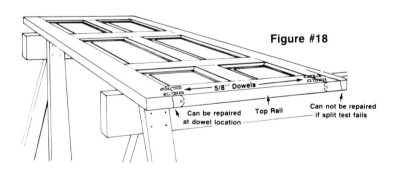

Figure #18

5/8'' Dowels

Can be repaired at dowel location

Top Rail

Can not be repaired if split test fails

Table 12-7 continued.

Repair of Stile and Rail Separation

Allowable Tolerance

A 1/64" separation can occur. This is normally caused by wood shrinkage and is easily repaired by slivering and using a good grade of exterior glue. (See Fig. #20.)

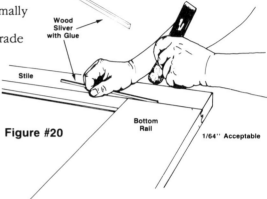

Wood Sliver with Glue

Stile

Bottom Rail

Figure #20

1/64" Acceptable

Testing for Possible Joint Failure

To test for glue failure at stile and rail joints, carefully place wood block on the inside edge of the stile nearest rail of the joint to be tested. Strike block with hammer. If joint moves appreciably, this would indicate a gluing failure. Note: Be careful not to destroy the sticking profile when placing and striking wood block. (See Fig. #21.)

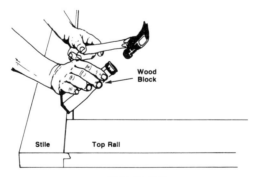

Wood Block

Stile   Top Rail

Figure #21

Table 12-8.

Door Repair

Repair of Stile and Rail Separation

Suggestions for field repair and out of warranty doors.

● ──────── **Material Needed**

1. Exterior water-proof glue - fast drying.
2. Furniture clamp - screw drawn.
3. 5/16" x 5" lag bolt with 3/4" diameter washer (one per location). Drill and bit (1/4" x 6 and 3/4" x 4 approx.).
4. Wood hole plug
5. Hammer
6. Plastic wood color matched to final finish, if stained.
7. 120 to 150 grit sandpaper.
8. Socket wrench and 1/2" socket.

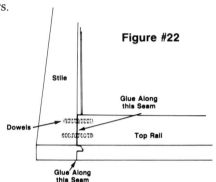

Figure #22

● ──────── **Procedure**

1. Separate joint enough to insert exterior glue on both sides of interior profile. Do not pull stile completely away from rail. Keep glue off face of components. (See Fig. #22.)

2. Clamp door with screw drawn furniture clamp and allow glue to set. (See Fig. #23.)

3. Using 1/4" x 6 drill bit, drill a hole between dowels approx. 6" deep from edge of stile. Use dowel locator or diagram to find dowel placement. (Pages 15, 16, and 17.) Now drill a 3/4" hole (using same hole) approx. 2" deep for counter sink lag bolt with washer. Repeat this step at each doweled location. (See Fig. #24.)

   Tighten lag bolt securely using socket wrench. Use caution to NOT over tighten which may strip wood.

   Apply glue and fill hole with wood plug to match species of door, sand and finish.

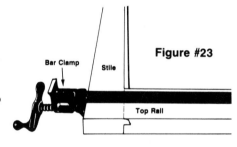

Figure #23

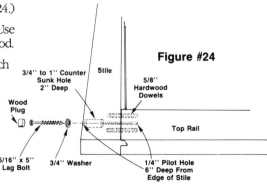

Figure #24

Table 12-9.

Replacing Wood Panels

Material Needed

1. Wide blade chisel (1" - 1-1/2")
2. 7/8" finish brads, and nail set
3. Sliver knife or utility knife
4. Plastic wood or stainable wood filler
5. Metal straight edge or framing square
6. Hammer
7. Wood glue (a good exterior grade)
8. 120 to 150 grit (medium) sandpaper
9. Small block plane (sharp)
10. Wood Block with leather
11. C-clamps (2)

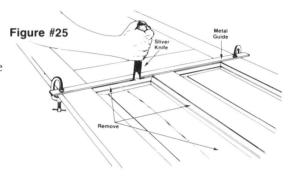

Figure #25

Procedure

Square Panel

1. Remove the three inside stickings on face of door only, either with a broad face chisel or a skill saw, set at 3/4" to 7/8" blade extension. *NOTE: Do not remove solid sticking on stile.* When removing panels in center of door - remove only three sticking sides, leaving one solid sticking on the mullion. (See Fig. #25.)

2. To remove panel - cut down toward panel using the shoulder of the rail or mullion as a guide. Remember that the panel is recessed into the rail or mullion about 1/8", therefore it is necessary to cut into panel to free. Be careful not to cut into shoulder of major component. (See Fig. #26.)

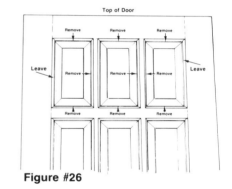

Figure #26

3. Once the three pieces of sticking have been removed, lift panel from door or if need be use chisel to split panel out of door. (See Fig. #27.)

4. When replacing panels - replacement size should be used. These panels are about 1/8" scant in all around dimension. If replacement size is not available, simply trim about 1/8" from each edge of the panel. (Be sure to measure before trimming.)

NOTE: Before replacing new panel, clean up area where sticking was removed, finish sand and prepare for new sticking installation.

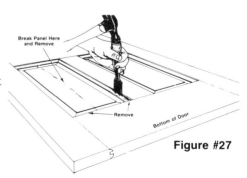

Figure #27

Table 12-10.

Door Repair

Replacing Wood Panels

5. Set panel into solid sticking first and let slip into place. (See Fig. #28)

6. After panel has been set apply glue to sticking and insert sticking into place. If requested, sticking will be supplied, however custom fit sticking can be easily cut to fit at the job site. To custom cut sticking, lay across area to size, mark, remove, set on scrap piece of cutting board and cut at 45 degree angles. (See Fig. #29) Shape inside sticking with knife using the contour as a pattern.

7. Using 7/8 " finish brad, tack sticking into place and draw knife blade over top of sticking next to component shoulder to seal the seam. Use care not to damage sticking profile. (See Fig. #30)

8. Fill with plastic wood or stainable wood filler as needed and sand lightly.

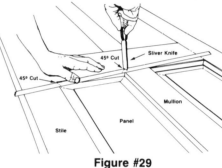

Slip Panel into Solid Sticking

Figure #28

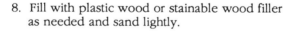

45° Cut   Sliver Knife

45° Cut

Mullion

Stile   Panel

Figure #29

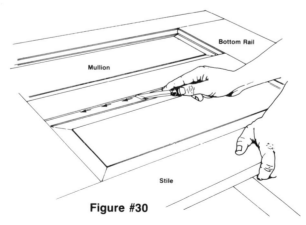

Bottom Rail

Mullion

Stile

Figure #30

Table 12-10 continued.

Replacing Wood Panels

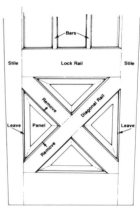

Figure #31

CROSSBUCK PANEL

1. Again, always leave stile solid sticking in place and remove the two pieces of sticking on the diagonal rail. (See Fig. #31.)

2. Repeat all steps for square panel.

CURVED PANEL

1. Leave the curved sticking in place and remove all other sticking. (See Fig. #32.)

2. Repeat all steps as used for square panel.

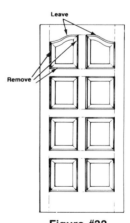

Figure #32

Table 12-10 continued.

Door Care

Handling Suggestions

The service information in this Manual deals with three species of wood doors: White Ponderosa Pine, Vertical Grain Douglas Fir, and Appalachian Red Oak.

1. Handle all doors carefully with clean hands and clean equipment.

2. Avoid creating drag marks or burnishes by dragging doors across one another or across other surfaces.

3. Store flat on a level surface in a dry, well-ventilated building. Avoid stacking on end.

4. Cover doors to keep clean but allow air circulation.

5. Avoid subjecting doors to abnormal heat, extreme dryness, humid conditions, sudden changes in climate or extreme wetness.

6. All wood doors should be conditioned to average prevailing relative humidity of the locality before hanging. (Approximately 3 weeks)

7. Deliver doors in clean truck and under cover in wet weather.

8. Deliver doors to building site only after plaster, texture and/or cement is dry.

9. If the doors are to be stored on the job site for more than a week, the entire door, including the top and bottom edges, should be sealed with a resin or pigmented base sealer.

Fitting and Hanging

1. Exterior glazed doors are to be hung with the removable bead side to the **interior** of the home or building.

2. Doors should be conditioned to the average prevailing moisture humidity of the locality before fitting. (Approximately 3 weeks)

3. When hanging door, allow approximately 1/8" clearance for swelling of door or frame in extremely damp weather.

Table 12-11.

Fitting and
Hanging (cont.)

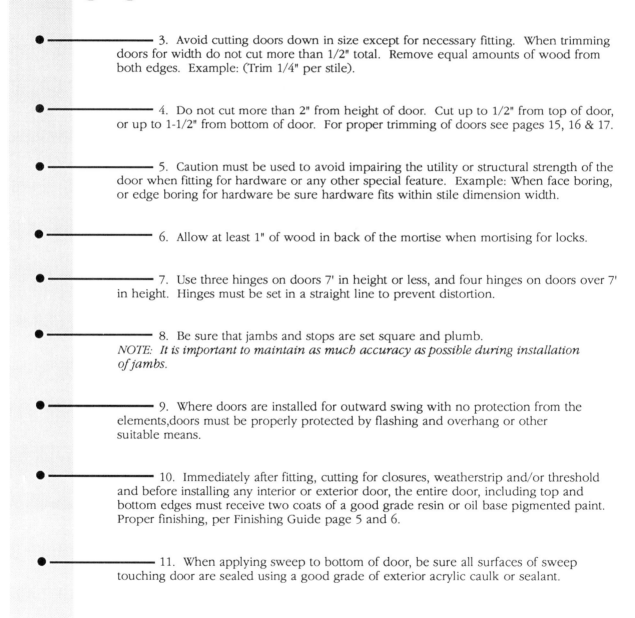

3. Avoid cutting doors down in size except for necessary fitting. When trimming doors for width do not cut more than 1/2" total. Remove equal amounts of wood from both edges. Example: (Trim 1/4" per stile).

4. Do not cut more than 2" from height of door. Cut up to 1/2" from top of door, or up to 1-1/2" from bottom of door. For proper trimming of doors see pages 15, 16 & 17.

5. Caution must be used to avoid impairing the utility or structural strength of the door when fitting for hardware or any other special feature. Example: When face boring, or edge boring for hardware be sure hardware fits within stile dimension width.

6. Allow at least 1" of wood in back of the mortise when mortising for locks.

7. Use three hinges on doors 7' in height or less, and four hinges on doors over 7' in height. Hinges must be set in a straight line to prevent distortion.

8. Be sure that jambs and stops are set square and plumb.
NOTE: It is important to maintain as much accuracy as possible during installation of jambs.

9. Where doors are installed for outward swing with no protection from the elements, doors must be properly protected by flashing and overhang or other suitable means.

10. Immediately after fitting, cutting for closures, weatherstrip and/or threshold and before installing any interior or exterior door, the entire door, including top and bottom edges must receive two coats of a good grade resin or oil base pigmented paint. Proper finishing, per Finishing Guide page 5 and 6.

11. When applying sweep to bottom of door, be sure all surfaces of sweep touching door are sealed using a good grade of exterior acrylic caulk or sealant.

Table 12-11 continued.

Door Care

Finishing Guide

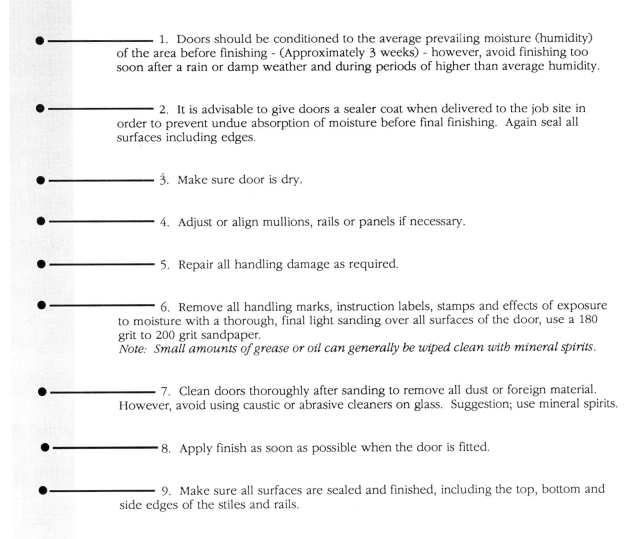

1. Doors should be conditioned to the average prevailing moisture (humidity) of the area before finishing - (Approximately 3 weeks) - however, avoid finishing too soon after a rain or damp weather and during periods of higher than average humidity.

2. It is advisable to give doors a sealer coat when delivered to the job site in order to prevent undue absorption of moisture before final finishing. Again seal all surfaces including edges.

3. Make sure door is dry.

4. Adjust or align mullions, rails or panels if necessary.

5. Repair all handling damage as required.

6. Remove all handling marks, instruction labels, stamps and effects of exposure to moisture with a thorough, final light sanding over all surfaces of the door, use a 180 grit to 200 grit sandpaper.
Note: Small amounts of grease or oil can generally be wiped clean with mineral spirits.

7. Clean doors thoroughly after sanding to remove all dust or foreign material. However, avoid using caustic or abrasive cleaners on glass. Suggestion; use mineral spirits.

8. Apply finish as soon as possible when the door is fitted.

9. Make sure all surfaces are sealed and finished, including the top, bottom and side edges of the stiles and rails.

Table 12-12.

Finishing Guide (cont.)

10. Finishing Systems

a. Painting

Use a good grade exterior oil based primer followed by at least two coats of a good grade exterior acrylic latex paint. If a water based primer must be used, be sure it is an acrylic latex primer, and apply two coats of a good grade exterior acrylic latex paint. Doors exposed to direct sunlight for extended periods should not be painted with dark colors. Refinishing may be required more often.

b. Clear Finishes or Stains

When applying a transparent or stain finish, use a semi-transparent stain or clear undercoat designed for exterior use followed by at least two coats of clear finish (gloss, semi-gloss or flat) designed for exterior use. All exterior finishes must have ultraviolet (UV) inhibitors in the finish. The first and second top coats should be identical. No longer than 24 hours should pass between each subsequent top coat. Avoid dark colored stain finishes on doors that are exposed to direct sunlight for extended periods.

11. Sand lightly between all coats with 180 to 200 grit sandpaper.

12. When finishing around joints where wood parts, or glass and wood come together, be sure to fill gaps with good quality wood filler before painting. This action should minimize moisture penetration through these joints.

13. You can make sure that all coatings in the finish system are as compatible as possible by using products from the same manufacturer. Finish manufacturers will be able to tell you which of their products may be successfully applied in combination with each other. Finishes should be applied in accordance with the manufacturer's instructions.

14. All stain and clear finishes will perform significantly better when protected by an overhang from the direct effects of sunlight and rain. Stain and clear finishes should be checked thoroughly each year for need to refinish. Regular maintenance, cleaning and refinishing will significantly extend the years of satisfied service from all exterior millwork.

15. For additional information concerning how to store, handle, finish, install and maintain wood doors, ask for separate flyer supplied by the NWWDA or ANSI/NWMA.

Table 12-12 continued.

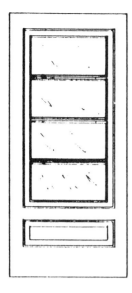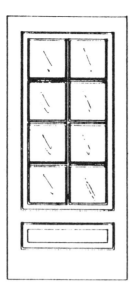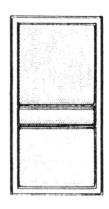

Illus. 12-26. Wood combination storm-and-screen doors.

get. There are many models to choose from, so comparison-shop before you buy.

Aluminum and vinyl doorways are usually available in colors like white, beige, and bronze, with custom shades also available from some suppliers. Storm panels and screens may be interchangeable (exchange them every spring and fall), or they may be self-storing (as in a combination storm window).

All glass in storm doors must, by law, be at least tempered safety glass. This makes it harder to break, and if it does break, it crumbles into less sharp pieces than regular glass. You should consider replacing an old storm door that contains regular glass. It's a safety hazard, especially for children.

Sizes

Combination storm-and-screen doors are available in a relatively limited variety of sizes, although many manufacturers will create custom sizes. Standard widths are 2′6″, 2′8″, and 3′0″. They can range in height from 6′7″ to 7′1″, depending on local custom in your part of the country. A door 6′9″ high is the most common. Note that these doors are 1″ higher than the primary doors. This is because the sill of the primary door frame is angled down to shed water, and the vertical opening becomes taller as you move towards the outside.

The width of the storm door depends on the type of jamb used in the door frame. Carefully measure the space between the two pieces of

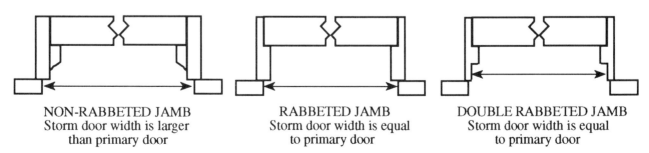

NON-RABBETED JAMB
Storm door width is larger
than primary door

RABBETED JAMB
Storm door width is equal
to primary door

DOUBLE RABBETED JAMB
Storm door width is equal
to primary door

Illus. 12-27. Three types of jamb that can be found in a frame.

outer casing at the far edge of your frame, as well as space between the two side jambs, and provide this information to your supplier along with the vertical measurement between the head casing, or head jamb, and the sill at the same spot. If you are replacing a storm door, simply measure what's there now. Illus. 12-27 shows the three types of jamb you may have in your frame. The use of the rabbeted jamb results in a storm door equal in width to the primary door. The nonrabbeted jamb results in a storm door approximately 1″ wider than the primary door. A non-rabbeted jamb is identifiable by the stop which has been added. However, after many applications of paint the joint may become invisible, so be careful when making your determination.

For odd-size or out-of-square installations, consider a wood door which can be trimmed to meet existing conditions.

Storm and screen doors are generally 1⅛ or 1¼″ thick.

Doorway Frames, Hardware, and Weather Stripping

The doorway frames, hardware, and weather stripping for combination storm-and-screen units are usually included with the door in a prehung package. The frames are usually made of aluminum and include all weather stripping, closers, hinges, knobs, and locks (Illus. 12-28). The quality of the frames, hardware, and weather stripping are dependent on the cost of the door. Pay attention to the quality of the hardware and weather stripping because they will determine how long the door will last and how well it will insulate.

Wood combination or screen doors are normally hung on the existing wood frame and do not come as a prehung unit.

Security

The security offered by combination storm-and-screen doors should not be a prime consideration in their selection. The best lock in the world won't deter a thief from gaining entry by cutting the screen or breaking the glass. Don't rely

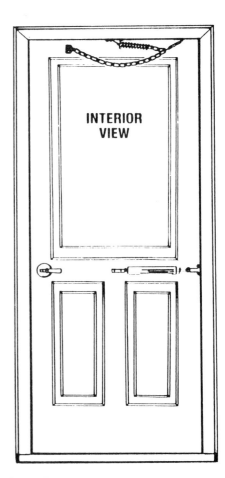

Illus. 12-28. Typical storm door hardware. (*Courtesy of The Combination Door Company*)

on these doors to prevent access.

Consider the safety of children and pets when choosing a design. Many styles include glass and screens, which create a potential hazard for these happy wanderers. Take precautions to protect the child or pet from coming in contact with the glass. Decorative grilles are available specifically for this purpose.

Energy Efficiency

Energy efficiency can be achieved in all seasons with the use of combination doorways. The screen insert saves on air conditioning, and the storm panel saves on heating. You must decide which design suits the climate you live in. Single-light doors with a large, full-length panel and screen are best for ventilation and provide the most complete view of your primary doorway, but may offer less efficient insulation because of all the glass. There are so many core and glass options available, you should have no difficulty in finding just the right product for your situation.

Cost

Combination storm-and-screen doors vary drastically in cost, from under $50 for a wood screen door to over $500 for an insulated, full-glass model with special brass hardware. Be on the lookout for the features needed, and then search for the best price. September and October are often the best months to shop for these doors because manufacturers and distributors create special sales in anticipation of the upcoming heating season.

Warranty

Manufacturer warranties for combination storm-and-screen doors range from one year to lifetime. Some manufacturers even supply an 800 telephone number to assist with installation and maintenance questions. The warranty is an important item to include on your shopping checklist.

Garage Doors

The overhead garage door is a mainstay on most homes within the United States. The word overhead refers to the method of opening the door by rolling it up on its overhead track. While swinging garage doorways are still available, they are not frequently used today. Manufacturers are continually coming up with new materials and designs to enhance both function and design. If it's time for you to replace that old door, you'll be surprised by the selection you now can choose from.

Construction

Garage doors generally have a core or stile-and-rail construction. Cores are normally insulating foam with steel, vinyl, or wood-composite (hardboard) faces. Stile-and-rail doors have wood stiles and rails with wood or wood-composite panels. The panels may be raised or flat. The steel and vinyl doors are usually factory-finished in various colors, while wood

doors are either left natural or are primed. Glazing is available in many functional and aesthetic patterns and is installed in the same fashion as previously described.

Sizes

Garage doors are available in relatively standard sizes. Common widths for single doors are 8'0", 9'0", or 10'0", and for double doors are 15'0", 16'0", or 18'0". Standard heights are 6'6", 7'0", and 8'0". Other sizes are available as special orders from certain manufacturers. The normal thickness of these doors is 1⅜".

If you are investigating garage doors sold by your supplier, bring along the measurement of your existing door as well as the width and height of the frame, the height of the ceiling in the garage, and the overall measurements of the garage itself. Allowances have to be made for hardware, and these measurements are important.

Door Frames

The door frames for garage doors are normally not supplied by the manufacturer of the doors, but are constructed at the job site by the installer.

Hardware and Weather Stripping

The hardware and weather stripping for these doors are generally supplied by the manufacturer along with the door. Hardware plays a large role in the efficiency of garage doorways and you should investigate the quality thoroughly. Optional hardware may include a key lock.

In order to facilitate the replacement of springs in the future, you should write down and save any information concerning the weight and size of the garage door. There are many different replacement springs to choose from, each geared to a specific size and weight. Automatic garage door openers are purchased and installed separately.

Weather stripping is important, even in unheated garages. Not only does it block drafts, it also helps keep out insects, dust and water. Check before you buy to ensure that you are getting a good-quality seal around the perimeter. If weather stripping is an optional item, purchase the best-quality weather stripping available.

Maintenance

In addition to performing the same maintenance tasks on garage doors that are performed on other doors, the operating system of garage doors must be inspected and lubricated. Keep tracks free of debris and keep wheels well lubricated. Replace springs as needed.

Security

Do not overlook security in the selection of these doorways. Garages are frequently targeted by unwanted visitors, and optional key-locks or other security devices should be considered.

Only use automatic garage door openers that come to an emergency stop if their pathway is impeded. Children and pets have suffered serious injury when they unknowingly stepped below a closing door.

Energy Efficiency

The energy efficiency of garage doors has been improved with the introduction of insulated core, steel or wood units. Test data is almost nonexistent, which makes comparison-shopping difficult. If your garage is connected to your heating system, you should not overlook this large area of exposure to the outside. Efficient perimeter weather stripping is at least as important as the type of door.

Cost and Warranty

Garage doors vary in cost, depending on material and construction type. Warranties run from one to 15 years.

INTERIOR DOORWAYS

Interior doorways play an important role in the function and decor of any structure. They provide the necessary privacy while making an important aesthetic statement. Carefully consider the type of doorways to use when planning your interior decor, because they can become the decorating focal point of a room. Choose from the large selection of types and finishes that will complement your design philosophy.

Construction Categories

There are two common construction techniques for interior doors: core and stile-and-rail construction. They are described below.

Core Interior Doors

The construction technique for interior core doors is the same as for exterior models. The cores are either solid or, more commonly, hollow. Wood flush doors came into prominence during the 1930s and continue to be very popular, especially to the price-conscious consumer. New skin designs, offering moulded panels, have increased the market share of this type of construction in recent years. Interior core doors are available with five different faces: steel, vinyl, glass, wood and wood composite. They are described below.

Steel- and Vinyl-Faced Core Doors

Steel- and vinyl-faced core doors are usually restricted to commercial or multifamily construction. They may be flush or moulded into louvre or panel designs. The flush steel skins are commonly found in utility rooms and apartment entranceways, while the moulded faces are frequently seen in folding or sliding closet doorways. These closet doors have a face on only one side, since the back is visible only from the closet. Steel- and vinyl-faced interior doors are prefinished at the factory. Sliding and folding doorways are normally prehinged and packaged with all necessary hardware.

These units provide a durable and relatively inexpensive method of enclosing a doorway, which is why they are so popular in apartment houses and offices.

Glass-Faced Core Doors

Glass-faced core doors, commonly known as "mirror doors," usually consist of an internal frame with a mirror face on one side only (Illus. 12-29). They are normally found in sliding or folding closet doorways. Mirror doors have become very popular in recent years because they create an expansive feeling in a small room.

Glass and Panels

The face of the individual mirror panel may be totally glass (unframed) or surrounded by metal or wood (framed). Framed panels are available in gold, white, bronze, and silver colors, as well as oak and other hardwoods. The glass may be flat throughout its surface or have bevelled edges. A safety factor is built into these units by applying a tape backing to the glass. With this sticky surface in place, glass does not fall away from the backing if it is broken.

Sizes

Mirror doors are available in relatively fixed sizes, although some manufacturers will create custom installations. Sliding units (also called bipassing units) come in standard widths of 4′0″ through 12′0″ in one-foot increments, depending on the number of panels in the unit (two, three, or four). They are generally available in heights of 6′8″ or 8′0″. Regardless of the size, no more than 50 percent of a sliding unit can be opened at any time. This may be an important consideration if large bulky items are contained in the closet.

Bifold Units

Bifold units are available in two- and four-door configurations. Two-door units come in standard widths of 2′0″, 2′6″, and 3′0″, while four-door units have measurements of 4′0″, 5′0″, and 6′0″. Bifold doors allow access to the entire closet at any one time, but require space in front of the doorway to fold into. Swinging mirror doors are now being produced in both core and stile-and-rail construction. Single, hinged doors with mirror faces on both sides allow for "pass through" installations in locations other than closets. Some manufacturers also produce a twin swinging door unit which contains two doors, one swinging to the left and one to the right. They range in size from 2′0″ to 3′0″ wide × 6′8″ tall. Full access to a closet is provided.

Hardware

The hardware for mirror doors is usually in-

Illus. 12-29. Sliding mirror door (*Courtesy of Ledco, Inc.*)

cluded in the overall package. Because of the glass, these are relatively heavy units and the hardware must be able to withstand the weight. Sliding doors usually have top and bottom tracks (Illus. 12-30), while folding units may include only a top track. You should compare the hardware package as well as the aesthetics when choosing a product. If you are purchasing five or more mirror units from the same manufacturer, consider buying an extra set of hardware to be held as insurance against possible future breakdowns.

All manufacturers include do-it-yourself installation instructions. Ask your supplier to show you these directions before you buy the unit and be sure you understand all the terminology and have the tools called for.

Wood-faced, Core Interior Doors

Wood-faced, core interior doors, commonly known as "flush doors," have been a mainstay of the door industry in the United States for 50 years. These relatively unsophisticated and inexpensive doors are commonly available with lauan, birch, or oak veneers. They can be stained or painted to blend with any decor.

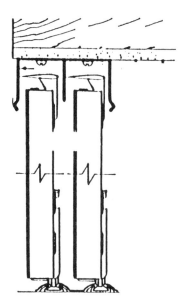

Illus. 12-30. Section view of a sliding mirror door. (*Courtesy of Ledco, Inc.*)

Cores

The cores may be solid, but hollow designs are much more common. Lights and louvres are available as inserts, which may be installed into a hole cut through the face of the door. There is a method of creating simulated panels (called plants) by mounting mouldings on the surface of the door in the shape of the desired panel. From a distance, it appears that there is actually a raised panel in the door.

Sizes Hollow-core doors offer the most size variations of any door on the market. Stock widths run from 1′0″ to 3′0″ in 2″ increments, and heights run from 6′0″ to 8′0″ with 6′8″ being the most common. A standard bedroom door is 2′6″ wide, and a bathroom door 2′0″ or 2′4″. Odd sizes are not difficult to manufacture and the do-it-yourselfer can easily perform moderate field trimming. Care must be exercised when cutting down these core doors. The stiles and rails of the internal frames are joined with metal fasteners that may come in contact with your saw blade. Also, the stiles and rails are normally only about 1″ wide, so no more than ½″ should be taken off any edge.

Solid-core flush doors are more limited in size availability, but, once again, a door of almost any size can be made. These doors are also used in furniture-making, especially as tabletops.

Hollow-core flush doors usually measure 1⅛″ thick or 1⅜″ thick, while solid-core models are usually 1⅜″ or 1¾″ thick.

Maintenance Maintenance is important. You must thoroughly seal all six sides of the door with a quality finish in order to keep moisture out of the core. An inadequate seal is the most common cause of warpage. This is especially true in doors with unequal moisture contents on either side, such as a bathroom door. The wood will actually bend towards the dry side if the moisture has no barrier.

Wood-Composite-Faced Core Interior Doorways

Wood-composite-faced core interior doors may have flush or moulded faces. The flush-faced units are the least expensive of all interior doors. They are constructed in the same fashion as the doors described above, but the skin is a piece of hardboard rather than a wood veneer. This is a paint-grade door commonly found in apartments or motels or wherever price is the major consideration.

The moulded door is also created with hardboard faces, but the appearance of the finished product is dramatically altered by moulding panels that are pressed into the skin during the manufacturing process (Illus. 12-31). In addition to the panels, grain lines are etched into the face to create the appearance of a wood stile-and-rail door. These moulded doors come with a factory-applied prime coat. The benefits of this type of construction are twofold: the price is substantially lower than true stile-and-rail construction, and the door is much less prone to warpage and panel shrinkage. The drawback is the inability of the hardboard to take a stain finish. Even though the manufacturers have come up with a prime coat that will allow for a stain top coat, it doesn't result in the same finished appearance as a true wood stile-and-rail door (Illus. 172). Since stain finishes are relatively new on the market, you should ask your supplier to show you the finished product.

Moulded door stock ranges in width from 1'0" to 3'0" in 2" increments, and is usually 6'8" high. Custom sizes are not generally available, but moderate trimming on the spot (up to 1" in width and height) can be accomplished. Be careful when cutting down doors to avoid the metal fasteners holding the internal frame together.

Stile-and-Rail Interior Doors
These doors are the standard against which all others are judged, and they continue to expand in design, thanks to the decorating renaissance presently underway in the United States. Interior stile-and-rail doors are available in a variety of different types, including panel, louvre, café, and French.

Panel Stile-and-Rail Doors
Panel stile-and-rail doors are the most common type of stile-and-rail door. The manufacturing technique has already been outlined in the exterior door section. Panel doors are available in many different designs (Illus. 12-32) and in various species of wood, with pine, fir and oak being the most popular. These doors are commonly hung as single- or double-door units and

Illus. 12-31. Typical moulded door designs. (*Courtesy of Ledco, Inc.*)

Illus. 12-32. Typical interior stile-and-rail doors.

are also widely available in prepackaged folding units.

There has been a recent revolution in the design of bifold doorways. Manufacturers have incorporated numerous glass patterns into these stile-and-rail doors to create a very decorative selection. Illus. 12-33 indicates only one of the many styles available.

The glass used in these doors should be tempered, but does not have to be insulated, since it is meant for interior use. You'll enjoy shopping the displays as there are many new and attractive products to enhance the decor of your home.

Size

Panel stile-and-rail doors are available in a variety of sizes. Common widths range from 1'0″ to 3'0″ in 2″ increments, and heights from 6'0″ to 7'0″ with 6'8″ as the most common. Bifold units range in width from 2'0″ to 6'0″, depending on whether they are two- or four-door units.

These doors range in thickness from 1⅛ to 1⅜″. Thickness is an important consideration. While 1⅛″ thick doors are less expensive, they do not provide a raised panel of the same thickness and are somewhat less resistant to warpage than a 1⅜″ door. Ask your supplier to show

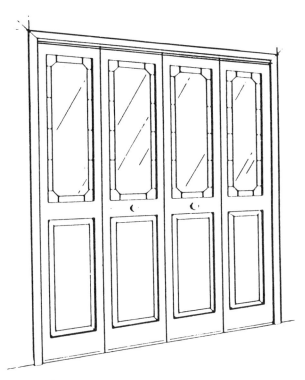

Illus. 12-33. A stile-and-rail bifold unit with a panel bottom and glass top. (*Courtesy of Ledco, Inc.*)

you both these thicknesses. Panel thickness does affect the aesthetic quality of the doorways. Prepackaged bifolds are usually 1⅛″ thick and you may have to special-order the bifold if you want thicker doors and panels. It should be noted here that some manufacturers offer different panel styles to accommodate various tastes. Once again, check with your supplier to see what's currently available. Wood stile-and-rail doorways are usually field-trimmable up to 1″ in width and height, possibly more in height on 1⅜″ thick doors.

Maintenance
Since interior stile-and-rail doors are generally made from wood, you must maintain a permanent seal on all six sides.

These doors may experience a slight panel shrinkage during the heating season when humidity within the home is lower. If this exposes an unpainted area, touch up the perimeter of the panel while it is available and the problem will be solved once and for all. If the shrinkage

is severe, check to see that all six sides of the door are properly sealed.

Louvre Doors and Blinds
Louvre doors and blinds are commonly found in all types of interior construction. The combination of light weight, attractive design, and ability to allow for air circulation make them unique within the doorway industry. These doors were originally an exterior product used to shutter doorways and windows. Their role was then expanded to a "between rooms" doorway, providing both privacy and ventilation.

Louvre doors typically come in two designs: louvre over louvre and louvre over panel (Illus. 12-34). The material is usually white pine. This is a complicated door to manufacture because each slat fits into an elongated hole in each stile. The slats of the door can be seen through more easily from one side, so care should be taken when positioning doors in bedrooms and closets, etc. Louvre doors do not block sound and may be ill suited for certain locations.

Sizes
Louvre doors are available in a variety of sizes. Common widths run from 1′0″ to 3′0″ in 2″ increments, and heights from 6′0″ to 7′0″, with 6′8″ as the most common. Bifold widths range from 2′0″

Illus. 12-34. Louvre doors.

to 6'0", depending on whether they are two- or four-door units.

These doors range in thickness from 1⅛" for bifold units to 1⅜" for single doors. As with panel doors, a thinner door is cheaper but does not resist warpage as well as a thick door.

Hardware
Louvre bifold prepackaged units come pre-machined with the necessary hardware attached to the doors. Illus. 12-35 shows a typical bifold setup. This hardware is relatively standard for all types of bifold doorway, but subtle changes do exist from manufacturer to manufacturer. If you are buying several units, consider purchasing an extra set of hardware as insurance against potential problems.

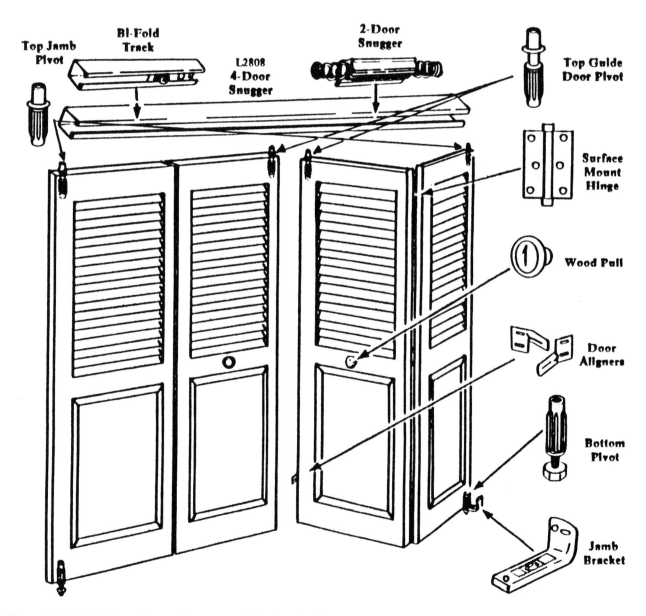

Illus. 12-35. Bifold hardware. (*Courtesy of Ledco, Inc.*)

Door and Window Blinds

Door and window blinds are really outside products, but since they are often manufactured with louvre construction, they are covered here. These are frequently referred to as "shutters." Originally, they had a dual purpose: to protect a window or door from the elements and to allow for ventilation with privacy. They have now evolved into a more decorative door that usually can't even be closed (Illus. 12-36).

Blinds are available in wood, vinyl, and steel in all-louvre, louvre/panel, and all-panel construction. The vinyl and steel models are available in a wide variety of colors and may have simulated slats. The sizes of the shutters are based on the window or door sizes, and range in thickness from ¾ to 1⅛″.

Hardware is available to create a working pair of shutters, but make sure you mount them so that the slats slope down and away from the window or door when they are closed.

Interior Window Blinds

Interior window blinds, sometimes called "shutterettes," are a further evolution of the exterior window blind. Illus. 12-37 shows two types of interior shutter commonly available.

These products are used to provide decorative privacy to the inside of the window. The vertical bar on the louvre unit is used to adjust the pitch of the slats to allow greater or less light infiltration. The nonlouvre door is usually finished with fabric to complement drapes or furniture. These units are compatible in size with standard windows and are often available in two- or four-wide prehinged units for easy installation.

Café Doorways

Café doorways do not enjoy the same level of popularity they once did, but are still found throughout the country. They are used in pairs, usually with "double-acting hardware" that allows them to open in either direction. The vertical measurement of the door is less than the full

Illus. 12-36. Window blinds (shutters).

height of the frame, similar to the saloon doors often seen in old Western movies (Illus. 12-38). They are available in various styles and run in sizes from widths of 2′6″ to 3′0″ by approximately 3′6″ in height. These doors are most frequently manufactured from white pine.

Maintenance
Louvre products are maintained the same as other wood doorways. All sides must be permanently sealed against moisture.

French Door
A French door is a stile-and-rail door with glass

Illus. 12-37. Interior shutters.

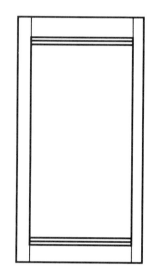

SHUTTERETTE

FABRIC PANEL

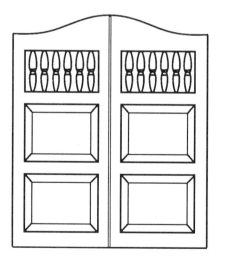

Illus. 12-38. Café doors.

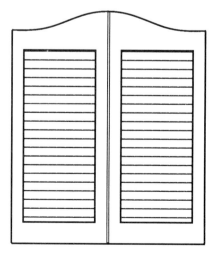

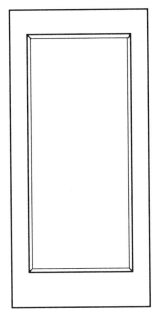

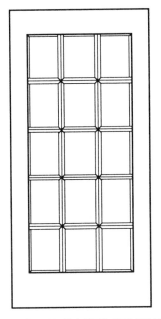

Illus. 12-39. French doors.

1 LIGHT STORE DOOR   15 LIGHT CASEMENT DOOR

occupying all the space between the stiles and rails (Illus. 12-39). The glass may be one light (called a "store door") or it may be divided into smaller individual lights by bars and muntins or grilles (called a "casement door"). Leaded glass, divided by metal cames, is also becoming a popular design element in French doors.

These doors are commonly used in pairs, with each door hinged and operable. A piece of moulding called a T astragal may be attached to one of the doors, and flush bolts mounted on this astragal allow for this door to be rigidly secured in place and act as a side jamb. With one door locked in place, you still have the other door for entering and exiting. If you want to open both doors, simply disengage the flush bolts at the T astragal and swing both doors open.

Interior French doors differ from exterior models in that they are usually 1⅜" thick rather than 1¾", and rarely contain insulating glass. Doorway frames and weather stripping also differ substantially, but it is not uncommon to use exterior doors in an interior installation.

French doors make excellent room dividers because they maintain an airy atmosphere and

can be fully opened if both rooms are needed simultaneously.

FIRE DOORS

In order to protect people from a rapidly expanding conflagration, fire-resistant materials are included in walls, floors, and ceilings to create a barrier against the flames and heat. These barriers are interrupted by doorways which must maintain the fire-resistant integrity of the entire room. Different core and face types offer varying levels of protection, which is rated by a time factor of from 20 minutes to 3 hours. Residential fire doors may be limited to the space between the garage and house or, in the case of multifamily construction, may be on every apartment entrance. Local building codes mandate minimum standards for fire doors and special attention should be paid to the requirements before any doorway modification is undertaken.

Special care is taken in the manufacture of these potential lifesavers. Manufacturers, by code, must be licensed by one of several underwriters (Underwriters Laboratory, Warnock Hersey, and Factory Mutual are the main licensers), and their factories are inspected on a monthly basis. A log, showing the type of door and to whom it was sold, is kept of all fire doors manufactured so that their authenticity can be checked in the future.

Not only must the manufacturers be licensed, but any firm that further modifies the door by putting in vision panels or louvres, etc., must also be approved. If the manufacturer simply makes the door and does not machine it for any hardware, a label showing the type of fire protection is placed on the top edge of the door. This label may be a rubber stamp or a metal plate. If a manufacturer or a modifier machines a fire door, the label is then placed on the hinge side of the door. According to the code, the only machine work that is allowed to be done on a fire door on location is preparation for surface-applied hardware, function holes for mortise locks, holes for labelled viewers, and a maximum ¾″ undercutting. Twenty- and thirty-minute doors may also, with proper reinforcement, be prepared in the field for fitting, hardware, and astragals. (A 20-minute door is a door that has a survival rate of 20 minutes in a fire.)

Door frames must also meet minimum requirements in order to create a fire-resistant doorway.

Construction

Fire doors have a core construction. Interior frames may be made of treated wood or steel. The cores in 20-minute doors may be made of foam or particleboard, but must be constructed of a mineral substance when longer ratings are called for. Their faces are made of either wood veneer or steel on all doors up to and including 90 minutes, and only steel on 180-minute doors. Typically, door labels refer to an alpha code or time that indicates the expected longevity of the doorway in a fire, as follows:

Time	Alpha Code	Door Face
20 minutes	None	Wood/Steel
30 minutes	None	Wood/Steel
45 minutes	C	Wood/Steel
60 minutes	B	Wood
90 minutes	B	Wood/Steel
180 minutes	A	Steel

Illus. 12-40. Fire door label. (*Courtesy of Warnock Hersey*)

Illus. 12-41. Fire door hardware. (*Courtesy of Warnock Hersey*)

Never remove a label from a fire door (Illus. 12-40).

Sizes
Manufacturers can create just about any size fire door up to $4'0'' \times 10'0''$. If cost is important, however, keep to the more standard sizes. Fire doors are usually $1\frac{3}{4}''$ thick.

Hardware
The hardware used with fire doors is regulated by the same building code. Locks require special latches, and other hardware must meet minimum standards. An automatic closing device is often mandated. If in doubt, check with your local building official before purchasing any of this special hardware (Illus. 12-41).

13
Door Frames

Simply put, door frames enclose and support doors. They provide an area to attach the hardware, weather stripping and door stop, and they help to create a decorative focal point in the wall. Door frames do not play a structural role in the house framework. They are independent of the framing system and are usually not installed until the roof is on the building. Exterior and interior door frames differ substantially in their construction and role.

EXTERIOR DOOR FRAMES

Exterior door frames consist of jambs, stops, casings, and a sill, all of which are more massive than their interior counterparts (Illus. 13-1). Most exterior door frames used are made of wood. Steel and aluminum are also used, although usually in fire-retardant or commercial doorways.

Residential exterior door frames commonly

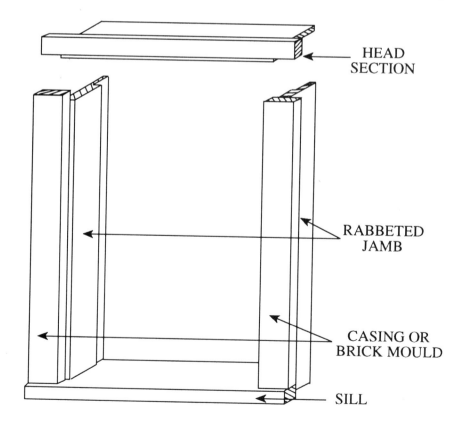

Illus. 13-1. Exterior doorway frame.

HEAD SECTION

RABBETED JAMB

CASING OR BRICK MOULD

SILL

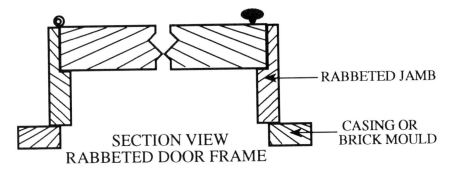

RABBETED JAMB

CASING OR
BRICK MOULD

SECTION VIEW
RABBETED DOOR FRAME

Illus. 13-2. Section view of a rabbeted door frame.

allow for the door to open into the home, while commercial units open out. If you have a choice, always select the in-swinging design. This will allow for an exterior-mounted storm-and-screen doors, and is safer if your view to the outside is obscured.

The jamb is the major component of the frame. A set of door frame jambs consists of one head and two sides (a left and a right). One side jamb will have the hinges mounted on it, and the other will contain the strike plate of the lock.

There are two main types of exterior door jamb: rabbeted and nonrabbeted. The rabbet in the rabbeted frame (Illus. 13-2) stops the door from swinging all the way through the opening. A nonrabbeted frame (Illus. 13-3) has a stop added on top of the jamb to accomplish this function. Each of these jamb types is common to certain parts of the country. The main reason some consider the stop to be better than the rabbet is that, in the case of door warpage, the stop can be moved to better fit the contour of the out-of-shape door. It seems that manufacturers are not interested in this advantage, and most of the new, insulated outer door units are being shipped with rabbeted frames.

Wood jambs and casings are usually made of pine, and paint-grade frame members are usually finger-jointed. Clear jambs are usually edge-glued and veneered in the same fashion as door stiles.

The *sill* of a door frame is the horizontal member at the bottom. The sill may be wood, aluminum, or plastic, or may be left off entirely if a masonry sill is provided at the site. Parts of the sill called "horns" extend beyond the side jambs and under the exterior casing.

The *threshold* is added to the top of or incorporated directly into the sill in order to create a weatherproof seal with the door bottom (Illus. 13-4). The combined sill and threshold may be fixed or adjustable. This part of the doorway is especially susceptible to leakage, and you should select an insulating system that will afford the most protection.

The *exterior casing* of the door frame consists of one head piece and two side pieces. The casing is attached to the exterior of the jamb, with the side pieces resting on the horns of the sill. There are two main functions of the casing: to cover the space between the house framing and the door jamb and to provide a means of secur-

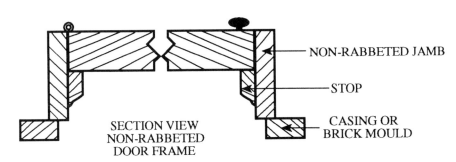

NON-RABBETED JAMB

STOP

CASING OR
BRICK MOULD

SECTION VIEW
NON-RABBETED
DOOR FRAME

Illus. 13-3. Section view of a nonrabbeted door frame.

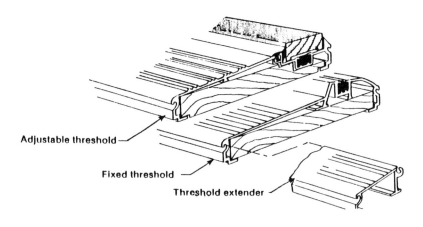

Illus. 13-4. Thresholds. (*Courtesy of Johnson Metal Products*)

Adjustable threshold

Fixed threshold

Threshold extender

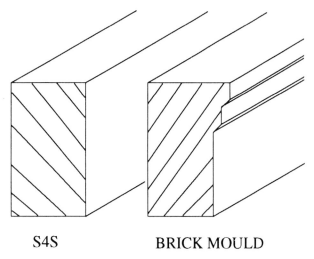

S4S   BRICK MOULD

Illus. 13-5. Exterior casings.

ing the door frame to the house. There are two common types of exterior casing: *S4S* and *brick mould* (Illus. 13-5).

Finishes

Wooden outer door frames are usually available either unfinished or primed. Some are now available with exteriors clad in aluminum or vinyl of various colors. These clad door frames do not include exterior casing because they are installed through the use of a fin system (Illus. 13-6).

Steel and aluminum door frames are somewhat different than wood door frames in that all the parts are formed into a head or side section. Casing is not added and sills are usually not included. Installation is accomplished by attaching the frame to the wall through the side and head jambs. These metal frames are usually prefinished in a variety of colors (Illus. 13-7).

Weather Stripping

Weather stripping is critical in door frames. Since a door must open, a space must exist all around the interior perimeter of the frame, and this space will admit drafts and dust unless it is weather-stripped. The type and quality of this weather stripping varies greatly from manufac-

Illus. 13-6. Aluminum-clad rabbeted jamb. (*Courtesy of JJJ Specialty Co.*)

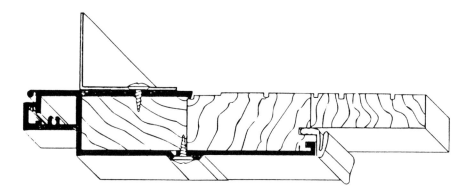

turer to manufacturer. It may be included with the frame or have to be added on later. You should be sure that any new frame is weather-stripped with a high-quality, long-lasting product that provides total perimeter protection. Check your existing frames and add weatherproofing if needed.

Sidelight, Transom, and Circle-Head Frames

Sidelight and transom frames are frequently used in combination with regular door frames. A transom frame is usually separate from the door frame and attached to it. Sidelight frames may be separate from the door frame or may be included in one continuous "sidelight door

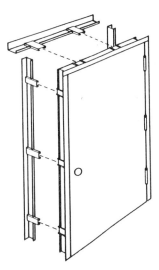

Illus. 13-7. Steel doorway frame installation. (*Courtesy of Johnson Metal Products*)

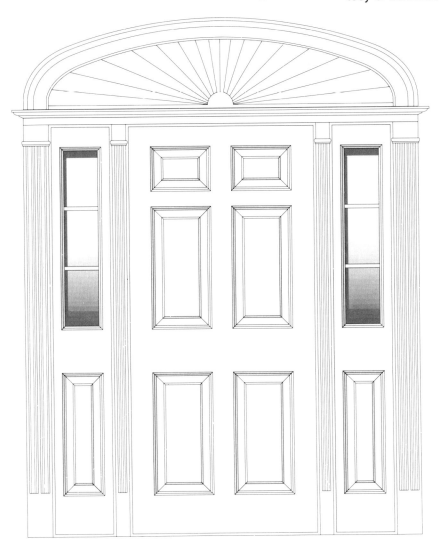

Illus. 13-8. Sidelight doorway frame with decorative trim. (*Courtesy of Morgan Products*)

frame." This method of construction is a good deal stronger than joining three separate frames together.

Circle-head frames are created in two different ways. The first method is to attach a semicircular transom unit over the door frame, which allows a regular door to be used. The second method is to actually create a semi-circular head jamb for the door frame; this mandates the use of a circle-head door. The "true" circle head unit is usually more expensive than the "created" circle head.

Specialty Exterior Trim

The main exterior doorway is likely to be the most prominent architectural feature of the

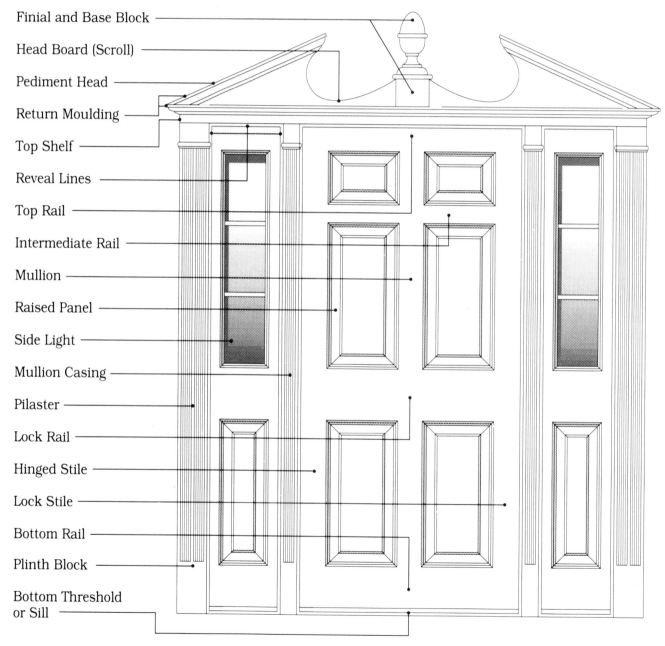

Finial and Base Block

Head Board (Scroll)

Pediment Head

Return Moulding

Top Shelf

Reveal Lines

Top Rail

Intermediate Rail

Mullion

Raised Panel

Side Light

Mullion Casing

Pilaster

Lock Rail

Hinged Stile

Lock Stile

Bottom Rail

Plinth Block

Bottom Threshold or Sill

Illus. 13-9. The parts of an exterior doorway. (*Courtesy of Morgan Products*)

home. In order to enhance the fenestration, special exterior trim may be applied to the door frame, often with dramatic results (Illus. 13-9).

This is a broad area of millwork consisting of many different designs. If you wish to enhance your exterior trim, take some door measurements and seek the advice of a knowledgeable supplier.

Traditionally, pine has been used to create these trim items. Recently, however, a polymer product has become very popular. This synthetic material looks like wood if it is painted and is resistant to weather and insects. It is available in a wide range of styles, including exterior mouldings and window trim, as well as other decorative items.

Sizes

Sizes of door frames reflect the size of the door that they are built to fit. Thus, if we see the description "3'0" × 6'8" door frame," this only indicates that the opening for the door is 36" × 80". We must still be sure to provide the measurements for the "overall size," the "frame size," the "rough opening," the "masonry opening," and the "wall thickness." Manufacturers should provide some or all of these measurements. Below is a description of each of them.

Overall Size

The "overall size," "unit size," or "unit dimension" (Illus. 13-10) is the overall width × the overall height of the entire door frame *excluding* any fins but *including* any exterior casing. This measurement indicates the exact dimension of the unit as viewed from the outside. This is also the measurement of that part of the door frame that fits inside the exterior siding, and, therefore, becomes critical in replacement applications.

Frame Size

The "frame size" is a measurement of the overall width × the overall height *excluding* fins and exterior casing.

Rough Opening

The "rough opening" (Illus. 13-11) is a widely used measurement which reflects the manufacturer's recommendation of the size of the hole in a wood-framed wall necessary to fit the door frame. Generally, the rough opening of an exterior doorway frame is approximately 3" wider and 4" taller than the door. The rough opening is needed when framing a wall to accept a door unit. To compute your own rough opening, add ½" to the "frame size."

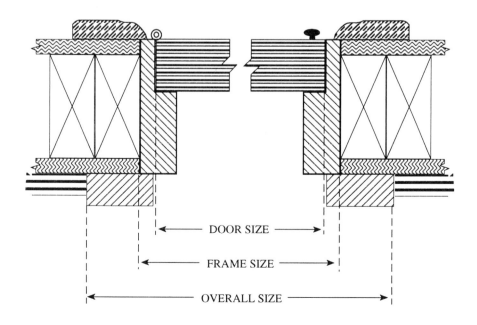

Illus. 13-10. Dimensions for a door frame.

DOOR SIZE

FRAME SIZE

OVERALL SIZE

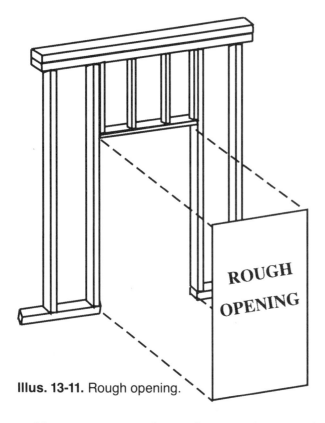

Illus. 13-11. Rough opening.

If you want to replace a doorway frame and need to determine the rough opening of the frame which is already installed, you must remove the interior trim and expose the wall framing. You can then measure the existing rough opening.

It is possible to estimate the rough opening size of an existing door frame, but this is best left to professionals.

Masonry Opening

The "masonry opening" is the manufacturer's recommendation of the hole size necessary to fit a door-unit frame into a block, brick, stone, or poured concrete wall. It is usually approximately ½ to 1″ larger than the overall size of the unit.

It should be noted that there is a difference between masonry walls and masonry *veneered* walls. It is common today to install a brick wall as a veneer over a wood-framed wall. In this type of construction, rough openings rather than masonry openings are used because the window unit will be installed into a wood wall.

Wall Thickness

Door frames have a third dimension (in addition to width and height) which is crucial to a successful installation. This measurement is the "wall thickness" or "wall construction" and must be provided by you when the door frames are specified. A formula for determining the wall construction is included in the window section. Jamb extenders are commonly used in door frames to accommodate wall thicknesses in excess of 4½″. These extenders are nothing more than pieces of trim made of the same material as the jamb and attached flush with the jamb. They effectively "extend" the jamb to cover a wider wall thickness.

INTERIOR DOORWAY FRAMES

Interior doorway frames differ from exterior frames in several ways. Since they generally support less door weight and don't have to keep out drafts, the jamb is thinner and does not contain a provision for weather stripping. Also, a sill or threshold is not included, and there is no exterior casing.

Frame Members

Residential frames are normally made of wood, but steel and aluminum frames are also found, especially in multifamily construction. Jambs may be rabbeted, but are most frequently non-rabbeted (flat or plain) with an added stop. Another type of jamb is the adjustable or "split" jamb. Illus. 13-13 indicates three different styles of wood interior doorway frame.

Adjustable jambs facilitate installation because they can be used on a variety of wall thicknesses, but they are generally more expensive because of the added material. Wood jambs and stops are usually made of pine, but mahogany, oak and other species are also popular. Finger jointing is common for paint-grade frame members. Clear jambs are generally edge-glued and veneered in the same fashion as door stiles.

Although sills are not commonly found on interior doorway frames, an oak or marble saddle is sometimes used under the door to cover

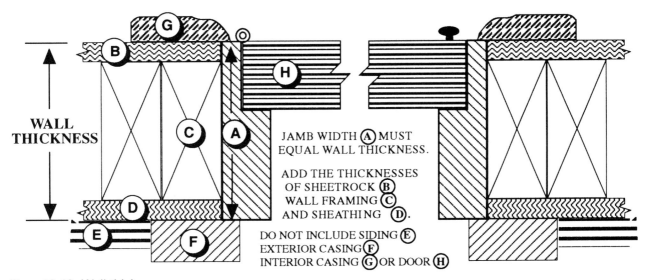

WALL THICKNESS

JAMB WIDTH Ⓐ MUST EQUAL WALL THICKNESS.

ADD THE THICKNESSES
OF SHEETROCK Ⓑ
WALL FRAMING Ⓒ
AND SHEATHING Ⓓ.

DO NOT INCLUDE SIDING Ⓔ
EXTERIOR CASING Ⓕ
INTERIOR CASING Ⓖ OR DOOR Ⓗ

Illus. 13-12. Wall thickness.

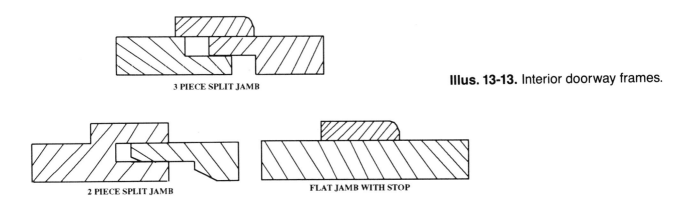

3 PIECE SPLIT JAMB

Illus. 13-13. Interior doorway frames.

2 PIECE SPLIT JAMB

FLAT JAMB WITH STOP

areas where different floor jambs meet. These saddles are usually thinner than exterior sills (Illus. 13-14).

Sizes

Interior doorway frames correspond in size to the size of the door the frame will take. A 2′6″ × 6′8″ door frame will have an interior opening of that size and you must then figure the rough opening needed to fit the frame. Plan your rough opening to be 2″ wider and 2″ higher than the door size. This formula is based on a jamb thickness of ¾″ plus space for shims, as well as floor or carpet clearance.

Purchasing Door Frames

If you are replacing a door and frame, you are better off purchasing a prehung door unit. The

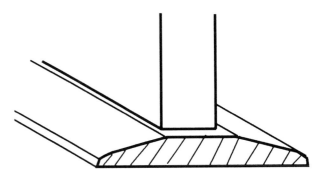

Illus. 13-14. Door saddle.

task of hanging the door is already completed, and you are assured of a good fit between the door and frame. If you need a door frame only, you have several options: a preassembled frame, a knocked-down set of parts, or individual pieces of jamb, casing, stop, or sill. You can also make jambs and casing from plain pine boards. You must provide two measurements when specifying a door frame: the size of the door and the size of the wall construction.

14
Prehung Door Units

As shown in Illus. 14-1, even the most simple door-unit installation requires considerable preparation. The door must be machined for the lock, latch, and hinges. The jambs must be machined for the hinges and the strike plate. All this work must be precise to ensure a proper fit between the frame and the door. This is why the prehung door unit has become so popular in the last 30 years. All the parts are joined together in a controlled atmosphere to create a product that even the most inexperienced person can handle.

PREHUNG DOOR FRAME

Prehung door frames are similar to the frames described above. They may be made of wood, steel, or aluminum. All machining for hinges and locks is performed in a factory setting where accuracy can be easily maintained. The doors are also machined and are then joined to the frame to create the finished unit, which may be shipped fully assembled or knocked down. Trim and locks are usually available as optional items with the prehung door unit.

MEASUREMENTS

The measurements of prehung doors are the same as for door frames. The "call out" size (the size given when ordering the door) is the door

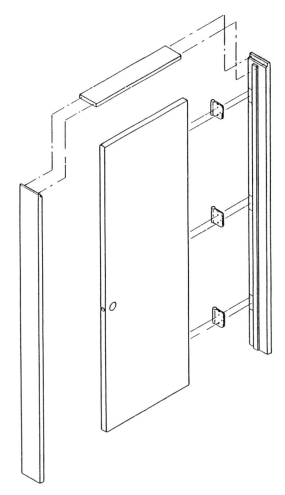

Illus. 14-1. The parts of a prehung door. (*Courtesy of "Norfield"*)

size (or combined door size in multidoor openings), and rough openings must be computed. The only difference from the normal rough opening formula occurs with the two-door sliding unit. Since these doors overlap by 1″, the rough opening width is only 1″ larger than the door width. An example would be a 5′0″-wide sliding door unit consisting of two 2′6″ doors. The doors overlap by 1″, which makes the interior width 4′11″ and the rough opening width 5′1″ (assuming ¾″ thick jambs are being used).

TYPES OF PREHUNG DOOR UNITS

Prehung door units are commonly available in several types other than the regular single exterior or interior swinging unit. They are described below.

Double-Door Swinging Units

Double-door swinging units, commonly called "twin doors" or "tudors," are available in exterior and interior models (Illus. 14-2). Exterior twin units should include a piece of T astragal, which contains weather stripping and flush bolt hardware to rigidly hold one door in the closed position. This is a critical function because the rigid door accepts the latch from the entry lock and provides much of the security for the entrance. Interior units may have a T astragal, but it is more common to allow both doors to swing at all times with dummy knobs and friction or magnetic catches located at the head stop. Unless one door is rigid, it is difficult to use a regular doorknob and latch.

The advantage of double-door swinging units is the uninterrupted space they provide for access to a closet or to enclose a wide opening between rooms. Their primary disadvantage is the amount of wall and floor space the open doors take up.

Sliding Door Units

Sliding door units, commonly called "bipass" doors, are frequently seen on closets (Illus. 14-3). They usually consist of two doors combined to make an overall width of between 4 and 6′, but other options are available with special hardware. They are most efficient in tight quar-

Illus. 14-2. Twin swinging doorway.

Illus. 14-3. Sliding doorway.

ters because they do not require any wall space outside the door opening. A double track is applied to the head jamb, and rollers attached to the tops of the doors allow the doors to slide past each other on separate tracks. Recessed pulls are installed in the outer side of each door to allow for opening and closing. A floor guide is usually provided to keep the doors separated at the bottom. The major disadvantage of sliding doors is that only half of the door opening is available at any time.

Folding Door Units

Folding door units, commonly called "bifold" doors, are used primarily in closets and as room dividers (Illus. 14-4). They are usually available in two-or four-door units up to 6′ wide, but larger widths are available with special hardware. Both doors in the two-door unit fold to one side, while the four-door model opens in the center with two doors going to each side. A track is applied to the head jamb, and L-shaped brackets to the side jambs. The doors are hinged together in pairs, and guides are placed in the tops and bottoms. Bifold units allow total access

Illus. 14-5. Accordian doorway.

Illus. 14-4. Four-door bifold doorway.

to closets, but require space in front of the door opening to allow doors to fold.

Another type of folding door unit is the "accordion door" (Illus. 14-5). Narrow panels are joined together and folded towards one or both sides. A top track is used to suspend the panels. This system allows total access with almost no space requirements.

Pocket Door Units

Pocket door units open into a wall (Illus. 14-6). They provide very efficient privacy in restricted spaces. The door frame on a pocket door unit is twice as wide as the door, and half of it is buried behind the wallboard. The door has rollers attached to the top and slides within a track. The locking device is rather unusual because it must not protrude from the face of the door. Double pocket units with doors meeting in the center and opening into separate pockets are also available. Pocket units may be available prehung, but are usually assembled on the job site.

A warped door can ruin a pocket unit. Be sure to maintain the seal on all six sides of a wood door to lessen this possibility.

Illus. 14-6. Pocket doorway.

Double-Action Door Units

Double-action door units swing both ways. They are sometimes found in diners leading from the eating area to the kitchen. Special hardware is used to allow the door to open in or out. Double-action door units are more difficult to hang than regular swinging door units, so purchase them prehung if available.

DOOR SWINGS

Doors open in or out and to the left or right. When you order a prehung unit, you must tell the manufacturer how the door will swing. There is a great deal of confusion about this specification, and it has caused many problems for manufacturers and consumers. You can avoid these problems by adapting the following system for specifying swings:

1. Using your imagination, position yourself facing the door as it opens towards you. Whether this is outside or inside makes no difference; just assume you are going to *pull* the door towards yourself.

2. Once you mentally position yourself, look at

Illus. 14-7. Door swings.

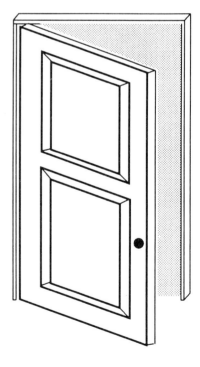

LEFT HAND (LH)   RIGHT HAND (RH)

the doorknob. If the knob is on the right, the door has a right-hand (RH) swing. If the knob is on the left, the door has a left-hand (LH) swing.

Use only this system. Many manufacturers will attempt to get you to adapt to their method, but to avoid confusion you should only use one system at any time. If the manufacturer wants

---

EXTERIOR DOORS

DOOR TYPE:_____   DOOR THICKNESS: 1 3/4 "; OTHER:_____

JAMB WIDTH (WALL THICKNESS)_____   SOLID; FINGERJOINT; ALUMINUM CLAD

JAMB TYPE: RABBETED; NON-RABBETED   WEATHERSTRIP INCLUDED?_____

SILL OR THRESHOLD TYPE:_____   DOOR OPEN: IN OR OUT

EXTERIOR CASING TYPE: BRICK MOULD; S4S; OTHER_____

SIDELIGHT(S)_____   TRANSOM_____

INTERIOR DOORS

DOOR TYPE:_____   DOOR THICKNESS : 1 1/8"   1 3/8 " 1 3/4 "

JAMB WIDTH (WALL THICKNESS)_____   SOLID;   FINGER JOINT.

JAMB TYPE: PLAIN;   SPLIT.

ALL DOORS

LOCKS: _____   INTERIOR TRIM TYPE:_____

OTHER OPTIONS:_____

QUANTITY	DOOR SIZE	ROUGH OPENING	SWING
_____	_____	_____	_____
_____	_____	_____	_____
_____	_____	_____	_____
_____	_____	_____	_____
_____	_____	_____	_____
_____	_____	_____	_____

Table 14-1. Checklist for exterior doorways.

clarification, draw a picture or tell him that when the door opens towards you, the knob is on the right/left side.

In order to save on inventory requirements, some manufacturers now provide reversible prehung door units which can be used as either righthand or lefthand swing by simply turning them upside down. These units are usually hollow-core flush doors, and the lock bores are halfway up from the bottom (40″ on a 6′8″ tall door). Normally, doorknobs are located 36″ up from the bottom of the door. Before purchasing one of these reversible models you should deter-mine if the knob height will affect the aesthetics of the whole room, which may have doors with lower knobs.

PURCHASING PREHUNG DOOR UNITS

Use Table 14-1 to gather the information you will need in order to place an order for a wood prehung unit. Remember to ask your supplier about warranties covering the products you are buying. Get copies of the certificates and be sure to follow all stipulations.

15
Installation Guidelines

The installation of door units (including pre-hung units) and door frames requires varying degrees of technical expertise, depending on the complexity of the task. If you can build a wall, you can surely install a prehung door unit in that wall. Replacing an existing front door unit, however, involves considerably more talent. Be sure your supplier can provide detailed instructions before you order any material. A general checklist for installing door frames and door units is as follows:

1. Check the rough opening for squareness and ensure that it is at least ½″ larger than the outer edge of the door frame. Also check that the swinging door will clear carpets or flooring.
2. Set the frame in the rough opening so that it is in the middle and lines up with the wall surfaces.
3. Install shims between side jambs and wall framing; they will provide equal spacing. Use a level or plumb bob to make sure the jambs are plumb and square.

4. Secure the frame in the opening according to the type of frame, as follows:
   A. *Exterior frames* are nailed through wood casing or metal fins.
   B. *Interior, plain-jamb frames* are nailed through the face of the jamb, into the shim, and then into the wall framing.
   C. *Interior, split-jamb* and *steel frames* are installed from each side of the opening.
5. Mark and cut out the area for the lock, and install the lock (this step is usually not necessary on prehung units).
6. Apply the trim and the finish. If you are installing a wood door, be sure to apply a seal coat to all six sides. This will help prevent warpage and preserve your warranty.

If you are installing only a door into an existing or new frame, your work must be very precise and will usually consist of the following:

1. Rough-fit the door to the frame. Create a slight bevel on the lock-side vertical edge, so that the face of the door that touches the stop is slightly narrower than the other face.

2. Mark and cut out the space for the hinges, paying close attention to the swing of the door and the outside and inside face.

3. Apply the hinges and install the door in the frame with hinge pins. Final-fit the door to the frame.

4. Cut out the space for the locks and install it and other hardware.

5. Apply the finish.

No matter who installs a door, you should be familiar enough with the process to identify good workmanship. Take the time to learn the correct procedure specified by the manufacturer.

Moulding

16
Basic Information

The ancient Greeks originated the concepts and designs that make up what is called moulding. These craftsmen were the first to accent their structures with components meant solely to beautify otherwise plain surfaces. They used mouldings to divide large areas into small parts, creating attractive highlights and shadows while concealing seams and protecting corners. Many of these ideas have been adopted and modified by woodworkers in the creation of modern moulding. In Colonial times, wood mouldings were individually planed by each carpenter; today an entire system of standard patterns can be mass-produced in a machine called a moulder.

The high cost of new house construction often mandates the purely utilitarian approach of hiding seams between the wall and floor or ceiling, as well as around doors and windows. This "contractor-installed" treatment is cheaper but uninspiring. The truly decorative work will take place later when it is installed by the homeowner. You can easily produce your own unique design by combining several standard profiles in the creation of truly elegant doorways, windows, stairways, mantels, and walls.

MATERIAL

Many different types of material are used in the

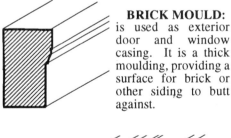

BRICK MOULD: is used as exterior door and window casing. It is a thick moulding, providing a surface for brick or other siding to butt against.

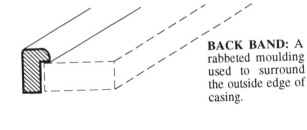

BACK BAND: A rabbeted moulding used to surround the outside edge of casing.

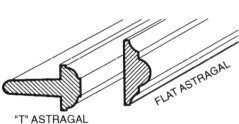

"T" ASTRAGAL

FLAT ASTRAGAL

ASTRAGAL: This catagory includes two types, "T" and "Flat". The "T" is attached to one of a pair of doors to keep one door from swinging through the opening. The flat astragal is used for decorative purposes.

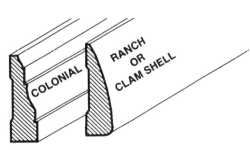

COLONIAL

RANCH OR CLAM SHELL

CASING: Used as interior trim for window and door openings. Many patterns available.

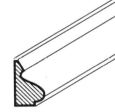

BASE CAP: A decorative member installed flush against the wall and the top of an S4S baseboard. Also a versatile panel moulding.

Illus. 16-1. Mouldings come in a wide variety of profiles and can be used in many different applications. Shown here are just a few of the basic profiles available.

manufacture of mouldings. The right product depends on the task at hand. Visit several retailers in order to get an overview of the wide variety of products available. Basically, mouldings are available in unfinished softwood, unfinished hardwood, veneered softwood and hardwood, and prefinished wood, metal, plastic, and foam. They are described below.

Unfinished Softwood Mouldings

Generally, softwoods come from trees that have cones (called coniferous) and do not drop their needles or leaves, while hardwoods come from trees with broad leaves that are shed annually (deciduous). Common softwood species are cedar, cypress, fir, hemlock, larch, pine, and spruce. Softwood mouldings are usually manufactured of pine, but fir and hemlock are also used.

Western white pine and ponderosa pine are the most commonly used woods for the manufacture of mouldings in the United States, and individual pieces may be clear or finger-jointed. *Clear* mouldings are also referred to as "solid," "stain" grade, or "N" grade, and are suitable for painting or staining. To be graded "clear," the moulding face must be relatively free of any defect.

Paint grade mouldings, also called "P" grade, allow the inclusion of finger jointing (Illus. 16-2) and/or stain. (The stain referred to under "P" grade is not a paint stain but a fungal or chemical stain, resulting in a blue or brown color.) Structurally, finger-joint mouldings are just as strong as solid, clear mouldings, and are usually available in longer lengths. Softwood mouldings are produced in random lengths from 3 to 20', with 6 to 16' being the most commonly available at the retailer. No more than 15 percent of a random selection of mouldings should be under 8'.

Unfinished Hardwood Mouldings

Unfinished hardwood mouldings are regaining the popularity they had in years past. Because of their tighter cell structure, hardwoods have the ability to take an even, less blotchy stain finish. The graining and color of red oak provides a unique appearance which is compatible with furniture, flooring, doors, stairways, and other millwork within the home. Likewise, birch, maple, and poplar may be used to provide a unique but less grainy material.

Hardwoods lend themselves to precise milling techniques and are available in more ornately detailed patterns. Illus. 16-3 shows information published by a moulding manufacturer and indicates some of the specialty items commonly associated with hardwood mouldings.

There are two readily available species of hardwood moulding: red oak and mixed white woods. The white woods consist of several species, all providing the same finish characteristics. These mouldings are graded the same as softwoods, but only "N"-grade products are readily available.

Hardwood mouldings are produced in random lengths from 3 to 16'. No more than 20 percent of a random selection of hardwood mouldings should be under 6'. Hardwood mouldings are relatively expensive, and you can usually save money by buying random rather than specified lengths.

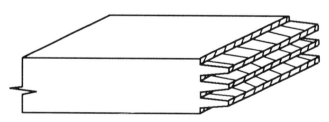

Illus. 16-2. Finger joint.

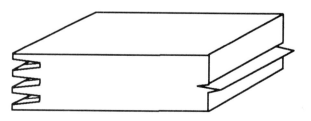

1. CROWN MOULDING:
Used where walls and ceilings meet. Bed or Cove Moulding can also be used.

2. CROWN CAPS:
Decorative, pre-assembled corner moulding. Crown butts to cap thus eliminating the need to miter and cope. Inside (**2a**) and outside (**2b**) available.

3. CASING: Moulding to trim interior of doors and windows.

4. ROSETTE: Decorative block used with casing to eliminate need for miter cuts. Various designs available.

5. PLINTH BLOCK:
Block used at bottom of door casing. Creates elegant look as well as a flush area for base moulding to meet.

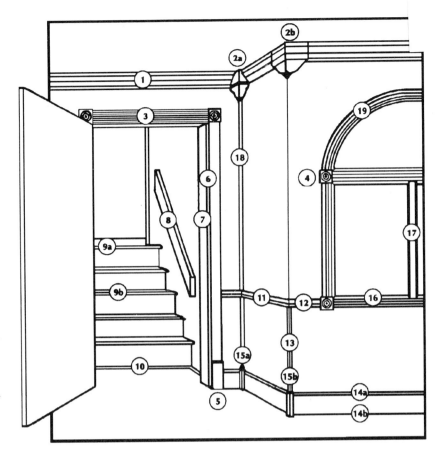

6. DOOR JAMB:
Avaiable in sets. Same wood species as mouldings.

7. STOP: Moulding attached to jamb to prevent door from swinging through. Also used on double hung windows.

8. HANDRAIL: Decorative stairway railing. Several styles available.

9. LANDING TREAD: (**9a**)
Used where floor meets riser at top of stairway. The TREAD (**9b**) is the horizontal step of the stairway.

10. QUARTER ROUND:
May be used in any 90° corner.

11. WAINSCOT CAP:
Covers rough edge at top of wainscoting.

12. CHAIR RAIL: Used to protect wall from chair backs or seperate two different wall coverings.

13. OUTSIDE CORNER:
Protect corner or cover seam where two wall coverings meet.

14. BASE: Applied where floor meets wall. May be built up using a BASE CAP (**14a**) and BASE SHOE (**14b**).

15. BASE BLOCKS: Fancy corner treatment. Base butts

into block, thus eliminating need to miter and cope. Inside (**15a**) and outside (**15b**).

16. STOOL: Window trim which covers sill of window.

17. MULLION CASING:
Window or door trim which conceals jamb edges in multiple openings.

18. COVE: May be used vertically or horizontally in any 90° corner.

19. CIRCULAR CASING:
Pre-manufactured in quarter, half and full round patterns to accomodate specialty windows and doors.

Illus. 16-3. Specialty items associated with hardwood mouldings. (*Courtesy of Webster Industries*)

Some hardwood moulding manufacturers offer premitred and coped corner sections (both inside and outside); these are real time-savers if you do not have much experience in applying trim.

Veneered Wood Mouldings

Veneered wood mouldings have thin veneers of clear pine or hardwood which are factory-applied over a finger joint or wood-composite substrate. The final product looks and is installed like a solid wood moulding. Veneered mouldings are produced in fewer patterns than solid wood, but are usually available in longer lengths. They are common in the wider patterns (over 2″) and especially common in door trim items such as jambs and casing. Veneered products are less expensive than solid wood products. Be cautious when using veneered material in close proximity to solid wood. Veneers, even though they come from the same species, may take a stain finish differently than a solid piece of wood. Test the final appearance before installation.

Prefinished Wood Mouldings

Prefinished wood mouldings are offered only for their laborsaving characteristics, and available mouldings are usually restricted to door and window trim. Mouldings with other prefinishing techniques, such as printing and vinyl wrapping, have become much less available in recent years. Plastic seems to be taking over as the material of choice when it comes to a prefinished moulding.

Metal Mouldings

Metal mouldings are used in specific situations. They are used on kitchen and bath countertops, as well as over the seam created where two flooring systems meet. Several finishes are available.

Plastic Mouldings

Plastic mouldings are available in many different patterns and colors. They are commonly used in conjunction with panelling installations.

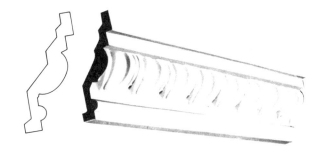

Illus. 16-4. Foam egg-and-dart moulding. (*Courtesy of Fypon Molded Millwork*)

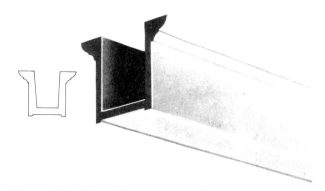

Illus. 16-5. Foam beam cover. (*Courtesy of Fypon Molded Millwork*)

Illus. 16-6. Happy Man Medallion. (*Courtesy of Fypon Molded Millwork*)

Use colored nails when installing plastic or any prefinished moulding.

Foam Mouldings

Foam mouldings are relatively new products. They are made of polymers with a density similar to that of pine. A prepainted skin covers the foam. This material can be sanded, cut, and nailed in the same fashion as wood, but foam-moulding joints usually call for an adhesive treatment.

Foam mouldings come in a wide variety of designs and in long lengths. They offer very ornate treatments of large areas. The "egg and dart" moulding shown in Illus. 16-4 is 1(and projects 5½" from the wall and ceiling of all, it comes in 16' lengths. This is a real time-saver for anyone wanting this type of effect in a painted finish. Other examples of foam mouldings are the "beam cover" (Illus. 16-5) and the "happy man medallion" (Illus. 16-6).

17

Selecting the Right Moulding

Don't be intimidated by the apparently myriad number of moulding patterns. Except for a few specialty items, mouldings fall into one of several categories based on function. Available designs may differ slightly, based on local preference, but the general categories still apply. Illus. 17-1–17-3 should clarify the nomenclature applicable to mouldings. Select a category that suits your need and then search within that category for the moulding that meets your aesthetic requirements.

There are four general types of base, casing, and stop patterns: "colonial," "ranch or clam shell," "sanitary or eased edge," and "S4S." Each serves the same function while creating a different architectural impression. Start your selection by choosing a base or casing pattern, and use that design in the selection of the rest of the items.

Basic Wood Moulding Profiles

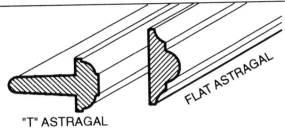

ASTRAGAL: This catagory includes two types, "T" and "Flat". The "T" is attached to one of a pair of doors to keep one door from swinging through the opening. The flat astragal is used for decorative purposes.

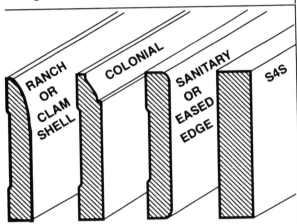

BASE: Covers joint where floor and walls meet and protects walls from kicks and bumps. Commonly available in four styles as shown above as well as built-up base, consisting of two or more members.

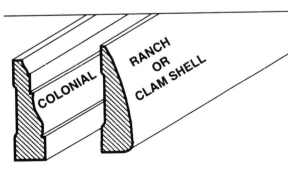

CASING: Used as interior trim for window and door openings. Many patterns available.

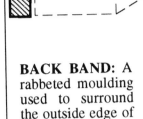

BACK BAND: A rabbeted moulding used to surround the outside edge of casing.

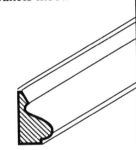

BATTEN: Symmetrical pattern used to conceal the line where two parallel boards or panels meet.

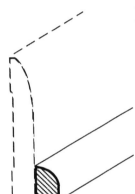

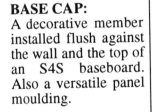

BASE SHOE: Applied where base moulding meets the floor. Protects base from damage by cleaning tools and conceals uneven lines or cracks where base meets floor.

BASE CAP: A decorative member installed flush against the wall and the top of an S4S baseboard. Also a versatile panel moulding.

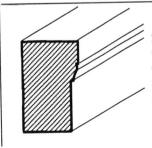

BRICK MOULD: is used as exterior door and window casing. It is a thick moulding, providing a surface for brick or other siding to butt against.

Illus. 17-1–17-3. Basic wood-moulding profiles.

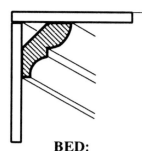

BED:

Used where walls and ceilings meet. Beds are usually smaller than crowns.

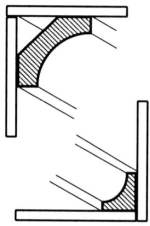

COVE:

Solid coves are often used as inside corners while sprung coves (hollow back) are generally found at the ceiling line.

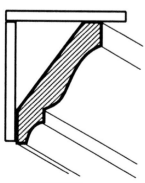

CROWN:

The largest of the ceiling mouldings. Usually sprung.

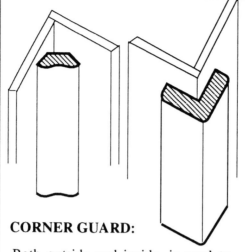

CORNER GUARD:

Both outside and inside, is used to cover and protect these accident prone areas. Also provides area to seperate contrasting wall treatments.

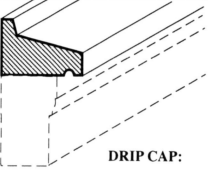

DRIP CAP:

Applied over exterior window and door frame head casing where it channels water away from siding and glass. Many decorative uses.

HALF ROUND:

The profile of this moulding is a half circle. Used as screen or panel mould as well as shelf edge.

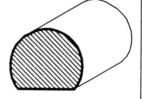

HAND RAIL:

Used as a stairway hand support.

Illus. 17-2.

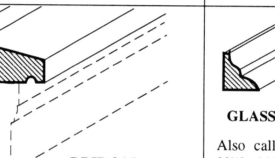

CHAIR RAIL:

Usually applied about one third the distance up from the floor. Protects walls and provides a divider between wall coverings. Different patterns and built-up designs available.

GLASS BEAD:

Also called glass stop, cove and bead, putty bead, glazing bead and staff bead. Used to hold glass in place.

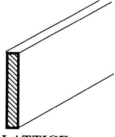

LATTICE:

Originally used in trellis work, this small, plain, S4S moulding is among the most versatile of profiles.

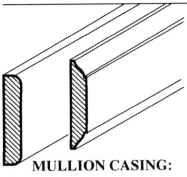

MULLION CASING:

Interior trim applied over the joint between two window or door frames. Sometimes called panel strip, it is also used for decorative wall treatments.

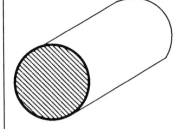

ROUND:

Commonly refered to as closet pole or full round, this moulding is usually available in fir or hemlock as well as pine.

STOOL:

Interior window sill cover

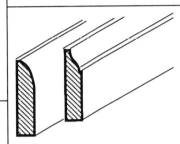

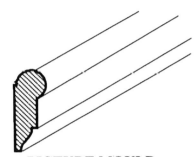

PICTURE MOULD:

Applied around a room's circumference near the ceiling line and used to support hooks for picture hanging.

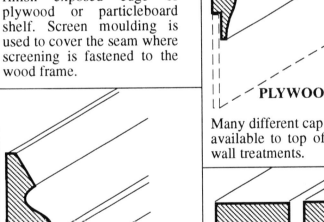

SHELF EDGE & SCREEN:

Shelf edge is often used to finish exposed edge of plywood or particleboard shelf. Screen moulding is used to cover the seam where screening is fastened to the wood frame.

STOP:

Common door and window trim. Also many decorative uses.

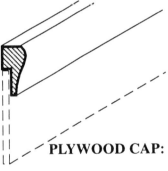

PLYWOOD CAP:

Many different cap mouldings available to top off wainscot wall treatments.

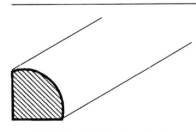

QUARTER ROUND:

Extremely versatile, may be used as a base shoe, inside corner or to cover any 90° recessed junction.

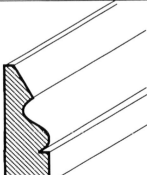

SHINGLE OR PANEL:

Also called BAND, these items have wide usage both inside & outside the home. May be used to create panel effect on walls.

Illus. 17-3.

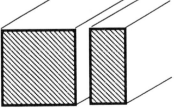

S4S:

Many sizes and uses in this special, clear, "moulding grade" material. Includes baluster.

18
Built-up Mouldings

By combining one or more standard profiles into a larger, more ornate moulding, you can greatly enhance the appearance of any room. Illus. 18-1–18-4 show just a few of the many possible combinations.

Other areas which lend themselves to built-up mouldings are door and window casing, mantels, wall panelling, and stairways. When installing the different pieces of the combined profile, it is better to completely install the first piece of the whole project before adding the second, etc.

BUILT-UP BASE MOULDING

Create unique base designs by combining 2 or more stock patterns. Here are a few mix-n-match suggestions using standard WM items.

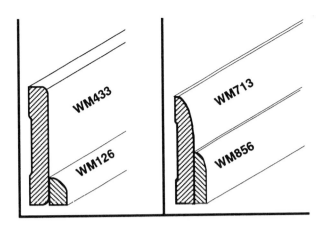

Illus. 18-1. Moulding for creating base designs.

BUILT-UP CHAIR RAIL

Here are a few ideas for creating that fancy chair rail from common wood mouldings. WM item number is shown.

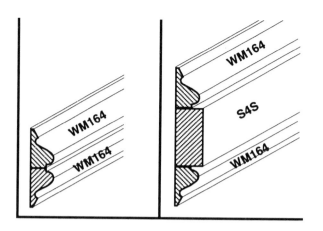

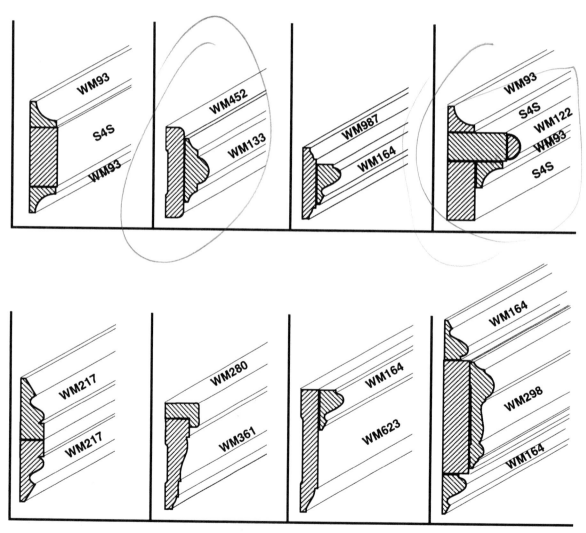

Illus. 18-2. Moulding for creating chair rails.

BUILT-UP CEILING MOULDING

Accent the transition between ceiling and wall with a special trim. You can create your own design by combining standard WM items.

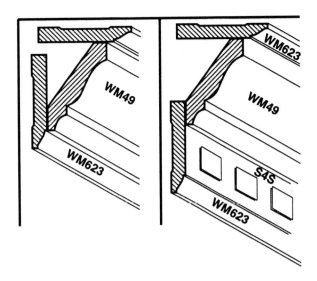

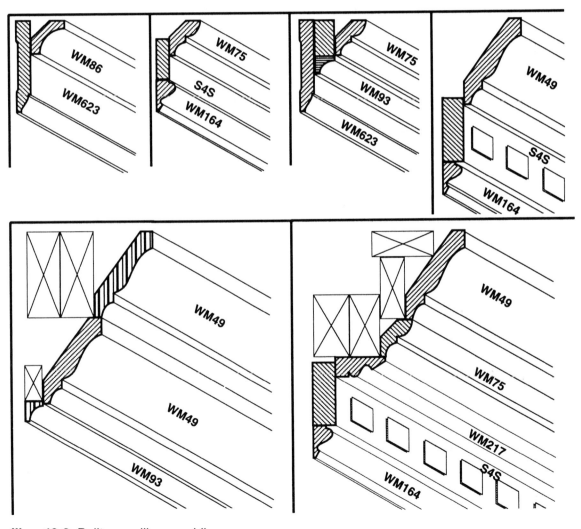

Illus. 18-3. Built-up ceiling moulding.

BUILT-UP PICTURE FRAMES

Here are a few suggestions for creating decorator frames at down to earth prices. All items are readily available.

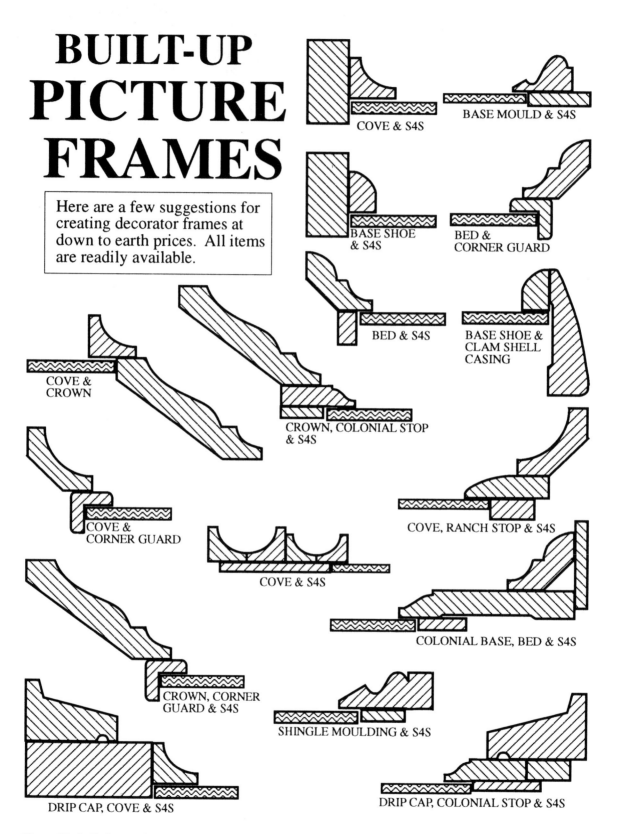

COVE & S4S

BASE MOULD & S4S

BASE SHOE & S4S

BED & CORNER GUARD

BED & S4S

BASE SHOE & CLAM SHELL CASING

COVE & CROWN

CROWN, COLONIAL STOP & S4S

COVE & CORNER GUARD

COVE & S4S

COVE, RANCH STOP & S4S

COLONIAL BASE, BED & S4S

CROWN, CORNER GUARD & S4S

SHINGLE MOULDING & S4S

DRIP CAP, COVE & S4S

DRIP CAP, COLONIAL STOP & S4S

Illus. 18-4. Built-up picture frames.

19
Buying Mouldings

Start your moulding purchase with a carefully computed list of each piece and its length. Round these measurements off to the next largest foot to allow for trimming, and take this list to your supplier. Know whether your existing base and casing pattern are colonial, ranch, sanitary, or S4S.

Everyone would prefer all 16′ lengths, but they are not always available, especially in hardwoods. You can usually save money by buying random lengths; however, for small quantities (under 100′) you are better off buying specified lengths. If you are going to paint the mouldings, ask about the availability of finger-joint material. This will be less expensive, and finger-jointed mouldings are available in all long lengths.

If you are attempting to match an existing pattern, bring a sample or at least its measurements. Illus. 19-1 shows how to obtain the needed specifications: the thickness and the width. The thickness is always less than or equal to the width.

If you are attempting to match a 50-year-old pattern, don't be surprised if today's product is slightly smaller than the old pattern. As long as you are not joining the new pattern to the old one, it will be impossible to tell the difference once they are installed.

The manufacturers of wood mouldings in the United States have an association to promote the use of their products. They are a great source of information on all aspects of the wood moulding industry, and can be contacted at the following address: Wood Moulding and Millwork Producers, P.O. Box 25278, Portland, Oregon 97225.

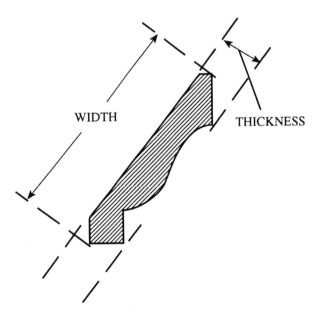

Illus. 19-1. How to determine the measurements for an existing moulding pattern.

20

Working with Mouldings

If you can use a saw and hammer, you can install your own mouldings. Equip yourself with the following tools: a hammer, a nail set, finishing nails, a tape measure, glue, sandpaper, wood filler, a mitre box and a backsaw (Illus. 20-1), and a coping saw (Illus. 20-2).

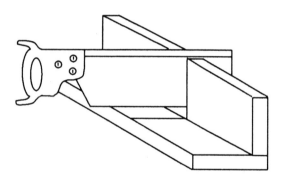

Illus. 20-1. Mitre box and backsaw.

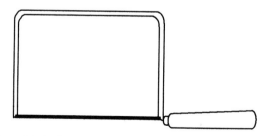

Illus. 20-2. Coping saw.

Installing mouldings means creating joints that are precise and neat. There are three joints you should be familiar with: the mitre, cope, and splice joint (Illus. 20-3). Regardless of the type, you should make a pencil mark on the moulding before making the cut. Hold the moulding in its intended position and draw the angle on the edge so that you can double-check your cut before you actually make it.

MITRE JOINT

Most mitre joints are at 45-degree angles, and each piece of moulding is trimmed at opposite angles. First, determine how the cut is to be made. The mitre joint between a piece of head and side casing is cut across its face (Illus. 20-4). A mitre joint between two pieces of S4S around an outside corner is cut across its edge (Illus. 20-5). Determine how the cut goes and position the moulding in the mitre box accordingly (either on the bottom or against the back, and either right side up or upside down). Adjust the saw to the appropriate 45-degree angle and make the first cut. Readjust the saw to the opposite angle and make the cut in the second piece. Finish the installation by gluing and nailing the joint.

COPE JOINT

Coping is a technique usually reserved for in-

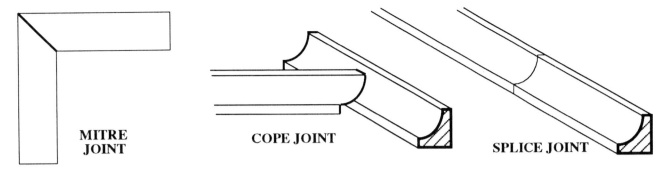

Illus. 20-3. Mitre, cope, and splice joints.

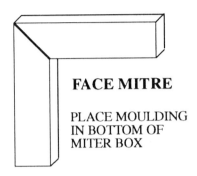

FACE MITRE

PLACE MOULDING
IN BOTTOM OF
MITER BOX

Illus. 20-4. Face mitre.

EDGE MITRE

PLACE MOULDING
AGAINST BACK EDGE
OF MITRE BOX

Illus. 20-5. Edge mitre.

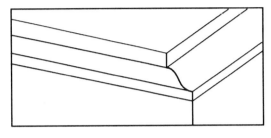

Illus. 20-6. Crown inside corner.

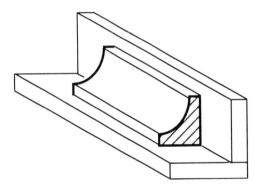

Illus. 20-7. Solid-back moulding.

side corners (Illus. 20-6). A cope joint is preferable because of its ability to cover irregularities more effectively than mitred joints. Only one of the two pieces of moulding being joined is coped; the other is cut square and tightly fitted to the corner.

One of two coping techniques is used, depending on the type of moulding being coped. If you are dealing with a "solid back" moulding (Illus. 20-7), use a piece of scrap moulding to trace the contour onto the back side of the piece to be coped. Cut along this outline with a coping saw; the remaining profile will then fit snugly against the face of the previously installed moulding.

If the pattern has a hollow or "sprung" back (Illus. 20-8), use the following technique: Place the piece upside down against the back edge of the mitre box and cut a mitre. The resulting slanted raw wedge exposed by the 45-degree cut is waste that must be trimmed away with a coping saw (Illus. 20-9). After making this final cut, it may still be necessary to use sandpaper or a utility knife on the joint. Coped joints can be complicated, so practise one or two before working on long material.

SPLICE JOINT

It may be necessary to join two shorter pieces of moulding together in order to cover an exceptionally long wall. This is accomplished by mitring both ends at the same 45-degree angle and joining the two edges over an area in the wall; this way the two edges can be nailed soundly to the wall.

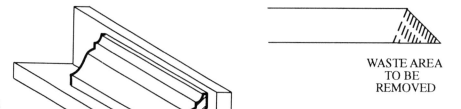

WASTE AREA
TO BE
REMOVED

Illus. 20-8 (right). Hollow-back (sprung) moulding placed upside down. **Illus. 20-9 (far right).** Waste area to be removed.

21
Window and Door Trim

There are two basic techniques used to trim windows (Illus. 21-1). In "picture trimming," four pieces of casing are mitred to each other. The window protrudes into the room an equal amount around its perimeter. In "stool trimming," three pieces of casing are mitred together, a piece of stool sits on top of the sill, and a piece of apron is mounted on the wall under the stool. The stool protrudes into the room, creating a shelf for the window treatment. Stool trim is most common on double-hung windows.

Another component of window trim may be the stop, but this depends on the type of unit being trimmed. You may be able to purchase window trim premitred or prepackaged.

Door trim consists of casing and stop. Each door gets two sides of casing (one head piece and two side pieces equal one side of door trim) and one set of stop (one head piece and two side pieces per set). You may be able to buy door trim premitred or even preassembled.

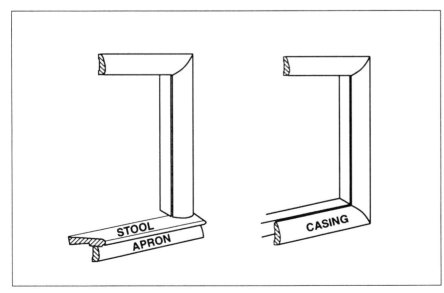

Illus. 21-1. Window-treatment techniques.

22
Moulding Patterns

The Wood Moulding and Millwork Producers publish a list of moulding patterns which are the most popular at the present time. These patterns are shown in Illus. 22-1–22-12. You will not be able to find every item listed here in your local lumberyard, but the patterns are those that are generally available.

BASE MOULDINGS

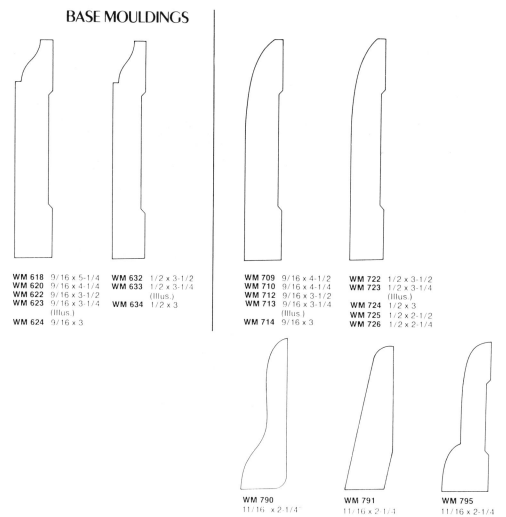

WM 618	9/16 x 5-1/4
WM 620	9/16 x 4-1/4
WM 622	9/16 x 3-1/2
WM 623	9/16 x 3-1/4
	(Illus.)
WM 624	9/16 x 3

WM 632	1/2 x 3-1/2
WM 633	1/2 x 3-1/4
	(Illus.)
WM 634	1/2 x 3

WM 709	9/16 x 4-1/2
WM 710	9/16 x 4-1/4
WM 712	9/16 x 3-1/2
WM 713	9/16 x 3-1/4
	(Illus.)
WM 714	9/16 x 3

WM 722	1/2 x 3-1/2
WM 723	1/2 x 3-1/4
	(Illus.)
WM 724	1/2 x 3
WM 725	1/2 x 2-1/2
WM 726	1/2 x 2-1/4

WM 790	11/16 x 2-1/4
WM 791	11/16 x 2-1/4
WM 795	11/16 x 2-1/4

Illus. 22-1–22-12. Popular moulding patterns. (*Courtesy of Wood Moulding and Millwork Producers Association*)

CASING

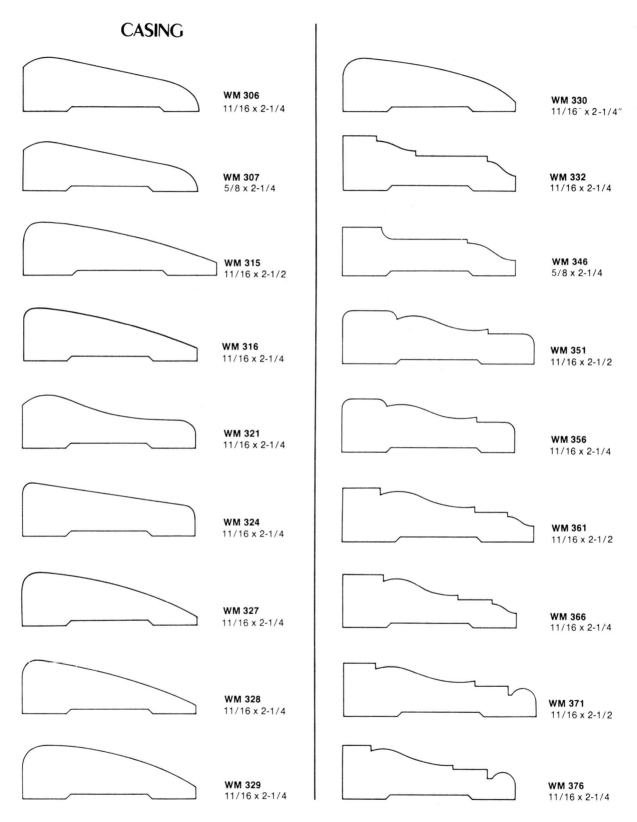

WM 306
11/16 x 2-1/4

WM 307
5/8 x 2-1/4

WM 315
11/16 x 2-1/2

WM 316
11/16 x 2-1/4

WM 321
11/16 x 2-1/4

WM 324
11/16 x 2-1/4

WM 327
11/16 x 2-1/4

WM 328
11/16 x 2-1/4

WM 329
11/16 x 2-1/4

WM 330
11/16" x 2-1/4"

WM 332
11/16 x 2-1/4

WM 346
5/8 x 2-1/4

WM 351
11/16 x 2-1/2

WM 356
11/16 x 2-1/4

WM 361
11/16 x 2-1/2

WM 366
11/16 x 2-1/4

WM 371
11/16 x 2-1/2

WM 376
11/16 x 2-1/4

Illus. 22-2.

CASING

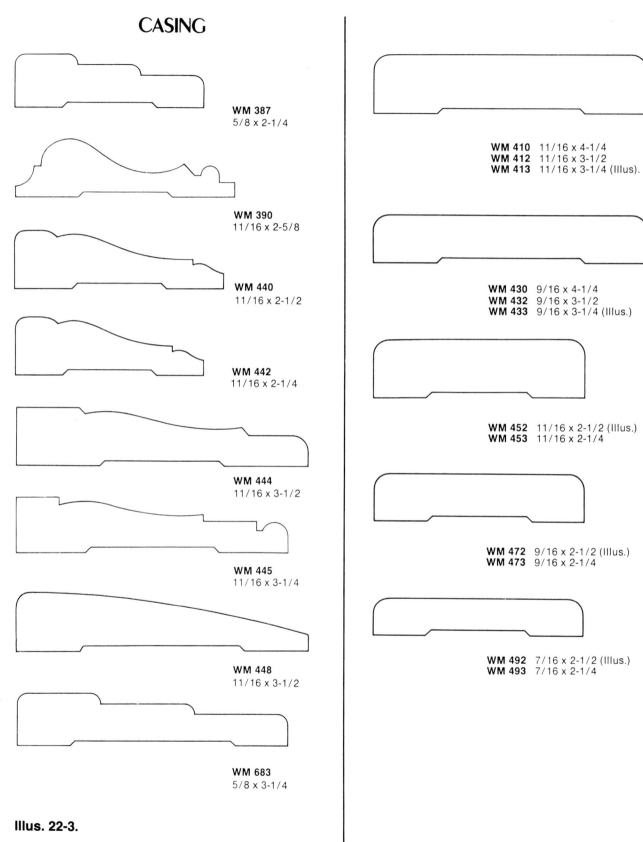

WM 387
5/8 x 2-1/4

WM 390
11/16 x 2-5/8

WM 440
11/16 x 2-1/2

WM 442
11/16 x 2-1/4

WM 444
11/16 x 3-1/2

WM 445
11/16 x 3-1/4

WM 448
11/16 x 3-1/2

WM 683
5/8 x 3-1/4

WM 410   11/16 x 4-1/4
WM 412   11/16 x 3-1/2
WM 413   11/16 x 3-1/4 (Illus).

WM 430   9/16 x 4-1/4
WM 432   9/16 x 3-1/2
WM 433   9/16 x 3-1/4 (Illus.)

WM 452   11/16 x 2-1/2 (Illus.)
WM 453   11/16 x 2-1/4

WM 472   9/16 x 2-1/2 (Illus.)
WM 473   9/16 x 2-1/4

WM 492   7/16 x 2-1/2 (Illus.)
WM 493   7/16 x 2-1/4

Illus. 22-3.

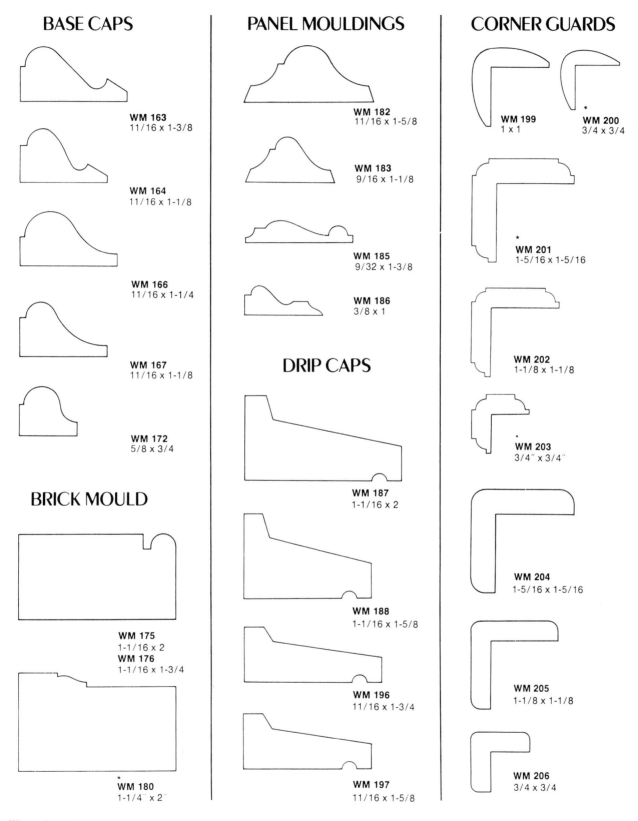

BASE CAPS

WM 163
11/16 x 1-3/8

WM 164
11/16 x 1-1/8

WM 166
11/16 x 1-1/4

WM 167
11/16 x 1-1/8

WM 172
5/8 x 3/4

BRICK MOULD

WM 175
1-1/16 x 2
WM 176
1-1/16 x 1-3/4

*
WM 180
1-1/4" x 2"

PANEL MOULDINGS

WM 182
11/16 x 1-5/8

WM 183
9/16 x 1-1/8

WM 185
9/32 x 1-3/8

WM 186
3/8 x 1

DRIP CAPS

WM 187
1-1/16 x 2

WM 188
1-1/16 x 1-5/8

WM 196
11/16 x 1-3/4

WM 197
11/16 x 1-5/8

CORNER GUARDS

WM 199
1 x 1

*
WM 200
3/4 x 3/4

*
WM 201
1-5/16 x 1-5/16

WM 202
1-1/8 x 1-1/8

.
WM 203
3/4" x 3/4"

WM 204
1-5/16 x 1-5/16

WM 205
1-1/8 x 1-1/8

WM 206
3/4 x 3/4

Illus. 22-4.

CROWNS

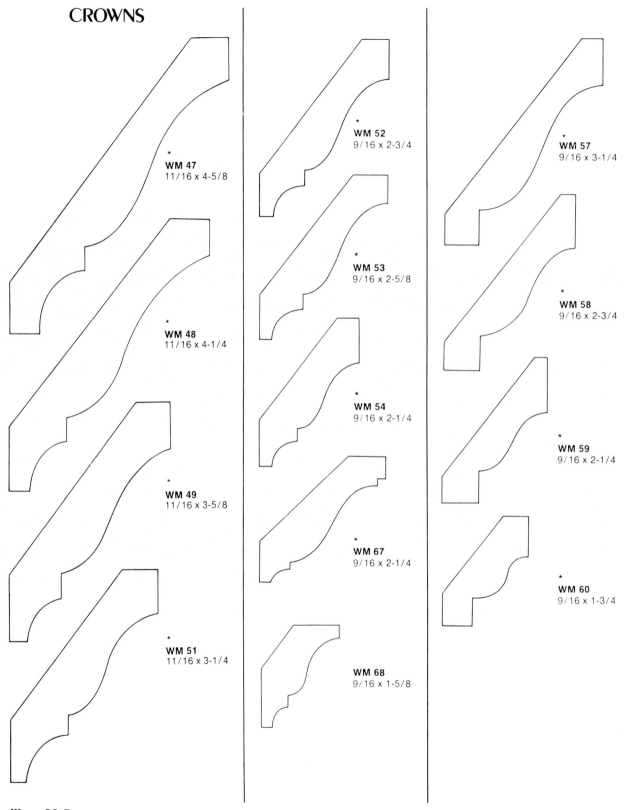

*
WM 47
11/16 x 4-5/8

*
WM 48
11/16 x 4-1/4

*
WM 49
11/16 x 3-5/8

*
WM 51
11/16 x 3-1/4

*
WM 52
9/16 x 2-3/4

*
WM 53
9/16 x 2-5/8

*
WM 54
9/16 x 2-1/4

*
WM 67
9/16 x 2-1/4

WM 68
9/16 x 1-5/8

*
WM 57
9/16 x 3-1/4

*
WM 58
9/16 x 2-3/4

*
WM 59
9/16 x 2-1/4

*
WM 60
9/16 x 1-3/4

Illus. 22-5.

222

BEDS

COVES

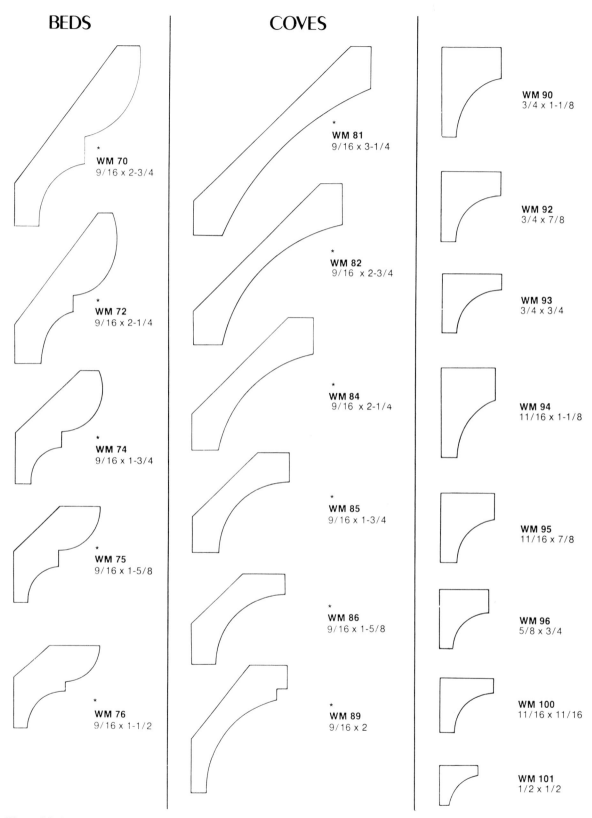

WM 70
9/16 x 2-3/4

WM 72
9/16 x 2-1/4

WM 74
9/16 x 1-3/4

WM 75
9/16 x 1-5/8

WM 76
9/16 x 1-1/2

WM 81
9/16 x 3-1/4

WM 82
9/16 x 2-3/4

WM 84
9/16 x 2-1/4

WM 85
9/16 x 1-3/4

WM 86
9/16 x 1-5/8

WM 89
9/16 x 2

WM 90
3/4 x 1-1/8

WM 92
3/4 x 7/8

WM 93
3/4 x 3/4

WM 94
11/16 x 1-1/8

WM 95
11/16 x 7/8

WM 96
5/8 x 3/4

WM 100
11/16 x 11/16

WM 101
1/2 x 1/2

Illus. 22-6.

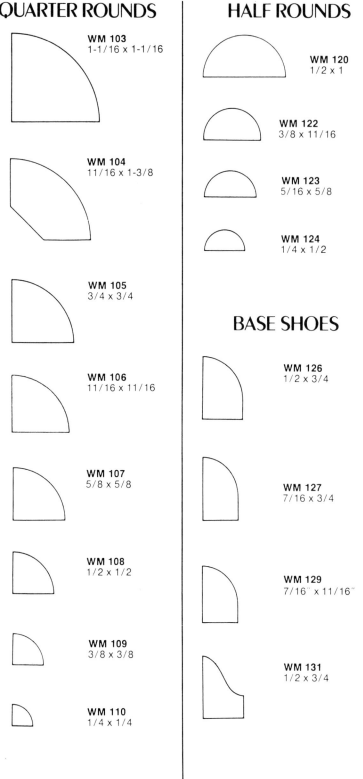

QUARTER ROUNDS

WM 103
1-1/16 x 1-1/16

WM 104
11/16 x 1-3/8

WM 105
3/4 x 3/4

WM 106
11/16 x 11/16

WM 107
5/8 x 5/8

WM 108
1/2 x 1/2

WM 109
3/8 x 3/8

WM 110
1/4 x 1/4

HALF ROUNDS

WM 120
1/2 x 1

WM 122
3/8 x 11/16

WM 123
5/16 x 5/8

WM 124
1/4 x 1/2

BASE SHOES

WM 126
1/2 x 3/4

WM 127
7/16 x 3/4

WM 129
7/16" x 11/16"

WM 131
1/2 x 3/4

FLAT ASTRAGALS

WM 133
11/16 x 1-3/4

WM 134
11/16 x 1-3/8

WM 135
7/16 x 3/4

SHELF EDGE/ SCREEN MOULD

WM 137
3/8 x 3/4

WM 138
5/16 x 5/8

WM 140
1/4 x 3/4

WM 141
1/4" x 5/8"

WM 142
1/4 x 3/4

WM 144
1/4 x 3/4

GLASS BEADS

WM 147
1/2 x 9/16

WM 148
3/8 x 3/8

Illus. 22-7

LATTICE

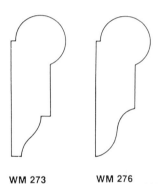

WM 265
9/32 x 1-3/4

WM 266
9/32 x 1-5/8

WM 267
9/32 x 1-3/8

WM 268
9/32 x 1-1/8

Lattice also available
in 1/4 thickness.

PICTURE
MOULDINGS

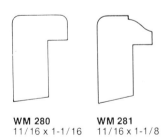

WM 273
11/16 x 1-3/4

WM 276
11/16 x 1-3/4

BACK BANDS

WM 280
11/16 x 1-1/16

WM 281
11/16 x 1-1/8

WAINSCOT/PLY
CAP MOULDINGS

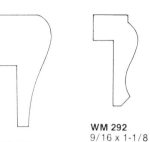

WM 290
11/16 x 1-3/8

WM 292
9/16 x 1-1/8

WM 294
11/16 x 1-1/8

WM 295
1/2 x 1-1/4

WM 296
3/4 x 3/4

CHAIR RAILS

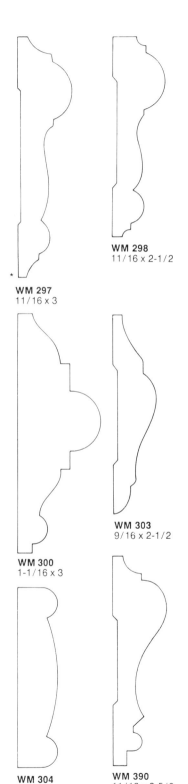

*
WM 297
11/16 x 3

WM 298
11/16 x 2-1/2

WM 300
1-1/16 x 3

WM 303
9/16 x 2-1/2

WM 304
1/2 x 2-1/4

WM 390
11/16 x 2-5/8

Illus. 22-8.

PANEL STRIPS/MULLION CASINGS

WM 955 3/8 x 2-1/4
WM 956 3/8 x 2
WM 957 3/8 x 1-3/4

WM 960 3/8 x 2-1/4
WM 962 3/8 x 2
WM 963 3/8 x 1-3/4

WM 965 3/8 x 2-1/4
WM 967 3/8 x 2
WM 968 3/8 x 1-3/4

WM 970 3/8 x 2-1/4
WM 972 3/8 x 2
WM 973 3/8 x 1-3/4

WM 975 3/8 x 2-1/4
WM 977 3/8 x 2
WM 978 3/8 x 1-3/4

WM 980 3/8 x 2-1/4
WM 982 3/8 x 2
WM 983 3/8 x 1-3/4

WM 985 3/8 x 2-1/4
WM 987 3/8 x 2
WM 988 3/8 x 1-3/4

SHELF CLEAT

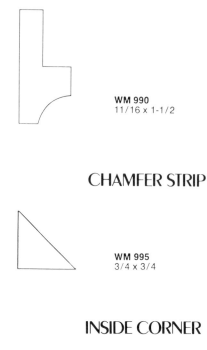

WM 990
11/16 x 1-1/2

CHAMFER STRIP

WM 995
3/4 x 3/4

INSIDE CORNER

WM 999
5/16 x 1

FLAT STOOLS

WM 1021
11/16" x width specified

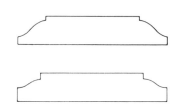

RABBETED STOOLS

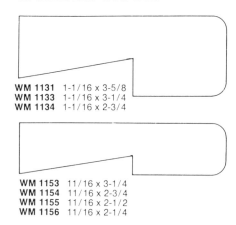

WM 1131 1-1/16 x 3-5/8
WM 1133 1-1/16 x 3-1/4
WM 1134 1-1/16 x 2-3/4

WM 1153 11/16 x 3-1/4
WM 1154 11/16 x 2-3/4
WM 1155 11/16 x 2-1/2
WM 1156 11/16 x 2-1/4

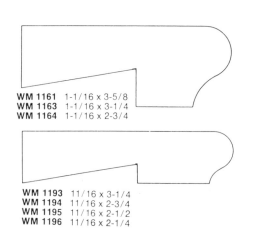

WM 1161 1-1/16 x 3-5/8
WM 1163 1-1/16 x 3-1/4
WM 1164 1-1/16 x 2-3/4

WM 1193 11/16 x 3-1/4
WM 1194 11/16 x 2-3/4
WM 1195 11/16 x 2-1/2
WM 1196 11/16 x 2-1/4

Illus. 22-9.

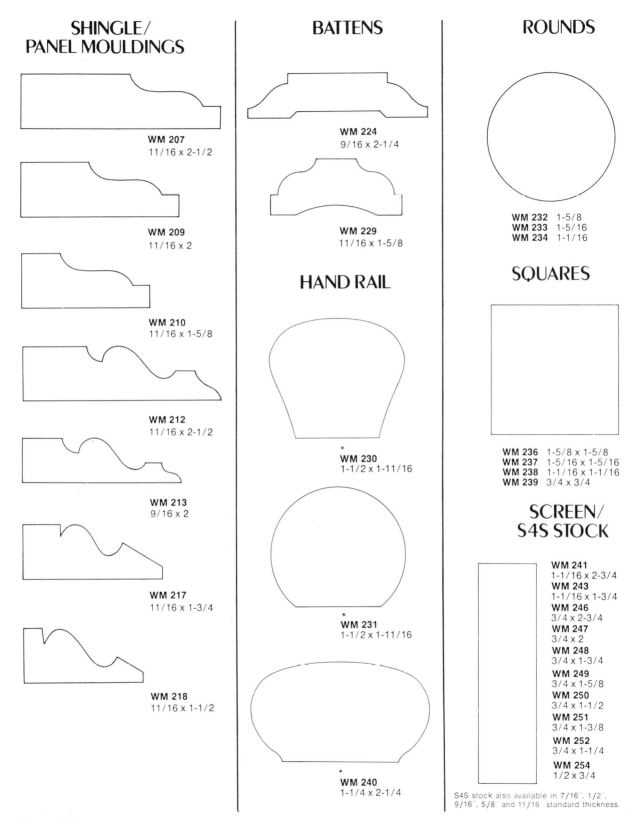

SHINGLE/ PANEL MOULDINGS

WM 207
11/16 x 2-1/2

WM 209
11/16 x 2

WM 210
11/16 x 1-5/8

WM 212
11/16 x 2-1/2

WM 213
9/16 x 2

WM 217
11/16 x 1-3/4

WM 218
11/16 x 1-1/2

BATTENS

WM 224
9/16 x 2-1/4

WM 229
11/16 x 1-5/8

HAND RAIL

*
WM 230
1-1/2 x 1-11/16

*
WM 231
1-1/2 x 1-11/16

*
WM 240
1-1/4 x 2-1/4

ROUNDS

WM 232   1-5/8
WM 233   1-5/16
WM 234   1-1/16

SQUARES

WM 236   1-5/8 x 1-5/8
WM 237   1-5/16 x 1-5/16
WM 238   1-1/16 x 1-1/16
WM 239   3/4 x 3/4

SCREEN/ S4S STOCK

WM 241
1-1/16 x 2-3/4
WM 243
1-1/16 x 1-3/4
WM 246
3/4 x 2-3/4
WM 247
3/4 x 2
WM 248
3/4 x 1-3/4
WM 249
3/4 x 1-5/8
WM 250
3/4 x 1-1/2
WM 251
3/4 x 1-3/8
WM 252
3/4 x 1-1/4
WM 254
1/2 x 3/4

S4S stock also available in 7/16", 1/2",
9/16", 5/8" and 11/16" standard thickness.

Illus. 22-10.

STOPS

WM 813	7/16 x 2-1/4
WM 814	7/16 x 1-3/4
WM 815	7/16 x 1-5/8
WM 816	7/16 x 1-3/8 (Illus.)
WM 817	7/16 x 1-1/4
WM 818	7/16 x 1-1/8
WM 820	7/16 x 7/8

WM 823	3/8 x 2-1/4
WM 824	3/8 x 1-3/4
WM 825	3/8 x 1-5/8
WM 826	3/8 x 1-3/8 (Illus.)
WM 827	3/8 x 1-1/4
WM 828	3/8 x 1-1/8
WM 830	3/8 x 7/8
WM 831	3/8 x 3/4

WM 843	7/16 x 2-1/4
WM 844	7/16 x 1-3/4
WM 845	7/16 x 1-5/8
WM 846	7/16 x 1-3/8 (Illus.)
WM 847	7/16 x 1-1/4
WM 848	7/16 x 1-1/8
WM 850	7/16 x 7/8
WM 851	7/16 x 3/4

WM 853	3/8 x 2-1/4
WM 854	3/8 x 1-3/4
WM 855	3/8 x 1-5/8
WM 856	3/8 x 1-3/8 (Illus.)
WM 857	3/8 x 1-1/4
WM 858	3/8 x 1-1/8
WM 860	3/8 x 7/8
WM 861	3/8 x 3/4

WM 873	7/16 x 2-1/4
WM 874	7/16 x 1-3/4
WM 875	7/16 x 1-5/8
WM 876	7/16 x 1-3/8 (Illus.)
WM 877	7/16 x 1-1/4
WM 878	7/16 x 1-1/8
WM 880	7/16 x 7/8
WM 881	7/16 x 3/4

WM 883	3/8 x 2-1/4
WM 884	3/8 x 1-3/4
WM 885	3/8 x 1-5/8
WM 886	3/8 x 1-3/8 (Illus.)
WM 887	3/8 x 1-1/4
WM 888	3/8 x 1-1/8
WM 890	3/8 x 7/8
WM 891	3/8 x 3/4

WM 903	7/16 x 2-1/4
WM 904	7/16 x 1-3/4
WM 905	7/16 x 1-5/8
WM 906	7/16 x 1-3/8 (Illus.)
WM 907	7/16 x 1-1/4
WM 908	7/16 x 1-1/8
WM 910	7/16 x 7/8
WM 911	7/16 x 3/4

WM 913	3/8 x 2-1/4
WM 914	3/8 x 1-3/4
WM 915	3/8 x 1-5/8
WM 916	3/8 x 1-3/8 (Illus.)
WM 917	3/8 x 1-1/4
WM 918	3/8 x 1-1/8
WM 920	3/8 x 7/8
WM 921	3/8 x 3/4

WM 933	7/16 x 2-1/4
WM 934	7/16 x 1-3/4
WM 935	7/16 x 1-5/8
WM 936	7/16 x 1-3/8 (Illus.)
WM 937	7/16 x 1-1/4
WM 938	7/16 x 1-1/8
WM 940	7/16 x 7/8
WM 941	7/16 x 3/4

WM 943	3/8 x 2-1/4
WM 944	3/8 x 1-3/4
WM 945	3/8 x 1-5/8
WM 946	3/8 x 1-3/8 (Illus.)
WM 947	3/8 x 1-1/4
WM 948	3/8 x 1-1/8
WM 950	3/8 x 7/8
WM 951	3/8 x 3/4

WM 953	7/16 x Width Specified

WM 954	3/8 x Width Specified

Illus. 22-11.

228

T-ASTRAGALS

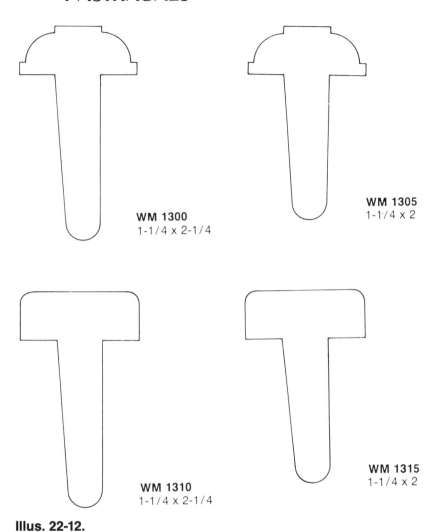

WM 1300
1-1/4 x 2-1/4

WM 1305
1-1/4 x 2

WM 1310
1-1/4 x 2-1/4

WM 1315
1-1/4 x 2

Illus. 22-12.

APPENDICES

Metric Equivalents

CONVERSION OF FRACTIONS OF AN INCH TO MILLIMETERS

Fraction	mm	Fraction	mm	Fraction	mm	Fraction	mm	Fraction	mm	Fraction	mm
1/64	0.40	3/16	4.76	23/64	9.13	17/32	13.49	11/16	17.46	27/32	21.43
1/32	0.79	13/64	5.16	3/8	9.53	35/64	13.89	45/64	17.86	55/64	21.83
3/64	1.19	7/32	5.56	25/64	9.92	9/16	14.29	23/32	18.26	7/8	22.23
1/16	1.59	15/64	5.95	13/32	10.32	37/64	14.68	47/64	18.65	57/64	22.62
5/64	1.98	1/4	6.35	27/64	10.72	19/32	15.08	3/4	19.05	29/32	23.02
3/32	2.38	17/64	6.75	7/16	11.11	39/64	15.48	49/64	19.45	59/64	23.42
7/64	2.78	9/32	7.14	29/64	11.51	5/8	15.88	25/32	19.84	15/16	23.81
1/8	3.18	19/64	7.54	15/32	11.91	41/64	16.27	51/64	20.24	61/64	24.21
9/64	3.57	5/16	7.94	31/64	12.31	21/32	16.67	13/16	20.64	31/32	24.61
5/32	3.97	21/64	8.33	1/2	12.70	43/64	17.07	53/64	21.03	63/64	25.00
11/64	4.37	11/32	8.73	33/64	13.10						

CONVERSION OF MILLIMETERS INTO INCHES

mm	0	1	2	3	4	5	6	7	8	9
					Millimeters					
					Fractions of an inch					
0	in.		3/64	5/64	1/8	5/32	13/64	15/64	9/32	5/16	23/64
10		25/64	7/16	15/22	33/64	35/64	19/32	5/8	43/64	45/64	3/4
20		25/32	53/64	55/64	29/32	15/16	63/64				
	1							1/32	1/16	7/64	9/64
30		3/16	7/32	17/64	19/64	11/32	3/8	27/64	29/64	1/2	17/32
40		37/64	39/64	21/32	11/16	47/64	49/64	18/16	27/32	57/64	59/64
50		31/32									
	2		1/64	3/64	3/32	1/8	11/64	13/64	1/4	9/32	21/64
60		23/64	13/32	7/16	31/64	33/64	9/16	19/32	41/64	43/64	23/32
70		3/4	51/64	53/64	7/8	29/32	61/64	63/64			
	3							1/32	5/64	7/64	
80		5/32	3/16	15/64	17/64	5/16	11/32	25/64	27/64	15/32	1/2
90		35/64	37/64	5/8	21/32	45/64	47/64	25/32	13/16	55/64	57/64
100		15/16	31/32								
	4			4/64	1/16	3/32	9/64	11/64	7/32	1/4	19/64

Example 38 mm 1-1/2 in., 65 mm 2-9/16 in.

CONVERSION OF METERS INTO FEET

m	0	1	2	3	4	5	6	7	8	9
0		3.28	6.56	9.84	13.12	16.40	19.69	22.97	26.25	29.53
10	32.81	36.09	39.37	42.65	45.93	49.21	52.49	55.77	59.06	62.34
20	65.62	68.90	72.18	75.46	78.74	82.02	85.30	88.58	91.86	95.14
30	98.43	101.71	104.99	108.27	111.55	114.83	118.11	121.39	124.67	127.95
40	131.23	134.51	137.80	141.08	144.36	147.64	150.92	154.20	157.48	160.76
50	164.04	167.32	170.60	173.88	177.17	180.45	183.73	187.01	190.29	193.57
60	196.85	200.13	203.41	206.69	209.97	213.25	216.54	219.82	223.10	226.38
70	229.66	232.94	236.22	239.50	242.78	246.06	249.34	252.62	255.91	259.19
80	262.47	265.75	269.03	272.31	275.59	278.87	282.15	285.43	288.71	291.99
90	295.28	298.56	301.84	305.12	308.40	311.70	314.96	318.24	321.52	324.80

CONVERSION OF FEET INTO METERS

ft.	0	1	2	3	4	5	6	7	8	9
0		0.30	0.61	0.91	1.22	1.52	1.83	2.13	2.44	2.74
10	3.05	3.35	3.66	3.96	4.27	4.57	4.88	5.18	5.49	5.79
20	6.10	6.40	6.71	7.01	7.32	7.62	7.92	8.23	8.53	8.84
30	9.14	9.45	9.75	10.06	10.36	10.67	10.97	11.28	11.58	11.89
40	12.19	12.50	12.80	13.11	13.41	13.72	14.02	14.33	14.63	14.94
50	15.24	15.54	15.85	16.15	16.46	16.76	17.07	17.37	17.68	17.98
60	18.29	18.59	18.90	19.20	19.51	19.81	20.12	20.42	20.73	21.03
70	21.34	21.64	21.95	22.25	22.56	22.86	23.16	23.47	23.77	24.08
80	24.38	24.69	24.99	25.30	25.60	25.91	26.22	26.52	26.82	26.21
90	27.43	27.74	28.04	28.35	28.65	28.96	29.26	29.57	29.87	30.18

CONVERSION OF CENTIMETERS INTO INCHES

cm	0	1	2	3	4	5	6	7	8	9
0		0.394	0.787	1.181	1.575	1.969	2.362	2.756	3.150	3.543
10	3.937	4.331	4.724	5.118	5.512	5.906	6.299	6.693	7.087	7.480
20	7.874	8.268	8.661	9.055	9.449	9.842	10.236	10.630	11.024	11.417
30	11.811	12.205	12.598	12.992	13.386	13.780	14.173	14.567	14.961	15.354
40	15.748	16.142	16.535	16.929	17.323	17.717	18.110	18.504	18.898	19.291
50	19.685	20.079	20.472	20.866	21.260	21.654	22.047	22.441	22.835	23.228
60	23.622	24.016	24.410	24.803	25.197	25.591	25.984	26.378	26.772	27.165
70	27.559	27.953	28.346	28.740	29.134	29.528	29.921	30.315	30.709	31.102
80	31.496	31.890	32.283	32.677	33.071	33.465	33.858	34.252	34.646	35.039
90	35.433	35.827	36.220	36.614	37.008	37.402	37.795	38.189	38.583	38.976

CONVERSION OF INCHES INTO CENTIMETERS

inch	0	1	2	3	4	5	6	7	8	9
0		2.54	5.08	7.62	10.16	12.70	15.24	17.78	20.32	22.86
10	25.40	27.94	30.48	33.02	35.56	38.10	40.64	43.18	45.72	48.26
20	50.80	53.34	55.88	58.42	60.96	63.50	66.04	68.58	71.12	73.66
30	76.20	78.74	81.28	83.82	86.36	88.90	91.44	93.98	96.52	99.06
40	101.60	104.14	106.68	109.22	111.76	114.30	116.84	119.38	121.92	124.46
50	127.00	129.54	132.08	134.62	137.16	139.70	142.24	144.78	147.32	149.86
60	152.40	154.94	157.48	160.02	162.56	165.10	167.64	170.18	172.72	175.26
70	177.80	180.34	182.88	185.42	187.96	190.50	193.04	195.58	198.12	200.66
80	203.20	205.74	208.28	210.82	213.36	215.90	218.44	220.98	223.52	226.06
90	228.60	231.14	233.68	236.22	238.76	241.30	243.84	246.38	248.92	251.46

Glossary

The National Sash and Door Jobbers Association is made up of wholesale millwork distributors around the United States. This group provides formal millwork training to its members and has allowed us to reproduce the following glossary and abbreviation guides. Hopefully, they will assist you in your millwork research.

Millwork and Associated Terms

(Contains current terms, as well as historical or obsolete terms, for reference purposes)

A

ACTIVE SOLAR HEAT GAIN—solar heat that passes through a material and is captured by mechanical means—ex-computerized solar collectors take advantage of active solar heat gain.

ADHESIVE—a substance capable of holding material together by surface attachment; it is a general term and includes many adhesives inclusive of "glue."

A FRAME—a method of moulding storage whereby the end piled mouldings on each side lean against a central bar; also a contemporary architectural design of a structure.

AIR DRIED—wood seasoned by exposure to the atmosphere, in the open or under cover, without artificial heat; varying percentages of moisture content can exist in "air dried" wood; also "air seasoned."

AIR INFILTRATION—the amount of air that passes between a window sash and frame, or a door panel and frame; for windows it is measured in terms of cubic feet of air per minute per square foot of area, and for doors, it is measured in terms of cubic feet of air per minute per foot of crack.

ANGLE BAY WINDOW—a composite of three or more windows, with flanking units projecting from the wall, usually at a 30-degree or 45-degree angle.

ANGLE BRACE—a wood member, usually 24″ in length, nailed across a sash or window frame at one or both of the upper corners while the frame is in the squared position in order to maintain squareness prior to installation; used in conjunction with a "spacer brace."

ANNUAL GROWTH RING—a tree's growth layer added during a single growth year, including springwood and summerwood; the discontinuity of cell size between summer growth and that of the following spring resulting in a so-called "ring."

APRON—a piece of horizontal sash or window trim applied against the wall immediately below the stool; serves to conceal the joint made by the sash or window frame sill and the plaster on interior finish surface.

ARCHITRAVE—the moulding or trim around a door opening, especially in regards to a front entrance; also a "surfaced four sides" member of a mantel or front entrance which forms part of the pilaster; a side-of-door trim; the lowest part of an entablature.

ASTRAGAL—an interior moulding attached to one of a pair of doors or sash in order to prevent swinging through; also used with sliding doors to ensure tighter fitting where the doors meet; also a small semi-circular moulding or bead encircling a column or post below the capital or cap.

Flat astragal—a non-rabbeted astragal applied to swing doors; the astragal is applied to the face of the meeting stile of one of the doors.

Sliding astragal—an astragal so worked so as to cover the meeting joint of sliding doors.

T astragal—an astragal, T-like in shape, which is rabbeted to the approximate thickness of the swinging door.

AWNING SASH—see Sash.

AWNING WINDOW UNIT—a combination of frame, one or more operative awning sash weatherstrip, operating device and at the option of the manufacturer screen and/or storm sash assembled as a complete and properly operating unit; unit may contain one or more fixed or nonoperative sash in combination with the operative sash.

B

BACKBAND—a narrow rabbeted moulding applied to the outside corner and edge of interior window and door casing to create a "heavy trim" appearance; increases both ornamentation and width of the trim.

BACK SPLASH—the extension of a counter top material up the wall in order to protect it; cove construction is most commonly employed.

BALANCE—see Overhead Balance; Sash Balance.

BALANCED CONSTRUCTION—arrangement of plies in pairs about the core so that the grains of opposite plies are parallel and at right angles to adjoining plies; contains an odd number of plies.

BALANCING—the raising and lowering of sash as well as holding its position at any desired level; sash activation.

BALUSTER—square or turned spindle-like vertical stair members supporting the stair rail.

Dovetail baluster—a baluster with a dovetail base for attachment to the stair tread.

Flat baluster—relatively thin slat-like sawn baluster.

Pin-turned baluster—a baluster with a dowel-like base to fit the bored hole of the stair tread.

Square baluster (baluster stock)—a square baluster which is surfaced four sides and primarily used for exterior balustrades; usually inventoried in lineal footage (nonspecified lengths).

Turned baluster—a baluster which has been turned or shaped on a lathe.

BALUSTRADE—a railing consisting of a series of balusters resting on a base, usually the treads, and supporting a continuous horizontal stair or hand rail; also applies to a roof and known as "belvedere"; see Belvedere.

BAND MOULDING—a flat decorative or protective strip that is flush or raised above the surface; a moulding somewhat similar to a panel moulding as well as an apron profile: used to trim mantels, china cabinets, etc.; "Band Board" is similar to fascia.

BAND-SAWN—sawn by means of a band saw as contrasted with circular saw.

BAR—a narrow rabbeted, horizontal or vertical sash or door member extending the total length or width of the glass opening; extends from rail to rail or stile to stile; also called "light bar"; diagonal bars may extend from stile to rail or vice versa.

Bar moulding—a rabbeted moulding used as nosing for a counter corner, specifically a bar; also bar nosing.

Transom bar—see Transom.

BARBED DOWEL PIN—steel pin driven into tenon of the door rail to prevent future withdrawal from the joint formed with the door stile.

BARGE BOARD—see Verge Board.

BARK—areas of fibre from outside the tree.

BASE—a moulding applied around the perimeter of a room at the point of intersection of the walls and finish floor; base shoe is generally used with it, forming a two-member base; also baseboard, mopboard or skirting.

Base block—see Plinth Block.

Base shoe—see Shoe.

Base shoe corner—a moulding applied in the corner of a room in lieu of mitring base shoe moulding; eliminates the collecting of dust in the corner; also corner block.

Base moulding—a relatively small moulding applied to the top of the base; when used with a two-member base it forms a three-member base; also base cap.

Pilaster base—see Plinth Block.

Three-member base—a base assembly formed by combining a base moulding with a two-member base.

Two-member base—see Base.

BASEMENT SASH UNIT (cellar sash unit)—a sash unit, usually of the inswinging or hopper sash type, used for basement or cellar sash openings; usually consists of one, two or three glass lights; may include screens and storm panels.

BATTEN—a moulding run to a pattern on both edges or surfaced four sides to conceal the joint of two adjacent boards in the same plane; also "batts"; see Door.

Reversible batten—a batten square edge on one face and reeded or beaded on the reverse.

BAY WINDOW—three or more individual windows projecting from the wall in a gently curved contour.

BEAD—a semicircular or rounded profile worked on wood; also a small moulding to secure glass or panels to doors, hence "glass bead."

Corner bead—a moulding used to protect corners, especially plastered corners; also corner guard, corner moulding, outside corner.

Glass bead—see Bead.

Return bead—see Corner Bead.

Staff bead—a moulding similar to "brick" moulding sometimes termed "staff" moulding.

BEAD AND COVE—a combination of a "bead" and a "cove" profile.

BEARING WALL—a wall which supports any vertical load in addition to its own weight.

BED MOULDING—a moulding "plain" or "sprung" applied where two surfaces come together at an angle; profile commonly consists of a "bead and cove."

BELVEDERE—a platform on the roof of a house with a row of balusters or balustrades around its perimeter; sometimes "captain's" or "widow's walk."

BENT RADIUS MOULDING—moulding which is bent to conform to a required profile, e.g., the cove moulding on a circle-end starting stair tread; such moulding may be bent or curved by one of several methods.

BETWEEN GLASS—the measurement across the face of any wood part that separates two sheets of glass.

BEVEL—to cut to an angle other than a right angle, such as the edge of a board or door.

BEVELED EDGE—an edge of the door which forms an angle of less than 90 degrees with the wide face of the door, such as a 3-degree beveled edge.

BILL OF MATERIAL—a list of the material (inclusive of the number, size, species and grade of each piece) required for an item of millwork.

BLEEDING—exudation or the coming to the surface of resin or pitch in some species of wood, usually due to temperature and solvents contained in wood finishes.

BLIND—a wood assembly of stiles and rails to form a frame which encloses wood slats; used in conjunction with door and window frames; blinds may contain a panel in combination with the slats or louvres; see Door.

Rolling slat blind—a blind in which the slats or louvres open and close; also "movable slat blind."

Stationary slat blind—a blind in which the wood slats are fixed or stationary.

BLIND CUTOUTS—decorative cutout in the top panels of blinds and shutters; more commonly used designs are the crescent, pine tree, squirrel, fleur-de-lis, candlestick, cloverleaf, rooster, sailboat and acorn.

BLIND STOP—a sash or window frame member applied to the exterior vertical edge of the side and head jamb in order to serve as a stop for the top sash and to form with the brick moulding and/or casing a rabbet for the storm sash, screens, blinds and shutters.

Extension blind stop—a moulded window frame member usually of same thickness as blind stop that is tongued on one or two edges in order to engage a groove in the unexposed or back edge of the blind stop, thus increasing its width and improving the weather tightness of the frame; also a means of securing the frame to the structure; also known as "blind stop extender"; also "blind casing."

Reversible blind stop—see Reversible Extension Blind Stop.

Reversible extension blind stop—an extension blind stop that is rabbeted to receive either ½" or ²⁵⁄₃₂" sheathing; sometimes the term "reversible blind stop" refers to a blind stop that is beveled on each end to the same shape as the window or sash frame sill and further machined to allow its use on either the left or right side of the frame.

Wide blind stop—a solid wood blind stop greater than 1¼ inches in width which also performs the function of an extension blind stop.

BLIND STOP EXTENDER—see Blind Stop.

BLISTER—spot or area where veneer does not adhere.

BLUE STAIN—see Stain.

BOLECTION MOULDING—a moulding that covers the joint between two members with surfaces at different levels and projects beyond both surfaces; also the part of a moulding that projects beyond the surface of a panel; also bilection.

BOLT HOLE PLUG—a small round wood plug used to fill the hole bored into a "stair crook" when joining another crook or stair rail.

BOND—glue line.

BOOK SIZE—the height and width of a door prior to prefitting.

BOW—a form of "warp"; deviation flatwise from a straight line from end to end of a piece, measured at the point of greatest distance from the straight line.

Bow window—see Window.

BOX BAY WINDOW—a composite of three or more windows, with flanking units projecting from the wall at a 90-degree angle.

BRACE—applied to an assembled window unit to maintain its squareness; see Angle Brace.

BRACKET—a wood member originally intended to support verge boards, hoods for porches or stoops, overhangs and cornices; today, primarily decorative.

BRASHNESS—condition of wood characterized by a low resistance to shock and by abrupt failure across the grain without splintering.

BREAD BOARD (cutting or slicing board)—a sliding wood board, generally ¾" in thickness and of varying width and depth, usually installed immediately below the base kitchen cabinet counter or below the top drawer of the base unit; often used for a "chopping block"; also termed a "pullout leaf."

BREAD BOX (bread drawer)—usually refers to a metal box with a sliding top which is inserted into the wood drawer of a base kitchen cabinet unit; metal insert also termed "metal drawer liner."

BREAST—the measurement between the outside edges of the casing or pilasters of an entrance or mantel; also "overall width" of the mantel.

Breast (chimney)—that part of a chimney which projects from a wall where the chimney passes through a room; distance between outside edges of a chimney as it projects from a wall inside a room.

BRICK MOULDING—a moulding of window and exterior door frames that abuts the exterior facing material of the structure; serves as (1) the boundary moulding for brick or other siding material; (2) forms a rabbet for the screens and/or storm sash or combination door; also staff mould, staff bed, staff bead, brick casing.

Beaded brick moulding—brick moulding containing a bead on its face.

Steel sash brick moulding—a moulding to receive the lip of a steel sash or window and serve as a brick moulding and blind stop; moulding is applied on the head and two sides; also steel sash surround.

BRICK VENEER—usually a facing of brick for a wood frame exterior wall; also brick facing wood frame exterior wall; see Wood Frame Wall (brick veneer).

BRUSHING WOOD PRESERVATIVE TREATMENT—application of wood preservative or water repellent to wood by means of brushing.

BUCK—a jamb stud or header; wood buck.

Buck opening—the opening in a wall formed by the rough framing members; also stud opening.

BUILT-ON-THE-JOB—the construction of cabinets, mantels and other members of a structure on the construction site from material which has not been previously manufactured and specifically intended to such use; opposed to factory-built or prefabricated; also on-site.

BUILT-UP—assembled as contrasted to "knocked down" or unassembled; also "set up."

BULLNOSE—the rounded end or edge of a wood member, e.g., "bullnose starting stair tread"; often used interchangeably with the term "nosed."

BUNDLING—the tying together of the same or different parts of a window or door frame for transportation and warehousing; styles of bundling are A, B and C.

Style A bundling—a number of pieces of the same frame part, e.g., 20 pieces of head brick moulding for 3° × 6 × 1¾"—Brick veneer door frame.

Style B bundling—frame parts to assemble a complete frame.

Style C bundling—includes the vertical or horizontal (cross) members of a frame.

BURL—twisted grain in wood surrounding the centers of undeveloped buds; usually present in trees as a tumorous growth.

BUTT—a door "hinge," one leaf being mortised or routed into the door frame jamb and the other into the edge of the door; incorrectly called a "butt hinge" as the term "hinge" is usually applied to one which is attached to the surface of a door rather than to its edge such as a strap or T-hinge; "butt" consists of the round central part (knuckle), flat portions (leaves or flaps), and the "pin" which is inserted into the "knuckle"; "pin" can be loose pin butt (removable) or "fast" (non-removable).

Removable pin butt (loose pin butt)—a butt which contains a "loose" or removable pin; if pin is not removable it is termed a "fast" pin; used on interior doors, as well as storm and screen doors, in order to facilitate removal of door.

BUTT JOINT—a joint formed by square edge surfaces (ends, edges, faces) coming together; end butt joint, edge butt joint.

C

CABINET—case or box-like assembly consisting of shelves, doors and drawers and primarily used for storage.

China cabinet—a cabinet consisting of several closed or open shelves above a counter or stool and storage space below enclosed by a door.

CABINET DRAWER—a four-sided rectangular assembly with a bottom, which slides in and out of a cabinet; drawers may be of two types, namely "flush front" or "lip or rabbeted front."

Flush front cabinet drawer—a drawer whose front in a closed position is flush with or very slightly recessed below the face or surface of the cabinet; also square edge or non-rabbeted.

Rabbeted front cabinet drawer—a drawer whose edges are "lipped" or rabbeted so that the drawer front, in a closed position, extends beyond the face or surface of the cabinet; also lip front drawer.

CABINET DRAWER GUIDE—a wood strip, surfaced four sides or rabbeted, to guide the drawer as it slides in and out of its opening; drawers may have "center guides", "side guides" or "suspended side guides."

CABINET DRAWER KICKER—a wood

cabinet member immediately above and generally at the center of a drawer to prevent its tilting downward when pullout out; a "kicker" is only required when a space exists above the drawer.

CABINET DRAWER RUNNER—a narrow wood member of the cabinet on which the bottom edges of the drawer sides rest; all cabinet construction does not contain drawer runners.

CABINET FILLER—narrow wood member (usually up to 4″ in width) used to fill the space between wall cabinet and soffit or ceiling or between the adjacent base cabinets or base cabinet and the wall.

CABINET WORK—woodwork involving a considerable amount of machine or hand joinery.

CAP—the upper member of an entrance, wainscot, partition or pilaster; also cap trim, wainscot cap, dado moulding, chair rail cap; also capital.

Dado cap—the upper edge or top of the wainscot; often analogous to "chair rail"; the cap for the dado of the wainscot, hence wainscot cap.

Drip cap—a moulding to direct water away from a non-masonry-faced structure so as to prevent seepage under the exterior facing material; usually employed over window and exterior door frames and sometimes around the perimeter of the structure immediately above the foundation wall; also "water table."

Entrance cap—the portion of an entrance above the door opening; also "entrance head."

Partition cap and shoe—partition cap is a ploughed (plowed) moulding serving as the top horizontal member of a partition (a wall that subdivides spaces within any story of a building); partition shoe is fastened to the floor and serves as a sole plate; it is ploughed (plowed) to receive the partition.

CAPITAL—marks termination of shaft and beginning of horizontal support of beam (entablature) or lintel or of arch and support; same as cap.

CAP MOULDING—a moulding sometimes used in conjunction with window or door head casing in order to elaborate on the simple trim design.

CAPE COD—an early American style of architecture particularly well suited to the wind-swept coast of Massachusetts; structure was set low with a massive roof calculated to deflect the breezes while offering a minimum of resistance to the Atlantic gales; roof swept down to the first-floor level, forming a plain pitched roof large in proportion to wall height at front and rear; never more than 1½ story in height and devoid of upstairs windows save in the gable ends; large chimney was always in center of front elevation.

CARPENTER ANT—large or small black or brown ants sometimes found in structural timbers or buildings; these ants use the wood for shelter rather than food and if left undisturbed can enlarge in a few years their tunnels to the point where replacement or repairs are necessary.

CARPET STRIP—a moulding, usually "quarter round," to secure the carpeting at the wall; base shoe is sometimes used.

CASED OPENING—an interior opening without a door that is finished with jambs and trim.

CASEMENT SASH—see Sash.

CASEMENT SASH UNIT—a combination of frame, casement sash, weatherstrip and operating device assembled as a complete and properly operating unit; screens and/or storm sash are optional.

CASEMENT WINDOW—window with sash hinged at the sides; it usually swings open by means of a crank-type hardware system.

CASEWORK—all the parts that constitute a finished case or cabinet, inclusive of doors, drawers and shelves; "casework" implies work which is three-dimensional.

CASING—moulded or surfaced-four-sides pieces of various widths and thicknesses for trimming out door and window openings; casing may be classified as "exterior" or "interior" as far as window and exterior door frames are concerned; also classified as "side" or "head" casing.

Blind casing—see Blind Stop (Extension blind stop).

Door casing—same as "casing"; may be "interior" or "exterior" door casing; "exterior" door casing installed only on the outside of exterior door frames, especially wood facing wood frame exterior walls; forms with the door jamb the rabbet for the combination or screen door.

Exterior casing (outside casing)—casing to trim the exterior of window and exterior door frames, to serve as the boundary moulding for the siding material, and to form a rabbet with the blind stop or jamb for the screen, storm sash, blind, shutter or combination door; exterior casing is most commonly used on wood facing wood frame exterior walls; three pieces of exterior casing are used for each frame, namely two side and one head; also exterior or outside lining.

Head casing—the horizontal casing across the top of the window or door opening.

Inner casing—an entrance member that fits over the outside edges of side and head jamb, thereby providing a base for the pilasters; entrance casing nearest the opening that provides base for pilasters; sometimes architrave.

Interior casing (inside casing)—casing to trim the interior of window and door frames; three pieces of casing are required, namely two of side casing and one of head; also

"window or door interior casing"; also inside lining.

Mullion casing—interior or exterior casing used to trim a mullion.

Outer casing—entrance casing furthest removed from the opening and which forms a foundation with the inner casing for the pilaster; also "back casing."

Side casing—vertical casing on either side of the window or door opening.

Window casing—same as "casing"; may be "interior" or "exterior" window casing; exterior window casing is most commonly installed on window frames for wood facing wood frame exterior walls; forms with the blind stop the rabbet for the storm sash or screen.

CAULK—to seal and make waterproof cracks and joints; e.g., joints around window and exterior door frames; also calk.

CAVETTO—a simple concave moulding; also termed "cove."

CELLAR SASH UNIT—see Basement Sash Unit.

CHAIR RAIL—an interior double-stuck moulding originally intended to be applied along the wall of a room to prevent the chair from marring the wall; sometimes used as "hook strip," batten and "wainscot cap"; also dado moulding, dado rail.

CHAMFER—a corner of a board beveled at a 45-degree angle; two boards butt-jointed and with chamfered edges form a "V" joint or right angle.

CHATTER—lines appearing across the panel at right angles to the grain giving the appearance of one or more corrugations resulting from bad setting of sanding equipment.

CHECK (season check)—a lengthwise separation of the wood that usually extends across the annual growth rings and commonly results from stresses set up in wood during seasoning.

Black checks—see Streak (Sound dark streaks; West Coast hemlock).

Door check—a mechanical device for self-closing of a door.

End check—a check occurring on the end of a wood member.

Surface check—a check occurring on the surface of a wood member.

CHECK STRIP—see Stop (Parting).

CHICKEN TRACKS—expression denoting scars which give the particular effect of a chicken's footprint, caused by air roots or vines. Small sections of chicken tracks appear to be part of the wood that are more highly densified. The problem of chicken track is the shape and number. It is approximately the same color as the surrounding wood but usually a little darker. Chicken track that generally follows the grain, and is of an individual line rather than a series of lines merging on each other, is not considered to be a defect.

CHIMNEY BREAST—see Breast.

CHINA CABINET COUNTER SHELF—the shelf of a china cabinet which separates the lower from the upper section or compartment; the lower compartment or section includes closed shelving (inclusive of drawers) whereas the upper section contains either open shelving or glazed cabinet doors; counter shelf usually extends beyond the front frame, thereby forming the stool.

CHOPPING BLOCK—a hardwood assembly, usually constructed of narrow hardwood strips which are laid on edge, glued and secured by metal bolts or dowels; the block comprises a section of the counter of the base kitchen cabinet units.

CLASSIC—refers to the orders of architecture as developed by the Greeks and Romans.

CLEAT (cleat joint)—a short narrow wood strip used to reinforce a butt edge joint; the strip may be joined to the butt edge members at their ends (drawing or bread boards) or across their faces; in either case, the grain of the wood strip or the cleat is at right angles to the other wood members; also used as end support for shelving; see Shelf Cleat and Screen Stock.

CLOSET POLE—a moulding circular in cross section, installed in clothes closets to accommodate clothes hangers; also "full round pole" and closet rod.

COLD SOAK TEST—a test to determine whether the bond between the plies of the plywood face, and between the plywood face and the stiles and rails of a hardwood veneered hollow-core flush door, will successfully withstand the effects of repeated wetting and drying.

COLONIAL—same as "traditional"; of or characteristic of the thirteen British colonies that eventually became the United States; sometimes separated into three periods, namely (1) Early American Colonial 1630–1700, (2) Georgian 1700–1790, and (3) Post-Colonial 1790–1820.

COLUMN—upright supporting member circular or rectangular in plan consisting of base, shaft and capital; when columns extend two or more stories to full height of structure they are sometimes termed "heroic columns."

COMBINATION STORM SASH AND SCREEN—a frame assembly of stiles and rails (usually 1⅛″ in thickness) containing a half screen and two glass storm panels; in summer the bottom storm panel is stored in the top of the combination frame and replaced by the screen panel; sometimes called "combination storm sash and screen unit" or simply "combination window unit."

COMPONENT BUILDING—various parts of a structure such as wall, floor or roof, assembled at the factory and transported to the building site for erection; also millwork component.

COMPOSITION FACE PANELS—a door face panel composed of a wood derivative.

CONCEALED NAILING—a technique of installation whereby a member of a structure does not expose the nail which secures it; e.g., an extension blind stop provides concealed nailing for a window unit.

CONDENSATION—add to present verbiage. (Usage—the higher the R-Value of a window or door, the less condensation will occur.)

CONDUCTION—the transfer of heat through matter, whether solid, liquid, or gas.

CONTEMPORARY—a style of architecture using today's materials, planning and methods; attention tends to be directed toward present family tastes and needs and free from full reliance on the traditional; a style of architecture lying somewhere between "traditional" and "modern" and partaking somewhat of both.

CONVECTION—a transfer of heat through a liquid or gas, when that medium hits against a solid surface. (Usage—"Forced convection" takes place outside when winds blow across a window pane; "natural convection" takes place inside when warmed or cooled air moves across the glass surface.)

CONVENTIONALLY HINGED—see Door (Hinged).

COPE—to cut or shape the end of a moulded wood member so that it will cover and fit the contour of the sticking coping.

CORE (Solid)—the innermost layer of section in flush door construction. Typical constructions are as follows:

Wood block—a solid core of wood blocks or strips.

Particleboard—a solid core of wood or other lignocellulose particles bonded together with a suitable binder, cured under heat and pressed into a rigid panel in a flat platen press.

Wood block, lined—a solid core of two parts: a central wood-block core bonded to two core liners of wood or other lignocellulose materials.

CORE (Hollow)—a core assembly of strips or other units of wood, wood derivative, or insulation board with intervening hollow cells or spaces which support the outer faces. Typical constructions are as follows:

Ladder—a hollow core composed of strips of wood, wood derivative, or insulation board, with the strips running either horizontally or vertically throughout the core area with air cells and/or spaces between the strips and supporting door faces.

Mesh or cellular—a hollow core composed of strips of wood, wood derivative, or insulation board, interlocked and running horizontally, vertically or diagonally throughout the core area with air cells and/or spaces between the strips and supporting the outer faces.

CORNER BLOCKS, MOULDED—square blocks used in lieu of mitring the side and head casing; "turns the corner" for door and window casing.

CORNER CABINET—see Kitchen Cabinet.

CORNER GUARD—see Bead (Corner).

CORNER MOULDING—see Bead (Corner).

CORNICE—the exterior trim of a structure at the meeting of the roof and wall; usually consists of boards and mouldings, namely bed moulding, soffit fascia and crown moulding; may be either "boxed" (closed), "open" or "plain" (simple); also the interior trim at the meeting of the ceiling and sidewalls; also the top part of the entablature.

Box cornice (closed cornice)—a cornice consisting of a fascia, plancier or soffit and frieze.

Open cornice—a cornice whereby the rafters are exposed at the eaves.

Plain cornice (simple cornice)—a cornice formed by a piece of crown moulding nailed to the end of the rafter and brought down against the side wall.

CORNICE MOULDINGS—mouldings such as crown, bed and cove applied in cornice construction.

COUNTER—top or working surface of a base kitchen cabinet.

COVE MOULDING—a moulding with a concave profile used primarily where two members meet at a right angle; a rounded inside corner; opposite to a bullnose; also scotia, cavetto, ceiling cornice.

COVE AND BEAD—a moulding profile consisting of a "cove" and a "bead"; also called "cove with a bead"; glass bead or stop.

CRACK PERIMETER—crack perimeter in feet of a door or window opening; also "sash crack perimeter"; for a double-hung window, equal to 3 times the width plus 2 times the height.

CROSSBAND—in 5-ply construction the layer of wood between the core and the face.

CROSSBANDED CONSTRUCTION—layers of wood glued together in which each layer has its grain at right angles to the adjacent layer or layers.

CROSS BREAK—separation (break) of the wood cells across the grain. Such breaks may be due to internal strains resulting from unequal longitudinal shrinkage, or to external forces.

CROSSBUCK—the panels of a door separated by intersecting diagonal rails and so arranged to simulate a sawhorse, especially one with the legs projecting above the cross bar; an arrangement of panels similar to the Roman numeral "X"; also sawbuck.

CROSSETTES—projecting "ears" formed by the casing at the top corners in a side of door trim; popular during Georgian period.

CROWN MOULDING—a sprung moulding used where two surfaces meet at an angle; usually applied wherever a larger angle is to be covered; also cornice moulding.

CUP—deviation flatwise from a straight line across the width of a piece measured at the point of greatest distance from the line; warp.

CUPOLA—a small vented four-sided roofed member usually installed on a roof; adds decoration to roof as well as provides ventilation for the attic.

CURTAIN WALL—a wall, usually nonbearing, between piers or columns.

CUT STOCK—relatively small pieces of surfaced, partially worked or rough lumber of specified sizes intended for further manufacture into millwork or other items of woodwork; generally cut at a sawmill or planing mill, bundled and shipped to the manufacturer.

CUT-UP—see Light.

CYCLE TEST—a method of exposing plywood or other glued-up assembles to alternating wet and dry conditions as a basis of determining waterproofness or durability of bond.

CYMATIUM—a combination of ovolo and cavetto; a reverse curve; ogee; see Inverted Cymatium.

D

DADO—a rectangular groove cut across the grain of a wood member; in contrast to plough (plow), which is cut with or parallel to the grain; in wainscot, the wide portion just above the base.

DAPPING—similar to "dado."

DECAY—disintegration of wood substance due to action of wood-destroying fungi; "advanced decay" or "incipient decay"; also rot, dote, punk and doze.

Advanced decay (typical)—the latter stage of decay in which disintegration of the wood substance is readily recognized because the wood has become punky, soft, spongy, stringy, shaky, pitted or crumbly and a decided discoloration or bleaching of the decayed wood is apparent.

Incipient decay—the early stage of decay in which the disintegration of the wood substance has not proceeded far enough to soften or otherwise perceptibly change the hardness of the wood; usually accompanied by a slight discoloration or bleaching of the wood.

DEHUMIDIFICATION—the artificial removal of moisture to attain a desired relative humidity.

DELAMINATION—separation of plies or layers of wood through failure of the adhesive.

DENSITY—the weight of a substance per unit volume, e.g., 23 lbs. per cubic foot.

DENTIL—a series of small square blocks uniformly spaced and projecting like teeth as used in cornice, front entrances and mantels; "dentil" moulding.

DIMENSIONAL STABILITY—the ability of a material to "stay put" or to resist changes in its dimensions due to temperature, moisture and physical stress variations; "stability" of a material.

DIPPING—the immersion of wood under atmospheric pressure in a solution or preservative (usually combined with a water-repellent); the wood is immersed for a period of time (usually 3 minutes) and then withdrawn and allowed to drain; nonpressure process of wood preservation.

DISCOLORATIONS—stains in wood substances. Some common veneer stains are sap stains, blue stains, stains produced by the chemical action caused by the iron in the cutting knife coming into contact with the tannic acid in the wood, and those resulting from the chemical action of the glue.

DIVIDED-LIGHT—same as "light."

DIVIDED LIGHTS—window or door panes separated by bars and muntins.

DOOR—a millwork assembly of stiles, rails and panels which swings, slides, tilts up or folds in order to close an opening in a wall or cabinet; may be exterior or interior, flush or panel type.

Access door—a small door, often a piece of plywood, to fill an opening in a ceiling or wall and trimmed with door casing; "scuttle door"; leads to plumbing concealed in wall partitions or attic areas.

Batten door—a door consisting of vertical boards or planking reinforced by horizontal strips or battens; also known as a "common ledged" door; when battens were reinforced by diagonal braces between them, it was termed a "ledged and braced" door.

Blind door—see Blind.

Bypass sliding door—one of two or more sliding doors that bypasses another door(s) in a door opening in a horizontal direction; a complete unit for such a door can be obtained consisting of two side jambs, header assembly with door track attached and necessary hardwood for hanging doors (doors may or may not be included); conserves space due to the exclusion of a required swing space.

Cabinet door (cupboard door)—a flush or panel door used on cabinets.

Casement door—see French Door.

Ceiling door, floor to—an interior door extending from the floor to the ceiling, utilizing surface-mounted or conventional hardware.

Combination door—a door assembly of stiles, rails and sometimes wood panels (usually 1⅛ inch thickness) containing interchangeable screen and glass storm panel inserts; in summer the glass storm panel(s) is replaced by the screen insert(s); also "combination storm sash and screen door"; usually occupies exterior rabbet of exterior door frame.

Conventionally hinged—see Hinged Door.

Dutch door—a door, usually exterior, with an upper and lower section that can be opened separately.

Entrance door—a door on the front entrance of a structure; also "front" or "main" entrance door; may be single or in pairs.

Fire door—a solid-core flush door incorporating noncombustible materials or fire-retardant chemicals to warrant specific fire ratings.

Folding door—one of two or more sliding doors hinged to move laterally in an opening; "accordion type" door; may be used for a folding partition; a complete unit for folding doors may be obtained consisting of doors with butts applied, track and guide hardware, door pulls and door frame (optional).

French door—an interior or exterior door consisting of stiles, top and bottom rail and divided glass panels or lights; often used in pairs; "casement" or "terrace" door.

Grade door—"service door"; derives its name from usual installation of door at grade (the level of the ground at the building).

Hinged door—an exterior or interior door hung by attaching butts to the stile so that the door swings on a vertical axis; may be single (swinging through 90 degrees) or double-acting (swinging through 180 degrees); double-acting doors do not require a door stop; conventionally hinged.

House door—interior door.

Jalousie door—see Jalousie.

Louvre door—a panel door with part or all of the panels replaced by louvres; blind door.

Non-prefit door—a door requiring further fitting prior to being hung; as opposed to "prefit door."

Panel door—consists of stiles, rails and one or more panels, the stiles and rails forming the frame around the panel; "stile and rail" door.

Patio door—see Terrace Door; French Door.

Prefit door—a door not requiring further fitting or sizing upon installation; "prefit" doors have eased edges and "skid blocks."

Prehung door—see Prehung Door Unit.

Rabbeted door—see Lip.

Rim door—consists of stiles and top and bottom rails and usually containing a single or divided-glass light(s); "store" door; French door.

Sash door—a panel with one or more panels replaced by glass.

Screen door—a door usually occupying the exterior rabbet of an exterior door frame to keep out insects by means of insect wire screening while admitting the maximum amount of air.

Service door—an exterior door other than an entrance door installed on rear or side elevations of a residential structure; "grade" door; side, rear or back door.

Sliding door—a door which slides in a horizontal direction parallel to a wall of the structure; may be of the "pocket" or "in-the-wall," "folding," "accordion" or the "bypass" type.

Store door—similar to rim or French door with a wide bottom rail and usually glazed with one glass panel or light.

Storm door—a panel or sash door occupying the exterior door frame to provide protection from cold weather.

Summer door—see Louvre Door.

Terrace door—exterior door, usually generous of glass, opening on the patio or terrace; see French Door.

Toilet door—a small louvre or panel door with stile extensions (lugs) and hinged as a swinging door; "café type" door.

Veneered door—a door made up of a core and face veneer and which may include crossbanding; may be hardwood or softwood veneered door.

X-Ray door—a solid-core flush door with one or more continuous sheets of lead fabricated in the door.

DOOR BEVEL—the bevel on the stile edge (lock edge) of a door, usually 1/16" for doors under 2" in thickness, so that the door may swing free of the door frame; bevel is approximately 3 degrees towards door stop.

DOOR BUCK—the rough frame door opening; also the jamb studs.

DOOR CLEARANCE—the space between the edge of a door and the door frame which enables the door to properly operate.

DOOR DOUBLER STUDS—studs doubled on each side of the rough door opening to (1) carry wall loads imposed on the opening, (2) provide support for door frame and (3) provide a nailing surface for plaster grounds and door trim or finish; door bucks.

DOOR FACE—the wide flat surface of a door.

DOOR FRAME—a group of wood parts machined and assembled to form an enclosure and support for a door; door frames are classified as exterior and interior door frames.

Adjustable door frame—a door frame including an adjustable or sliding jamb which can be used for walls of varying thicknesses.

Bypass door frame—an interior door frame to accommodate two or more sliding doors that slide by or bypass each other in a horizontal direction; sliding door frame.

Casing bead door frame—a door frame using a metal casing bead which eliminates the door casing; bead serves both as a plaster ground and casing.

Exterior door frame—a door frame installed in an exterior wall of a structure.

Folding door frame—see Bypass Door Frame; doors fold accordion-like; bifold door frame; see Door (Folding).

Interior door frame—a door frame installed in an interior wall of a structure.

In-the-wall sliding door frame—see Pocket-Type Door Frame.

Irregular-head door frame—door frame for a nonrectangular opening; the head may be circular, elliptical, Gothic, segment, peak or rake.

Pocket-type door frame—an interior door frame to accommodate a door that slides into a partition; pocket-type door frames are often sold as a unit consisting of outside jamb, header assembly with door track attached, split jamb pocket assembly and hardware for hanging door.

Structural exterior door frame—an exterior door frame installed in a conventionally framed (usually 4-foot) wall panel or section.

DOOR JAMB—the part of a door frame which surrounds and contacts the edges of the stiles and top rail of a door; jambs may be classified as (1) "head" or "side" jambs and (2) "plain" or "rabbeted."

Adjustable door frame—a two (sometimes three) piece split jamb consisting of a rabbeted and adjusting jamb section for walls of varying thicknesses; the rabbeted jamb contains a plough (plow) to receive the rabbeted edge of the adjusting jamb.

Beveled door jamb—a jamb with edges beveled 1/16" in order to provide a better foundation or bearing for the casing.

Head door jamb—the horizontal member forming the top of the door opening and inserted into the dado of the side jambs of the door frame.

Hinge jamb—side jamb in which the door hinges (butts) are applied.

Plain door jamb—a jamb surfaced four sides to which a wood door stop is applied.

Rabbeted door jamb—a jamb with a rabbet on one or both edges; if both edges, "double-rabbeted door jamb"; if one edge, "plain rabbeted door jamb."

Side door jamb—the upright or vertical member forming the side of the door opening; the side jamb is generally dadoed to receive the head jamb of the door frame.

Strike jamb—jamb opposite the hinge jamb; jamb on which the lock or passage-set strike plate is installed.

DOOR PANEL—a sheet of thin lumber, plywood or composition material inserted into the frame formed by the stiles, rails and mullions of a door.

Bevelled raised door panel—a raised door panel with the edges of the raised face at an angle of approximately 30 to 45 degrees.

Composition door panel—a door panel of material other than solid wood or plywood.

Flat door panel—a door panel consisting of a flat piece of plywood, solid wood or other material; contrasted to "raised door panel."

Hip-raised door panel—a raised door panel with the edges of the raised face perpendicular.

Raised door panel—a door panel whose face(s) is raised above the panel edges which are moulded and shaped to fit in the grooves of the door stiles and rails; contrasted to "flat panel."

Solid door panel—a door panel consisting of solid wood raised or beveled one or two sides.

DOOR RAIL—see Rail.

DOOR SKIN—face panel (usually two or more plies) of a flush door.

DOOR STILE—see Stile.

DOOR TRIM, SIDE OF—the mouldings required to "finish or trim" the side of a door frame consisting of two pieces of side and one of head casing.

DOORWAY—door, frame and trim.

DORMER WINDOW—see Window.

DOTE—see Decay.

DOUBLE-ACTION DOOR—a door, usually interior, with special hinges or pivots which allow the door to function in both directions.

DOUBLE-HUNG WINDOW UNIT—see Window Unit.

DOUBLE STUCK—a wood member with both edges moulded.

DOVETAIL—see Joint.

DOWEL—a wood peg or pin used to strengthen a wood joint; dowelled construction.

DOZE—see Decay.

DRIP CAP—see Cap.

DRIVE-FIT—dowel base slightly smaller than dowel, requiring some pressure to be exerted to engage dowel and close the joint.

DROP—see Turned Drop.

DROP CEILING—see Soffit.

DRY—see "seasoned"; varying degrees of "dryness" can exist for wood, varying from no moisture to relatively high moisture content.

DRY WALL—an interior wall finish material usually consisting of a layer of gypsum plaster board ⅜ to ⅝ inches in thickness; as contrasted to "wet wall"; should two layers be employed, it is termed "laminated gypsum dry wall"; wood panelling, hardboard, plywood or fibreboard when used for an interior finish is also termed "dry wall."

DURABILITY—permanence or resistance to wood deterioration.

DUTCHMAN—see Patch (Boat).

DUTCH CUT—the meeting point of the lower and upper section of a Dutch door.

E

EASED EDGE—a corner rounded or shaped to a slight radius to lessen splintering and paint failure; is not machined from an appearance standpoint, as in "round edge," but rather from a utility standpoint.

EASEMENT—a stair crook whereby the stair rail is curved primarily in a vertical plane; a "ramp"; also easing.

Concave easement—concave in profile; upeasing.

Convex easement—convex in profile; also "overhand easement" (easing).

Overhand easement—see Convex Easement.

Starting easement (easing)—see Easement with Newel Cap.

Turnout easement (easing)—an easement with newel cap whereby the newel cap extends either to the left or right of the easement and is in a horizontal plane; "turnout easement" with newel cap, right (left) as one observes the stairs from the initial point of ascent.

EASEMENT WITH NEWEL CAP—an easement (concave) with a dowel or pin top newel; same as "starting easement"; upeasing and newel cap.

EDGE BAND—a strip along the outside edges of the two sides and/or top and bottom of the door.

Wood edge band—a separate strip of wood, not less than ½ inch thick (12.7 mm) applied either to the edges of the stile or rails or directly to the edges of the core.

High-pressure decorative laminate edge band—a separate strip of high-pressure decorative laminate, applied to the edges of the stile or rail.

EFFECTIVE DEPTH OF STAIR STRINGER—the minimum distance from the intersection of the tread and bottom edge of the riser to the lower edge of the stringer; the minimum is between 3½ and 5 inches; also effective depth of rabbet.

EGG AND DART—a moulding design using an egg and dart alternately; the egg is said to represent life and the dart death.

ELECTRIC MOISTURE METER—an electrical apparatus to determine the moisture content of wood, based on the electrical resistance of wood being dependent on its moisture content.

EMISSIVITY—the relative ability of a surface to radiate heat, with emissivity factors ranging from 0.0 (or 0 percent) to 1.0 (or 100 percent).

EMITTANCE—heat energy radiated by the surface of a body, usually measured per second per unit area—syn. Emissivity.

END STRIP—an "edge strip" of the top and bottom rails of a door.

ENTABLATURE—the portion of a building faced with horizontal mouldings lengthwise above a series of columns or pilasters and comprising the architrave, frieze and cornice; the structure that rests on the top of the capital of a column.

ENTRANCE (front entrance)—an exterior door frame with or without transom or sidelights (usually used for the main or front entrance of a structure) with decorative exterior trim; trim may include pilasters, entrance head or cap or a decorative exterior casing.

Entrance head—the portion of the entrance above the door opening; also entrance cap; entablature; commonly used when head is other than a pediment.

EQUILIBRIUM MOISTURE CONTENT—the moisture content at which wood neither gains nor loses moisture when surrounded by air at a given relative humidity and temperature.

ESCUTCHEON—in builders' hardware, the plate containing the keyhole.

EXTENSION HINGE (casement hinge)—a hinge whereby an outswinging sash swings away from the frame to provide a space between the frame and the sash for washing or cleaning from the inside; space provided varies between 2 and 4 inches.

EXTENSION JAMBS—flat parts which are nailed to the inside edges of the window or door frame, so that it will fit a wider wall.

F

FABRICATOR—the person or firm that assembles all of the component parts into a complete window or sash unit.

FAÇADE—the main or front elevation of a building.

FACE—outer or exposed ply in cross-banded construction; surface from which lumber grade is determined.

FACE MEASURE—the measurement across the face of any wood part exclusive of any solid mould or rabbet.

FACE NAIL—a nail driven perpendicular to the surface of a piece.

FACTORY AND SHOP LUMBER—lumber primarily for manufacturing or cut-up purposes; e.g., millwork.

FALSE CABINET DRAWER FRONT—a simulated cabinet drawer front installed in the kitchen cabinet unit immediately below the sink level.

FASCIA (facia)—a wood member, surfaced four sides, used for the outer face of a "box cornice" where it is nailed to the ends of the rafters and "lookouts"; sometimes refers to the "face" of a mantel.

FEDERAL STYLE—a style of American architecture, 1780–1820, which exhibited feminine delicacy, replacing the heavy ornamentation of the Georgian style.

FENESTRATION—the placement or arrangement and sizes of the windows and exterior doors of a building.

FIBREBOARD—a broad term used to describe wood sheet material of widely varying densities manufactured or refined of partly refined wood fibres; usually manufactured by the "wet process" whereby the wood fibres are put into suspension and pressed into a board.

FIBER SATURATION POINT—the stage in the drying or wetting of wood at which the cell walls are saturated and the cell cavities are free from water; it is assumed to be 30 percent moisture content based on oven-dry weight; the point below which shrinkage occurs in wood.

FIGURE—patterns or designs on wood formed by annual growth rings, rays, knots, deviation from regular grain such as interlocked and wavy and irregular coloration; due to different types of sawing.

FILL (Putty Repairs)—a repair to an open defect, usually made with fast-drying plastic putty. Should be well made with non-shrinking putty of a color matching the surrounding area of the wood. To be flat and level with the face and panel, and to be sanded after application and drying.

FILLER STRIP—in a casement sash frame analogous to an extension blind stop; also blind stop; in factory-built kitchen cabinets, strips inserted between wall cabinets and walls or between base cabinets and appliances or between cabinets.

FILLET—a narrow band of wood between two flutes in a wood member; a flat, square moulding separating other mouldings; in stairwork, a thin narrow strip of wood which fits into the plough (plow) of the stair shoe or subrail between balusters; sometimes "neck" moulding.

FINGER JOINT—see Joint.

FINIAL—an ornament at the top of a gable or spire or at the end of certain structures.

FINISH—the "interior or exterior finish" of a structure; the "finish" or "actual" size of a piece of lumber; the protective coating given a wood member; upper or select grades of softwood lumber; an ambiguous term.

Exterior finish—a general term for those items of lumber and millwork used to provide a "finish" appearance to the exterior of the structure.

Interior finish—a general term for those items of lumber and millwork, inclusive of panelling, used to provide a "finish" appearance to the interior of the structure.

Prime coat finish—a hardware finish of baked enamel intended for a later application of paint.

FIREPROOF CONSTRUCTION—construction designed to withstand a complete burnout of the contents for which the structure was intended without impairment of structural integrity.

FIRE-RATED DOORS—a door which has been constructed in such a manner that when installed in an assembly and tested it will pass ASTM E-152 "Fire Test of Door Assemblies," and can be rated as resisting fire for 20 minutes (⅓ hour), 30 minutes (½ hour), 45 minutes (¾ hour) (C), 1 hour (B), or 1½ hours (B). The door must be tested and carry an identifying label from a qualified testing and inspection agency.

FIRE RETARDANT TREATMENT—impregnation of wood by fire-retardant chemicals to increase its fire resistance by (1) retarding the normal increase in temperature under fire conditions, (2) decreasing the rate of flame spread, (3) lessening the rate of flame penetration and (4) making fires more easy to extinguish.

FIREWALL—a wall with qualities of fire resistance and structural stability which subdivides a building into fire areas and which resists the spread of fire.

FIVE-PLY CONSTRUCTION—a crossbanded assembly consisting of a core, crossbands and face veneers.

FLAME SPREAD—the propagation or progress of flame over a surface; in wood, usually compared to the rate of spread over oak used as a control.

FLASHING—a metal or plastic strip used to prevent water and air leakage between the window or door frame and the surrounding wall; it is attached to the outside face of the head jamb and side jambs.

FLOOR GUIDE PLATE—hardware applied to the floor of the structure to guide bypass, folding and pocket-type sliding doors.

FLUSH DOOR—a door consisting of a core, crossbanding and flat face veneers or a core and flat face veneers only.

Hollow-core flush door—a flush door with a core assembly of strips or other units of wood, wood derivative or insulation board which supports the outer faces and with intervening hollow cells or spaces.

Solid-core flush door—a flush door consisting of a core of solid wood blocks or strips with crossbanding and face veneers or face veneers only.

FLUTE—a long, rounded groove machined along the grain of a wood member, e.g., a pilaster; may be "through fluted" or "stop fluted"; shallow or deep concave or groove cut-back of surface; repeated flutes produce texture.

Feather-edge flute—a flute which joins the adjacent parallel flute at a point; contrasted to a flute which joins the adjacent parallel flute by a flattened separation or fillet.

Regular flute—a flute which joins the adjacent parallel flute by a flattened separation or fillet; contrast to "feather-edge flute."

Stop flute—a flute terminated from the ends of a wood member and not visible from the ends as in "through flute."

Through flute—a flute running from end to end in a wood member and visible from the ends.

FLYER—see Tread.

FOLDING DOOR—one of two or more sliding doors hinged to move laterally in an opening; "accordion type" door; may be used for a folding partition; a complete unit for folding doors may be obtained consisting of doors with butts applied, track and guide hardware, door pulls, and door frame (optional). A two- or four-door unit is usually called a bifold door.

FRAME—parts which enclose the window or door sash; they are attached to the wood members lining the rough opening. (Usage—Vertical frame members are called "side jambs"; the top, horizontal piece is the "head jamb"; the bottom, horizontal piece is the "sill.")

FRAMING—

Balloon—wood frame construction that carries the stud the full height of the exterior wall.

Platform—wood frame construction that terminates the stud at each level; also "western frame," "repeat story frame" or "braced frame" construction.

FRANKING—fitting or joining muntins to bars.

FREE-STANDING RANGE—a conventional-type appliance which is not part of a built-in cabinet unit; term may also be applied to other appliances.

FRENCH DOOR—a door with rectangular panes extending its full length—also called Garden Door. See Window (French).

FRIEZE—derived from French "frise" border; a box cornice wood member surfaced four sides nailed to the wall of the structure where the soffit (plancier) and building wall meet; the part of an entablature between architrave and the cornice; the space between the top of the lintel and/or ceiling joists and the bottom of the plate.

FRONT ASSEMBLY—as used in china cabinets, consists of the front frame and may be inclusive of stool or counter shelf, drawers, doors, mouldings and shelving.

FULL BOUND—sash having stiles and rails of same width; "same rail all around."

FUNGI—low parasitic forms of plant life which deteriorate wood by using it as a source of food; may be wood-staining or wood-destroying.

FURRED-DOWN CEILING—see Soffit.

FURRING (STRIP)—narrow strips of wood spaced to form a nailing base for another surface; furring is used to level, to form an air space between the two surfaces, especially in damp situations, and to give a thicker appearance to the base surface.

G

GAIN—similar to "dado"; also a notch or mortise made to receive a door butt or strike.

GAP—open splits in the inner ply or plies, or improperly joined veneer when joined veneers are used for inner plies.

GEORGIAN STYLE—a style of American architecture popular between 1700 and 1780; characterized by symmetry, elaborate front entrances and cornices, belvederes and other heavier ornamentation.

GLASS—a transparent, translucent or opaque material formed by fusing silicates with soda or potash, lime and sometimes various metallic oxides.

Corrugated glass—glass rolled to produce a corrugated contour; when wired, it is used especially for skylights, roofs and sidewalls; may be plain or wired.

Figured glass—rolled glass having a patterned or figured surface(s).

Greenhouse-quality glass—the lowest quality of window glass; a double-strength clear sheet or window glass made in very limited quantities; of little interest to millwork industry.

Heat-absorbing glass—glass which intercepts appreciable portions of radiant energy, especially solar energy; obtainable as polished plate, window or other types of glass; color varies among different glass manufacturers.

Insulating glass—two or more (generally two) pieces, lights or panes of glass separated by a hermetically sealed air space $\frac{3}{16}$ to $\frac{1}{2}$ inch in width.

Laminated glass—two or more layers of glass, usually plate, with inner layers of tough transparent plastic, bonded tightly together with the aid of heat and pressure.

Leaded glass—small, usually irregular panes of glass, sometimes vari-colored, joined together by lead or zinc muntins and bars and used primarily for decorative purposes; zinc bar glazing.

Plate glass—glass from which surface irregularities have been removed by grinding and polishing so that the surfaces are approximately plane and parallel; also polished plate glass.

Pressed figured glass—glass with a determinate figure pressed on one side; this process makes possible a clear, sharp, even-figured pattern which is not obtainable by other methods.

Processed glass—glass whose surface(s) has been altered by etching, sandblasting, chipping, grinding, etc., to increase the diffusion.

Rolled glass—glass having a patterned or irregular surface and which varies in transparency; more or less diffusing, depending on pattern; the surface pattern is formed in the rolling process.

Tempered glass—plate glass with increased mechanical strength.

Wire glass—flat, rolled glass having a layer of meshed wire completely imbedded in the sheet.

GLASS PANE—see Light.

GLAZIER'S POINTS—small, flat generally triangular (sometimes diamond-shaped) thin pieces of metal (usually zinc) used in glazing to hold the glass in the putty or glass rabbet; after the glass has been placed in the putty or glass rabbet of the sash, glazier's points are forced into the wood (usually left

projecting $\frac{1}{8}$–$\frac{3}{16}$ of an inch) and the putty or glazing compound applied; also "sprigs" or glazing points.

GLAZING—glass or other transparent materials, used for windows; also the act of installing the glass.

Double-glazing—glazing with two panes of glass separated by an air space; double-glazing may be accomplished by storm sash (panels) or insulating glass; term sometimes refers to storm sash.

Groove glazing—glazing in which the glass is inserted into a groove machined on the stiles and rails of the sash; a bedding or glazing compound is placed in the groove prior to inserting the glass.

Leaded-glass glazing—see Glass.

Putty glazing—glazing by use of putty; the glass is inserted into the putty rabbet, glazier's points driven and the putty or glazing compound applied to the putty rabbet.

Triple-glazing—glazing with three panes of glass with an air space between each pane.

Wood-stop glazing—glazing whereby a thin layer of putty or glazing compound is placed in the putty or glass rabbet, the glass pressed into the "bed" and secured by wood stops.

Zinc-bar glazing—see Glass.

GLAZING BEAD—a strip surrounding the edge of the glass in a window or door; applied to the sash on the outside, the glazing bead holds the glass in place.

GLAZING COMPOUND—a plastic substance of such consistency that it tends to remain soft and rubbery when used in glazing sash and doors; unlike putty, it resists hardening, cracking and eventual failure; sometimes refers to "putty."

GLUE BLOCK—a wood block, triangular or rectangular in shape, which is glued and nailed into place to reinforce a right-angled butt joint; sometimes used at the intersection of the tread and riser in a stairs.

GLUE JOINT—see Joint.

GOOSENECK—a stair crook-shaped in the profile of a goose's neck; composed of a long curved vertical section of stair rail with a short horizontal section at the top; used at the point of "winders" in an open stairs, at the landing or the head of stairs.

Gooseneck with landing return, 1(2) riser(s)—a gooseneck with the stair rail in the short horizontal section making a 180-degree turn (return) on the level; may be right or left; also gooseneck with level half-turn.

Gooseneck with level quarter-turn—a gooseneck with the stair rail in the short horizontal section making a 90-degree turn on the level (on a horizontal plane); may be termed right or left.

Gooseneck with (without) newel cap—a gooseneck with (without) a newel cap and no stair rail outlet therefrom in the short horizontal section of the stair crook; a "gooseneck without newel cap" is synonymous with the term "gooseneck"; adaptable for use with either one or two risers.

Gooseneck with newel cap and easing—a gooseneck with the stair rail in the short horizontal section ending in a newel cap and with an easing leading out of the newel cap at right angles to the stair rail; either right or left.

Gooseneck with newel cap and level outlet right (left)—a gooseneck with a newel cap and a rail outlet in the short horizontal section of the stair crook; the rail outlet is at 90 degrees to the newel cap and on level (in horizontal plane); stair crook is termed right or left.

Gooseneck with newel cap and level outlet; straight—a gooseneck with a newel cap and a rail outlet in the short horizontal section of the stair crook; the rail outlet is opposite its entry into the newel cap.

Gooseneck with quarter-turn and easement—a gooseneck with the stair rail in the short horizontal section of the stair crook making a quarter-turn on level and then curving upward (easement) either right or left.

GOTHIC HEAD—an entrance or door head in the form of a pointed arch.

GRAIN—arrangement and direction of alignment of wood elements or fibres, e.g., straight grain, spiral grain; used loosely to indicate "texture."

Coarse grain—a commonly used term denoting wood with wide conspicuous annual growth rings in which there is considerable difference between springwood and summerwood.

Cross grain—wood fibres deviate from a direction parallel to the axis of tree.

Edge grain—see Vertical Grain.

Flat grain—annual growth rings which form an angle of less than 45 degrees with the surface of a piece of wood; also "slash grain," "plain sawn" or "flat sawn."

Mixed grain—any combination of edge (vertical) and flat grain.

Raised grain—a commonly used term denoting the roughened condition of the surface of dressed or surfaced lumber in which the hard summerwood is raised above the softer springwood but not torn loose from it.

Rift grain—generally refers to "edge" or "vertical" grain; when referring to hardwoods implies that the annual growth rings make an angle of 30–60 degrees with the faces of the board; "rift sawn" hardwoods, in such species as white oak, produce a figure where the saw cuts across the rays at an angle, producing pencil-like stripes with no large, quartered flakes.

Torn grain—part of the wood torn out in dressing or surfacing where the tearing is deep enough to warrant measurement; slight torn grain—not over 1/32" deep; medium torn grain—over 1/32" but not over 1/16" deep; heavy torn grain—over 1/16" but not over 1/8" deep; deep torn grain—over 1/8" deep.

Vertical grain—annual growth rings which form an angle of 45 degrees or more with the surface of a piece of wood; also "edge grain"; known as "quarter sawn" when referring to hardwood lumber.

GREEK REVIVAL STYLE—a style of classic architecture popular in the United States from 1820 to the War Between the States.

GREEN—freshly sawn wood or wood which has received no intentional drying or seasoning; also "unseasoned."

GRILLE—an ornamental item that visually divides a piece of glass into separate panes; snapped into the window or door sash from the inside, the grille replaces muntins and bars. See Bar; Muntin.

GROOVE—a hollow three-surface cut in the edge or face of a wood member; a groove across the grain is a "dado" while parallel with the grain, a plough (plow).

Drip groove—a semicircular groove on the under side of drip cap or the lip of a window sill which prevents water from running back under the drip cap or sill; "weep"; water drip groove.

GROUND—a narrow strip of wood which serves as a guide for plaster as well as a base to which trim members are nailed; grounds are applied to rough interior openings, especially doors, along the interior walls at the finish floor line and wherever wainscot may be installed; the thickness of a ground is that of the combined lath and plaster while the width varies from one to three inches; often called "plaster grounds" (around interior or exterior openings) and "base grounds" when used around base of rooms.

GROUT—a mixture of sand and cement of such consistency that with the addition of water it will just flow into the joints and cavities of structure members, especially in masonry work.

GROWTH RING—see Annual Growth Ring.

GUIDE, DOOR—hardware installed on the floor directly under the head jamb of a sliding door frame to keep the door from swinging out (tilting) of its plane of action.

GUM SPOTS—well-defined openings between rings of annual growth, usually containing gum or pitch.

GUTTER—concave-like moulding used to carry off rainwater from the roof to the downspouts or conductors; also moulded wood gutter.

H

HANDRAIL—see Rail (Stair).

HAND—A term describing the swinging direction of a door as one stands on the side of the door from which security is desired, namely the outside.

Left hand—door butts or hinges on left side of person with door swinging away from him.

Left-hand reverse—same as left hand except door swings towards person.

Right hand—door butts or hinges on right side of person with door swinging away from him.

Right-hand reverse—same as right hand except door swings towards person.

HANG—fitting a door to its opening or frame and installing the hardware essential for its operation.

HARDBOARD—a board material manufactured of wood fibre, refined or partly refined and formed into a panel having a density range of approximately 50 to 80 pounds per cubic foot under carefully controlled optimum combinations of consolidating pressure, heat and moisture so that the board produced has a characteristic natural ligneous bond; other materials may be added during manufacture to improve certain properties such as stiffness, hardness, finishing qualities, strength and durability; the smaller-size wood particles used in hardboard manufacture is the essential difference between this material and particleboard.

HARDWARE, FINISH—all hardware exposed in a structure such as butts, locks, drawer pulls.

HARDWARE, ROUGH—all hardware used in the construction and concealed in the house such as bolts and nails.

HARDWOOD—one of the botanical groups of trees that has broad leaves in contrast to the needle-like leaves of the conifers or softwoods; hardwoods are (1) deciduous (shed their leaves in the fall or at end of each growing season), (2) have shorter-length wood fibres than softwoods, (3) contain cells (vessels) of relatively large diameters (in addition to the wood fibres) and (4) have seeds enclosed by an ovary.

HARDWOOD VENEERED DOOR—see Door (Veneered).

HEADBOARD—a flat board cut to fit the contour of a bow or bay window; it is installed between the window frame and the surrounding wall surface, to create a kind of ceiling.

HEADER—a horizontal structural member (also "lintel") that supports the load over an opening, such as a window or door.

HEARTWOOD—the wood extending from the pith or center of the tree to the sapwood, the cells of which no longer participate in the life processes of the tree.

HEAT LOSS—the Heat Transmission Coefficient ("U" value) multiplied by the area of the door or window opening or other member of a structure; see Total Heat Loss.

HEAT TRANSMISSION COEFFICIENT—hourly rate of heat transfer for one square foot of surface when there is a temperature difference of one degree F of the air on the two sides of the surface; also known as "U" value.

HEAVY CONSTRUCTION—as opposed to light construction.

HEEL (of a door)—the "hinge" edge of a door.

HOLES (Worm)—holes resulting from infestation by worms greater than 1/16 inches in diameter and not exceeding 5/8 inches in length.

HOLLOW-BACK—to groove or remove a portion of the wood on the unexposed face of a wood member to more properly fit any irregularity in bearing surface; conserves on transportation charges, assists in prevention of warping and allows a moulding more or less warped to hug the jamb and plaster more closely; also "backed out."

HOOK STRIP—a wood member, moulded or surfaced four sides, nailed along the walls of a closet to support clothes hooks; see Chair Rail.

HOPPER—an upside-down awning window, hinged at the bottom and opening inward from the top; many basement windows are this type. Also, frequently referred to as a ranch-type window. (Add.: Hopper under Window Unit, between Frame Building Window Unit and Horizontal Sliding Window Unit.)

HORN—the extension of a stile, jamb or sill.

Double horn—horns at both ends; also "horns two ends."

Jamb horn—the extension of a window frame side jamb beyond the sill and head jamb.

Sill horn—the extension of the "lip" of a window sill to the outside edge of the casing, brick moulding or sometimes wide blind stop or blind stop extension; the extension of a door sill beyond the frame; sometimes "lugs."

Sill long horn—the extension of the "lip" of the window sill beyond the outside edge of the casing, brick moulding or blind stop; long horns are "left end or hand" or "right end or hand" as one views the frame from the outside; long horns may be required on both ends.

Stile horn—the extension of the stile of a panel door beyond the top and bottom rail; "stile lug" or "stile extension."

HOUSED—the "notching" or "grooving" of one member to receive another.

HUMIDIFICATION—artificial introduction of moisture to attain a certain desired relative humidity.

HYGROSCOPIC—the ability of wood to "take on" and "give off" moisture.

I

INCOMBUSTIBLE CONSTRUCTION (noncombustible)—construction consisting of all structural elements of incombustible materials with fire-resistance ratings of one hour or less.

INFILTRATION HEAT LOSS—heat loss due to air infiltration through cracks and other spaces around windows and doors; crack perimeter multiplied by infiltration factor (cubic feet of air per foot of crack) and the temperature differential between outside and inside surfaces gives the number of BTU's lost to heat up infiltrated air; see Total Heat Loss.

INNER FRAME (insert frame)—on a panel door, the intermediate panel member between the stile and door panel which accentuates the sticking of the door.

IN-THE-WHITE—natural or unpainted; the natural unfinished surface of the wood.

INVERTED CYMATIUM—reverse of cymatium, being convex at the top and concave at the bottom; ogee.

IRONING BOARD CABINET UNIT—a shallow cabinet assembly (approximately 3½ inches in depth, 12 inches in width, and six feet in height) containing an ironing board and installed in a wall.

J

JACK STUD—vertical wood member at each side of the rough opening for a window or door; the jack stud supports the header.

JALOUSIE—a series of small horizontal overlapping glass slats, sections, jalousies or louvres held together by an end metal frame attached to the faces of window frame side jambs or door stiles and rails; the slats or louvres move simultaneously like a Venetian blind in an outward direction; a louvred window or door; admits air and light but excludes rain and sun; glass storm panels and screen inserts are available.

JAMB—the top and two sides of a door or window frame which contact the door or sash; top jamb and side jambs.

Back jamb—the side jamb of a box (pocket and pulley type) window frame for a masonry wall which is next to the rough opening; also called "back lining."

Extender jamb—see Sub-Jamb.

Face of jamb—the exposed surface of a jamb next to the door or sash.

Jamb liner—see Liner.

Sill jamb—side jamb.

Split jamb—a split jamb to enable a pocket-type sliding door or a vertical sliding sash to enter the partition; see Door Jamb (Adjustable).

JAMB BLOCK—a concrete or cinder block used when window units are installed in a concrete or cinder-block masonry wall; two types of jamb blocks, "slotted" (with a ¾″ slot in the middle of one end of the block) or with a 2-inch-wide, 4-inch-deep cut on one end of an 8-inch-block.

JOINERY—the work, trade or skill of a carpenter, especially one who works on interior woodwork; a joiner.

JOINT—the joining of two pieces of wood by nails, glue, adhesives or other means; may be joined end to end, edge to edge, end to edge, or end to face; also glue or wood joint.

Blind mortise-and-tenon joint—a mortise-and-tenon joint in which the tenon does not extend through the mortise and does not remain visible once the joint is completed; also "blind tenoned."

Butt joint—a joint formed by square edge surfaces (ends, edges, faces) coming together; end butt joint, edge butt joint.

Coped joint—a joint at the meeting of moulded members.

Dado joint—a rectangular groove across the grain of a wood member into which the end of the joining member is inserted; also a housed joint; variations include "dado and tenon" and "stopped dado" joints.

Dovetail joint—a joint formed by inserting a projecting wedge-shaped member (dovetail tenon) into a correspondingly shaped cut-out member (dovetail mortise); variation includes the "dovetailed dado."

Dowelled joint—a joint using "dowels" ("dowelled construction"); also "dowelled edge joint."

Edge joint—a joint formed by joining together the edges of wood members; the edges may be square edge (plain edge joint) or machined (tongue and groove, dowelled); edge butt joint sometimes termed "rubbed" joint.

End joint—a joint formed by the ends of wood members; the more common end joint is the "finger-joint."

Finger joint—a series of fingers machined on the ends of two pieces to be joined, which mesh together and are held firmly in position by a water-resistant adhesive.

Haunched mortise-and-tenon joint—a mortise-and-tenon joint in which the tenon is not the same width as its wood member.

Lap joint—a joint formed by extending (lapping) the joining part of one member over the joining part of the other member; also "ship-lap," "shouldered rabbet" or "plain rabbet" joint.

Locked-mitre joint—a mitre joint employing a tongue and groove working to further strengthen the joint.

Lock sill joint—formed by dadoing the side jamb and sill of a window frame.

Mitre joint—the joining of two members at an angle that bisects the angle of junction.

Mortise-and-tenon joint—a joint formed by the tenon of one member being inserted into the mortise of the other member; the tenon may be secured in the joint by means of steel pins or nails (pinned mortise-and-tenon).

Open mortise-and-tenon joint—a mortise-and-tenon joint in which the inserted tenon extends completely through the mortise and the end of the tenon remains visible once the joint is completed; also through or full mortise-and-tenon.

Rabbet joint—a joint formed by the rabbet(s) on one or both members; also rabbeted edge joint; rabbeted right-angle joint.

Right-angle joint—a 90-degree joint formed by end to face, edge to face or edge to end of wood members; the joint may be formed with the grain, at right angles or parallel to it.

Scarf joint—an end joint formed by having the two ends of the members bevelled to form sloping plane surfaces.

Slotted mortise-and-tenon joint—a mortise-and-tenon right-angle joint in which the tenon is visible on two edges once the joint is completed; also "bridle" or "slip" joint.

Spline joint—a joint formed by the use of a spline; also "slip tongue" joint.

Starved joint—a glue joint poorly bonded because of an insufficient quantity of glue that remained in the joint.

Stub mortise-and-tenon—see Joint (Blind Mortise-and-Tenon).

Tongue-and-groove joint—a joint formed by the insertion of the "tongue" of one wood member into the "groove" of the other; modifications include tongue-and-groove rabbet joint, dado tongue and rabbet, tongued shoulder joint, dado and rabbet joint, dado and lip joint.

"V" joint—a joint formed by two adjacent boards in the same plane which have faces with chamfered edges; the wood joint may be center-matched, butt joint or other working.

Wedged mortise-and-tenon joint—similar

to the through mortise-and-tenon joint save that two saw cuts are made in the tenon and fitted with wedges; since the sides of the mortise are flared the tenon cannot pull out after the wedges have been driven and glued into place.

JOINTER—a machine for the preparation of an edge.

JOIST TRIMMER—a joist doubled or tripled, to support a header and form part of the opening for a stairway or fireplace.

K

KERFING—longitudinal saw cuts or grooves of varying depths (dependent on the thickness of the wood member) made on the unexposed faces of millwork members to relieve stress and prevent warping or to allow insertion of integral weatherstrip or for spliner in casing or prehung units.

KICKPLATE—a thin polished metal plate applied to the bottom rail or bottom of a door to prevent denting and soiling of the wood surface caused by the kicking action of persons in opening the door; kickplates may be applied to one or both sides of a door.

KILNBURN, LIGHT RED—see Red KilnBurn.

KILN-DRIED—wood seasoned in a kiln by means of artificial heat, humidity and circulation; "kiln dried" wood may refer to wood with various moisture content percentages.

KITCHEN—the area of a structure primarily reserved for food storage, preparation and maintenance.

Corridor kitchen assembly—the placing of the three kitchen work centers on two parallel walls.

Kitchen work triangle—a triangle formed by the paths between the three kitchen work centers.

"L" kitchen assembly—the placing of the three kitchen work centers on two walls at right angles to one another.

One-wall kitchen assembly—the placing of all of the kitchen work centers in a straight line or on a single wall.

"U" kitchen assembly—the placing of each of the kitchen work centers on one of three walls which form a "U" shape.

KITCHEN CABINET—case or box-like assembly consisting of doors, drawers and shelves primarily used for storage for food, utensils, linen, cleaning devices and the like.

Base corner cabinet—a base kitchen cabinet which makes use of corner space at the intersection of two lines of cabinets.

Base end kitchen shelf unit—semicircular shelves employed on the end of base cabinets.

Base kitchen cabinet—kitchen cabinet resting on the floor and providing storage and counter space, access to which is provided by doors and/or drawers.

Built-in kitchen cabinet—soffit-high kitchen cabinet to accommodate oven or refrigerator.

Custom-built kitchen cabinet—a term generally applied to a kitchen cabinet which is constructed on the job site from material which was not prefabricated or manufactured in a factory; also cabinets not considered to be available from any existing inventory; as opposed to "factory-built" kitchen cabinet.

Drawer-unit base kitchen cabinet—a base kitchen cabinet consisting entirely of drawers.

Factory-built kitchen cabinet—a kitchen cabinet manufactured in a factory or plant and available (1) knocked down, (2) semi-assembled, (3) assembled and not finished or (4) assembled and finished.

Island base kitchen cabinet—a base kitchen cabinet entirely removed from any row of kitchen cabinets; two cabinet ends are exposed.

Peninsula base kitchen cabinet—a base kitchen cabinet which extends outward at right angles from a row of base cabinets and presents one exposed end.

Utility kitchen cabinet—a relatively tall cabinet extending from floor to soffit or ceiling, to provide storage for brooms, sweepers, mops, clothing and the like.

Wall-corner kitchen cabinet—a wall cabinet to "turn-a-corner."

Wall-end kitchen shelf unit—semicircular or quarter-round shelves with a standard for attachment to a wall cabinet.

Wall kitchen cabinet—a kitchen cabinet attached to wall or suspended from ceiling for providing kitchen storage.

KITCHEN WORK CENTER—one of the three principal work areas in which a kitchen is organized: "work centers" are (1) food storage, (2) food preparation and (3) range.

KNEE SPACE—an outward extension of the upper part of a base kitchen cabinet, directly under the counter and above the cabinet door, to accommodate the knee while working close to the counter.

KNEE WALL MOULDING—a crown-like moulding suitable for installation at oblique joints.

KNIFE MARKS—very fine lines that appear across the panel that can look as though they are raised resulting from some defect in the lathe knife that cannot be removed with sanding.

KNOB LATCH SET—door hardware for keeping a door closed and with a spring-operated latch bolt activated by a knob; also passage set.

KNOCKED-DOWN—unassembled as contrasted to assembled or "built-up."

KNOT—branch or limb embedded in the tree and cut through during lumber manufacture; size of a knot is determined by averaging the maximum length and width.

Large knot—a knot over 1½" in diameter.

Medium knot—a knot over ¾" but not over 1½" in diameter.

Pin knot—a knot not over ½" in diameter.

Small knot—a knot over ½" but not over ¾" in diameter.

Sound knot—solid across its face, as hard as the surrounding wood, shows no indication of decay and may vary in color from natural color of the wood to reddish brown or black.

Tight knot—so fixed by growth or position as to retain its place.

KNOTS, OPEN—openings where a portion of the wood substance of the knot was dropped out, or where cross checks have occurred to present an opening.

KNOTS, PIN—sound knots less than ¼ inches in diameter.

L

LAMBS TONGUE—a moulding, of considerable projection as compared to its width, of two opposed ogees separated by a fillet.

LAMINATED—layers of veneer or lumber bonded with an adhesive so that the grain of all layers is essentially parallel; contrasted to plywood, in which the adjacent layers are usually at right angles to one another.

LAMINATED GYPSUM DRY WALL—see Dry Wall.

LANDING, STAIR—see Stair Landing.

LAP—a condition where the veneers composing plywood are so misplaced that one piece overlaps the other and does not make a smooth joint.

LATCH SET—see Knob Latch Set.

LATHE—a woodworking machine for turning and shaping wood members.

LATTICE—a thin strip of wood, surfaced four sides, originally used in lattice-work; lattice strip.

LAZY SUSAN—a circular revolving cabinet shelf employed in corner kitchen cabinet units.

LEADED GLASS—see Glass.

LEVEL—on a horizontal plane or line.

LEVEL HALF-TURN—a stair crook; stair rail with a 180-degree turn on the level (in a horizontal plane).

LEVEL QUARTER-TURN—a stair crook; stair rail with a 90-degree turn on the level (in a horizontal plane).

LIGHT—a framed opening in a sash or door containing a pane of glass (glass panel); light opening, lite; divided-light; cut-up.

Glass light—see Light.

Horizontal light—a light or cut-up formed by a horizontal bar extending from stile to stile of a sash or door.

Marginal light—a light or cut-up so formed by bars and muntins in a sash or door that unequal lights result.

Sidelight—an assembly of stiles and rails, with or without a wood panel, containing a single row of glass panels or lights and installed on one or both sides of an exterior door frame, especially a front entrance door frame; provides light, especially for an entry hall, as well as decorative appeal.

Vertical light—a light or cut-up formed by a vertical bar extending from rail to rail of a sash or door.

LIGHT CONSTRUCTION—construction generally restricted to the conventional wood stud walls, floor and ceiling joists and rafters; "light frame construction"; as opposed to "heavy construction"; primarily residential in nature although it does include small light commercial buildings such as one- or two-story stores.

LINEAL FOOT—having length only; used in designating quantities of mouldings; "linear," "foot," or running foot; "lineal" usually designates nonspecified lengths.

LINEAR—see Lineal Foot.

LINER—most commonly a jamb or sill extension member.

Door frame liner—see Windbreak.

Jamb liner—a small strip of wood, either surfaced four sides or tongued on one edge, which, when applied to the inside edge of a window jamb, increases its width.

Sill liner—serves same purpose for "sill" as "jamb liner" does for "jamb"; also sill extender.

LINING—

Exterior door frame lining—see Windbreak.

Outside lining—see Windbreak.

LINTEL—see Header.

LIP—a rabbet run on the edges of a cabinet door or drawer causing it to project in a closed position beyond the face or surface of the cabinet; a rounded overhanging edge; see Sill Lip.

LOCK—hardware which keeps windows or doors shut. (Usage—Locks for swinging windows have a "keeper," a protruding, hook-shaped piece attached to inside face of the stile; Sliding Windows have "latches," two-piece units attached to adjoining rails.)

LOCK BLOCK—a solid or glued-up block of wood, the thickness of the hollow-core flush door stile, which is joined to the inside edge of the stile and to which the lock is fitted; flush doors have a lock block on each stile.

LONGITUDINAL—a direction in wood along the grain or the longitudinal axis of the tree.

LOUVRE—an opening of various shapes with a series of horizontal slats (louvre boards) so arranged (sloping downwards) so as to permit ventilation but excluding rain, sunlight or vision; may be square, rectangular, triangular, quarter- or half-circle; horizontal slats may be stationary or movable (rolling); also "attic or gable louvre"; see Slat.

LOW-EMISSIVITY GLASS—glass which restricts the passage of radiant heat, in and out; a metal and metal oxide coating is either suspended between the two layers of glass, or affixed to one of the panes, separated by a small air space.

LUG—an extension of the stiles beyond the meeting rails of a sash, usually ogee-shaped; usually sawn ornamentally on the inside of the stile; "ogee lug"; sometimes the interior door side jamb extension beyond the dado is termed the "lug"; also "joggles"; see Horn (Sill).

LUMBER—a manufactured product derived from a log in a sawmill, or in a sawmill and planing mill, which when rough shall have been sawed, edged and trimmed at least to the extent of showing saw marks on the wood on the four longitudinal surfaces of each piece for its overall length, and which has not been further manufactured than by crosscutting, ripping, resawing, joining crosswise and/or endwise in a flat plane, surfacing with or without end matching, and working.

Factory and shop lumber—see Factory and Shop Lumber.

Yard lumber—lumber of grades, sizes and patterns intended for ordinary construction and general building purposes.

M

MANTEL—the facing of wood, stone, marble, brick or similar material around a fireplace and which usually includes a projecting slab or shelf above it; mantelpiece.

MANTEL FACE—horizontal member directly under the mantel shelf; also fascia or frieze of the mantel.

MANTEL MOULDING—see Surround.

MANTEL SHELF—upper part of a mantel projecting into the room.

MASONRY WALL—a wall consisting of clay, shale, concrete, gypsum, stone or other similar nonwood materials bonded together with mortar; the masonry units may be hollow or solid.

Brick-facing masonry wall—a masonry wall constructed of cinder or concrete blocks, concrete, or clay tile as backing and faced with a single wall of brick.

Cavity-type solid brick masonry wall—a masonry wall constructed of two or more units or walls of bricks with a 2″ air space between each tier; the inner and outer walls are called "wythes."

Concrete block masonry wall—a hollow masonry wall constructed of concrete or cinder blocks; usually 8″ in thickness.

Hollow masonry wall—a masonry wall in which the voids in the units exceed 25 percent of the cross-sectional area.

S.C.R. brick masonry wall—a masonry wall constructed of one unit or wall of "SCR bricks," the actual size of the brick being 2⅛″ × 5½″ × 11½″.

Solid brick masonry wall—a masonry wall generally constructed of two units of four-inch brick (8″ wall); three units are sometimes employed making a wall approximately 12 inches in thickness.

Solid masonry wall—a masonry wall in which the voids in the units do not exceed 25 percent of the cross-sectional area at any plane parallel to the bearing surface.

Stucco masonry wall—a masonry wall constructed of brick, block, concrete or clay tile as backing and faced with a layer(s) of stucco.

MEDALLION—a raised decorative wood design sometimes used on flush doors.

MEDIUM-DENSITY FIBREBOARD (MDF)—the generic name for a panel manufactured from lignocellulosic fibres combined with a synthetic resin or other suitable binder and bonded together under heat pressure in a hot press by a process in which the entire bond is created by the added binder.

MESH—the number of meshes or open spaces per lineal inch in width and height in insect wire screening.

METAL WALL BRACKET—hardware used to secure the wall rail to the wall; installed at a maximum spacing of 10 feet; "wall rail support or bracket."

MILLING IN TRANSIT—a privilege extended to a rail shipper whereby carload shipments of lumber, unglazed doors, plywood and other articles taking lumber rates may be billed to a final destination and stopped somewhere en route in order to permit manufacture.

MILLWORK—a term to describe those products which are primarily manufactured from lumber in a planing mill or woodworking plant; includes mouldings, door frames and entrances, blinds and shutters, sash and window units, doors, stairwork, kitchen cabinets, mantels, china or corner cabinets and porch work; woodwork.

Architectural millwork—see Special Millwork.

Custom millwork—see Special Millwork.

Packaged millwork—the wrapping or packaging of items of millwork; "packaged trim."

Special millwork (custom millwork)—millwork not manufactured in a standard size, pattern or layout and which must be specially made in meeting a particular set of specifications; also architectural woodwork (millwork).

Stock millwork—millwork manufactured in a standard size, pattern and layout, readily available from a distributor's inventory and ready for installation upon delivery to the construction site.

MILLWORK COMMISSION MAN—one who sells millwork in quantity on a commission basis for millwork manufacturers to millwork jobbers and lumber and building materials dealers.

MILLWORK ESTIMATION—the number, sizes, types and cost of millwork items required for a structure.

MILLWORK JOBBER—an organization that buys millwork in quantity from millwork manufacturers, wholesalers or commission men, assembles or fabricates, maintains an inventory and ultimately sells to lumber and building materials dealers.

MILLWORK MANUFACTURER—an organization that manufactures millwork and distributes it either through its own or other sales organization to millwork distributors or jobbers; sometimes sales are made directly to the lumber retailer or ultimate customer.

MILLWORK RETAILER—an organization that purchases millwork from the millwork jobber, wholesaler or commission man for subsequent sale to the ultimate user; also termed lumber and building materials dealer.

MINERAL STREAK—see Streak.

MIRROR MOULDING—a moulding applied to the surface of a door to provide a frame for and to secure the mirror; may be "one-member" or "two-member" mirror mouldings.

One-member mirror moulding—forms a base or frame as well as secures the mirror.

Two-member mirror moulding—consists

of a base member applied to the surface of the door and a second member or bead to secure the mirror.

MITRE—see Joint.

MODERN STYLE—a style of architecture, practically devoid of the traditional and incorporating the more recent construction techniques, design and planning; simple structural planes and such construction techniques as post and beam, flat roofs and glass walls are emphasized.

MODULAR COORDINATION—the dimensioning of a structure and use of building materials based on a common unit of measurement, namely a module.

MODULAR SIZE—conforming to a module (a unit of measurement) or multiples thereof, the most common being 4 inches.

MOISTURE CONTENT—the amount of water, usually expressed as a percentage of the weight of oven-dry wood, contained in wood; obtained by one or two methods, namely (1) oven-drying or (2) electric moisture meter.

MORTISE—a notch or slot cut into a member to receive a projecting part (tenon) of another member to form a "mortise-and-tenon" joint.

MORTISER—a woodworking machine for "mortising."

MOULDED—worked into a form or shape and referring to wood member other than those "surfaced four sides"; also "stuck."

MOULDER—a woodworking machine designed to run mouldings and other wood members with regular or irregular profiles; a sticker.

MOULDING—a relatively narrow strip of wood, usually shaped to a curved profile throughout its length; used to accent and emphasize the ornamentation of a structure and to conceal surface or angle joints.

Applied moulding—see Planted Moulding.

Flush moulding—a moulding on the same level or plane as the wood member or assembly to which it is applied; a member is flush with another when they form an unbroken or even surface; in contrast to "raised" or "recessed" moulding; "flush-moulded."

Raised moulding—an applied moulding which partly covers or extends above the face or surface of an assembly.

MOULDING SERIES—mouldings of a certain pattern and size to which individual numbers have been assigned; the mouldings are designated as comprising a moulding series, e.g., "8,000 Series of Mouldings."

MULLION—the upright or vertical member dividing the panels in a door; the vertical member of a sash, window or door frame between openings in a multiple-opening frame; the mullion is known as the "mullion

center"; frames are termed "mullions," "triples," or "quadruples," depending on whether they have one, two or three mullions respectively; in doors, sometimes "muntings."

Door mullion—see Mullion.

Exterior door frame mullion—see Mullion.

Window frame mullion—see Mullion.

MULTIPLE-OPENING FRAME—a window or door frame consisting of at least one mullion.

MUNTIN—a short "bar," horizontal or vertical, extending from a bar to a stile, rail or another bar.

N

NAILING MARKER—a small "V" groove cut into one member to position a nail to correctly enter a second wood member.

NAIL—a slender piece of metal consisting of a head and pointed opposite end which when driven serves as a fastener for wood.

Bright nails—steel nails noncoated or otherwise treated.

Casing nails—thin wire nails with a countersunk head to engage the point of the nail set; shank and head are a little longer than finish nails.

Coated nails—steel nails given a surface treatment or covering to increase the nails' withdrawal resistance as well as resistance to corrosion and staining; "cement coated" nails are coated with a resinous substance whereas other coatings employ zinc, cadmium and tin.

Finish nails—see Casing Nails.

Galvanized nails—steel nails which are coated with zinc as a protection against rust and staining; hot-dipped galvanized; nonferrous.

NEWEL—the main post at the start of a stairs and the stiffening post at the landing; a stair newel.

Angle newel—see Landing Newel.

Landing newel—a newel installed on a landing or at the turn of a set of stairs; intermediate newel; "angle newel."

Starting newel—the newel installed at the beginning of the flight of stairs; newel post.

NEWEL CAP—a turned decorative cap or top into which the dowel or pin of the newel top fits.

Newel cap with 1 rail outlet—a newel cap with a stair rail extension.

Newel cap with 2 rail outlets—a newel cap with two stair rail extensions which are opposite to one another.

Newel cap with 2 rail outlets at right angle (quarter-turn)—a newel cap with two stair rail extensions at right angles to one another.

NEWEL COLLAR—a turned wood collar used in lengthening the base of certain stair newels.

NONBEARING WALL—a wall which supports no vertical load other than its own weight.

NONPRESSURE WOOD PRESERVATIVE PROCESS—a process of wood preservation or treatment carried out without the use of artificial pressure to force the preservative solution into the wood.

NOSE AND COVE MOULDING—see Nosing Moulding.

NOSED—the rounded edge of a wood member; also "rounded one edge"; see Nosing.

NOSING—in stairwork, the rounded edge of the stair tread which projects beyond the face of the riser; "tread nosing"; also applied to the rounded edge of a wood member, "nosed one edge" or "nosed two edges"; see Sill; Tread (Landing).

Return nosing—the nosing of an open stair tread that continues around to the open end(s) of the stairs; the return nosing is applied to the open end(s) of the stair tread and mitred to the nosing of the tread.

Sill nosing—the nosing of a "main sill and nosing" of a window frame.

Stair nosing—see Nosing.

NOSING MOULDING—a moulding consisting of a profile that is "nose and cove" and which is sometimes used on the exposed edges of flooring (especially porch work) to give a rounded or "returned nosing" effect; also "nose and cove."

NOTCHING—rectangular cut consisting of two surfaces cut on end of a member across the grain.

O

OFFSET CENTER OF STAIR CONVERGENCE—a method of "winder" construction whereby the risers do not converge at a point at the turn of the stairs, and afford some width to the winders.

OGEE—having an "S"-shaped or reverse-curve profile; the "ogee" arch was pointed with an "ogee" curve on each side and was prominent in Gothic architecture; also O.G.; see cyma recta (cymatium) and cyma reversa (inverted cymatium).

OLD GROWTH—timber from a mature naturally propagated forest; usually possesses narrower and more uniformly wide annual rings compared to second-growth timber; virgin; a rather inconclusive term.

OPENING—a discontinuity in an exterior or interior wall to admit a door or window.

Buck opening—see Rough Opening.

Outside opening—the measurement from outside of a millwork assembly.

Rough opening—the opening formed by the framing members; buck opening.

OPERATOR—crank-type hardware for opening a window which swings outward; a jointed, metal arm keeps the window open at any position.

ORIEL WINDOW—see Window.

OVERHANG—a projection of 2nd-floor joists beyond an exterior wall of the structure; projection usually 12 to 18 inches.

OVERHEAD BALANCE—a steel tape which coils up into a metal case installed in the head jamb of a window frame; the end of the tape attaches to each sash, providing activation or balancing; "overhead balance" when installation is in head jamb; patent balance; see Sash Balance.

OVERHEAD TRACK—metal or wood tracks for sliding doors or sash.

OVERMANTEL—wall panelling with moulded plaster-like decoration installed above the mantel shelf.

OVOLO—a convex profile; usually a quarter-section of a circle and similar to the profile of "quarter-round."

P

PAINT-PRIMED—see Prime Coat.

PALLADIAN—a generic term for classical architecture during the 17th and 18th centuries and widely adapted in England following the publication of the designs of the Italian architect, Andrea Palladio (16th century); Palladian window.

PANEL—a wood surface within a surrounding frame; all panels have structural frames, the interstices of which are filled with sheets or fields called "panels"; the frame is necessary for adequate strength only with the panels occupying considerable more area than the frame; the panel may be raised above or recessed below the surrounding frame and set off from it by moulding or other decorative treatment; "panel" also refers to a sheet of plywood or thin lumber as well as to a section of a floor, wall, ceiling or roof prefabricated of a large size and handled as a single unit in the operations of assembly and erection.

Dust panel—a panel consisting of a thin sheet of lumber or plywood used in cabinet work to prevent dust from entering drawer, shelving or other cabinet compartment areas.

Laying panel—grain of panel running horizontally.

Screen panel—see Combination Storm Sash and Screen.

Storm panel—see Combination Storm Sash and Screen; Sash.

Upright panel—Grain of panel running vertically.

PANEL DIVIDER—a moulding which separates two vertical wood panels along their common edges.

PANEL MOULDING—a decorative moulding used in panel work.

PARTICLEBOARD—a formed panel, consisting of particles of wood flakes, shavings, slivers, etc., bonded together with a synthetic resin or other added binder; the particles are classified by size, dried to a uniform moisture content, mixed with binder, mat-formed, compressed to density and then cured under controlled heat and pressure.

PARTING STRIP—see Stop.

PARTITION CAP AND SHOE—see Cap.

PASSIVE SOLAR HEAT GAIN—solar heat that passes through a material and is captured naturally, not by mechanical means—example, large windows facing south will take advantage of passive solar heat gain.

PATCH—an insertion of sound wood placed and glued into veneers or panels from which defective portions have been removed.

Boat patch—oval-shaped with sides tapering to a point or a small rounded end; "dutchman."

Router patch—parallel sides and rounded ends.

Sled patch—rectangular with feathered ends.

PATENT BALANCE—see Sash Balance; Overhead Balance.

PEAKED HEAD—similar to "pediment"; also applies to a door head; peaked cap.

PEDIMENT—a low-pitched triangular entrance head or cap; triangle formed by sloping roof and horizontal cornice; also may apply to window and door openings.

Broken pediment—a pediment broken along its perimeter; not solid; often contains an urn in its broken portion; may be scroll-like (swan's neck).

Rounded pediment—arc-like as contrasted to triangular; accepted, in practice, but does not satisfy definition of "pediment."

Solid pediment—a triangular head unbroken along its perimeter; peaked cap.

PENETRATION—the depth of penetration in wood by the preservative after treatment.

P.G.—a solid mould consisting of a long bevel with a small fillet on each side.

PICTURE FRAME MOULDING—rabbeted moulding forming a frame for pictures; also the trimming of window units by the use of casing on four sides, resulting in the deleting of stool and apron.

PICTURE MOULDING—a narrow moulding along the perimeter of the walls near the ceiling line to support hooks for picture hanging.

PIECE-BILL—to assemble a "bill of materials" item by item.

PILASTER—a rectangular, circular or semi-circular member used as a simulated column in entrances and other door openings and fireplace mantels; usually contains base, shaft and capital.

Fluted pilaster—see Flute.

Plain pilaster—a pilaster surfaced or dressed four sides.

Reeded pilaster—see Reed.

Reversible pilaster—a pilaster plain on one face and reeded, fluted or otherwise worked on the reverse.

PILASTER CAP—a "plinth-like block" used at the top of a pilaster.

PITCH—accumulation of resin in the wood cells in a more or less irregular patch; see Resin.

PITCH POCKET—an opening between annual growth rings which usually contains or has contained resin, bark or both.

PITCH SEAM—shake or check filled with pitch or resin.

PITCH STREAK—well-defined accumulation of pitch in a more or less regular streak; designated as small, medium or large.

PLAIN MOULDING—nonsprung; see Sprung.

PLAIN-SAWN—see Grain (Flat).

PLANCIER—also "plancher," "plancer," "planceer," and "plancia"; see Soffit.

PLANER-MATCHER—a woodworking machine which surfaces lumber on four sides and which may match or shiplap the edges; sometimes referred to as planing machine.

PLANING MILL—a mill where rough lumber (generally dry or seasoned) is dressed or surfaced (planed), run to pattern, matched or shiplapped.

PLANTED MOULDING—a moulding applied to a surface which projects or remains above it; "raised moulding"; as opposed to "solid-sticking"; "applied moulding."

PLASTER BASE—a wood member surfaced three sides, bevelled on the fourth and used as both a base plaster ground and a finish base.

PLASTERED ARCH—a door opening in which the plaster is carried on through the opening; no interior door frame or trim is used.

PLATE, TOP—a wood member, usually a double 2 × 4, which joins the top of the wall studs and upon which the ceiling joists (and sometimes rafters) rest; see Sole.

PLINTH BLOCK—a square block at the base of a pilaster; a block of wood placed at the bottom of side door casing to terminate the casing as well as the base; since the door casings and bases are moulded, "plinth blocks" offer a sturdier member and a better appearance; "plinth blocks" are thicker and wider than the abutting members; also base block, foot block or pilaster base.

PLOUGH (PLOW)—a rectangular groove or slot of three surfaces cut parallel or with the grain of a wood member; in contrast to "dado," which is cut across the grain.

PLOUGHED (PLOWED) AND BORED SASH—a "box window frame" sash where the edges of the stiles are "ploughed and bored" to receive the sash weight cord and to tie the knot.

PLUG—sound wood of various shapes for replacing defective wood portions which have been removed; plugs are usually held in veneer by friction only until veneers are bonded into plywood; also synthetic plugs of fibre and resin aggregate used to fill openings and provide a smooth, level, durable surface.

PLUMB—exactly perpendicular or vertical; at right angles to the horizon or floor.

PLY—veneer which has been assembled into a panel; a layer of veneer, veneer ply; also "skin."

PLYWOOD—a crossbanded assembly of layers of veneer or veneer in combination with a lumber core or plies joined with an adhesive; the grain of the adjoining veneer or plies is approximately at right angles; an odd number of plies is generally used; two types of plywood are recognized, "veneer plywood" (layers of veneers only) and "lumber core plywood" (lumber core with veneers or plies bonded to it).

Banded plywood—a strip of wood applied to the edges of a lumber core or veneer plywood to facilitate the shaping of the edges as well as to conceal the core and cross-banding.

Exterior plywood—plywood for outdoor or marine uses and bonded with adhesived affording the ultimate in water and moisture resistance.

Interior plywood—plywood with a high degree of moisture resistance and suitable for construction where its application requires that it shall retain its original form and practically all of its strength when occasionally subjected to a thorough wetting and subsequent normal drying.

Lumber core plywood—plywood made of layers of veneer in combination with a lumber core; lumber cores are seldom less than ⅜″ in thickness and give lengthwise stiffness to the plywood, as well as greater resistance to warping than "veneer" plywood.

Veneer plywood—plywood made of layers of veneer only.

POCKET—a removable section of a pulley stile (side jamb) of a box window frame (pocket and pulley) which gives access to the weight box; the standard width is roughly 2″–2½″ with the height determined by the length of the sash weight; the lower end of the pocket is located about 6″ above the window sill and may extend midway to the meeting rail; also weight access pocket, weight pocket.

POCKET AND PULLEY-TYPE WINDOW FRAME—see Window Frame (Box Window).

POCKET-TYPE DOOR FRAME—see Door Frame.

POLE—see Closet Pole.

PORCH COLUMN—a turned, built-up or solid column in porch work both to support a load and for decorative purposes.

PORCH RAIL, BOTTOM—a porch rail that joins the bottoms of the balusters of a porch balustrade.

PORCH WORK—millwork items used primarily in the porch balustrade, i.e., porch rails, balusters, newels and columns.

PORTICO—a porch or covered walk consisting of a roof supported by columns; a colonnaded (continuous row of columns) porch.

POWDER POST BEETLE—small insects whose larvae bore through both seasoned and unseasoned wood and leave holes ¹⁄₁₆ to ¹⁄₁₂ inch in diameter when they emerge on the surface as adults; the galleries are filled with dry, powdery, partly digested food.

PREFABRICATION—essentially component building; this term is applied to an entire wall section as contrasted with a panel or part of the entire wall; also "manufactured"; see Component Building.

PREFINISHED—millwork with an applied finish coating.

PREFITTING—trimming of the door for width and/or width and height.

PREHUNG DOOR UNIT—a precut and assembled unit consisting of a wood door with preparation for lock hardware that is hung on hinges in a wood frame; the wood frame includes the one- or two-piece jamb adjustable or as-ordered width as well as the door stop mouldings and casings (trim); also hinged interior wood door unit; door units other than conventionally hinged are also available.

PRESERVATION, WOOD—the penetration of wood by selected chemicals or wood preservatives; two general processes employed are (1) pressure and (2) non-pressure.

PRESERVATIVE—any substance that, for a reasonable length of time, will prevent the development and action of wood-destroying fungi, borers of various kinds and other harmful insects that deteriorate wood after the wood has been properly treated with it; also wood preservative.

PRESSURE WOOD PRESERVATIVE PROCESS—a process of wood preservation or treatment in which the wood preservative is forced into the cells of the wood under greater than atmospheric pressure.

PRIME COAT—the first coat of paint in an application that consists of two or more coats; also refers to the paint used for such an initial coat; priming; primer; paint-primed.

PRIME SASH—see Sash.

PUNK—see Decay.

PUTTY—a precipitated whiting (chalk or calcium carbonate) ground in linseed oil with approximately 5 percent white lead added; see Glazing Compound.

Face putty—glazing whereby glass is inserted into the glass rabbet, glazier's points driven and the glass rabbet filled with putty, which is bevelled back against the glass.

PUTTY GROOVE—a small groove worked in the putty or glass rabbet of a sash to secure a better bond between putty and wood.

PUTTY SMEAR—where putty has been incorrectly placed in surrounding area of wood as well as into the open defect that the putty was intended to repair. Putty smears are not allowed where the expression "well puttied" is used.

Q

QUARTER-ROUND WINDOW—stationary or operating window with glass shaped as a quarter-circle; it is divided into separate panes or comes with a removable grille, installed on the interior.

QUARTER-SAWN—applies specifically to hardwoods; see Grain (Edge, Vertical).

R

R-VALUE—an industry measurement of the resistance to heat flow through a given material. (Usage—the higher the R-Value, the greater the resistance to heat flow.)

RABBET—a rectangular cut consisting of two surfaces cut on edge of a member parallel with the grain; a rabbet has two surfaces and a "plough" (plow) three; also "rebate," rabbit.

Glass rabbet—see Putty (Face).

Lath and plaster rabbet—a rabbet on a window or door jamb or sill to receive the lath and plaster; serves as a ground for interior finishing material.

Putty rabbet—the rabbet in stiles, rails, muntins and bars of a sash that receives the glass; glass rabbet.

Screen rabbet—the rabbet in the stiles and rails of a flush moulded screen that receives the screening.

Secondary putty rabbet—a small rabbet worked on the exposed corner or edge of the glass or putty rabbet next to the glass; after the sash has been "face-puttied," the sash is turned over and putty run into the "secondary putty rabbet" to fill any voids that might exist between glass and wood.

RABBETED TO (IN) PAIRS—a pair of sash or doors with rabbeted meeting stiles to prevent swinging through; each sash or door has its meeting stile rabbeted on an opposite edge or corner.

RADIAL—direction in wood passing across the annual growth rings and through the pith.

RADIATION—energy released in the form of waves or particles, due to a change in temperature within a gas or vacuum. (Usage—"Short wave radiation" refers to energy emitted from a high temperature source, such as the sun; "long wave radiation" refers to energy emitted by low temperature sources, such as the human body.)

RADIUS MOULDING—a moulding run to a specified radius.

RAIL—horizontal member of a window or door sash.

Bottom rail—the bottom rail of a sash, door, blind or other panel assembly.

Center rail—a rail, approximately at the midlength point of the frame of a hollow-core door.

Check rails—meeting rails sufficiently thicker than the window to fill the opening between the top and bottom sash (two adjacent sash on a horizontal sliding window) made by the parting stop of the frame; check rails are usually bevelled and rabbeted.

Cross rail—the rail of a door.

Diagonal rail—a diagonal rail of a crossbuck or sawbuck of a panel or sash door; see Crossbuck.

Door rail—the cross or horizontal members of the framework of a door.

Frieze rail—see Intermediate Rail.

Intermediate rail—a rail of a door located between the top and bottom rails.

Kick rail—a rail located approximately 10–12 inches from the bottom of a hollow-core flush door frame; used primarily on institutional doors.

Lock rail—the intermediate rail of a door at lock height.

Meeting rail—one of the rails of a window that meets when the window is closed; also middle rail; see Check Rail and Plain Rail; may be used collectively to designate both sash meeting rails.

Oval bottom edge—the bottom rail of a screen with an oval bottom edge; contrast to bevelled edge.

Plain rail—a meeting rail the same thickness as the window; see Check Rail.

Plain bevelled sash rail—the bottom rail of a sash bevelled to conform to the slope of the window frame sill and with no other working.

Porch rail—a moulded wood member that joins either the tops or bottoms of the balusters of a porch balustrade; "porch rails" are classified as "top" or "bottom" porch rails.

Solid door rail—see Stile.

Stair rail—the moulded wood member of a balustrade that connects the tops of the balusters and serves as a hand support and guard; sometimes "handrail."

Top rail—the top rail of a sash, door, blind or other similar panel assembly.

Top porch rail—see Porch Rail.

Veneered door rail—see Stile.

Wall rail—a moulded linear wood member secured to the wall of a closed flight of stairs and which serves as a hand support.

RAISED MOULDING—a moulding not on the same level or plane as the wood member or assembly to which it is applied; as contrasted to "flush moulding."

RAKE MOULDING—a moulding applied to the rake or the exposed inclined ends of a gable roof; term is sometimes applied to any moulding installed in a direction other than horizontal or vertical; also barge moulding.

RAMP—a stair rail steeper than the normal rake of a stairs; see Easement.

RANDOM LENGTHS—unspecified lengths as contrasted to "specified lengths."

REBATE—see Rabbet.

RED KILNBURN—a chemical discoloration of wood, primarily softwoods, which usually occurs during the kiln drying or air seasoning process; usually penetrates deeply.

REED—small semicircular profile similar to a "bead" worked on a wood member; used commonly in pilasters (reeded pilasters); opposite of "flute"; reeds are occasionally below the surface.

RELATIVE HUMIDITY—ratio of the amount of water vapor in the air to that the air would hold at saturation at the same temperature.

RESILIENCY—the ability of a material to withstand temporary deformation, the original shape being assumed when the stresses are removed.

RESIN—any of various solid or semisolid organic substances exuded from various plants and trees or prepared synthetically; see Pitch.

RESIN-SEALER PRIME COAT—a coating applied to resinous species of wood to prevent "bleeding."

RETURN—continuation in a different direction of a moulding or projection, usually at right angles.

RETURN MANTEL—the measurement from the surface of the interior wall to the masonry face of a fireplace opening; also "mantel reveal."

REVEAL—the margin visible between the window or door sash and the surrounding frame.

Door panel reveal—see Reveal.

RIBBON STRIPE—a veneer figure which consists of alternate light and dark stripes running primarily the length of the veneer and produced by quarter-sawing.

RIM SECTION—the frame assembly of a combination door.

RISE—in stairwork, the vertical or perpendicular measurement between the faces of two consecutive treads; also "stair tread rise."

Total rise—the vertical or perpendicular measurement from the lower-level finish floor to the finish floor of the landing or upper floor level where the flight ends.

RISER—the vertical stair member between two consecutive stair treads.

ROD BOARD—a board used to "lay out" the various sizes of members required in manufacturing an item of millwork, e.g., a window or sash frame; the board contains the correct measurements of each required member.

ROOF WINDOW—window designed to be installed on a sloping surface; see also Skylight. (Usage—"Stationary Roof Windows" are nonoperating; "Venting Roof Windows" have the sash hinged at the top, swing outward, and are operated by manual or automatic equipment.)

ROSETTE—a turned (usually circular or oval) decorative wood plaque secured to a plastered wall and abutted by the end of the stair rail.

ROT—see Decay.

ROTARY-CUT FACE VENEER—veneer cut on a lathe which rotates a log or bolt against a broad cutting knife; the veneer is cut in a continuous sheet much the same as paper is unwound from a roll.

ROUGH LUMBER—lumber that has not been dressed or surfaced but which has been sawed, edged and trimmed at least to the extent of showing saw marks in the wood on the four longitudinal surfaces of each piece for its overall length.

ROUGH OPENING—an unfinished wall or ceiling opening, where a window or door will be installed. (Usage—Rough Openings are lined by wood members; the top one is the "header," the side ones are the "jack studs," and the bottom one is the "rough sill"; also Rough Openings in brick walls are known as "masonry openings.")

ROUGH SILL—the horizontal wood member lining the bottom of a rough opening for a window or door.

ROUND—a moulding whose profile is one-quarter, one-half or a full-circle.

Full-round—see Closet Pole.

Half-round—a moulding whose cross section is one-half of a circle; also screen moulding, screen bead, flat half-round.

Quarter-round—a moulding whose cross section is one-quarter of a circle; sometimes "carpet strip."

ROUND EDGE—the corner of a piece shaped to a radius; generally implies a greater radius than for an "eased edge": shaped primarily for appearance.

ROUNDED ONE EDGE—see Nosed.

ROUND-TOP WINDOW—see Circle-Top Window.

ROUT—to groove or hollow out a wood member with a router, e.g., housed stair stringers; also "hinge rout" on door.

Concealed rout(ing)—routing the bottom of cabinet doors and drawers to provide a means of opening and closing; such routing is concealed (gives the door or drawer a flush design) and eliminates cabinet door or drawer pulls.

RUN—in stairwork, the horizontal measurement between the faces of two adjacent or consecutive risers; also "stair tread run" or "going"; also "sash run" or "runway."

Total run—the horizontal measurement between the face of the first riser and the face of the last riser of a flight of stairs.

RUNNING FOOT—see Lineal Foot.

S

SADDLE—see Threshold.

SANDED—

Belt-sanded—sanded on a "belt sander," a machine consisting of a relatively long endless abrasive belt driven between two rollers and designed to smooth flat surfaces ready for finishing; also for sanding millwork, especially mouldings, with curvilinear profiles.

Drum-sanded—sanded on a "drum sander"; a drum sander has a power feed similar to a planer or surfacer and consists of several drums each covered with a different grade of abrasive, the coarser drums being first while the final drum is covered with a fine abrasive; a drum sander doesn't produce as fine a work as a "belt sander"; belt sanders are often used after the drum-sanding operation.

Hand-sanded—non-machine-sanded.

Machine-sanded—sanded by one of various types of sanders or sanding machines, most common types being the "drum" and the "belt sander."

SAP STAIN—see Stain (Blue).

SAPWOOD—the living wood of pale color (usually white) near the outside of the tree immediately under the bark.

SASH—a single assembly of stiles and rails into a frame for holding glass, with or without dividing bars or muntins, to fill a given opening; it may be either "open" or "glazed."

Awning sash—a sash the bottom of which swings outward (awning type) or the top of which swings inward (hopper type).

Barn sash—a sash usually installed in a rough built-on-the-job type of frame for farm, utility and temporary structures, where economy is a prime prerequisite; utility sash.

Basement sash—an awning-like sash usually consisting of one, two or three vertical lights; sash swings inward from the top (hopper type).

Cabinet sash—a sash door used in cabinets; also cupboard sash.

Casement sash—a sash hinged at the stile to swing outward (swing-out) or inward (swing-in); also French sash or window.

Combination storm sash and screen—see Combination Storm Sash and Screen.

Fixed sash—see Stationary Sash.

Gable sash—a decorative sash, commonly utilized in the gables of structures; may be one-quarter circle, one-half circle, full circle or octagonal in shape; usually contains divided-lights and may be installed as a sash or as a frame unit; may be vented.

Glazed sash—a sash in which the glass has been installed.

Hopper-type sash—see Awning Sash.

Hotbed sash—a sash used in plant cold frames for forcing plants or other greenhouse activities; also "cold frame."

Jalousie sash—see Jalousie.

Open sash—a sash in which the glass has not been installed.

Picture sash—same as Stationary or Fixed Sash; "picture sash or window" usually implies a relatively large size sash.

Porch sash—sash intended for use in porch work.

Prime sash—the balanced or activated sash of a window unit.

Sash condensation—see Condensation.

Stationary sash—a fixed or nonoperative sash; as a View Sash or "picture window" often used in combination with other types of window and sash units; intended primarily for view purposes and to admit light; see Picture Sash.

Storm sash—a glazed panel or sash placed on the inside or outside of an existing sash or window as protection against the elements; an insulated air space is formed between the sash or window and the storm sash; also "double-glazing"; "storm panels"; "storm window."

Studio sash—see Picture Sash.

Transom sash—a sash installed in a "transom."

Utility sash—see Barn Sash.

View sash—see Stationary Sash, Picture Sash.

SASH BALANCE—one of several types of mechanical sash-activation devices; primarily these "balances" include coiled springs, spiral springs or other spring-type devices for raising and lowering the sash.

SASH CLEARANCE—difference between the width of window frame guide or runway and the sash thickness.

SASH CORD—a rope to connect the sash with the sash weight in a "box window frame."

SASH CRACK—sash crack thickness is equivalent to one-half the difference between the inside window frame dimension and the outside sash width.

SASH FRAME—see Window Frame.

Gable sash frame—a sash frame for a "gable sash."

SASH PIN—a steel nail-like pin driven into the joint formed by the sash rail and stile to penetrate the rail tenon; sash pins are also used at each end of at least one bar; pins may be either smooth or barbed; also a pin

or bolt capable of being engaged in one or two holes bored in the side sash jamb to maintain position of sash.

SASH PULLEY—a metal or wood pulley installed in the "pulley stile" of a box window frame to accommodate the sash cord or chain; the pulley is generally located approximately 4″ from the face of the head jamb.

SASH RUNWAY—the space between the parting stop and the window stop in which the bottom sash of a double-hung window slides when raised or lowered; also the space between the blind stop and the parting stop in which the top sash of a double-hung window slides when raised or lowered; any space in which a sash slides; also "sash run."

SASH TRACK—head or sill sash guides; see Sill Track.

SASH WEIGHT—solid, usually cast-iron cylindrical weights to balance or activate the sash in a box window frame (pocket-and-pulley type); sash weights are hung either on sash cords or chains and are of different sizes and weights for each sash size.

SAWBUCK—see Crossbuck.

SCALLOP—a decorative wood member which contains a series of curves or areas of circles sawn or shaped on one of its edges; a scalloped member.

SCARF JOINT—see Joint.

SCIENTIFIC NAME—a universal system of nomenclature for plants and animals that can be used not only within the boundaries of a single country but throughout the world; scientific names are in Latin, e.g., Pinus ponderosa—Ponderosa pine; in the above example Ponderosa pine is the common name; the scientific name is further broken down into the "genus" (pinus) and the "species" (ponderosa).

SCOTIA—a deep concave moulding more than a one-quarter round in section; reverse of torus; cove moulding.

SCREEN—a frame assembly of stiles and rails with inserted screening; screens may be of two types, "rigid" and "flexible"; a rigid screen is similar to a storm sash with the screening replacing the glass; a flexible screen is similar in operation to a window shade.

Combination screen—see Combination Storm Sash and Screen.

Flexible screen—also called "roll screen"; see Screen.

Flush moulded screen—see Screen Moulding.

Full screen—a screen which fills the entire window opening of a double-hung window.

Half-screen—a screen which does not fill the entire window opening of a double-hung

window but only the bottom sash of the window; "sliding half-screens" may cover either the top or bottom sash; screen panel.

Raised moulded screen—see Screen Moulding.

Rigid screen—see Screen.

Sliding half-screen—a half-screen which slides vertically in order to cover either the top or bottom sash of a double-hung window.

SCREENING—a mesh of fine aluminum, galvanized steel or bronze wire; "insect wire screening," "wire cloth" or "insect wire"; also "plastic and fibreglass."

Groove-with-a-spline screening—see Rolled-into-a-Groove Screening.

Rolled-into-a-groove screening—the inserting of screening into a flush moulded screen frame by rolling or pressing the screening into a groove worked into the screen frame rabbet; a flush screen moulding is then placed in the rabbet; if plastic screening is used, a "spline" must be inserted into the groove after the plastic screening has been inserted.

Stapled screening—the application of screening to a "raised moulded screen" frame, stapling the screening to the faces of the stiles and rails, and then covering with a screen moulding.

SCREEN MESH—see Mesh.

SCREEN MOULDING—a small moulding of several different patterns to cover screening when it is nailed or stapled to the screen frame; if screen moulding is "flush" with the frame, a "flush moulded screen"; if raised above the frame, a "raised moulded screen."

Beaded screen moulding—screen moulding with three semicircular beads.

Cloverleaf screen moulding—screen moulding with a clover-like profile.

Flat screen moulding—flat screen moulding with both edges slightly round or "eased."

Half-round screen moulding—see Round.

SCREEN STOCK—moulding stock generally 1″ × 2″, 1″ × 3″, ⅝″ × 2″, or ⅝″ × 3″ nominal size for use as stiles and rails in screens; screen stock may be surfaced four sides, rabbeted on one edge as in "combination" screen stock or ploughed (plowed) on one edge as in "sliding" screen stock; also shelf cleat, cleat or clear strips.

Combination screen stock—screen stock that is rabbeted on one edge; the rabbet receives the screening and the screen moulding; moulding usually beaded, and a member of the combination screen stock; combination screen stock is used for "flush moulded screens."

Combination sliding screen stock—sliding screen stock is rabbeted on one edge

253

to receive the screening and screen moulding.

Sliding screen stock—screen stock with a groove or plough (plow) on one edge that received a "T" slide nailed to the window frame side jamb; used for sliding half-screens; the screen stock includes the "T" slide member.

Square-edge screen stock—surfaced four-side screen stock.

SCRIBING—drawing a line parallel with an existing surface; fitting millwork to an irregular surface.

SCROLL HEAD—the head or cap of an entrance with a scroll-like design.

SCROLL HEAD AND URN—a scroll head with an urn comprising the cap or head of an entrance.

SCUFF STRIP—see Skid Block.

SEASONED—wood which has lost varying amounts of moisture from a green or partially dry condition, such moisture loss having been accomplished either by "air seasoning" or "kiln-drying"; an indefinite term; see Dry.

SEAT BOARD—a flat board cut to fit the contour of a bow or bay window; it is installed between the sills and the surrounding wall surface, to provide a seat or shelf space.

SECOND GROWTH—timber that has grown after the removal, whether by cutting fire, wind or other agency, of all or a large part of the previous stand.

SEED—a minute bubble appearing in plate or window glass.

SEGMENT HEAD—an entrance or door head in the form of the arc of a circle.

SET, NAIL—driving a nail by means of a nail set below the surface of the wood so that the nail hole may be filled with putty prior to finishing and concealed.

SETTING BLOCK—a wood block placed in the glass groove or rabbet of the bottom rail of an insulating glass sash to form a base or bed for the glass.

SHADING COEFFICIENT—a ratio established by the American Society of Heating, Refrigerating, and Air Conditioning Engineers, to compare solar heat gain, through a glazing system, to the total solar heat gain (1.0) through a single sheet of clear glass, ⅛ inch thick. (Usage—The lower the shading coefficient, the lower the solar heat gain.)

SHAKE—a separation along the grain of wood, the greater part of which occurs between the rings of annual growth; shaky lumber.

SHAPER—a woodworking machine with knives mounted on a vertical shaft on a table for shaping wood members.

SHEATHING—a surface, usually of wood or fibreboard, applied to the exterior faces of the studs or wall frame.

SHELF CLEAT—a moulding commonly used in closets to support the shelves; also shelf strip.

SHELVING—usually surfaced four sides, boards used as shelves in clothes closets, linen closets, kitchen cabinets and other locations.

Adjustable shelving—shelving which employs metal side clips (other methods may be used) that enable shelves to assume different spacings or clearances.

Closed shelving—shelving in cabinets concealed by a door.

Open shelving—exposed shelving not in a cabinet and not concealed by a door.

SHIM—a thin strip of wood, sometimes wedge-shaped, for plumbing or levelling wood members, especially door and window frames.

SHINGLE MOULDING—a moulding used on the rake of a structure.

SHIPLAP—lumber whose edges are rabbeted to make a "lap joint."

SHOE—a moulding installed at the base of various members of a structure.

Base shoe—a small narrow moulding running around the perimeter of a room where the base meets the finish floor; also "shoe moulding" and floor mould; see Carpet Strip.

Bent shoe—base shoe moulding curved or on a radius and used on starting stair treads.

Partition shoe—moulding that is ploughed (plowed) out to receive the bottom of a partition.

Stair shoe—a stair member which lies on the top of a curbed stringer and into whose groove or plow the balusters are inserted; also "stair subrail" or "shoe rail."

SHORTS—a general term for lumber and moulding lengths under 8 feet; 8 feet is commonly used in determining short lengths although this may vary.

SHOW THROUGH—irregular surfaces visible on the face of a wood flush door (such as depressions, bumps, mechanical marks, or core, or frame outlines).

SHUTTER—a wood assembly of stiles and rails to form a frame which encloses panels used in conjunction with door and window frames; may also consist of vertical boards cleated together (batten-type shutters); see Blind.

Reversible shutter—a shutter which resembles a slat-like blind on one side and a panel-like shutter on the reverse side; also "reversible shutter-blind."

SIDE JAMB—vertical member of the window or door frame.

SIDE-OF-WINDOW TRIM—the mouldings and/or trim necessary to "finish" or "trim" the interior side of a sash or window frame.

SIDELIGHT—see Light.

SIDING GROOVE—a groove on the underside of a window sill to accommodate the wood siding or facing of the exterior wall of the structure.

SILL—lower, horizontal member of the window or door frame.

Door sill—see Sill.

Main sill and nosing—a narrower exterior extension fastened to the outside face of a main window sill.

Main sill and undersill—an upper thinner member of a two-piece window sill resting on top of a thicker lower member (formerly subsill).

Plain bevel sill—an exterior door sill which employs a wood or nonwood threshold.

Sill horn—see Horn.

Sill liner—see Liner.

Sill nosing—see Nosing.

Sill windbreak—see Windbreak.

Steel sash sill—a sill to receive the bottom lip of a steel sash.

Threshold sill—a door sill with the threshold worked on it.

Two-piece sill—"main sill and nosing" and "main sill and undersill."

Window sill—main sill; see Sill.

SILL LIP—that part of the window sill extending beyond the outside face of the blind stop; if sill includes an offset, that part of the sill beyond it.

SILL OFFSET—the rabbet(s) on the surface of a window sill to accommodate the window sash and the storm sash and/or screens; originally called "weatherings"; when sill contained two weatherings, known as "double-sunk sill."

SILL TRACK—metal, wood or plastic tracks or grooves which guide the sash in a horizontal-sliding window unit; also "sill sash guides."

SINK FRONT—a base kitchen cabinet shallow-front assembly that contains a false drawer front directly below the counter and a pair of doors below to complete the assembly.

SIZE—measurement of millwork items and members.

Actual size—the true or actual dimensions or size as opposed to "nominal size."

Finished size—the overall measurement of any wood part including the solid mould or rabbet.

Glass size—one of the three measurements of a window or sash unit; glass size is measured from stile to stile and from rail to rail inclusive of the muntins and bars and is always in inches; the size of a pane of glass of any sash or door light.

Modular size—see Modular Size.

Outside opening size—measurement from outside to outside of any given item; unit measurement.

Stud opening size—see Rough Opening.

Window opening size—the dimensions of the window frame required to accommodate the window, in feet and inches.

Window rough opening size—the size of the rough frame wall opening to receive the window or sash unit; given in feet and inches; also "buck opening."

SKID BLOCK—a small wood or metal block applied to the bottom edge of a "prefit door" in order to prevent damage; "scuff strip."

SKIM—long narrow repair not more than 3/16 inches wide.

SKIRTING—see Base.

SKYLIGHT—a window installed in a roof and assuming the same slope.

SLAT—a thin narrow strip of wood used in door and window blinds, doors and transoms; a louvre.

Chevron slat—a "V"-shaped slat which assures maximum privacy and ventilation.

Diagonal slat—a rectangular-like slat rounded or bevelled and installed diagonally as in Venetian blinds; stationary or movable.

Movable slat—see Blind.

Stationary slat—see Blind.

SLOTTED—see Joint (slotted mortise-and-tenon joint).

SLIDING DOOR, POCKET-TYPE—a door which slides horizontally into a wall pocket or slot recessed into the wall of a structure; imparts additional space to a room compared to the conventionally hinged door since no swing space is required; see Door Frame (pocket-type door frame).

SLUDGING—sediment of a muddy mass which settles to the bottom of the container of a wood-treating solution when solids are precipitated from the solvent.

SNAP-IN GRID—wood or plastic removable divided-lights for sash and windows.

SOFFIT—the under side of a box cornice; in kitchens, the lowered ceiling directly above the top of the wall cabinets which seals off cabinet space too high to utilize; known as "drop ceiling," "furred-down ceiling," or "furred ceiling"; also plancier.

SOFTWOOD—one of the botanical groups of trees that has persistent needle-like or scale-like leaves; softwoods are evergreen (only three important native species being deciduous), have longer-length fibres than hardwoods, do not contain vessels and have seeds naked; also known as "cone bearers" or "conifers."

SOLAR ENERGY—thermal radiation from the sun, as measured by short radiation wavelengths. (Usage—The three kinds of solar radiation are ultra-violet, visible, and near-infrared.)

SOLAR ORIENTATION—placement of a structure on a building site to obtain the maximum benefits of sunlight.

SOLE—a horizontal wood member, usually a 2 × 4, on which wall and partition studs rest; soleplate, bottom plate.

SOLID MOULDING—non-finger-jointed moulding, solid length.

SOLID-STICKING—a mould or profile worked on the article itself; also "solid-stuck."

SOLID-STUCK—see Solid-Sticking.

SOLID WOOD—nonveneered.

SOUND—free of decay; see Knot.

SPACER BLOCK—a thin strip of wood placed on the edges of a prehung door to take up the door clearance while in transit; also spacer wafer.

SPECIFIED LENGTHS—specific lengths as contrasted to "random" or assorted lengths; see Random Lengths.

SPIRAL DOWEL—a wood dowel with spiral grooves allowing the glue to flow in the grooves and prevent "starved joints"; dowels with glue grooves.

SPIRAL SPRING BALANCE—see Sash Balance.

SPLINE—a small strip of wood that fits into a groove or slot of both members to form a joint; the "groove" into which the spline fits; a small piece of metal, often corrugated, driven into two members at the joint to strengthen it, especially mitre joints.

SPLIT—lengthwise separation of wood extending from one surface through the piece to the opposite or an adjoining surface.

SPRAYING, WOOD-PRESERVATION TREATMENT—application of wood preservative or water-repellent to wood by means of spraying.

SPRIGS—see Glazier's Points.

SPRING BALANCE—see Sash Balance.

SPRINGWOOD—the portion of the annual growth ring of the tree formed during the early part of the season's growth; due to relatively thin-walled cells it is usually less dense and weaker mechanically than the summerwood; see Summerwood.

SPRUNG—the interior corner of a moulding "bevelled off" to better fit a right-angle joint; in contrast to nonsprung or plain.

SQUARE EDGE—the corner of a piece that forms a 90-degree angle.

SQUARENESS TOLERANCE—difference in lengths of diagonals that extend from upper right to the lower left and from the upper left to the lower right corners of a door.

STABILITY—see Dimensional Stability.

STACKING—the vertical joining of awning sash units.

STAFF MOULDING—see Brick Moulding.

STAIN—discoloration on or in lumber other than its natural color and commonly confined to the sapwood (sap stains); stain is classified as "light, medium or heavy stain."

Blue stain—a bluish or grayish discoloration of sapwood caused by the growth of certain mould-like fungi on the surface and in the interior of wood; has little or no effect on strength of wood although it can seriously affect wood from an appearance standpoint; a "sap stain."

Heavy stain—difference in color so pronounced as practically to obscure the grain of wood.

Light stain—slight difference in color which will not materially impair the appearance of the wood if given a natural finish.

Medium stain—pronounced difference in color which, although it does not obscure the grain of the wood, is customarily objectionable in a natural but not in a painted finish.

Water stain—thought to be staining of certain species due to chemical reaction between relatively prolonged water accumulations and the wood elements; usually superficial.

STAIR BRACKET—thin decorative wood member nailed to the face of an open stair stringer immediately under the return nosing of each stair tread; "scroll bracket."

STAIRCASE—same as "stairs," especially when a balustrade is included.

STAIR CARRIAGE—a rough structural stair member (stringer) which is cut out to receive the treads and risers, stair carriages may or may not be used in stair construction; "stair carriages" are nonexposed structural supporting members of the finished stairs; also "rough stair stinger," "horse" or "springing tree."

STAIR CLEARANCE—measurement from the tip of the tread nosing perpendicular to the overhead rake of the stairs.

STAIR CROOKS—irregularly shaped stair rail which when properly joined to straight runs of stair rail completes the handrail of the balustrade. Also referred to as fittings.

STAIR FILLET—see Fillet.

STAIR FLIGHT—a series of steps unbroken by a landing that extends from (1) one main floor level to a landing, (2) landing to landing, (3) landing to main floor level or (4) main floor level to main floor level; a stairs or stairway may consist of one or more flights.

STAIR HEADROOM—the clear vertical height measured from the nosing of a stair tread to any overhead obstruction.

STAIR HORSE—see Stair Carriage.

STAIR LANDING—a level platform between two flights of stairs.

STAIR RAIL—see Rail.

STAIR RAIL BOLT—a metal bolt consisting of a lag at one end and a nut at the other used in joining a "stair crook" to "stair rail."

STAIRS—one or more flights of a series of steps leading from one main level of a structure to another.

Basement stairs—extend from an uninhabitable to an inhabitable level; service stairs.

Box stairs—see Closed Stairs.

Closed riser stairs—a stair with risers.

Closed stairs—a stairs entirely "walled in" on both sides; does not contain a balustrade; also "boxed" or "box stairs"; "closed string stairs."

Closed and open stairs—stairs both closed and open in the same flight.

Disappearing stairs—a sectional-type stair assembly that folds up and recesses into an opening in the ceiling; also folding stairs.

Double "L"-type stairs—a platform stairs with two intermediate landings, one near the top and one near the bottom with a change of direction of 90 degrees for each landing.

Finish stairs—extends from one habitable level or floor to another; also main stairs.

Geometric stairs—a stairs without newels, usually including a circular or elliptical stairwell, the handrail continuing in a smooth unbroken line from top to bottom; a winding stairs.

"L"-type stairs—a platform stairs with flights at right angles to each other.

Open riser stairs—a stairway without risers.

Open stairs—a stairs having one or both sides open to a hall or room and containing a balustrade; open stairs are "right" or "left" hand open or "open both sides" depending on the location of the open or nonwalled side(s) as one observes the stairs from the bottom level; also "open string stairs."

Platform stairs—stairs that include an intermediate landing(s) in going from one main floor level to another; also "dog-legged" or "broken flight" stairs.

Service stairs—see Basement Stairs.

Straight-run stairs—stairs from one main floor level to another without turns or landings; also "straight stairs."

"U"-Type stairs—platform stairs with an intermediate landing in which the direction of the stairs returns on itself or reverses direction 180 degrees; should flights be relatively close to one another (narrow well hole), a "narrow U" stairs; flights further apart, "wide U" stairs.

Winding stairs—scroll or circular stairs containing well holes which are circular or elliptical; a geometric stairs.

STAIR SHOE—see Shoe.

STAIR STRINGER—the inclined side of a stairs that supports the treads and risers; also "stair string."

Box stair stringer—see Closed Stair Stringer.

Closed stair stringer—a plain stringer used to conceal the ends of the treads and risers in an open stairs and also known as a "curb stair stringer"; also refers to a housed stringer installed in a closed stairs.

Curb stair stringer—see Closed Stair Stringer.

Face stair stringer—see Open Stair Stringer.

Finish stair stringer—the exposed or finished stringer of a stairs as contrasted to the unexposed or "rough stair stringer" or stair carriage.

Housed stair stringer—a finish stair stringer which contains horizontal and vertical grooves or routs on the face to receive the treads and risers; also closed or box stringer.

Open stair stringer—a finish stair stringer (string) which is cut out to receive the treads and risers; an open stair stringer always requires a balustrade; also "cut," "return string" or "cut and mitred string."

Plain stair stringer—a nonhoused stair stringer surfaced four sides; also solid stair stringer.

Rough stair stringer—see Stair Carriage.

Wall stair stringer—see Closed Stair Stringer.

STAIR SUBRAIL—see Shoe.

STAIR TREAD—see Tread.

STAIRWAY—used synonymously with "staircase" or "stairs."

STAIR WEDGES—wood wedges glued and driven into the grooves of a housed stair stringer after treads and risers are inserted to assure a tight fit.

STAIRWELL—the rough framed opening which receives the stairs.

STAIR WINDER—see Winder.

STAIRWORK—a general term applying to the building and erection of stairs.

STANDARD DOOR GUARANTEE—a guarantee for one year by the manufacturers of the National Woodwork Manufacturers Association of doors produced by them; certain requirements must be met by the purchaser to make such guarantee valid.

STANDARD MILLWORK LIST—a millwork price list for sash, windows, screens and doors commonly used in the millwork industry; also Standard Lists.

STAPLING—fastening of millwork by staples rather than nails.

STARTING RAIL DROP—a stair crook which consists of a stair rail with a 90-degree turn (drop) in a vertical plane and which is returned at its end.

STARTING STEP—a separate stair assembly of stair tread, riser, cove and usually base shoe, joined to a flight of stairs at the main lower level; also "curtail step."

Bullnose starting step—similar to "half-circle starting step."

Half-circle starting step—a starting step with a one-half circle on one or both ends; also "circle end."

Quarter-circle starting step—a starting step with a one-quarter circle on one or both ends.

Reversible starting step—a starting step that can be employed for either a right-hand or left-hand open stairs.

Scroll-end starting step—a starting step with a spiral-like or scroll design on one or both ends.

STEPPING—lumber surfaced three sides and "nosed" one edge; it is generally finished $1\frac{1}{16}$" in thickness by $9\frac{3}{8}$" or $11\frac{3}{8}$" in width and may be classified as "lineal stair tread stock."

STICKER—see Moulder.

STICKING—see Solid-Sticking.

STILE—the upright or vertical outside pieces of a sash, door, blind or screen; "style."

Angle stile—narrow strips, usually not moulded, to close the space between the front assembly and the wall of a corner china cabinet.

Hanging stile—a door stile to which the butts or hinges are applied; also hinge stile; also refers to the side jamb of a window or sash to which pulleys, balances or hinges are applied.

Inside entrance stile—the vertical entrance member immediately under the pilaster and next to the entrance opening.

Outside entrance stile—the vertical entrance member immediately under the pilaster and away from the entrance opening.

Pulley stile—in a box window frame the side window jamb in which the pulley is installed.

Solid door stile—door stile of solid lumber as contrasted to "veneered stile."

Stile plate—thin polished metal plate on the stile face of the door in the vicinity of the lock or passage set to prevent soiling; also "push plate."

Striking stile—the door stile containing the lock.

Veneered door stile—door stile of lumber core and face veneers; in "five-ply" construction crossbanding veneers are also used; as contrasted to "solid stile."

STOOL—a moulded interior trim member serving as a sash or window frame sill cap; stools may be "bevelled-rabbeted" or "rabbeted" to receive the window frame sill or "nonbevelled" or "nonrabbeted"; some nonbevelled or nonrabbeted stools include a tongue to fit in the groove of the window frame sill; also window stool, stool cap.

Bevelled-rabbeted window stool—window stool bevelled-rabbeted (usually a 10- or 14-degree bevel) to accommodate the pitch or slope of a window frame sill.

China cabinet stool—the extension of the china cabinet countershelf beyond the front frame.

Rabbeted window stool—window stool rabbeted to receive the flat surface of a window frame sill; nonbevelled stool.

STOP—a moulding primarily used in window and door trim.

Cabinet drawer stop—a wood strip or stop fastened to the drawer side guide, the back end of the drawer or the runner near the back to prevent a filled drawer from tearing off the "lip" of the drawer front.

Door stop—a moulding nailed to the faces of the door frame jambs to prevent the door from swinging through; door stops are sometimes larger in size than window stops although they are usually interchangeable.

Glass stop—see Bead.

Head stop—the horizontal door or window stop across the top of the window or door frame opening.

Parting stop—a small strip of wood let into the plough (plow) of the jambs of a double-hung check-rail window frame to separate the top sash from the bottom sash; also parting bead, parting strip or check strip.

Side stop—the vertical window or door stop on either side of the window or door frame opening.

Window stop—a moulding to hold the bottom sash of a double-hung window in place (sometimes called "check stop"); the weatherstripping of the side window jambs has generally taken over this function, although window stops are still generally employed in trimming out windows and sash; also "check stop."

STORM SASH—see Sash.

STRADDLE MOULDING—a two-member decorative glass bead-like moulding around the light opening of a flush door.

STRAIGHT-GRAINED WOOD—wood in which the fibres (grain) run parallel to the axis of the tree.

STREAK—discoloration in wood from various causes, which imparts a streak effect.

Mineral streak—an olive to greenish black or brown discoloration of undetermined cause in hardwoods (particularly hard maples) which occurs in streaks usually containing accumulations of mineral matter.

Pitch streak—a well-defined accumulation of pitch in a more or less regular streak.

Sound dark streaks—a chamber formed by the maggots of a small black fly which results in a black streak appearing on the surface of West Coast Hemlock; also "black check" and "bird pecks."

STRESSED SKIN—two facings, one glued to one side and the other to the opposite, of an inner structural framework to form a panel; facings may be of plywood or other suitable material.

STRIKE PLATE—a metal piece mortised into or fastened to the face of a door frame side jamb to receive the latch or dead bolt when the door is closed; also strike.

STRINGER MOULDING—a moulding, often a wood or window stop, along the top edge of the stringer of a closed stairs; stringer moulding may also be solid-stuck on the stringer.

STRUCTURAL WINDOW WALL PANEL—a window unit framed into a wall panel in a factory as a structural member of the wall; also factory-assembled structural wall panel.

STUCCO MOULDING—moulding similar to "brick moulding" save the inclusion of a groove to receive and hold the "stucco"; the groove prevents plaster cracks where the moulding and stucco meet.

STUCK—see Moulded.

STUD—a vertical wall framing member usually $2'' \times 4'' \times 8'$ nominal size; also "studding".

Cripple stud—a short supporting stud such as used above the header of a window or door rough opening or below the window sill.

SUB-JAMB—a jamb-like member, usually surfaced four sides, which increases or extends the width of the exterior door frame jamb; sub-jambs imply a larger width than "jamb liners"; can also be used with window units; extension jamb.

SUBSILL—see Sill.

SUMMER—a term formerly used for the principal beam in a floor or partition; also a "louvre door."

SUMMERWOOD—the portion of the annual growth ring of the tree formed after the springwood growth has ceased; due to relatively thicker-walled cells it is usually denser and stronger mechanically than springwood; see Springwood.

SUNBURST—a semi-elliptical area, the lower center of which contains a sun-like figure with sun rays radiating therefrom; may consist of a wood panel or glazed sash; sunburst entrance; sometimes fanlight or elliptical head.

SUNLIGHT—the portion of solar energy which is detectable by the human eye; sunlight accounts for about 44 percent of the total radiation wavelength spectrum.

SUNROOM—a glass-enclosed porch or living room with a sunny exposure; called also a sun porch, sun parlor.

SURROUND—applied to a moulding which extends around an opening such as a fireplace and termed mantel moulding or mantel surround.

SWEEP—a rubber or vinyl strip applied to the bottom of a door to create an effective seal against the sill (threshold).

T

TANGENTIAL—direction in wood tangent to or along the annual growth rings and at right angles to the radius of the log.

TAPE—strips of gummed paper used to hold the edges of the veneer together at the joints prior to gluing.

TEARDROP—a term given to mouldings with a gradual curved profile.

TELEGRAPHING—visible irregularities in the surface of the face of plywood caused by corresponding irregularities in the underlaying plies such as core laps, voids, or extraneous matter.

TENON—a projecting tongue-like part of a wood member to be inserted into a slot (mortise) of another member to form a "mortise-and-tenon joint."

TENONER—a woodworking machine for running tenons on wood members.

TERMITES—ant-like insects which attack and destroy wood.

Nonsubterranean termites—termites that live in dry or damp wood without outside moisture or contact with the ground.

Subterranean termites—termites that develop their colonies and maintain their headquarters in the ground, from which they build their tunnels through earth and around obstructions to attack wood for a source of food.

TEXTURE—size and arrangement of wood cells, and classified as fine or coarse texture; for the most part, those woods with the smaller-diameter cells are finer-texture.

THREE-PLY CONSTRUCTION—a crossbanded assembly consisting of a lumber core and two face veneers, skins or plies.

THRESHOLD—a wood or aluminum member, bevelled or tapered on each side, and used with exterior or interior door frames; classified as "interior" or "exterior"; also "saddle."

Interior threshold—a threshold, symmetrically bevelled, which when installed provides door clearance for carpeting, ceramic tile and other floor coverings.

Exterior threshold—a threshold non-symmetrically bevelled (the more gradual and longer bevel facing the exterior) which, when secured to the exterior door frame sill and/or finished floor, prevents water from driving under the door.

TOE BOARD—the wood member that forms the vertical face of the "toe space" in a kitchen cabinet.

TOENAIL—to drive a nail diagonally to the surface of a vertical member to fasten it to a horizontal member; usually done when end-nailing is not practical.

TOE SPACE—a recessed space at the floor line of a base kitchen cabinet to enable one to more closely approach it.

TONGUE—a projection (usually ¼" to ⅜" in width, ¼" to ¾" in thickness and with a curved edge) on the edge or end of a wood member that is inserted into a groove of similar size to form a joint; "tongue and groove."

TOP PLATE—see Plate, Top.

TOP ROLLER GUIDE—hardware fastened to the top of a sliding door and which contains a roller which glides in the door's overhead track.

TORUS—a large bead; opposite of scotia; rope-like moulding.

TOTAL HEAT LOSS—the total heat loss from a structure equal to the sum of the heat loss (transmission) and infiltration (air leakage).

TRADITIONAL—styles of architecture used in the early period of this country symbolizing the American heritage in house design.

TRANSOM—a small opening above a door separated by a horizontal member (transom bar) and which usually contains a sash or a louvre panel hinged to the transom bar; the "transom bar" or "transom" may act as a door frame head jamb for the door opening and as a sill for the transom or may be built up and separated; "transom" also refers to the "transom bar."

TRANSVERSE—direction in wood at right angles to the wood fibres and includes both "tangential" and "radial" sections.

TREAD—the horizontal stepping of a stairs supported by the stringers; also "flyer"; stair tread.

Landing tread—a partial tread, usually 4" in width, which forms the "nosing" of a stair landing or main floor level; rabbeted for finish floor thickness, namely ²⁵⁄₃₂" or ¹³⁄₁₆"; also used around stair wells; also stair nosing.

TREATING CYCLE—the time consumed in the nonpressure vacuum process of wood preservation from the initial vacuum until the treated material is taken from the cylinder.

TRIM—millwork primarily mouldings and/or trim to finish-off (trim around) window and door openings, fireplaces, walls and other members.

Door trim—trim for a door opening usually consisting of casing.

Exterior trim—trim used on the exterior of a structure.

Interior trim—trim used on the interior of a structure; sometimes refers to interior finish.

Running trim—interior or exterior trim ordered in linear or lineal measurement and which extends for runs around the perimeter of a room or structure; as opposed to standing trim.

Side of trim—trim required to finish one side of a door or window opening.

Standing trim—interior or exterior trim around window and door openings.

Window trim—see Window Trim.

TRIMMING-OUT—installing "trim"; sometimes refers to interior finish.

TRUSS—an assembly of framing members so arranged and fastened together as to form a rigid framework for spanning openings, usually long spans; the truss cannot be deformed by the application of an exterior force without deformation or one or more members.

TURNED DROP—usually an acorn-like turned wood ornament used under the overhang of a Colonial-type two-story structure; originally were carved corner posts.

TWIST—a distortion caused by the turning or winding of the edges of a board or surface so that the four corners of any face are no longer in the same plane.

U

ULTRA-VIOLET—type of radiation with wavelengths shorter than those of visible light and longer than those of X-Rays.

UNDERSILL—see Sill (Main Sill and Undersill).

UNITED INCHES—the sum in inches of the width plus the height of a sash.

UNIT MEASUREMENT—see Size.

UNSEASONED—see Green.

UNSELECTED—as applied to hardwood veneered doors, unselected from the standpoint of color; heartwood (generally exhibiting a definite color in many species) is mixed with sapwood (usually white in most species) and gives a nonuniform color.

UPEASING—see Easement (Concave Easement).

URN—a turned-wood member commonly used in a broken pediment of an entrance.

"U"-VALUE—the overall heat transfer rate through a combination of materials; it is measured by the BTU's (energy units) per hour per square foot per degree of temperature difference. (Usage—The lower the "U"-value, the lower the heat transfer rate in specified conditions.)

V

VACUUM PROCESS OF WOOD PRESERVATION—a nonpressure process of wood preservation in which a vacuum is applied to the millwork in an airtight cylinder, the preservative solution admitted at atmospheric pressure (filling the cylinder) and the excess preservative solution finally removed by drawing a final vacuum; the partial exhaustion of the air from the wood cells (initial vacuum) draws the preservative into the wood cells when the preservative is introduced at atmospheric pressure.

VAPOR BARRIER—generally, a building paper with a low rate of vapor transmission and installed on the warm side of walls.

VENEER—a thin sheet or layer of wood, usually rotary cut, sliced or sawn from a log, bolt or flitch; thickness may vary from ¹⁄₁₀₀ to ¼ of an inch; also skin, ply, veneer ply.

Face veneer—the veneer or ply used on the exposed side of plywood; the exposed veneer surfaces of a veneered door.

Rotary-cut veneer—see Rotary-Cut Face Veneer.

Sawn veneer—veneer produced by sawing.

Sliced veneer—veneer that is sliced off a bolt, log or flitch with a knife.

VENT—sawkerf run on top and bottom rails of hollow-core flush door to equalize the inside and outside atmospheres of the door.

VERGE BOARD—an exposed member nailed along the rake of a gable-end roof open cornice; also implies the larger rake member of an exterior cornice; also barge board.

V-GROOVE—A V-shaped groove cut into the surface of a wood member for decorative purposes; V-grooving is often done on the exterior surface or face of solid flush doors; see Joint.

VICTORIAN—the name assigned to the style of architecture prominent in the United States during the period 1860 to 1893.

VINE STREAKS (MARK)—scars in the wood generally caused by the stems of clinging vines or by their hair-like roots which cling to the tree trunk. Live vine streaks produce sound scars. Dead vine streaks contain either dead residue of the vine, or the remaining pocket similar to bark pocket. Most vine streaks run across the grain, and therefore all vine streaks are considered defects in accordance with restrictions described in these rules.

VIRGIN GROWTH—the original growth of mature trees.

VOLUTE—a stair crook consisting of an easement with a spiral section of stair rail, inclusive of a newel cap, extending to the left or right of the easement in a horizontal plane; also volute with easement.

W

WAINSCOT—a lower interior wall surface (usually 3 to 4 feet above the floor) that contrasts with the wall surface above it; an interior wall composed of two different Interior wall surfaces one above the other.

WALL RAIL—see Rail.

WALL THICKNESS, EXTERIOR—the measurement from the inside face of the interior wall surface to the outside face of the sheathing.

WALL THICKNESS, INTERIOR—the measurement from face to face of the interior wall surfaces.

WARDROBE CLOSET—a closet or cabinet for holding clothes.

WARP—any distortion in the plane of the item itself and not its relationship to the frame or jamb in which it is to be hung. The term "warp" includes bow, cup, and twist, which are defined as follows:

Bow—a flatwise deviation from a straight line drawn from top to bottom; a curvature along the length of the item.

Cup—a deviation from a straight line drawn from side to side; a curvature along the width of the item.

Twist—a deviation in which one or two corners of the item are out of plane with the other corners.

WATER DRIP—a moulding sometimes used on the exterior surface of the bottom rail of an in-swinging casement sash in order to prevent water from being driven in over the sill; may be installed along bottom rail of the door to direct water away from threshold or sill.

WATER DRIP GROOVE—see Groove (Drip Groove).

WATER REPELLENT—a solution, primarily paraffin wax and resin in mineral spirits, which upon penetrating wood retards changes in its moisture content.

WATER-REPELLENT PRESERVATIVE—a solution of a water repellent and wood preservative.

WATER-RESISTANT BOND—a bond or glue joint which retains practically all of its strength when occasionally subjected to a thorough wetting and drying.

WATER STAIN—see Stain.

WATER TABLE—see Cap (Drip Cap).

WEATHERING—the mechanical or chemical disintegration and discoloration of the surface of wood caused by exposure to light, the action of dust and sand carried by winds and alternate shrinking and swelling of the surface fibres with continual variation in moisture content due to changes in the weather; also an inclined surface on a member such as a cornice or sill which directs away rainwater.

WEATHERSTRIP—variously shaped metal, vinyl plastic or moulded-fibre strips which fit tightly against sash or door frame parts to prevent air infiltration through cracks.

Adjustable-pressure weatherstrip—sash or window weatherstripping on which sash tension is maintained by means of spring action.

WEEP—see Groove (Drip Groove).

WEIGHT BOX—in a box window frame (pocket-and-pulley type) the space enclosed by the side jamb, pulley stile, blind stop, inside rough casing (subcasing) and the 2 × 4 doubler (back jamb); contains the sash weights and space for their up and down movement; sometimes "pulley pocket."

WEIGHT POCKET—see Pocket.

WELL HOLE—the clear floor-to-floor space around which a stairs turns or between handrails.

WET WALL—an interior wall finish surface usually consisting of ⅜ inch gypsum plaster lath and ½ inch gypsum plaster applied to the lath surface; as contrasted to "dry wall."

WHITE SPECK—a form of "white rot"; appears on the wood as "white specks" or "white pits"; decay; white pocket.

WIDOW'S WALK—see Belvedere.

WINDBREAK—an exterior door frame member, usually surfaced four sides, rabbeted into the unexposed outside corner of the door frame jamb and flush with the sheathing to provide a weathertight seal between the door frame and structure and a nailing surface to secure the frame to the structure; the brick moulding and/or casing conceals the joint made by the windbreak and the jamb; usually deleted from the door frame; also "outside lining" or "liner"; also may apply to sill of window frame ("sill windbreak").

Reversible windbreak—a "windbreak" adaptable for either ½″ or ²⁵⁄₃₂″ (¾″) sheathing.

Sill windbreak—a window frame member occasionally used to prevent air infiltration around the sill and secure the frame to the structure; generally installed in a groove in the bottom of the window frame sill immediately in back of the sill siding groove.

WINDER—radiating or wedge-shaped stair tread at the turn of a non-platform-type stairs.

WINDOW—consists of two or more single sash to fill a given opening; may be open or glazed.

Bay window—one or a series of windows installed in a "bay" or projecting section of a building; a "bay" may be an arc or polygon; when a "bay" is or closely approaches an arc, the window is termed a "bow."

Bow window—a series of adjoining window units, commonly five in number, installed on a radius; radial bay window; see Bay Window.

Casement window—see Sash.

Check rail window—a double-hung window whose meeting rails are of the "check rail" type; see Rail.

Cottage window—a window with unequal-size top and bottom sash; front window.

Dormer window—any window installed in a roof.

Double-hung window—consists of two sash, top and bottom, which (1) slide vertically past each other, (2) are joined by a meeting rail and (3) are held in any open position by means of weights or one of several types of balancing devices.

Fire window—sash or window constructed and glazed to give protection against the passage of fire.

French window—two-casement sash each hinged on one stile and opening in the middle; the sash extend down to the floor and serve as a door to a porch or terrace.

Front window—see Cottage Window.

Horizontal-sliding window—consists of two or more sash which slide horizontally past each other; one or more of the sash may be fixed or nonoperative or all sash may operate; the sash come together and form a vertical-meeting rail (stile) in a closed position.

Oriel window—a bay window at an upper floor level supported upon corbels or a pier attached to the main wall; found in most houses of importance during 15th and 16th centuries.

Picture window—see Sash.

Plain rail window—a double-hung window whose meeting rails are of the "plain," non-check rail type; a "plain rail window" frame (1) does not use a parting stop, (2) the bottom rail is usually not bevelled, (3) the thickness of the sash is 1⅛", (4) the top rail of the bottom sash contains a putty rabbet (none is employed in a "check rail window") and (5) either sash may be fixed.

Ribbon window—a relatively long, narrow line or strip of windows or sash such as two or more single awning sash units adjoined horizontally.

Single-hung window—similar to a double-hung window with the top sash stationary or nonoperative while the bottom sash operates freely; vertical slider.

Storm window—see Sash.

Window clearance—the measurement between the interior and exterior face of the sash and the corresponding parallel surfaces of the window stop and parting strip; the difference between the width of the sash runway and the sash thickness; also "sash clearance"; window face clearance.

Window condensation—see Condensation.

Window crack—the measurement between the edges of the sash and the corresponding parallel surfaces of the jambs or one-half the difference between the inside window frame dimension and the outside width of the sash; also "sash crack" or "crack"; window edge clearance.

WINDOW FRAME—a group of wood parts so machined and assembled as to form an enclosure and support for a window or sash.

Box window frame—a window frame in which the sash are activated or balanced by sash weights attached to the end of sash cords or chains which are fastened to the sash, the sash cord or chain carried over a pulley, installed in the side jamb (pulley stile); the sash weights are contained in the weight box; also pocket-and-pulley type.

Pocket-and-pulley type window frame—see Box Window Frame.

Split-head—a frame whereby a sash is raised through a split-head jamb; similar to a barn sash installed in a frame.

WINDOW JAMB—the part of the window frame which surrounds and contacts the window or sash that the frame is intended to support.

Head window jamb—the horizontal jamb forming the top of the window or sash frame.

Rabbeted window jamb—a window jamb with a rabbet on one or both edges to receive a window or sash.

Side window jamb—the vertical jamb forming the sides of the window or sash frame.

WINDOW STOOL, NONBEVELLED, NON-RABBETED—a window stool without a bevel or rabbet and which may or may not contain a tongue or rabbet on its exterior edge; see Stool.

WINDOW TRIM—the mouldings and/or trim necessary to "finish" or "trim" a sash or window frame.

Side of window trim—see Side-of-Window Trim.

WINDOW UNIT—consists of a combination of the frame, window, weatherstripping, sash-activation device and at option of manufacturer screens and/or storm sash assembled as a complete and properly operating unit.

Brick veneer window unit—refers to a window unit for brick facing, wood frame exterior wall although it may also be used in other types of wood frame walls.

Casement window (sash) unit—a combination of frame, casement sash, weatherstripping, operating device and at the option of the manufacturer screen and/or storm sash assembled as a complete and properly operating unit.

Double-hung window unit—consists of a window frame, double-hung window, weatherstrip, balancing device and at the option of the manufacturer screen and/or storm sash assembled as a complete and properly operating unit.

Frame building window unit—usually refers to a window unit for a wood-facing wood frame exterior wall; casing, rather than brick moulding, and drip cap are a part of the unit.

Horizontal-sliding window unit—combination of the window frame, horizontal-sliding window, weatherstrip and at the option of the manufacturer screen and/or storm sash assembled as a complete and properly operating unit.

Single-hung window unit—similar to double-hung window unit save single-hung window rather than double-hung; see Double-Hung Window Unit.

WOOD ALLOWANCE—the difference between the outside opening and the total glass measurement of a given window or sash.

WOOD BUCK—see Buck.

WOOD FRAME—a group of wood parts so machined and assembled as to form an enclosure and support for a window or door; also frame.

WOOD FRAME STRUCTURE—a structure whose structural frame consists primarily of wood members, inclusive of exterior and interior frame walls that support the floors and roof; exterior facing of the wall may be brick, stone, stucco or other nonwood material; frame structure.

WOOD FRAME WALL—a wall basically framed or constructed of wood members; wood members usually employed are studs, plates and sheathing; may be faced on the exterior with wood or nonwood facing materials such as brick, stucco, stone; also "frame wall."

Brick-facing wood frame wall—a wood frame wall with an exterior facing of a single layer of brick usually a nominal 4 inches in thickness; usually a one-inch air space between the sheathing and the brick; also "brick veneer wood frame wall."

Brick veneer wood frame wall—see Brick-Facing Wood Frame Wall.

Brick and wood-facing wood frame wall—a wood frame wall with both wood and brick as facing materials.

Stucco wood frame wall—a wood frame wall with "stucco" as a facing material; stucco is generally furred out from the sheathing approximately ¼" to ⅜".

Wood-facing wood frame wall—a wood frame wall with a wood facing material such as wood shingles, vertical panelling, siding or shakes; same type of wall may accommodate asbestos shingles, siding and other nonwood siding materials; "frame building" wall.

WOOD JOINT—see Joint.

WOODWORK—used interchangeably with Millwork; may apply to anything made of wood.

WORM TRACK OR SCAR—the groove or resulting scar tissue in the wood caused by worms or other borers.

WORM-TYPE HARDWARE—a device op-erated by a handle which when turned opens and closes a casement or awning-type sash.

WREATH—the curved part of a stair stringer in a winding stairs; also refers to a curved portion of the stair rail; curved sec-tion of a stair rail curved in both the vertical and horizontal planes (volute).

X

X-RAY DOOR—see Door.

Y

YOKE—in a box window frame, the head window jamb.

MILLWORK
ABBREVIATIONS

AD—Air dried
ALS—American Lumber
    Standards
ALW—Allowance
AMT—Amount
APR—Apron
APRX—Approximately
ASBLY—Assembly
ASTG—Astragal
AV
AVG } —Average
ADH—Adhesive
ARCH—Architectural
AWN—Awning
AWWI—American Wood Window
    Institute

B—Base
B&C—Bead & Cove
B&B
B&BTR } —B and Better
B of M—Bill of Material
B1S—Beaded one side
B2S—Beaded two sides
BAL—Balance (sash or window);
    also baluster
BASMT—Basement
BAT—Batten
BB
BBD } —Backband
BD—Board; also bead
BDFT—Board feet
BDL—Bundle
BDM—Bed moulding
BET GL—Between glass
BET—Between
BET JBS—Between jambs
BEV—Bevelled
BK SH—Bookshelves
BKT—Bracket
B/L—Bill of lading
BLD—Blind
BLDG—Building
BLD ST—Blind stop
BLK—Block

BLT-IN—Built-in
BM—Board measure; also brick
    moulding
BOT—Bottom
BOT RL—Bottom rail
BOT SH—Bottom sash
BP—Bypass
BRKT—Bracket
BRNZ—Bronze
BR OPG—Brick opening
BR VEN—Brick veneer
BS—Base
BS MLDG—Base moulding
BSMT—Basement
B SH—Barn sash
BTR—Better

C—Closet; also hundred
CAB
CABT } —Cabinet
CABWK—Cabinet work
CASG—Casing
CAS SH—Casement sash
CASWK—Casework
CAT—Catalog
CB—Center bead
CB1S—Center bead 1 side
CB2S—Center bead 2 sides
C&B—Cove and bead
CC—Cement coated (nails)
CCD—China closet door
CEL—Cellar
CEL SH—Cellar sash
CSF—Cellar sash frame
CG—Comb grain (hdwds); also
    corner guard
CG2E—Center groove 2 edges
CHAM—Chamfer
CH CAB—China cabinet
CH CL—China closet
CH RL—Chair rail
CIN BL—Cinder block
CIR—Circle (circular)
CIR E—Circle end
CIR HD—Circle head

CIRCUM—Circumference
CK RL—Check rail
CK R WDS—Check rail windows
CL—Clearance; also closet, and
    carload
CLF—Hundred lineal feet
CLG—Ceiling
CLO—Closet
CLR—Clear
CLRCE—Clearance
CM—Center-matched; also crown
    moulding, and cap moulding
CMC—Crown moulded cap
CND—Checks no defect
CO—Cased opening; also cutout
COL—Column; also colonial
COMB—Combination
COM—Common
CONC—Concrete
CONC B
CONC BL } —Concrete block
CONST
CONSTR } —Construction
CONTEMP—Contemporary
COR—Corner
COR BD—Corner board
CP—Clothes pole
CP M—Cap moulding
CPR—Copper
CS—Commercial Standard
CSG—Casing
CSMT SH—Casement sash
CTR—Center; also counter
CUP—Cupboard
CV—Center Vee
CV1S—Center Vee 1 side
CV2S—Center Vee 2 sides
CYC—Cycle
CYP—Cypress

D/S
D/SDG } —Drop siding
D&CM—Dressed and center-
    matched
D&M—Dressed & matched

D&SM—Dressed & standard-
 matched
D2S&CM—Dressed two sides and
 center-matched
DA—Double acting (door)
DB CLG—Double beaded clg.
DBL—Double
DB PART—Double-beaded
 partition
DC—Drip cap
DEG—Degree
DEN—Dense
DET—Double end trimmed; also
 detail
DF—Douglas fir
DG—Double glass
DH
DHW } —Double-hung window
DIA
DIAM } —Diameter
DIAG—Diagonal
DIM—Dimension
DIN RM—Dining room
DIV—Divided
DR—Door; also double-rabbeted;
 and dining room
DR FR
DR FRA } —Door frame
DR JB—Door jamb
DR TR—Door trim
DRWS—Drawers
DS—Double strength; also double
 sash; and drop siding
DSA—Double strength A (glass)
DT—Dinette
DV1S—Double Vee 1 side
DVTL—Dovetail
DWL—Dowel
DWR—Drawer

E—Edge; also entrance
EA—Each
EASEMT—Easement
E&CB1S—Edge & center bead 1
 side
E&CV1S—Edge & center V 1 side
EB1S—Edge bead 1 side
ECM—Ends center-matched
EE—Eased edges
EG—Edge (vertical) grain
EM—End-matched
EMC—Equilibrium moisture
 content
ENT—Entrance
ESC—Escutcheon
ESM—Ends standard-matched

FB—Frame building
FBK—Flat back
FBD—Full bound
FBM—Foot (feet) board measure
FC—Furred ceiling
FCTY—Factory
FDR—Fire door
FG—Flat grain
FIL—Fillet
FIN—Finish(ed)
FIN S—Finished size
FL—Flashing; also flush, flute;
 flooring and flat
FL B—Flour bin
FLG—Flooring
FLOR—Florentine (glass)
FL PAN—Flat panel
FLR—Floor
FM—Flush-moulded; also face
 measure
FOH—Free of heart
FOHC—Free of heart center
FOK—Free of knots
FP—Fireplace
FR—Frame; also front
FR DR—French door
FRGT—Freight
FRM—Framing
FRT—Freight
FR WD—French window
FS—Federal specification
FT—Flush threshold; also feet
FT SH—Front sash
FT SM—Feet surface measure
FT WD—Front window
FUR—Furring
FXD—Fixed

G—Grooved
GALV—Galvanized
GL—Glass (glazed)
GL SZ—Glass size
GM—Grade-marked
GND—Ground
GOTH—Gothic
GR—Green; also grade and grain
GS—Glass size

EST—Estimate(d)
EST WT—Estimated weight
EV1S—Edge Vee 1 side
EX—Extra
EXT—Exterior; also extension

FAS—Firsts and seconds (hdwds)
H—Height; also high and house

H&M—Hit and miss
H or M—Hit or miss
HB
HBK } —Hollow back
HC—Head casing
HDWD—Hardwood
HDWE—Hardware
HEM—Hemlock
HEX—Hexagonal
HF—Half
HFRD—Half-round
HGT—Height
HOR
HORIZ } —Horizontal
HR—Hour
HRD—Half-round
HRT—Heart
HRTWD—Heartwood
HSE—House
HSG—Housing
HT—Height

IB—Ironing board
ID—Inside diameter
IM—Inside measure
IN—Inch
INDIV—Individual
INS—Inside; also inches
INT—Interior
INTER—Intermediate
IRG BD—Ironing board
IS—Inside
ISD—Inside door
IW—Inside width

JBS—Jambs
JNT
JT } —Joint
JTD—Jointed

K—Kitchen
KD
KLD } —Kiln-dried
KD
KDN } —Knocked down
KLND—Kiln-dried
KP—Kick plate

L—Left; also length
LAM—Laminated
LAT—Lattice
LBR—Lumber
LCL—Less than carload; also linen
 closet
LDG—Landing
LF
LFT } —Linear feet

LG—Leaded glass
LGR—Longer
LGTH—Length
LH—Left hand
LIN—Lineal (linear)
LIN FT—Lineal foot (feet)
LIV RM—Living room
LL—Longleaf pine
LNG—Lining
LOA—Length overall
LR
LRL } —Lock rail
LT—Light (glass)
LV—Louvre
LVD—Louvre door

M—Thousand; also mesh, member
    and measurement
MACH—Machine
MARG—Marginal
MAT
MATL } —Material
MATRL
MAX—Maximum
MBM—Thousand (feet) board
    measure
MBR—Member
MC—Moisture content; also
    moulded cap
MCH-SAND
MCH SD } —Machine-sanded
MDSE—Merchandise
MEAS—Measurement; measure
MED—Medium
MED CAB—Medicine cabinet
MEM—Member
MFG—Manufacturing
MFR—Manufacturer
MG—Mixed grain; also medium
    grain
MID—Middle
MILLWK—Millwork
MIN—Minimum
MIR—Mirror
MISC—Miscellaneous
MIT—Milling in transit
ML—Mixed lengths
MLD
MLDG } —Moulding (moulded)
MLF—Thousand lineal feet
MO—Masonry opening
MOD—Modern
MOLD—Moulding
MR—Mill run; also meeting rail
MSM—Thousand surface measure

MSRY—Masonry
MST—Measurement
MT—Muntin
MTAL
MTL } —Material
MTRL—Meeting rail
MULL—Mullion
MULT—Multiple-opening frame;
    multiple
MUN
MUNT } —Muntin
MW—Mixed widths

N—Nosed; also nail and net
N1E—Nosed 1 edge
NA—Nail
NO—Number
NOM—Nominal
NT—Net
NW—Narrow widths
NWL—Newel

O—Oak
OA—Overall
OBS—Obscure
OC—On center
OCT
OCTG } —Octagon; octagonal
OD—Outside diameter
OG—Ogee
OP—Opposite
OPG—Opening
ORD—Order
OS—Outside
OS CASG—Outside casing
OSD—Outside door
OSM—Outside measure
OSOPG—Outside opening
OVHD—Overhead
OVO—Ovolo

P—Planed; also surfaced, porch
    and plaster
P&B—Ploughed (plowed) and
    bored
P&P—Pocket & pulley
PA—Plastered arch
PAN—Panel
PAR—Paragraph
PART—Partition
PAT—Pattern; also patent balance
PAT NO—Pattern number
PC—Piece; also plain cap
PCS—Pieces
PCT MLD
PCT MO } —Picture moulding

PE—Plain end
PERI—Perimeter
PIL—Pilaster
PKT—Pocket
PKY—Pecky
PL—Plate; also plaster
PL ARCH—Plastered arch
PLAS—Plaster
PLG—Planing
PLGL—Plate glass; also plain glass
PL GUM—Plain gum
PLR
PLRL } —Plain rail
PL R OAK—Plain red oak
PL R WDS—Plain rail windows
PLT—Plate
PN—Partition; also paragraph
PNL—Panel
PP—Ponderosa pine
PP GL—Polished plate glass
PR—Pair
PR BLDS—Pair of blinds
PR CSMT—Pair of casements
PREFAB—Prefabricated
PRM—Premium
PS
PST } —Pulley stile
PSTP—Parting stop

Q—Quarter
QNTY—Quantity
QR—Quarter
QR RD—Quarter-round
QR SD—Quarter-sawn
QTD—Quartered
QTR—Quarter
QUAD—Quadruple
QUAN—Quantity
QUINT—Quintuple

R—Radius; also right and riser
R/L—Random length
R/W—Random width
R/W/L—Random width & length
RAB
RABT } —Rabbet(ed)
RAD—Radius; radial
RAN—Random
RD—Round
RD HD—Round head
RDM—Random
REG—Regular
RES
RESN } —Resawn
RET
RETD } —Return(ed)

RGH—Rough
RH—Right hand
RIP—Ripped
RL—Rail; also random length
RM—Room
RMO—Raised moulding
RND—Round
R PAN—Raised panel
RS—Rolling slat; also rift sawn (hdwds)
R SDG—Rustic siding
RT—Right; return

S—Sash
S/L ⎱
S/LAP ⎰ —Shiplap
S1E—Surfaced 1 edge
S1S—Surfaced 1 side
S2S & CM—Surfaced 2 sides and center-matched
S2S & S/L—Surfaced 2 sides and shiplap
S2S & SM—Surfaced 2 sides and standard-matched
S4S—Surfaced four sides
S&E—Side and edge
S&S4S—Sanded and surfaced 4 sides
S2S1E S1S—Surfaced 2 sides and one edge and sanded 1 side
SAP—Sapwood
SB—Standard bead
SB1S—Single bead 1 side
SC—Screen; also surface coat
SCN ⎱
SCR ⎰ —Screen
SD—Sash door; also seasoned
SDG—Siding
SD LTS—Side lights
SE—Square edge
SEG HD—Segment head
SEG TOP—Segment top
SEL—Select
STSH—Storm sash
STUD—Studding
STWY—Stairway
SU—Set up
SURF—Surface
SW—Sound wormy
SF—Surface foot
SFCE—Surface
SFTWD—Softwood

SG—Straight-grained; also slash grain
SGL—Single
SH—Shelves; also sash
SHOPG—Sash opening
SH D—Shipping dry
SH DR—Sash door
SHTRS—Shutters
SIT SPR—Sitka spruce
SL—Shiplap; also short lengths
SLDG—Sliding
SM—Surface measure; also solid mould and standard-matched
SND—Sap no defect; also sound
SO—Single opening
SP—Special
SPEC ⎱
SPECS ⎰ —Specifications
SPR—Simplified Practice Recommendations
SQ—Square
SQE—Square edge
SS—Single-strength
SR—Single-rabbeted
SS BLDS—Stationary slat blinds
SSND—Sap stain no defect
ST—Stile; also stairs
STA SL—Stationary slat
STD—Standard
STDR—Storm door
STDM—Standard-matched
STGS—Stringers
STK—Stock
STKG—Sticking
STL—Stool; also stile
STND—Stained
STP—Stops; also stepping
STPG—Stepping
STR—String; also structural
STRUC ⎱
STRUCT ⎰ —Structural

T—Top; also transom and tread
T&G—Tongue and groove
TB&S—Top, bottom and sides
TH ⎱
THK ⎰ —Thick; also threshold
THRES—Threshold
TK—Thick
TR—Transom; also trim and tread
TRAD—Traditionally
TRANS—Transom

TR BR—Transom Bar
TRD—Tread
TREL—Trellis
TRIP ⎱
TRIPL ⎰ —Triple

UNS BIR—Unselected birch
UNSD—Unseasoned
UP—Upper
UT—Utility

V1S—Vee one side
VEN—Veneered
VENT—Ventilator
VERT—Vertical
VG—Vertical (edge) grain
VEST—Vestibule

W—Wall; also width and wider
WAINS CAP—Wainscot cap
WAL—Wider all lengths
WC—Water closet; also West Coast
WCH—West Coast hemlock
WD—Wood; window
WD FR—Window frame
WDR—Wider
WD SC—Wood screen
WDT—Width
WDW—Window
WF—White fir
WGHT—Weight
WGI—Wire glass
WI—Wrought iron
WKG—Working
WKT—Worktable
WND—Window
WP—White pine
WPP—Western Ponderosa pine
WRC—Western red cedar
WS—Weatherstripping
WT—Weight
WTH—Width

X—By
X Cut—Cross cut
X Pan—Cross panel
X SECT—Cross section

YP—Yellow pine

Z—Zinc

SIGNS AND SYMBOLS

× —By

∥ —Parallel

⊥ —Perpendicular

< —Angle

∟ —Right Angle

△ —Triangle

□ —Square

▭ —Rectangle

◯ —Circle

° —Degree

′ —Minute (also foot)

″ —Second (also inch)

Design Gallery

The placement of millwork in a structure is known as the fenestration.

This doorway becomes the focal point of the home. (Courtesy of Morgan Products Ltd.)

Typical progression of millwork. Original double-hung window units are now joined by a roof-mounted solar water heater and one-light sliding glass doors.

A pair of 10-light casement doors mounted in a double-pocket unit. (Courtesy of Velux-America Inc.)

Effective use of skylights provides an excellent light source.

This ceiling fan used in conjunction with ventilating skylights creates an excellent potential for air flow.

Leaded glass creates a unique decorating touch. (Courtesy of Morgan Products Ltd.)

Pocket units afford an efficient use of space in tight quarters. (Courtesy of Johnson Pocket Door Hardware)

This basic door is made more attractive and efficient with the addition of two sidelights. (Courtesy of Morgan Products Ltd.)

An unusual and beautiful pair of circle-head doors. (Courtesy of Weather Shield MFG Inc.)

– Index –

This is John Hiro's first book. He writes and presents seminars dealing with millwork and customer service. If you wish to consult him, please write % Sterling Publishing, 387 Park Avenue South, New York, NY 10016.